The Rhetoric
of Soft Power

LEXINGTON STUDIES IN POLITICAL COMMUNICATION

SERIES EDITOR: ROBERT E. DENTON, JR.,
VIRGINIA POLYTECHNIC INSTITUTE AND STATE UNIVERSITY

This series encourages focused work examining the role and function of communication in the realm of politics including campaigns and elections, media, and political institutions.

RECENT TITLES IN THE SERIES:

The Rhetoric of Soft Power

Public Diplomacy in Global Contexts

Craig Hayden

LEXINGTON BOOKS
Lanham • Boulder • New York • Toronto • Plymouth, UK

Published by Lexington Books
A wholly owned subsidary of The Rowman & Littlefield Publishing Group, Inc.
4501 Forbes Boulevard, Suite 200, Lanham, Maryland 20706
www.lexingtonbooks.com

Estover Road, Plymouth PL6 7PY, United Kingdom

British Library Cataloguing in Publication Information Available

Library of Congress Cataloging-in-Publication Data

Hayden, Craig, 1972-
  The rhetoric of soft power : public diplomacy in global contexts / Craig Hayden.
    p. cm.— (Lexington studies in political communication)
  Includes index.
  ISBN 978-0-7391-4258-5 (cloth. : alk. paper) — ISBN 978-0-7391-4259-2 (pbk: alk. paper) —ISBN 978-0-7391-4260-8 (electronic)
  1. International relations. 2. Diplomacy. 3. Communication in politics. I. Title.
JZ1305.H39 2012
327.2—dc23   2011036917

Printed in the United States of America

Contents

Acknowledgments

This book came together over the course of three years, and drew from an ongoing personal research program to compare different kinds of public diplomacy and strategic communication around the world. The project became a book only after I thought about this project with the help of an eclectic community of friends and colleagues who share an interest in public diplomacy. This research would not have been possible without the encouragement of my colleagues at the University of Southern California, the University of Virginia, and my home institution, the School of International Service at American University. At American University, Nanette Levinson of the SIS International Communication Program worked diligently to provide the kind of institutional support necessary to write a book while on the tenure track. I also owe a debt of gratitude to colleagues, friends, and advisors who have helped me along the way by sharing their ideas and comments on this book and project, including Bruce Gregory, Shawn Powers, Amelia Arsenault, Matthew Armstrong, Nicholas Cull, Jan Melissen, R. S. Zaharna, Robert Albro, Robert Kelley, Patrick Thaddeus Jackson, and Dan Sreebny, among many others. I am also grateful for the help of my research assistants and student colleagues at American University, including Jacquelyn Chi, Kia Hall, Rena Hinoshita, Shanti Shoji, Anna Cheung, Efe Sevin, and Yelena Osipova. I am also quite thankful for the patience of Lexington-Rowman and Littlefield as I slowly put the pieces of this puzzle together.

Chapter 1

Introduction

Why do international political actors increasingly believe that to *communicate* to foreign audiences is crucial to their interests? When material resources such as military and economic assets offer visible measures of potency on the global stage—why should communicative resources like information, culture, and other symbolic factors be considered vital to the practice of international relations? These questions are posed in this book to address the growing number of foreign policies around the world designed to influence, persuade, and to cultivate support in foreign audiences. These policies reveal the pervasive influence of *soft power*—Joseph Nye's intuitive and sweeping amendment to the traditional field of international power politics that asserts the inclusion of persuasion and culture to the instruments of nation-state power. Soft power's currency is most readily observable in the spread of "public diplomacy" initiatives and similar policies. This book presents a comparative analysis of the words and actions surrounding such programs from a selection of actors around the world.

The idea that *information* and *communication* are important to the relative power of the state is not new.[1] Nor is the place of persuasion in the conduct of international relations.[2] While public diplomacy after September 11, 2001, is often discussed in the United States as a battle of "ideas," the notion of struggle between competing ideologies broadly framed international relations throughout the twentieth century.[3] The context of the twenty-first century, however, presents new challenges for nation-states and other actors on the global stage—in part because the role of information, culture, and communication in the practice of international politics has changed.[4] The erosion of informational sovereignty in the wake of rapid media globalization, the widespread dissemination of communication and information technologies (ICTs),

1

and the concurrent use of such ICTs to organize and assert a political presence presents new challenges to nation-states.[5] These trends form a backdrop to the events of 9/11 in the United States, which forced a renewed focus on identity, culture, and communication for U.S. diplomatic strategy—a move that coincided with widespread recognition of soft power as an essential component of foreign policy thinking.[6]

Soft power has since proven to be a compelling justificatory logic from which to argue for and implement a range of programs—from media-based advocacy to nation-branding. It transforms the calculus of international influence by describing how the relative "attractiveness" of an actor's culture, policies, or actions can be leveraged to achieve foreign policy ends.[7] In Nye's formulation, soft power is both an *asset* to cultivate and a *tool* to use, a kind of public opinion capital that has raised the profile of communication-centric foreign policies such as public diplomacy, international broadcasting, and other forms of strategic communication. The widespread currency of this notion has lead many countries to pursue communication-based goals, such as to improve their credibility, to influence media representation, and to establish stronger ties with foreign publics.

This book provides a critical examination of how soft power is articulated in public diplomacy and strategic communication policies across a range of international actors. This book examines the cases of China, Venezuela, Japan, and the United States. These are certainly not the only international actors engaged in public diplomacy, but each case illuminates a different aspect of how the notion of soft power has been interpreted and implemented. For each of these actors, public discourse (from leaders, analysts, and media) and related policy initiatives reveal fundamental assumptions about soft power as an orientation toward the practice of international affairs and the role that communication plays in sustaining global relations.

The *discourse* and *practices* of soft power are presented here to illustrate comparative perceptions of what constitutes such relations—such as the meaning of "public," the relation between media and audience, and fundamental expectations about influence via such policies. This body of evidence is presented as a *rhetoric* of soft power; an instructive selection of policy discussion and public argument from which can be derived the contextual fields of reasoning that shape how such programs are imagined and more broadly, particularistic views of what constitutes necessary international political action through communication.

Each case was selected to represent a diversity of interpretations about soft power that captures the distinctive context of each actor, as well as how the components of soft power (culture, audience, etc.) are reflected in the practice of public diplomacy programs. The United States has a well established tradition of public diplomacy programs that is fraught with internal debate over its efficacy and the content of its "message." China has embarked on a multimodal campaign to confront what it believes to be a kind of "hegemony" over its representation in the global media sphere that threatens its rise to power. Venezuela's public diplomacy includes an international broadcasting campaign to capitalize and cultivate a regional identity through an alterative news service. Japan is a post-industrial power that seeks to leverage its considerable cultural industries into a strategic asset for its foreign policy. Each of these cases elaborate a situated understanding of soft power, and in the process recontextualizes the relationship between media, foreign policy, and the developing norms of international politics in a globalized age.

In the course of the analysis, this book provides a general introduction to how soft power is understood in order justify and implement programs that can generally be categorized under the term "public diplomacy." Public diplomacy represents practices of transnational communicative engagement or, as diplomacy scholar Paul Sharp describes, "the process by which direct relations with people in a country are pursued to advance the interests and extend the values of those being represented."[8] This expansive definition accommodates the increase in both the types of actors apparent in international politics, as well as the proliferation of new communication tools. Former public diplomacy practitioner Bruce Gregory captures the interplay of time, policy goals, and methods involved in this process:

> Public diplomacy operates though actions, relationships, images, and words in three time frames: 24/7 news streams, medium range campaigns on high value policies, and long-term engagement. Its tools range from electronic media to cultural diplomacy to "the last three feet" of personal communication.[9]

Gregory's depiction suggests that the study of public diplomacy transcends the traditional domains of communication, media, and foreign policy analysis. Therefore, the research in this book draws on theoretical and methodological insights from both communication studies and international relations. As Gregory notes, public diplomacy has "no consensus on its analytical boundaries."[10] The goal of this book is also relatively straightforward—to develop a theoretical treatment soft power and public diplomacy through an interdisciplinary investigation of what is demonstratively a transnational, interdisciplinary phenomenon. There are two arguments that illustrate the significance of this study, aside from the general pervasiveness of soft power-inspired programs.

First, this study is arguably a step toward redressing what some of called a serious lack in the development of theory-based scholarship about public diplomacy.[11] It moves beyond the historical reflection that currently defines most of the public diplomacy scholarship, and is responsive to the need for systematic understanding of public diplomacy as form of communicative action in international politics.[12] While historical scholarship is a valuable foundation for insight, the global context of public diplomacy has shifted dramatically. Diplomacy scholar Jan Melissen argues that it is "not advisable to make a forward projection of historical practices into the present international environment."[13] Instead, this book offers that public diplomacy should be assessed synchronically—across different examples to gauge the broader implications of the context of global communication and politics.

Second, the study of soft power and its manifest influence on public diplomacy programs demonstrates the possibilities of interdisciplinary inquiry toward building a coherent understanding of public diplomacy. While there are numerous examples of research potentially pertinent to public diplomacy sequestered in disparate academic fields, the methods and insights here are purposefully synthetic and ideally, collaborative.[14] Interdisciplinary analysis may be increasingly *necessary* for informed observation of social and political phenomena within a highly globalized world, as the conceptual boundaries of nation, culture, and the political are blurred. For Gregory, the confluence of events has transformed the context described in the histories of statecraft to necessitate new thinking on public diplomacy.[15] Ever increasingly, the business of soft power links the resources of communication with the imperatives of politics.

This study, therefore, addresses the question of soft power as expressed in instances of communicative action. While the conclusions may be pertinent to enduring questions in international relations, the method and subject matter are grounded in communication studies. Rhetorical analysis of policy discourse is deployed to illustrate the consequences of such texts as both functional knowledge *and* practice. The study is framed as a communication design in part because soft power and public diplomacy are ultimately about *communication itself;* how international actors wrestle with the communication infrastructure that both constrains and enables their actions.[16]

The remaining sections of this introduction provide a brief overview of soft power and public diplomacy as analytic concepts, a short explanation of the study conducted for this book, and finally an overview of the chapters.

SOFT POWER: ADAPTATION TO GLOBAL CONDITIONS

Soft power is understood to be the ability to "affect others to obtain the outcomes you want" without coercion or economic inducement[17] Its mechanism is relatively straightforward. Nye's notion of soft power is a kind of *co-optation*—where objectives are achieved by getting others to "want what you want." Soft power encompasses three broad categories: (a) influence, (b) the force of an actor's argument, and, perhaps most important, (c) the "attractiveness" of an actor's culture and institutions—the supposed "intangible assets" that draw other actors toward wanting the same objectives and viewing the scene of international politics in roughly the same normative frame.

This conception of soft power is not a predictive theory political effects, but a recognition that traditional metrics of "power" in international affairs should be inclusive of ideational factors: what people believe can shape or constrain the agency of a political actor and their ability to effect change. This formulation therefore brings communication back to the center of international strategy, since to leverage soft power implies efforts to influence or cultivate attitudes.[18] Soft power's relative simplicity makes it a readily exportable strategic notion; it is not just a policy corrective designed for the United States but a general indictment of how global politics gets resolved in the present context.

In Nye's terms, soft power reflects the "attraction" that a nation-state enjoys in relation to others.[19] A nation-state's values, cultural products, and other characteristics are the resources of soft power—and theoretically enable increased agency, much like how military or economic resources bestow their own form of power. For Nye, soft power suggests both a *post hoc* measure of effectiveness in achieving foreign policy objectives, as well as implies a *means* to achieve these political goals by leveraging the assets that cultivate "attraction." In sum, soft power is thus both a measure of "resources" as well as a reflection on "behavioral outcomes."[20]

Yet the idea of soft power has not escaped criticism or controversy. Even Nye himself has acknowledged that soft power is but a necessary *complement* to still-viable metrics of military and economic power, and cannot stand as on its own as a strategic orientation.[21] For others, its dynamic of attraction either masks a form of hegemony, or elides the coercive aspect of international argumentation.[22] These critiques, which are discussed at greater length in the subsequent chapter, suggest that the term is not fixed, but a malleable signifier of political action. Its significance for this study lies in the term's *potentiality* across contexts as a resource for policy argumentation.

Nye's formulation offers that soft power is international politics by other means—it suggests that persuasion and communicative acts can yield political ends, and that international actors may possess or cultivate resources in order to exert soft power. Nye also claims that because soft power represents both resources for achieving objectives and measurable behaviors, policies like public diplomacy have become necessary instruments of soft power. He states that public diplomacy provides a crucial link between these two aspects; it is "an instrument that governments use to mobilize these resources to communicate with and attract the publics of other countries."[23] For soft power to "work," it renders the audience of soft power efforts as *targets*, susceptible to campaigns of "attraction" and yet empowers them with a valuable potential of political agency. These are crucial assumptions. They reflect profound changes in the context of politics and communication—as well as implicit relations of media, message, and effect.

Given its core assumptions, why has soft power become such an important addition to contemporary strategic discourse on international politics? The events of September 11, 2001, catalyzed an increasingly international trend toward the promotion of public diplomacy efforts and other forms of communication interventions.[24] These programs in turn emerged amidst significant developments in the global political environment. The rise of ideologically charged global networks of terrorism, an international news and information ecology that ignored national boundaries, and the growing efficacy of transnational social advocacy via NGOs—all signified that international politics is increasingly ideational as it is material. As a result, soft power has become a kind of catch-all term to describe how nation-states engage the global political landscape, and proffers ways to achieve objectives that account for newly emergent challenges to the traditional means of power politics.

Soft power is distinct, however, from merely recasting politics *as* communication. Communicative action is discussed in some IR scholarship to be a venue for the resolution of conflict and the promotion of norms—often within a largely rationalist paradigm.[25] Soft power, however, does not necessarily rely upon a rationalist model of persuasion and influence.[26] Its implications cast international politics as more rhetorical argument than public reasoning that brackets cultural and instrumental influences. Rather, purposive instruments of soft power like public diplomacy present a "means to persuasion" that leverage influential "resources" to achieve desired behaviors. Soft power depicts a broadly applicable set of arguments for why actors should engage with the pluralistic ideoscapes and mediascapes that constrain contemporary political action.[27] As the global proliferation of public diplomacy programs imply, soft power is an idea that is widely applicable.

The fact that soft power is recognized as important by so many nation-states and nonstate actors reflects increased attention to the role of publics in political change, information and communication technologies, and the transnational flows of culture and news. The idea of soft power, explicitly or otherwise, establishes grounds for justifying foreign policies and programs that specifically leverage the assets of attraction, for soft power reveals a complementary dimension to the strategic assumptions of realist politics—and justifies a reallocation of resources to policies like public diplomacy, international broadcasting, and strategic communication. At the same time, it broadens the scope for how international actors take inventory of their own strategic assets, and suggests new applications for cultural products, industries, and communicative competencies.

Soft power, therefore, provides a new conceptual terrain from which to imagine, articulate, and enact policies designed to engage foreign publics and achieve political goals. It contains assumptions about how influence works, both domestically and internationally. External influence is the first order effect of soft power, and suggests that exposure to attempts at persuasion (some form of communicative engagement) and other symbolic activity can have a tangible effect on the target audience. Also implicit is the idea that foreign publics have some sort of *internal* influence over their own governments, and that public opinion matters in some shape or form to the course a nation-state's foreign policy objectives. As stated previously, soft power implies a rudimentary model of domestic power dynamics and of communication effect, and thus invites attempts to cultivate and manage the symbolic economy of international influence.

Given its basic precepts, there is considerable latitude in how the imperatives of soft power are interpreted and deployed around the world. Even Nye's own description does not provide an absolute prescriptive for the cultivation and exertion of soft power.[28] And as this book will describe in greater detail—soft power's theoretical assumptions are inevitably refracted through the existing political and policy imaginary of the country or actor embracing a soft power strategy. While soft power may signal the salience of communication to international relations, what "communication" actually means varies from actor to actor.

Nevertheless, there are some relatively ubiquitous conditions that might suggest why "soft power" has become an important touchstone for international politics. First, the political economy of global media has forced nation-states to reckon with communication flows that ignore boundaries.[29] Nation-states must contend with the erosion of their institutional sovereignty through media regulatory regimes that increasingly favor transnational corporations while dismantling cultural protections.[30] Consequently, the volume and scale of message flows challenge the ideational monopoly once enjoyed by the nation-state.[31] The growth of transnational media conglomeration coupled with the rapid dissemination of participatory technologies like social networking platforms only magnify the lack of informational control. Admittedly, the growth of global media platforms has not been universal as the global digital divide reveals persistent information inequalities.[32] Yet despite its uneven growth, media globalization and the transnational flows of information have altered traditional communication-based foundations for nation-state power.[33] This has taken the form of protectionist measures, and increasingly proactive attempts to engage the global media sphere—such as South Korea's development of its cultural industries for export and Qatar's Al-Jazeera satellite news network.[34]

Another signal that soft power represents an alternative measure of political potency is the increased effectiveness of nonstate political action. The much-lauded success of transnational advocacy movements to the virtual media production centers that cultivate support for global Islamic extremist organizations—there is ample evidence of nonstate activity that increasingly impacts the agenda of nation-states.[35] The global communication infrastructure has empowered actors to connect, organize, and influence.[36] At the same time, however, this communication infrastructure reveals an increased media *dependency.* Credibility and trustworthiness—measures that contribute to perceptions of an actor's attractiveness—increases the relative importance of media and communication outlets for actors seeking to cultivate soft power.[37]

As Nye states clearly, "fifty years ago political struggles were about the ability to control and transmit scarce information. Today, political struggles are about the creation and destruction of credibility."[38] If communication outlets ultimately disseminate and package the information that form perceptions, then the communication infrastructure becomes the fulcrum for managing credibility deemed essential to soft power. Thus the global circuits of media framing provide a crucial context for international actors to consider methods to both leverage and cultivate their soft power.[39] The most readily apparent of such methods for international actors are the instruments of public diplomacy and strategic communication.

For Nye, public diplomacy remains a necessary instrument for those actors seeking leverage their soft power assets.[40] His endorsement of public diplomacy is largely driven by the context of information itself. Public opinion matters, because governments are increasingly held accountable for their actions—and this has much to do with the availability of information. As Steven Livingston argues, the transparency provided by the proliferation of information and communication technology (ICT) outlets has rendered nation-states increasingly susceptible to scrutiny.[41] Such transparency has empowered a range of actors, from global civil society activists to extremist and criminal organizations, to influence the global agenda. Kristin Lord states that this has increased the importance of global public opinion: "public opinion holds more sway than any previous time in history . . . A dense network of private companies, non-governmental organizations, and social movements exert even more influence relative to governments."[42] Information transparency and access have redistributed influence to other actors.

At the same time, the availability of information also offers unprecedented choices to information consumers. For Nye this choice is a "paradox of plenty," forcing nation-states to compete with other actors in order to gain the attention of publics crucial to their foreign policy objectives—where politics becomes a struggle of 'asymmetric credibility.'"[43] As Arquilla and Ronfeldt presciently argued in 1999, the conflicts of the future may increasingly be about "whose story wins."[44] To focus the attention of important global audiences, international actors turn to instruments that attempt to shape the communication landscape—instruments of soft power like public diplomacy.

PUBLIC DIPLOMACY—LEVERAGING SOFT POWER

The term *public diplomacy* reflects "an international actor's attempt to manage the international environment through engagement with a foreign public."[45] Yet what exactly does "engagement" mean—and what kind of programs and policies can be derived from this idea? Matthew Armstrong argues that public diplomacy "is not about changing public opinion unilaterally, but the proactive engagement of global audiences in support of a foreign policy that will stand alone and influence public opinion positively."[46] Armstrong's mandate for engagement incorporates what R. S. Zaharna offers as the two principal conceptions of communication in public diplomacy—the *information* and the *relation-building* frameworks that have defined previous public diplomacy programs.[47] Giles Scott-Smith describes these as a range of activities, "[from] the direct advocacy of specific policies to the more 'noble' pursuits of cultural diplomacy and the use of the arts gains sympathizers abroad."[48] These varied conceptions reveal a common thread: the relevance of communicating to foreign publics that transcends method, time, and purpose. Engagement via public diplomacy, then, is neither new nor distinct to specific international actors, but ultimately about the cultivation of influence.[49]

The common emphasis on *influence* suggests a strong link between public diplomacy and soft power. Nancy Snow states that soft power is "the most referenced term in the public diplomacy lexicon."[50] For Snow, soft power is "a new concept for an old habit"—meaning public diplomacy has been practiced in some form for some time, while soft power represents recent terminological scaffolding. Brian Hocking, however, cautions that public diplomacy represents neither a "new paradigm of international politics," nor is it "uniquely the expression of soft power."[51] Public diplomacy is a policy label with a historical trajectory that has converged with the salience of soft power's practical implications.

The term *public diplomacy* is used throughout this chapter and the remainder of the book as a descriptive term to capture the scale and scope of what are loosely described herein as "communication interventions"—or purposive attempts to communicate in global media, cultural, and informational spaces. "Public diplomacy" as it is used here encompasses but does not conflate other terms such as "propaganda," "strategic communication," "nation-branding," "international broadcasting," "cultural diplomacy," and other labels used interchangeably or in conjunction with public diplomacy. Talking about these terms in relation to "public diplomacy" is not meant to diminish their often controversial usage, but rather to capture the different interpretations of soft power and how it has been *justified* through public diplomacy programs.

Words like "propaganda" and "strategic communication," for example, are often the focus of controversy over the ethics and utility of influence-oriented communication. Robert Kelley argues, however, that instead of focusing on definitional debates about public diplomacy, we should attend to the impact of contexts: the substance of foreign policymaking and the landscape of international communication. These ultimately shape the motivations and strategies that take shape in public diplomacy programs.[52] Rather than strive for an essential definition of public diplomacy, this study views the myriad concepts related to international influence as an integral part of the analysis, and will be discussed in greater detail as they relate to the case of each international actor.

Of course, public diplomacy as a term continues to generate controversy.[53] It conjoins two normative concepts, *public* and *diplomacy*, and has since been the subject of some skepticism in the wake of its renewed importance to policymakers in the United States.[54] The term carries connotations of propaganda, due in part perhaps to how the United States has explicated its need to influence foreign parties.[55] Public diplomacy in the U.S. context is both a description of policy programs and a terminological strategy to euphemize communication interventions.

As is evident in the U.S. case, the problem of defining and evaluating public diplomacy is that it often reflects its own complicated institutional arrangement. Public diplomacy in the United States represents what veteran U.S. public diplomacy practitioner Barry Zorthian described as a label of "convenience" for budgetary purposes—linking often disparate policy programs under the mantle of agencies that must reconcile both long and short term communication mandates.[56] As John Brown has argued, public diplomacy is often at "cross-purposes"—at once aiming to cultivate long-term goodwill through educational and culture programs, maintaining the presence of U.S. perspectives in the news media sphere, and reacting to the increasingly short cycle of news and information.[57]

This book investigates how these varied programs, often not articulated as public diplomacy, cohere around basic justifications often drawn from the tenets of soft power. The following chapter will provide a more thorough discussion of soft power as a historical and theoretical construction and the implications for how the term is deployed in subsequent policy discourse around the world.

DESIGN OF THE STUDY

This book presents a comparative study of how the idea of soft power has been implemented through public diplomacy programs of four nation-states. In many respects, this kind of study is unprecedented. Eytan Gilboa observes there are few examples of theory-driven scholarship of public diplomacy aside from historical accounts.[58] Existing studies are often from the perspective of former practitioners from the United States, or represent a diluted pool of white papers, essays, and policy recommendation papers.[59] Public diplomacy as a subject for scholarly analysis is thus both lacking in theory and in danger of being conceptually distorted by U.S. foreign policy history. This book is an attempt to remedy both of these concerns, through a series of case studies presented as an interdisciplinary investigation of soft power and communication interventions.

The study is *comparative,* in order to address the concern voiced by diplomacy scholar Jan Melissen—that public diplomacy (and to some extent, the idea of soft power) is too grounded in the U.S. experience, especially when so many countries around the world now engage in some form of public diplomacy activity. Public diplomacy is no longer a U.S.-centric enterprise, but the shared concern of nation-states around the world.[60]

Comparative analysis of public diplomacy also provides insight that is relevant to both policymakers and researchers seeking insight from a diversity of evidence. Aside from Melissen's path-breaking volume, comparative studies of public diplomacy are relatively few in number. The most recent example of a systematic, comparative study of public diplomacy comes not from the academy, but from a 1979 study conducted by the United States General Accounting Office. The GAO report focused on the structures, themes, and practices of public diplomacy in seven countries: Britain, France, the Federal Republic of Germany, China, the Soviet Union, and the United States.[61] The report was justified as both a means to understand the range of available public diplomacy programs and also a source for best practices for the United States. Surprisingly, no report of the same scale or scope of that study has since been produced.[62]

The objective for this study is to build a theoretical understanding of how soft power is conceived and implemented in four global actors: China, Japan, Venezuela, and the United States. To accomplish this objective, the study is framed around the following thematic questions that address how soft power has been "translated" into each context:

1. How do actors articulate their expectations and goals through public diplomacy and strategic communication policies?

   This is accomplished by a focus on how the "outcomes" or "objectives"
   of soft power are discussed. By looking at the policy rhetoric, in press
   statements, public events, and arguments from policymakers—we get at
   the larger question of why do countries believe that soft power is important. The reasons given provide a complex, contextualized notion of soft
   power. How soft power is articulated through local contexts and strategic
   imperatives reveal the emergent perceptions about what constitutes norms
   of international politics and the distinctions between actors and resources.
   This question assesses what Robert Kelley calls the public diplomacy
   "model" used by different international actors, emphasizing the linkages
   between public diplomacy and other instruments of foreign policy.[63]

2. What do policies reveal about how the global communication infrastructure mediates political goals and expectations?

   This question refers to the issue of "scope" at stake in soft power—the
   ways in which audiences (the subjects of soft power) are rendered as relevant to soft power and significant to the objectives of public diplomacy.
   The practice of public diplomacy is illustrative of constitutive moves to
   transform international politics. As actors engage in communication interventions like public diplomacy, they reveal contingent norms of political
   agency and significance that reflect how global communication constrain
   and enable action. Reading the policies in this way helps to reveal which
   audiences "matter" in the process of international politics, what appeals
   are necessary to facilitate foreign policy goals, and finally, how the communication infrastructure of global media systems are depicted as a terrain
   of political action.

3. What assumptions about influence and communication effects are
   expressed in public diplomacy?

   This question is fundamental to the specific interpretations of soft
   power, and reflects each country's sense of what "mechanisms" work
   effectively to link soft power resources with outcomes. In other words,
   the question addresses the "how" of the soft power process. Public diplomacy programs and the reasons used to justify and warrant such policies
   reveal assumptions about the nature of influence and persuasion. Public diplomacy initiatives reflect expectations about what messages and
   actions are persuasive, what audiences do with information, and how the
   larger context of communication and media constrain acts of influence
   across borders and between publics. Soft power is based upon a basic
   premise of what constitutes influence—yet this is by no means a universal

[Handwritten margin notes: "PD models used by diff. int'l actors · their assumptions about influence + communication effects · 3 fund. elements of soft power: 1. role of publics 2. impact of global comm. flows 3. workings of influence"]

...plomacy programs indicates. By ...question refers to the communicator's public diplomacy profile.[64]

...all deal in some way with three ...le of publics, the impact of global ...influence. These elements are the ...he empirical evidence of discourse ...nework of the conclusions. These ...mechanism, and outcome—ideal-concept of soft power is translated ...Vhile there are other categorical ...nalyzing comparative public diplo-ework provides a means by which to compare the range of arguments and related policies in a cohesive and inclusive manner.

The method by which the research questions are investigated is primarily interpretive, though based firmly on available empirical evidence of public discourse, news content, and policy details. Additional evidence is drawn from direct observation and interview data obtained from representatives in the respective ministries responsible for public diplomacy. Translated material is used when necessary. Interpretation of the evidence is supported with relevant political, cultural, and historical information and is presented as separate case studies.

To clarify, this study is an in-depth look at the linkages between ideas and policies that result in public diplomacy-style initiatives and strategies, and is not meant to be an evaluation of soft power or public diplomacy *effectiveness*.[65] The research approach in this study follows a trajectory established at the intersection of communications and international relations research.[66] The analysis provides both a set of interpretive conclusions and a comparative categorical mapping of policy programs.

As the second chapter elaborates in greater detail, the study of public argument and policy rhetoric builds on insight derived from communication scholarship that is directly relevant to recent international relations (IR) scholarship.[67] Recent developments in constructivist IR scholarship posit links between discourse and practice that shed insight on how ideas translate into specific policy formulations.[68] This insight is mirrored in the development of communication studies scholarship of foreign policy. Argument theorist Thomas Goodnight claims that studying the public discourse surrounding foreign policy allows us "to see the limits and inventive possibilities of the cultural, social, practical contexts within which actions and judgments are contested."[69] Goodnight claims that the profoundly new strategic context of the post–Cold War world invites the contribution of communication studies to IR and foreign policy scholarship.

This insight warrants further attention toward how arguments reveal the available commonplaces from which to imagine and enact policy. Kenneth Burke, a pivotal thinker within communication and rhetorical studies, noted that "there is kind of a terministic compulsion to carry out the implications of one's terminology."[70] The point of this study is not, however, to show that the policies of public diplomacy *necessarily* follows the discourses of soft power. Rather, it is that we can see how in various contexts the discourse functions as a kind of resource, what rhetorical scholar Robert Asen terms a political *imagination*.[71] The interpretive analysis and the comparative framework presented here in this book together provide a comprehensive assessment—one that presents the linked significance of ideational and contextual factors for how soft power ideas have translated into public diplomacy programs.

While the presented evidence is wide-reaching, it is important to note that it is not exhaustive. The reason for this limitation is in part related to the expansive definition of public diplomacy itself. International actors engage in actions that often have implications for public diplomacy—in that such actions may be freighted with symbolic meaning that can translate into public diplomacy objectives—yet they are not purposively envisioned as public diplomacy from an institutional perspective. So, for example, foreign aid programs and presidential speeches may not be reflexively justified as public diplomacy, but nevertheless function as a kind of public diplomacy. This analysis attempts to describe as much activity and policy discussion as possible, acknowledging that other policies may fall outside the purview of overt public diplomacy discourse and institutions.

It is also important to clarify that the focus on comparative nation-state cases is not intended to reaffirm the centrality of the *national* as the most relevant boundary of analysis. As much of the recent writing on public diplomacy and soft power suggests, citizens, NGOs, and other international actors are no longer simply the targets of PD, but also producers of it.[72] If anything, the concept of soft power crystallizes the anxieties over the relevance of the nation-state as a unitary actor among peers. As nation-states struggle to affirm their credibility and navigate the complex policy networks that constrain international political action—the increasing salience of public diplomacy and international communication is a hallmark of how the nature of state action has been transformed. Case studies of nation-states presented here are illustrative snapshots of just how these bounded entities are transformed and adaptive to broader global transformations.

OVERVIEW OF THE CHAPTERS

Chapter Two provides an in-depth exploration of the term "soft power" and its relation to the historical construction of the term "public diplomacy." It introduces soft power as a historical concept within international relations scholarship, and analyzes the internal logic of the notion along with its conceptual deficiencies, in order to set up a more stable set of assumptions about soft power that are sufficient for comparative analysis. The chapter draws upon contemporary insights in constructivist IR and communication studies to elaborate how soft power can be understood as a justification for a wide range of public diplomacy policies, both implicitly and explicitly.

Chapter 3 provides analysis of contemporary debates over public diplomacy and soft power in Japan. The Japan case focuses in particular on the contemporary debates over the utility of soft power as strategic policy orientation and on efforts to leverage the considerable success of Japanese cultural industries into tangible public diplomacy outcomes.

Chapter 4 describes Venezuela and its attempts to cultivate a regional narrative surrounding its representative status as the Bolivaran Republic—via the use of rich, historical imagery and the rhetorics of international crisis and emancipation via its international broadcasting platforms, development aid, and symbolic regional institutions. These representational tactics are assessed alongside Venezuela's ambitious attempt to construct an alternative communication infrastructure through its *Telesur* international broadcasting service, a regional collaboration to provide news from a distinct regional identity position.

Chapter 5 covers the case of China, and provides a comprehensive overview of Chinese public diplomacy programs and the significant body of Chinese literature on the necessity of soft power for China's future role in international politics. The chapter covers both official efforts to marshal domestic resources toward an international advocacy campaign, as well as delves into the ways in which attitudes toward communication are translated into specific models of advocacy and relationship-building.

Chapter 6 analyzes the evolving debate within the United States over the purpose and methods of public diplomacy in the wake of rampant anti-Americanism around the world. The analysis focuses primarily on continued attempts to reconcile the imperatives of strategic communications with those of public diplomacy within the existing institutional framework of U.S. foreign policy, and the efforts to redefine public diplomacy activities through collaborative, "public diplomacy 2.0"—style communication interventions that rely on increasingly technology-driven platforms of communication facilitation.

The book concludes with a recapitulation of the observations in the previous chapters, and how the practices and discourse in each case signal a contingent evolution of soft power as a globally relevant strategic orientation. The diversity of public diplomacy perspectives and instruments are presented as evidence of public diplomacy as an increasingly viable, if not universally necessary, complement to existing foreign policy tools in a networked, highly connected field of global political action.

CONCLUSION

Soft power and public diplomacy represent terministic developments that highlight the salience and perhaps inevitable convergence of communicative action with the imperatives of international politics. Yet as public diplomacy historian Nicholas Cull argues, public diplomacy is not a *new* aspect of foreign policy, but one made "more prominent with the increased role of the public in the affairs of state and the proliferation of mechanisms for communication."[73] In the case of this book, the comparative study of soft power public argumentation provides both a needed theoretical perspective on public diplomacy discourse and a way to systematically assess the communicative dimension of the programs and campaigns that public diplomacy represents.

The study of public diplomacy and soft power could conceivably be reduced to an uncritical survey of policies. But a descriptive catalog of policy actions does little to advance theoretical inquiry into the motivations, ideas, and attitudes that ultimately shape how international actors perceive the field of international politics. This study aims to provide insight into how policies represent perceptions of necessary action and the constraints imposed by the communication environment.

Of course, this volume does not assert that the previous metrics of power (e.g. "hard" power) are irrelevant. The continued prevalence of transnational violence and economic struggle underscores the persistent centrality of concerns that have defined paradigmatic debates within international relations. The rise of soft power discourse and the growth of public diplomacy initiatives suggest, rather, that these "traditional" concerns for international actors are increasingly mediated through what Nye himself described as "the complex machinery of interdependence."[74] In the global discussion of "power" (soft or otherwise) and the recognized need to communicate, countries and organizations indirectly reconsider the meaning of international *actorhood* itself.[74]

NOTES

1. Manuel Castells, ""Informationalism, Networks, and the Network Society: A Theoretical Blueprint," in *The Network Society: A Cross-Cultural Perspective*, ed. Manuel Castells (Northampton, MA: Edward Elgar, 2004); "Communication, Power, and Counter-Power in the Network Society," *International Journal of Communication* 1 (2007):238–266.

2. See E. H. Carr, *The Twenty Years' Crisis 1919–1939: An Introduction to the Study of International Relations* (Basingstoke: Macmillan, 1983); Ronald Krebs and Patrick Thaddeus Jackson, "Twisting Tongues and Twisting Arms: The Power of Political Rhetoric," *European Journal of International Relations* 13 (2006): 35–66.

3. Samuel Huntington, "The Clash of Civilizations?" *Foreign Affairs* 72 (1993): 22–49.

4. Ronald Deibert, *Parchment, Printing, and Hypermedia: Communication in World Order Transformation* (New York: Columbia University Press, 1997); Elizabeth Hanson, *The Information Revolution in World Politics*, (Lanham, MD: Rowman and Littlefield, 2008); see also Jerry Everard, *Virtual States: The Internet and the Boundaries of the Nation-State* (London: Routledge, 2000).

5. Monroe Price, *Media and Sovereignty: The Global Information Revolution and Its Challenge to State Power* (Cambridge: The MIT Press, 2002); Report of the Defense Science Board Task Force on Strategic Communication (Washington DC: Department of Defense, 2004). www.fas.org/irp/agency/dod/dsb/commun.pdf, 12.

6. Joseph Nye, "Public Diplomacy and Soft Power," *The ANNALS of the American Academy of Political and Social Science* 616, no. 1 (2008): 94–109.

7. J. Nye, *Soft Power: The Means to Success in World Politics* (New York: Public Affairs, 2004), 31, 32.

8. Paul Sharp, "Revolutionary States, Outlaw Regimes and the Techniques of Public Diplomacy," in *The New Public Diplomacy: Soft Power in International Relations*, ed. Jan Melissen (New York: Palgrave Macmillan, 2007): 106–123.

9. Bruce Gregory, "Public Diplomacy and National Security: Lessons from the U.S. Experience," *Small Wars Journal*, August 14, 2008. http://smallwarsjournal.com/mag/2008/08/public-diplomacy-and-national.php.

10. Bruce Gregory, "Public Diplomacy: Sunrise of an Academic Field," *The ANNALS of the American Academy of Political and Social Science* 616, no. 1 (2008):274–290.

11. Eytan Gilboa, "Searching for a Theory of Public Diplomacy," *The ANNALS of the American Academy of Political and Social Science* 616, no. 1 (2008): 55–77; Jan Melissen, "The New Public Diplomacy: Between Theory and Practice," in *The New Public Diplomacy: Soft Power in International Relations*, ed. Jan Melissen (New York: Palgrave Macmillan, 2007), 5.

12. John Robert Kelly, "Between 'Take-offs' and 'Crash Landings': Situational Aspects of Public Diplomacy," in the *Routledge Handbook of Public Diplomacy*, eds. Nancy Snow and Philip Taylor (New York: Routledge, 2008): 72–85; R. S. Zaharna, "Mapping Out a Spectrum of Public Diplomacy Initiatives: Information and

Relational Communication Frameworks," in *Routledge Handbook of Public Diplomacy* (2008): 86–100.

13. Jan Melissen, "The New Public Diplomacy: Between Theory and Practice," in *The New Public Diplomacy: Soft Power in International Relations.* (New York: Palgrave, 2007): 11.

14. Kristin Lord, "What academics (should have to) say about public diplomacy." Paper presented at the American Political Science Association Conference on International Communication and Conflict, Washington, DC (2005), www8.georgetown .edu/cct/apsa/papers/lord.doc.

15. Bruce Gregory, "Public Diplomacy: Sunrise of an Academic Field."

16. Rhetorical analysis of policy is increasingly conducted in both international relations and communication studies. Rhetorical scholarship, in particular, focuses on how public argument both constructs and constrains the social imagination of policy alternatives. For a recent demonstration of this research, see Jason A. Edwards, *Navigating the Post-Cold War World: President Clinton's Foreign Policy Rhetoric* (Lanham, MD: Lexington, 2008).

17. Joseph S. Nye Jr., *The Future of Power*, 1st ed. (PublicAffairs, 2011); Joseph S. Nye, Jr., "Public Diplomacy and Soft Power," *The ANNALS of the American Academy of Political and Social Science* 616, no. 1 (March 2008):94.

18. See Thomas Risse,"'Let's Argue!': Communicative Action in World Politics," *International Organization* 54, no. 1 (2007): 1–39; Krebs and Jackson.

19. Nye Jr., *The Future of Power*, 94.

20. See 2008 Nye citation in endnotes 16, page 95.

21. Joseph Nye, "Security and Smart Power," *Journal of the American behavioral Scientist* 51, no. 9 (2008):1351–1356. See also Center for Strategic and International Studies, *CSIS Commission on Smart Power: A Smarter, More Secure America* (Washington DC, 2007).

22. Paul Robinson, *Dictionary of International Security* (Malden, MA: Polity, 2004), 94; Zahran and Ramos, "From Hegemony to Soft Power: Implications of a Conceptual Change," in Inderjeet Parmar and Michael Cox, eds., Soft Power and U.S. Foreign Affairs (London: Routledge, forthcoming 2009); Janice Bially Mattern, "Why 'Soft Power' Isn't So Soft: Representational Force and the Sociolinguistic Construction of Attraction in World Politics" *Millennium—Journal of International Studies* 33, no. 3 (2005):583–612.

23. Joseph Nye, "Public Diplomacy and Soft Power," 95.

24. Melissen, "The New Public Diplomacy," 6–7.

25. See Risse, "Let's Argue!"; Rodger Payne and Nayef Samhat *Democratizing Global Politics: Discourse Norms, International Regimes, and Political Community* (Albany, NY: SUNY University Press, 2004); Neta Crawford, *Argument and Change in World Politics: Ethnics, Decolonization, and Humanitarian Intervention,* (Cambridge, Cambridge University Press, 2002).

26. Both Brian Hocking and Janice Bially Mattern argue that Nye's notion of soft power suffers from a logical inconsistency tied to its reliance on a Habermasian framework for communicative action—simply put, public diplomacy isn't necessary

if shared cultural frameworks (necessary for communicative action) imply already shared norms and values. This critique is discussed in Chapter 1.

27. Both *ideoscape* and *mediascape* are both terms popularized by Arjun Appadurai's treatment of social transformation within globalization. These terms provide a useful contextual metaphor for the complicated interactions and "disjunctures" imposed on the institutions of modernity caused by globalization. See his *Modernity at Large, Cultural Dimensions of Globalization* (Minneapolis: University of Minnesota Press, 1996).

28. Joseph S. Nye Jr., "Responding to My Critics and Concluding Thoughts," in *Soft power and US Foreign Policy: Theoretical, Historical and Contemporary Perspectives*, ed. Inderjeet Parmar and Michael Cox (New York: Routledge, 2010), 215–227.

29. Daya Kishan Thussu, "Mapping Global Media Flow and Contra-Flow," in *Media on the Move: Global Flow and Contra-Flow*, ed. Daya Kishan Thussu (New York: Routledge), 10–29.

30. Oliver Boyd-Barrett, "Cyberspace, Globalization, and Empire," *Global Media and Communication*, 2, no. 1 (2006):21–41; see also Joseph Straubhaar *World Television: From Global to Local* (Thousand Oaks, CA: Sage, 2007).

31. Monroe Price, *Media and Sovereignty*, 2002.

32. Wenhong Chen and Barry Wellman, "The Global Digital Divide—Within and Between Countries," *IT & Society* 1, no. 7 (2004):39–45.

33. Castells, "Communication, Power, and Counter-Power in the Network Society," 2007.

34. Youna Kim, "The Rising East Asian Wave: Korean Media Go Global," in *Media on the Move: Global Flow and Contra-Flow*, ed. Daya Kishan Thussu (New York: Routledge): 121–135; see also Shawn Powers and Eytan Gilboa, "The Public Diplomacy of Al Jazeera," in *New Media and the New Middle East*, ed. Philip Seib (New York: Palgrave Macmillan, 2007): 53–80.

35. Michelle Betsill and Elisabeth Corell. *NGO Diplomacy: The Influence of Nongovernmental Organizations in International Environmental Negotiations* (Cambridge, MA: The MIT Press, 2008); Margaret Keck and Kathryn Sikkink, *Activists beyond Borders* (Ithaca, NY: Cornell University Press, 1998); Daniel Kimmage, *The Al-Qaeda Media Nexus: The Virtual Network behind the Global Message*. RFE/RL Special Report, 2008, www.rferl.org/content/article/1079736.html.

36. W. Lance Bennett, "New Media Power: The Internet and Global Activism," in *Contesting Media Power*, eds. N. Couldry and J. Curran (Lanham, MD: Rowman and Littlefield, 2003), Jeffrey Juris, "The New Digital Media and Activist Networking within Anti–Corporate Globalization Movements," *The ANNALS of the American Academy of Political and Social Science* 597, no .1 (2005):189–208.

37. Robert Gass and John Seiter, "Credibility and Public Diplomacy," in the *Routledge Handbook of Public Diplomacy*, eds. Nancy Snow and Philip Taylor (New York: Routledge, 2008), 154.

38. Joseph Nye, *The Paradox of American Power* (Oxford: Oxford University Press, 2002), 67.

39. Robert Entman, "Theorizing Mediated Public Diplomacy: The U.S. Case," *The International Journal of Press/Politics* 13, no. 2 (2008):87–102; Z. S. Justus and

Aaron Hess, "One Message for Many Audiences: Framing the Death of Abu Musab al-Zarqawi," *Report #0605 Consortium for Strategic Communication, Arizona State University* (June 23, 2006).

40. Nye, "Public Diplomacy and Soft Power" 107–8.

41. Steven Livingston, "Diplomacy in the New Information Environment," *Georgetown Journal of International Affairs* (summer/fall 2003):111–116.

42. Kristin Lord, "Voice of America: U.S. Public Diplomacy for the 21st Century" (Washington DC: Brookings, 2008), 1.

43. Report of the Defense Science Board Task Force on Strategic Communication (Washington DC: Department of Defense 2004, 20–24; Joseph Nye, *Paradox of American Power* 2002, 67.

44. David Ronfeldt and John Arquilla, "The Promise of Noöpolitik," *First Monday* 12, no. 8–6 (August 2007).

45. Nicholas Cull, *Public Diplomacy: Lessons from the Past* (Los Angeles CA: University of Southern California, 2007), 6.

46. Matthew Armstrong, "Defining Public Diplomacy," http://mountainrunner.us/public_diplomacy.html.

47. R. S. Zaharna, "Mapping Out a Spectrum of Public Diplomacy Initiatives: Information and Relational Communication Frameworks," 86–87.

48. Giles Scott-Smith, "Exchange Programs and Public Diplomacy," in the *Routledge Handbook of Public Diplomacy* (2008), 51.

49. Ali Fisher, *Bridging the Gap between Theory and Practice in Public Diplomacy*, Presentation to the International Studies Association Conference (February 16, 2009).

50. Nancy Snow, "Rethinking Public Diplomacy," in the *Routledge Handbook of Public Diplomacy*, 2.

51. Brian Hocking, "Rethinking the 'New Public Diplomacy,'" in *The New Public Diplomacy: Soft Power in International Relations*, ed. Jan Melissen (New York: Palgrave Macmillan, 2007), 33, 34.

52. John Robert Kelley, "Between 'Take-offs' and 'Crash Landings': Situational Aspects of Public Diplomacy," 72.

53. John Brown, "Public Diplomacy and Propaganda: Their Differences," *AmericanPublicDiplomacy.org* (September 16, 2008), www.unc.edu/depts/diplomat/item/2008/0709/comm/brown_pudiplprop.html.

54. Barry Zorthian, "Public Diplomacy Is Not the Answer," *PublicDiplomacy.org*, June 2004, www.publicdiplomacy.org/29.htm; R. S. Zaharna, "The Network Paradigm of Strategic Public Diplomacy," *Foreign Policy in Focus* 10, no. 1 (2005): 1–4; Giles Scott-Smith, "U.S. Public Diplomacy and the New American Studies: No Logo," 49th Parallel, summer 2006, www.49thparallel.bham.ac.uk/back/special/ScottSmith_USPDNewAmStud.pdf.

55. See "U.S. Public Diplomacy: Interagency Efforts Hampered by the Lack of a National Communication Strategy," report to the Chairman, Subcommittee on Science, State, Justice, and Commerce, and Related Agencies, Committee on Appropriations, House of Representatives. Government Accountability Office (GAO-5–323, April 2005).

56. Barry Zorthian, comments at the Smith-Mundt Symposium: A Discourse to Shape America's Discourse. January 13, 2009. http://mountainrunner.us/symposium/.

57. John Brown, "The Purposes and Cross-Purposes of American Public Diplomacy," *American Diplomacy*, August 15, 2002, www.unc.edu/depts/diplomat/ archives_roll/2002_07–09/brown_pubdipl/brown_pubdipl.html.

58. Eytan Gilboa, "Searching for a Theory of Public Diplomacy."

59. See Kristen Lord, "Voice of America: U.S. Public Diplomacy for the 21st Century"; Marwan Kraidy, "Arab Media and U.S. Policy: A Public Diplomacy Reset," *The Stanley Foundation Policy Analysis Brief* (2008).

60. Jim Murphy, "Engagement," in *Engagement: Public Diplomacy in a Globalized World*, eds. Jolyon Welsh and David Fearn (UK Foreign Commonwealth Office, 2008).

61. "The Public Diplomacy of Other Countries: Implications for the United States," report to The Congress by the Comptroller General of the Unites States, GAO Report ID-79–28, July 23, 1979.

62. Perhaps the closest approximation for this kind of study was issued in 2003 by the Foreign Policy Centre in the UK. See M. Leonard, C. Stead, and C. Smewing, *Public Diplomacy*, (London: Foreign Policy Centre, 2003).

63. John Robert Kelly, "Between 'Take-offs' and 'Crash Landings,'" (2008).

64. Ibid.

65. How actors perceive policies *as* effective, however, is certainly a focus of the study.

66. For a ground-breaking collection of essays demonstrating the possibility of this kind of research, see *Post-Realism: the Rhetorical Turn in International Relations*, eds. Francis Beer and Robert Hariman (East Lansing, MI: Michigan State University Press, 1996).

67. For more examples of these points of intersection, see Gordon Mitchell, "Rhetoric and International Relations: More Than 'Cheap Talk'" in the *Sage Handbook of Rhetorical Studies*, eds. Andrea Lunsford, Kirt H. Wilson, and Rosa Eberly (Thousand Oaks, CA: Sage, 2008), 247–264.

68. Iver Neumann, "Returning Practice to the Linguistic Turn," *Millenium—Journal of International Studies* 31 (2002):627–651; Vincent Pouliot, "The Logic of Practicality: A Theory of Practice of Security Communities," *International Organization* 62 (2008):257–288.

69. Thomas Goodnight, "Public Argument and the Study of Foreign Policy," *American Diplomacy* (1998), www.unc.edu/depts/diplomat/AD_Issues/amdipl_8/ goodnight.html; see also Thomas Goodnight, "The Nuclear Age as Argument Formation: On Rhetorical Construction and Epochal Change, working paper for the USC IIDAS (International/Interdisciplinary Discourse Analysis Series), February 2006.

70. Kenneth Burke, *Language as Symbolic Action: Essays on Life, Literature, and Method* (Berkeley: University of California Press, 1968), 45.

71. Robert Asen, *Visions of Poverty: Welfare Policy and Political Imagination* (East Lansing: Michigan State University Press, 2002).

72. Brian Hocking, "Reconfiguring Public Diplomacy: From Competition to Collaboration," in *Engagement: Public Diplomacy in a Globalized World*, eds. Jolyon Welsh and David Fearn (UK Foreign Commonwealth Office, 2008), 62–75.

73. Nicholas Cull, "Public Diplomacy: Seven Lessons for Its Future from Its Past," in *Engagement: Public Diplomacy in a globalized world*, eds. Jolyon Welsh and David Fearn (UK Foreign Commonwealth Office, 2008), 18.

74. Joseph Nye. "Misleading Metaphor of Decline," *The Atlantic*, March 1990.

75. Brian Hocking, "Rethinking the 'New Public Diplomacy,'" in *The New Public Diplomacy: Soft Power in International Relations*, ed. Jan Melissen (New York: Palgrave Macmillan, 2007), 33.

REFERENCES

Arjun Appadurai, *Modernity at Large, Cultural Dimensions of Globalization* (Minneapolis: University of Minnesota Press, 1996).

Matthew Armstrong, "Defining Public Diplomacy," http://mountainrunner.us/public_diplomacy.html (2008).

Robert Asen, *Visions of Poverty: Welfare Policy and Political Imagination* (East Lansing: Michigan State University Press, 2002).

Francis Beer and Robert Hariman (eds.) *Post-Realism: the Rhetorical Turn in International Relations* (East Lansing, MI: Michigan State University Press, 1996)

W. Lance Bennett, "New Media Power: The Internet and Global Activism," in *Contesting Media Power*, eds. N. Couldry & J. Curran (Lanham, MD: Rowman and Littlefield, 2003).

Michelle Betsill and Elisabeth Corell. *NGO Diplomacy: The Influence of Nongovernmental Organizations in International Environmental Negotiations* (Cambridge, MA: The MIT Press, 2008).

Oliver Boyd-Barrett, "Cyberspace, Globalization, and Empire," *Global Media and Communication*, 2, no. 1 (2006), 21–41

John Brown, "Public Diplomacy and Propaganda: Their Differences," *American publicdiplomacy.org*, September 16, 2008, www.unc.edu/depts/diplomat/item/2008/0709/comm/brown_pudiplprop.html.

John Brown, "The Purposes and Cross-Purposes of American Public Diplomacy," *American Diplomacy*, August 15, 2002, www.unc.edu/depts/diplomat/archives_roll/2002_07–09/brown_pubdipl/brown_pubdipl.html.

Kenneth Burke, *Language as Symbolic Action: Essays on Life, Literature, and Method* (Berkeley: University of California Press, 1968).

E. H. Carr, *The Twenty Years' Crisis 1919–1939: An Introduction to the Study of International Relations* (Basingstoke: Macmillan, 1983)

Manuel Castells, ""Informationalism, Networks, and the Network Society: A Theoretical Blueprint," in *The Network Society: A Cross-Cultural Perspective*, ed. Manuel Castells (Northampton, MA: Edward Elgar, 2004)

Manual Castells, "Communication, Power, and Counter-Power in the Network Society," *International Journal of Communication* 1 (2007):238–266.

Wenhong Chen and Barry Wellman, "The Global Digital Divide—Within and Between countries," *IT & Society* 1, no. 7 (2004):39–45.

Neta Crawford, *Argument and Change in World Politics: Ethnics, Decolonization, and Humanitarian Intervention* (Cambridge, Cambridge University Press, 2002).

Nicholas Cull, "Public Diplomacy: Seven Lessons for Its Future from Its Past," in *Engagement: Public Diplomacy in a Globalized World*, eds. Jolyon Welsh and David Fearn (UK Foreign Commonwealth Office, 2008).

Nicholas Cull, *Public Diplomacy: Lessons from the Past* (Los Angeles CA: University of Southern California, 2007).

Ronald Deibert, *Parchment, Printing, and Hypermedia: Communication in World Order Transformation* (New York: Columbia University Press, 1997).

Jason A. Edwards, *Navigating the Post–Cold War World: President Clinton's Foreign Policy Rhetoric* (Lanham, MD: Lexington, 2008).

Robert Entman, "Theorizing Mediated Public Diplomacy: The U.S. Case," *The International Journal of Press/Politics* 13, no. 2 (2008).

Jerry Everard, *Virtual States: the Internet and the Boundaries of the Nation-State* (London: Routledge, 2000).

Robert Gass and John Seiter, "Credibility and Public Diplomacy," in the *Routledge Handbook of Public Diplomacy*, eds. Nancy Snow and Philip Taylor (New York: Routledge, 2008).

Eytan Gilboa, "Searching for a Theory of Public Diplomacy," *The ANNALS of the American Academy of Political and Social Science* 616, no. 1 (2008): 55–77.

Thomas Goodnight, "Public Argument and the Study of Foreign Policy," *American Diplomacy* (1998), www.unc.edu/depts/diplomat/AD_Issues/amdipl_8/goodnight.html.

Thomas Goodnight, "The Nuclear Age as Argument Formation: On Rhetorical Construction and Epochal Change," working paper for the USC IIDAS (International/Interdisciplinary Discourse Analysis Series, February 2006).

Bruce Gregory, "Public Diplomacy and National Security: Lessons from the U.S. Experience," *Small Wars Journal*, August 14, 2008. http://smallwarsjournal.com/mag/2008/08/public-diplomacy-and-national.php.

Bruce Gregory, "Public Diplomacy: Sunrise of an Academic Field," *The ANNALS of the American Academy of Political and Social Science* 616, no. 1 (2008): 274–290.

Elizabeth Hanson, *The Information Revolution in World Politics* (Lanham, MD: Rowman and Littlefield, 2008).

Brian Hocking, "Reconfiguring Public Diplomacy: From Competition to Collaboration," in *Engagement: Public Diplomacy in a Globalized World*, eds. Jolyon Welsh and David Fearn (UK Foreign Commonwealth Office, 2008), 62–75.

Brian Hocking, "Rethinking the 'New Public Diplomacy,'" in *The New Public Diplomacy: Soft Power in International Relations*, ed. Jan Melissen (New York: Palgrave Macmillan, 2007).

Samuel Huntington, "The Clash of Civilizations?" *Foreign Affairs* 72 (1993):22–49

Jeffrey Juris, "The New Digital Media and Activist Networking within Anti–Corporate Globalization Movements," *The ANNALS of the American Academy of Political and Social Science* 597, no. 1 (2005):189–208.

Z. S. Justus and Aaron Hess, "One Message for Many Audiences: Framing the Death of Abu Musab al-Zarqawi," *Report #0605 Consortium for Strategic Communication, Arizona State University* (June 23, 2006).

Margaret Keck and Kathryn Sikkink, *Activists Beyond Borders* (Ithaca: NY: Cornell University Press, 1998).

John Robert Kelly, "Between 'Take-offs' and 'Crash Landings': Situational Aspects of Public Diplomacy," in the *Routledge Handbook of Public Diplomacy*, eds. Nancy Snow and Philip Taylor (New York: Routledge, 2008), 72–85.

Youna Kim, "The Rising East Asian Wave: Korean Media Go Global," in *Media on the Move: Global Flow and Contra-Flow*, ed. Daya Kishan Thussu (New York: Routledge, 2008), 121–135.

Daniel Kimmage, *The Al-Qaeda Media Nexus: The Virtual Network behind the Global Message* (RFE/RL Special Report, 2008), www.rferl.org/content/article/1079736 .html.

Marwan Kraidy, "Arab Media and U.S. Policy: A Public Diplomacy Reset," *The Stanley Foundation Policy Analysis Brief* (2008).

Ronald Krebs and Patrick Thaddeus Jackson, "Twisting Tongues and Twisting Arms: The Power of Political Rhetoric," *European Journal of International Relations* 13 (2006):35–66.

M. Leonard, C. Stead, and C. Smewing, *Public Diplomacy* (London: Foreign Policy Centre, 2003).

Steven Livingston, "Diplomacy in the New Information Environment," *Georgetown Journal of International Affairs* (summer/fall 2003): 111–116.

Kristin Lord, "What Academics (Should Have to) Say about Public Diplomacy," paper presented at the American Political Science Association Conference on International Communication and Conflict, Washington DC (2005), www8.georgetown.edu/cct/apsa/papers/lord.doc.

Kristen Lord, "Voice of America: U.S. Public Diplomacy for the 21st Century," Brookings Institute (2008).

Janice Bially Mattern, "Why 'Soft Power' Isn't So Soft: Representational Force and the Sociolinguistic Construction of Attraction in World Politics," *Millennium—Journal of International Studies* 33, no. 3 (2005):583–612.

Jan Melissen, "The New Public Diplomacy: Between Theory and Practice," in *The New Public Diplomacy: Soft Power in International Relations*, ed. Jan Melissen (New York: Palgrave Macmillan, 2007).

Gordon Mitchell, "Rhetoric and International Relations: More Than 'Cheap Talk,'" in *The Sage Handbook of Rhetorical Studies*, eds. Andrea Lunsford, Kirt H. Wilson, and Rosa Eberly (Thousand Oaks, CA: Sage, 2008), 247–264.

Jim Murphy, "Engagement," in *Engagement: Public Diplomacy in a Globalized World*, eds. Jolyon Welsh and David Fearn (UK Foreign Commonwealth Office, 2008).

Iver Neumann, "Returning Practice to the Linguistic Turn," *Millenium—Journal of International Studies* 31 (2002):627–651.

Joseph Nye, "Public Diplomacy and Soft Power," *The ANNALS of the American Academy of Political and Social Science* 616, no. 1 (2008): 94–109.

Joseph Nye, "Security and Smart Power," *Journal of the American behavioral Scientist* 51, no. 9 (2008):1351–1356.

Joseph Nye, *Soft Power: The Means to Success in World Politics* (New York: Public Affairs, 2004).

Joseph Nye, *The Paradox of American Power* (Oxford: Oxford University Press, 2002).

Joseph Nye, "The Misleading Metaphor of decline," *The Atlantic* (March 1990).

Rodger Payne and Nayef Samhat, *Democratizing Global Politics: Discourse Norms, International Regimes, and Political Community* (Albany, NY: SUNY University Press, 2004).

Vincent Pouliot, "The Logic of Practicality: A Theory of Practice of Security Communities," *International Organization* 62 (2008):257–288.

Shawn Powers and Eytan Gilboa, "The Public Diplomacy of Al Jazeera," in *New Media and the New Middle East*, ed. Philip Seib (New York: Palgrave Macmillan, 2007).

Monroe Price, *Media and Sovereignty: The Global Information Revolution and Its Challenge to State Power* (Cambridge: The MIT Press, 2002).

Report of the Defense Science Board Task Force on Strategic Communication (Washington DC: Department of Defense, 2004).

Thomas Risse, "'Let's Argue!': Communicative Action in World Politics," *International Organization* 54, no. 1: 1–39

Paul Robinson, *Dictionary of International Security* (Malden, MA: Polity, 2004).

David Ronfeldt and John Arquilla, "The Promise of Noöpolitik," *First Monday* 12, no. 8–6 (August 2007).

Giles Scott-Smith, "Exchange Programs and Public Diplomacy," in the *Routledge Handbook of Public Diplomacy* (2008).

Giles Scott-Smith, "U.S. Public Diplomacy and the New American Studies: No Logo," 49th Parallel, summer 2006. www.49thparallel.bham.ac.uk/back/special/ScottSmith_USPDNewAmStud.pdf.

Paul Sharp, "Revolutionary States, Outlaw Regimes and the Techniques of Public Diplomacy," in *The New Public Diplomacy: Soft Power in International Relations*, ed. Jan Melissen (New York: Palgrave Macmillan, 2007), 106–123.

Nancy Snow, "Rethinking Public Diplomacy," in *The Routledge Handbook of Public Diplomacy* (2008).

Joseph Straubhaar, *World Television: From Global to Local* (Thousand Oaks, CA: Sage, 2007).

"The Public Diplomacy of Other Countries: Implications for the United States," report to the Congress by the Comptroller General of the Unites States, GAO Report ID-79–28, July 23, 1979.

Daya Kishan Thussu, "Mapping Global Media Flow and Contra-Flow," in *Media on the Move: Global Flow and Contra-Flow*, ed. Daya Kishan Thussu (New York: Routledge, 2007), 10–29.

"U.S. Public Diplomacy: Interagency Efforts Hampered by the Lack of a National Communication Strategy," report to the Chairman, Subcommittee on Science, State, Justice, and Commerce, and Related Agencies, Committee on Appropriations, House of Representatives. Government Accountability Office (GAO-5–323, April 2005).

R. S. Zaharna, "Mapping Out a Spectrum of Public Diplomacy Initiatives: Information and Relational Communication frameworks," in *Routledge Handbook of Public Diplomacy* (2008), 86–100.

R. S. Zaharna, "The Network Paradigm of Strategic Public Diplomacy," *Foreign Policy in Focus* 10, no. 1 (2005).

Zahran and Ramos, "From Hegemony to Soft Power: Implications of a Conceptual Change," in *Soft Power and U.S. Foreign Affairs*, eds. Inderjeet Parmar and Michael Cox (London: Routledge, forthcoming 2009).

Barry Zorthian, "Public Diplomacy Is Not the Answer," *PublicDiplomacy.org*, June 2004, www.publicdiplomacy.org/29.htm.

Chapter 2

Evaluating Soft Power

Toward a Comparative Framework

INTRODUCTION

This chapter provides an overview of the idea of soft power, the controversy surrounding its definition within the study of power, and the analytical approach informing the research contained in this book. The primary goal of this chapter is to establish a conceptual and methodological basis for comparing idealizations of soft power present in various strategies of public diplomacy and strategic communication across nation-state contexts. The chapter begins with a discussion of the issues at stake in the study of soft power, by situating soft power within a contemporary understanding of power. It then reviews key contentions by the original author of the concept, Joseph Nye, and arguments put forth in other academic treatments of soft power. The chapter concludes with a discussion of the methodology deployed in this study.

The argument presented here is that the soft power concept be understood *in practice* as a complex of assumptions about the modalities of influence that are distinctive from coercive and "command" power behaviors typically associated with what Nye calls "hard power."[1] When soft power is invoked in foreign policy discourse and embodied in particular actions or interventions, it reveals the tacit logics of how soft power is supposed to "work;" how resources will be *translated into outcomes* desired by the agent seeking influence. These logics are proposed here as configurations of rhetorical procedures and relations, including what *audiences* are deemed significant within a strategic foreign policy calculus, how particular *communication forms* are expected to contribute to influence, and how *messages*, formed as either contingent arguments or symbolic action, are purported as viable to

27

achieve outcomes. By examining the justificatory and descriptive arguments for soft power as presented by Nye and others, this chapter provides an analytical basis to assess soft power as a set of assumptions about persuasion and identification in international relations.

Joseph Nye's term "soft power" is a pivotal development in the conceptual vocabulary of international politics, the practice of diplomacy, and the study of power. While perhaps not a "strategy" in the strictest sense, soft power has informed the logic behind particular strategic choices in public diplomacy and strategic communication.[2] The term clarifies the increasingly perceived necessity for non-coercive *influence*, derived from attributes of the nation-state (and other nonstate actors) that can facilitate foreign policy objectives without recourse to material, "hard" power or economic incentives. While the term "soft power" is not always explicitly invoked across the cases discussed in this book and elsewhere by policy planners—it remains a *generative* concept—justifying a host of supposedly noncoercive international communication and symbolic acts in the service of influence.

The imperative for soft power reflects growing recognition among scholars and practitioners that certain qualities of the nation-state yield particular forms of power other than those based on material or economic resources and that characteristics of the international system itself necessitate a concept like soft power.[3] The term illuminates the seemingly uncontroversial point that power can be derived from intangible sources, and, that international actors ultimately require such power in a time when military power is often asymmetrically monopolized by the United States and ubiquitous communication technology politically empowers and enable a host of *non*state actors. Within the sphere of international politics, soft power is an increasingly *necessary* component of statecraft.

Yet the soft power concept is also controversial in the sense that it has sparked debate amongst scholars over its meaning and impact, furthering its conceptual refinement and application.[4] The idea that soft power is distinguished from "hard power" by a focus on intangible attributes, co-option, and attraction seems elegantly straightforward, yet soft power remains difficult to deploy in an analytically consistent fashion. Nye's concept requires further specification of its vehicles, its relationships, and its context.

The idea of soft power carries some intuitive sense: international actors can accomplish objectives without material coercion. Yet soft power also raises a number of questions. What constitutes soft power? How do we know it when we see it? How do actors use or possess soft power? The simplicity of soft power's basic notion relies on some unelaborated assumptions about what counts as influence, persuasion, and the supposed values of symbolic and cultural attributes in relation to a concept of power. Soft power also relies on a conception of power that does not clearly specify distinctions between capacities (the resources an actor might possess), vehicles (policies or other attempts to wield soft power resources), and effects (the outcomes that can be derived from soft power). And because soft power supposedly operates in contexts outside of traditional IR-centric disciplinary concerns (e.g., communication, media, cultural flows, social structures), unpacking the idea of soft power invites contribution from disciplinary perspectives on communication, persuasion, and culture from outside the sphere of international relations scholarship.

WHAT IS SOFT POWER?

The description of soft power as elaborated by Joseph Nye is the basis for the comparative analysis presented in this book. In Nye's *The Future of Power*, he defines soft power as "the ability to get preferred outcomes through the co-optive means of agenda-setting, persuasion, and attraction."[5] Soft power is thus a *capacity* that can be leveraged by international actors. According to this definition soft power involves three kinds of "behaviors": agenda-setting (which Nye often conflates with "framing"), persuasion, and attraction. These are what actors do in the wielding of soft power in order to achieve preferred outcomes. The behaviors are not necessarily exclusive to soft power, though attraction is clearly the archetypical soft power behavior.

Soft power behaviors represent means to achieve outcomes that reflect the reality of "competitive struggles over legitimacy," as perceived by international actors.[6] As Nye argues, soft power "depends upon credibility."[7] Yet credibility plays a complicated role in Nye's argument. It can be both an outcome *and* a resource in the transaction that is soft power. To clarify, Nye argues that an international actor's soft power derives from: "primarily . . . three resources: its culture (in places where it is attractive to others), its political values (when it lives up to them at home and abroad), and its foreign policies (when they are seen as legitimate and having moral authority)."[8]

To summarize, soft power involves an ability to get preferred outcomes through specific behaviors (agenda-setting, persuasion, attraction) that draw upon specific types of resources (culture, political ideas, and foreign policy legitimacy). Yet as Nye argues, soft power is not as straightforward as this model suggests. It can operate both directly between governments, or alternatively, on environments that enable an actor to get what it wants. It is ultimately contingent on a host of contextual factors—which lead Nye to offer that the "crucial intervening variable" is *power conversion*.[9] How international actors get from "resources to behavioral outcomes" is key to understanding how soft power works.[10]

Nye argues against reasoning about soft power based solely on examination of resources or solely through what actors do; rather, Nye claims to be focused on "outcomes."[11] Thus, "we must pay more attention to contexts *and* strategies."[12] Following this claim, soft power as conceived in this study is not an essentialized, universal aspect of power politics, but rather a reflection of particular historical and culturally situated reactions to the requirements of international influence. The analytic treatment of soft power presented here is a pragmatic one, conceived to examine the diversity of idealizations that are linked to particular political imperatives and historical contingencies. It involves a focus on how the imagined relations between *agents* (those actors that seek to leverage soft power) and *subjects* (the "target" of a soft power intervention) are realized in the deployment of soft power programs like public diplomacy.

Soft power is not a trans-historical constant of power politics, but, as Nye explains it, a concept that reflects particular exigencies facing agents in international affairs. In other words, soft power is a product of a particular moment. Soft power's original articulation helped to explain a historical moment in the transformation of U.S. global leadership at the end of the Cold War, and continues to provide justification for more recent reinvigoration of US public diplomacy.[13] Yet the concept has chained out to inform, explicitly other otherwise, the strategies of other international actors. And many of the analytical "problems" with soft power—such as the somewhat unclear specification of soft power's function and resources—stem from its origins as a corrective for *U.S.* foreign policy, which underscores the larger theme of this book: soft power is now a global phenomenon that is refracted through domestic, historical, and technological contexts.

The overarching objective of the book is to examine how idealizations of soft power, as component arguments about the relationship of communication to international power, have spread out to manifest in particular examples of public diplomacy and strategic communication around the world. This chapter provides a starting point for the exercise: a resource to chart the conceptual issues and inconsistencies at stake within the debate over soft power, which ultimately inform the repertoire of ideas and strategies that animate soft power programs and initiatives in countries around the world.

The intention is to provide a basis for the examination of soft power as articulated by policy leadership, public discourse, and in the design of programs that appear to reflect a soft power imperative. The method choice adopted here is a textual analysis derived, in part, from interpretive rhetorical and argumentation studies—in that evidence for how soft power manifests as a meaningful strategic position coheres in justificatory language and soft power-based programs and initiatives.[14] When policymakers, pundits, and other public intellectuals talk about soft power, they endow the notion with an operative significance that extends beyond the straightforward explanation originally voiced by Nye. Likewise, programs like public diplomacy are also encoded with an intrinsic sense of ideal modes for communication, intended audience, and outcomes.

This approach toward understanding soft power also draws from the constructivist position articulated by Stefano Guzzini and others within the postfoundationalist tradition of international relations—that analysts should look to the performative nature of power, how it comes to mean what it does in its articulation around specific circumstances and perceived exigencies.[15] Instead of drawing sharp conceptual boundaries around soft power, the methodology proceeds from identifying ideal-typical aspects that build up, emphasize, or reformulate ideas from the original soft power arguments elaborated by Nye. The analysis reveals how such typifications are visible in discourse *and* practice by practitioners, policymakers, and leaders in the cases illustrated in this volume. This approach is presented as a more pragmatic means by which we can come to understand the broader implications of soft power within the intersubjective constitution of international politics.[16]

FROM POWER TO SOFT POWER

Understanding soft power as a concept available to comparative, interpretive study requires some definitional clarification. To analyze soft power as a complex of arguably *rhetorical* assumptions requires the elaboration of what goes into the exercise and possession of soft power—how resources are deployed in some fashion in order to bring about expected soft power outcomes. A good place to start is to distinguish *power* as it is typically treated in international politics and international relations (IR) scholarship from *soft power*.

Conceptions of power in international contexts are often expressed within terms articulated by Realist scholarship in international relations, and understood as how international actors (states) use material resources to "compel another state to do something it does not want to do."[17] *Soft power*, however, is an alternative to power as a reflection of material capacities to effect outcomes. While traditional conceptions of power in IR may explain consequences of resource asymmetries and very often, particular threats to security, soft power describes the impact of norms, ideas, and culture on the capacity of to effect change. Given this distinction, soft power is not easily reconciled with Realist assumptions about international relations.

Liberal and Constructivist approaches within IR studies offer less explicit attention to power, and often locate it in the form of institutional leverage, the force of normative factors on interests, and in the various manifestations of social process to define (and limit) actor identities and culture. As such, soft power is more readily justifiable within these two paradigmatic approaches to international relations—yet Nye admits that soft power can also derive from "material" resources of power. Thus, soft power doesn't fit neatly into liberal and constructivist approaches. Clearly, power remains present in *some* form across paradigmatic depictions of international relations—and this suggests that power is a more heterogeneous concept, one that seemingly should accommodate different kinds of power variants, like soft power.

Put another way, given the different explanatory narratives offered by international relations scholarship—it is evident that power is more than the "ability to effect outcomes" or an "agent's abilities to bring about significant effects."[18] To analyze power in a way that acknowledges the *diversity* of power vehicles, actions, and outcomes requires a more comprehensive range of power types. Soft power carves out such a distinction.

Michael Barnett and Raymond Duvall assess the scholarly treatments of power to build up a taxonomy to capture power diversity, which provides a basis from which to understand soft power.[19] Their treatment of power is offered here to provide a foundation from which to assess the assumptions of soft power. Barnett and Duvall acknowledge that some power is derived from attributes of actors, while others are found in the social processes that constitute actors in their relations.[20] Their survey of power scholarship suggests that power is not reducible to individual dynamics of particular relationships nor to systemic properties that endow actors with interests and abilities. Power, in other words, can be "soft," "hard," or "sticky"—but it is rarely just one of those things to the exclusion of others. As Peter van Ham has noted, this complexity reveals the profoundly *social* determination of why and how power inhabits particular cases—power is not a caricature of nation-state potential, but a quality of social relations *within* and *among* nation-states.[21] Thus power can be seen as a *probability*, in the Weberian sense, assessed on the basis of particular assets or as a consequence of relations between agents and subjects.

Yet traditional notions of power within North American IR/political science scholarship rest on a presumed capacity for one particular actor to affect the behavior and/or options of another.[22] Barnett and Duvall's notion of power attempts to acknowledge this trend while recognizing other forms of power, in a way that is not reductive to just agent or structure centric accounts and, incidentally, can accommodate something like soft power. They define power as "the production, in and through social relations, of effects on actors that shape their capacity to control their fate."[23] This abstraction of power allows Barnett and Duvall to identify two dimensions of power relations and how these dimensions are manifest in specific kinds of effects.

Relations of power are either expressed as "interactions" or as "constitutions."[24] While interaction relations yield power effects, such as where an agent compels a subject through some particular action, a constitutive power relation suggests that the nature of the agent and the subject are *a product of that relation*, where an agent is legitimized or authorized to act in a certain way as a consequence of social arrangements.[25] This distinction of power relations maps onto the oft-described difference between the idea of "power over" versus "power to."[26] *Interaction* relations focus on how agents exercise influence *over* subjects, while *constitution* relations reflect how power may be found in "structures or discourses" that are not agent-specific, but may grant an agent the power *to* act.[27] For example, a state may utilize its credibility as a democracy to justify its actions in some way.

Barnett and Duvall argue that interactions and constitutions are specified in a variety of effects, which they identify as either *direct* or *diffuse*. In other words, power can be found in *direct* relations between agents and subjects, which they identify as either compulsory or structural power, or power operates *indirectly* through institutional or "productive" power (the latter term they use to capture the diffuse effects of network relations and discourses on subjectivity).[28]

This comprehensive framework encapsulates different ways of thinking about power to distinguish a focus on *effects or outcomes* as well as *actions or behaviors*. It allows for the fact that power can "do" different things through a variety of means. Where does soft power figure in this taxonomy?

Nye's notion of soft power is difficult to place in Barnett and Duvall's taxonomy because soft power can effectively be both diffuse and direct. It can also involve relations of constitution and interaction. Soft power can be seen as a consequence of an agent's active attempt to leverage its resources (institutional power) or a structural consequence of relations that make resources like cultural values effective *as* soft power (either structural or productive power). The only type within Barnett and Duvall's framework that does not apply easily to soft power is "compulsory power"—which closely resembles what Nye calls "command power." Perhaps not surprisingly, Nye has argued that Barnett and Duvall's treatment of power is "abstract,"[29] and that soft power is best understood as a concept policymakers recognize as informing their strategic capabilities. Power may be ideal—typically divided into Barnett and Duvall's typology—but Nye is just as concerned with the distinctions of power as understood in practice.

In Nye's formulation, soft power is something policymakers can actively pursue by linking resources to expected outcomes (e.g., the cultivation of credibility through public diplomacy programs, to facilitate attraction.). Yet while soft power may be an *accessible* concept that suggests alternatives for practitioners to "get what they want"—its conceptual flexibility carries some analytical uncertainty. If soft power is potentially *everywhere*, such as within the popularity of a country's culture or as a consequence of normative structures that sustain international cooperation, what does that say about the capacity of influence in either a predictable or at least analytically consistent way?

For Nye, soft power can be identified *post hoc* through careful process tracing—where analysts observe how an international actor translates resources into effective outcomes.[30] Nye gets around the problems of resources or behaviors as being essential *causes* of power effects by claiming that soft power is only effective in the conversion of resources through behaviors. From this perspective, we can come to understand soft power as distinct from other forms of power in reconstructing the factors that lead to particular outcomes.

Like power more generally, the concept of soft power suffers from ambiguities which often manifest in analysis that either reduces soft power to the tagging of particular resources (e.g., political values) as *inherently* possessing a particular influential "power" quality or in *post hoc*, case-based assessments of a given situation (e.g., soft power was instrumental in an outcome). Neither approach is ultimately satisfying, in part because neither captures the way in which the meaning of soft power is itself emergent in the way resources are translated into policy outcomes. For example, while one might argue that Japanese popular culture may have some inherent soft power potential, it's not entirely obvious how Japan could actively endeavor to translate this popularity into specific outcomes. No singular resource has an inherent soft power quality across contexts, nor, do behavioral outcomes (like co-option) appear as *distinctly* the result of an action, direct exposure to a resource, or as the result of a structural relation of some sort.

Soft power operates between international actors, over varied amounts of time, and very often reflects constitutive elements of the actors themselves. Nye's basic notion of "getting others to want and do what you want without the resort to material compulsion" gets complicated quickly when one considers just what things (resources, processes, etc.) incentivize action and indeed, what relations constitutes competitive actors in a field of international power relations.[31] Nye argues that the *scope* (the parties involved in a transaction of power) and the *domain* (the issue at stake) are inevitably contingent and dependent on how an actor leverages their "contextual intelligence" to translate resources into "behaviors" that lead to preferred outcomes.[32] Clearly, soft power can represent a variety of power configurations found within Barnett and Duvall's typology. This suggests that the more significant lesson of soft power is not its typological distinction of power relations and resources, but in its *usage* within strategic justifications and worldviews; the way in which the concept renders certain resources and behaviors as available to actors in international relations.

Soft Power: Meaning in Use

Power is, in Nye's words, a "contested subject."[33] Stephen Lukes likewise describes the category of "power" as a "primitive."[34] Soft power suffers similar conceptual ambiguity. It has been appropriated, critiqued, and equivocated in a variety of ways; perhaps indicative that it is difficult to reduce into a statement of theory.[35] Indeed, Nye has argued that soft power is *not a theory*—it is an "analytical concept."[36] Not surprisingly, the term has become an ideograph for noncoercive influence; it grants particular significance to resources like culture and media in foreign affairs. Soft power has grown beyond its domestic origins in Joseph Nye's arguments against U.S. declinism in the 1990s, to become a flexible signifier, explicitly or otherwise, for new and pressing requirements of international strategies of engagement, communication, and influence. This definitional flexibility has also left the notion subject to critique by skeptics such as Janice Bially-Mattern and Niall Ferguson.[37]

A generic understanding of soft power is intuitively justified in a media-saturated, post–Cold War world of ideational conflict, yet also easy to critique in the face of supposed soft power "failures"—where actors like the United States, with seemingly limitless soft power resources, struggle to retain global credibility.[38] Soft power may not be a theory, *per se*, but it does reflect an intersection or indeed, an *assemblage* of theoretical assumptions: about the requirements of international persuasion, the nature of the relationship between message and audience, and on the distinct implications of communication technology for the conduct of foreign policy. And this list is by no means exhaustive.

So what does "soft power" mean for the discourse and practice of international relations? A more appropriate question for this study is: "what *can* it mean?" Drawing loosely on Nye's descriptive language—a provisional explanation is that soft power describes the increasing importance of *intangible* elements in the workings of power—in Nye's terms—persuasion, attraction, and agenda-setting—that do not rely upon material or incentive-based resources. As Nye argues, the resources of soft power are culture, values, and perceptions of policy legitimacy. But this definition does not fully elaborate causal processes, specify the nature of the *agent* or the *subject* of power, nor really anticipate the structural context of such power. What remains to be more fully explained in a conceptual treatment of soft power is how intangible resources work to enhance or establish *co-option*—that ultimately enable an actor to get what it wants in international politics without necessarily resorting to "hard" power.

Nye's numerous writings on soft power have aimed for accessibility and clarity, perhaps at the expensive of specification.[39] This lack of specification, while at times frustrating for analysts, leaves room innovative interpretation and creative re-articulation. Soft power, since its introduction in 1990, has proven to be a flexible conceptual architecture, ready for adaptation in particular contexts. Yet it is not a prescriptive calculus of influence.

What soft power does offer is that actors, be they states or nonstates, can possess, cultivate, and deploy particular resources like political values or cultural products to achieve policy ends. It implies both a description of international affairs and a slate of possible strategic alternatives. The soft power concept is predominantly *agent* focused—actors do things with these resources to influence subjects, and to influence the agendas and preferences that would alter the attractiveness of soft power resources.

But Nye also acknowledges that the processes of soft power are impacted by contextual factors like globalization—which affect both "receiver" and the "sender."[40] Statements such as these are an invitation to consider how particular agents come to recognize what counts as persuasive, how they articulate the subjects of soft power initiatives, and how power resources are understood as useful given the contextual challenges. In this sense, soft power is both a product of contemporary conditions as much as a field of strategic possibilities. Building on this insight, Yusashi Watanabe and David McConnell argue for attention to how "attraction" and "persuasion" are socially constructed through the "indigenization of soft power."[41]

It follows that if soft power is at some level socially constructed—either as a strategic concept or as an observable dynamic of influence—then it *cannot* be reduced to a universally prescriptive calculation of influence. Nye argues that, "[a]ttraction and persuasion are socially constructed. Soft power is a dance that requires partners."[42] Therefore, soft power should be understood in terms of how certain resources and capacities are seen by international actors as both *available* to them and likely to be *effective* in persuasion or some form of influence. Nye's formulation offers a set of roughly sketched ideal-types, establishing pertinent actors, resources, behaviors, and outcomes that comprise soft power. These types provide both a range of strategic options and a guide for subsequent analysis.

To understand soft power types, deductive-nomethetic prescriptions about how actor A may get actor B to be affected in a specific way given certain parameters, are likely to be less than useful. Rather, soft power analysts are perhaps better suited to understand how presupposed soft power "resources" are put to use or are imagined to be of certain value in articulations of strategic discourse and in policy initiatives. Following this logic of inquiry, to understand soft power we need to examine the intersection of policies, strategies and discourses about such things like public diplomacy, nation-branding, cultural diplomacy, media diplomacy, etc. that embody elements of soft power. Nye calls the process by which policymakers engage in soft power as "conversion—getting from resources to behavioral outcomes."[43] Attention to this process may reveal how other concepts imbricated in soft power, such as culture, social relationships, values, and institutions are deployed in practice and endowed with significance.

Therefore, a crucial step toward understanding soft power is to ascertain how international actors understand the concept and make use of it, explicitly or implicitly, in their strategies and actions. The cases presented in this volume reveal some of the tacit and explicit assumptions that guide policy worldviews—made visible in the policies that are imbued with the *primitives* of soft power yet inevitably transformed by the social, historical, and political context of each actor. The following section elaborates Nye's terms and arguments about soft power, in order to provide a fuller account of the conceptual idealizations that have been deemed controversial by some writers, yet have also been *indigenized* in soft power programs around the world.

ORIGINS: NYE'S ANALYTICAL CONCEPT

In order to assess how nation-states have appropriated the tenets of soft power in some fashion, it is instructive to understand the original argument for soft power. Nye's version of the concept has its origins in his 1990 book *Bound to Lead* and in a *Foreign Policy* article of the same year, which was then elaborated in subsequent books, *The Paradox of American Power* (2002) and *Soft Power: The Means to Success in World Politics* (2004).[44] Soft power was a response to a trend in declinist depictions of United States at the close of the Cold War.[45] Nye claimed that hard power, the power to command that rested on a predominance of military and coercive economic power, was an insufficient measure to account for the way in which the United States sustained its position in the international system. In other words, the analytical concept is bound up in the U.S. experience.

The concept of soft power was offered as a way to describe the ability to get "others to want what you want"—rather than the ability to get others to do what you want.[46] This power is derived from the presumed strength of ideas and is demonstrated in the ability to set the political agenda, persuade through noncoercive means, and to alter the preferences of subjects to soft

power. This notion was tied to historical developments in understanding the
international system. The evolution of "complex interdependence" and the
values that sustained the international system until the end of the Cold War
lead Nye to believe that the United States was "bound to lead."[47] International
relations at the end of the Cold War represented a system sustained by values
and ideas congruent with those represented by the culture, ideology, and policies of the United States.

Soft Power or Hegemony?

Nye argues that the ability to "get what you want" via soft power, works
"through attraction rather than coercion or payments."[48] In this sense, soft
power relies on the possession of particular resources, or, the prospect of cultivating the perception that one possesses such resources in order to achieve
soft power outcomes. At first glance, this kind of power appears to be the
ability of an actor to leverage structural or *hegemonic* power over the preferences of others—or at the very least, the ability to recognize and adapt to the
perceived institutions that are valued by others:

> A state may achieve the outcomes it prefers in world politics because other
> states want to follow it or have agreed to a situation that produces such effects.
> This . . . aspect of power . . . [that] occurs when one country gets other countries
> to *want* what it wants might be called co-optive or soft power in contrast with
> the hard or command power of *ordering* others to do what it wants.[49]

The nature of influence contained in soft power owes some conceptual debt to
Antonio Gramsci's notion of hegemony, which describes how elites can sustain domination over a class differentiated society—where elites make their
own ends commonsensical, or even *desirable* by the dominated.[50] Gramscian
hegemony operates by submission and cooptation, made possible through the
domination of a particular field of ideas and norms that sustain the power of
an elite social group. In Althusserian reasoning, the power of this group manifests in the varied apparatus of norms and practices across societal institutions
and culture.[51] Nye acknowledges this debt, though curiously does not identify
his work with subsequent neo-Gramscian scholarship in IR theory.[52]

Indeed, if there is an unelaborated aspect to Nye's notion of soft power, it
is the underemphasized reliance on hegemonic means of control over subjects
rather than brute symbolic coercion. Nye's vision of soft power provides an
uncritical argument for hegemonic control over both the political agenda and
the ordering of preferences in foreign audiences. Soft power is a translation
of Gramsci's hegemony thesis into a relatively value-neutral concept for
policymakers.

Nye's description of soft power appears to reject by definition the basic Gramscian notion that coercion and cooptation are in practice inseparable— which for Geraldo Zahran and Leonardo Ramos takes some of the explanatory force out of the notion and masks what they see as the implicit goals of soft power: to sustain hegemonic domination.[53] As a result, soft power is neither a critical nor explicitly structural depiction of the workings of power. Considered as a diluted translation of hegemony, the force of soft power cannot be solely isolated from the coercive and often very material contexts that condition soft power.

For Gramsci, the power transactions involved in hegemony takes place within the political terrain of civil society, intellectuals, and the domestic institutions, while Nye is focused on recognizing the potential of co-option free of coercion as a tool for *statecraft*. To be fair, however, Nye's later writing on the relationship between hard and soft power acknowledges how coercion and co-option may be inextricable—as they represent points on a spectrum of behaviors available to agents seeking power outcomes.[54] Nye acknowledges that noncoercive behaviors and the often intangible resources of soft power are not divorced from history or the very real material asymmetries that structure relations.

But Nye does not call the effective fungibility of coercive and cooptive power resources "hegemony." Nye's later notion of *smart power* is offered instead as a corrective to categorical reasoning that assumes hard and soft power resources and behaviors can be in practice isolated and proposes a holistic view on how power resources can be translated into hard *and* soft power effects given the contextual complexities that agents and subjects confront.[55] Yet soft power continues to factor in Nye's overarching conception of power, and remains viable as a distinctive strategy for nation-states. To understand how *soft power* fits into Nye's own range of power concepts, it is first necessary to unpack Nye's basic equation for how power unfolds; how power resources are mobilized in contexts through behaviors.

From Resources to Behaviors

Soft power ultimately rests on the assumption that certain qualities can be translated into international influence that do not involve traditional material components of coercive power behaviors. One such process of translation is the capacity of an international actor (presumably in Nye's earlier work: a *nation-state*) to establish itself as representative of a "universal" cultural value or institution. If successful, then it is in a position to achieve influence without necessarily resorting to the "command power" that Nye associates with military and economic levers.

Nye argues that "the universality of a country's culture and its ability to establish a set of favorable rules and institutions that govern areas of international activity are critical sources of power."[56] Despite the fact that Nye emphasizes soft power as an agent-centric concept, his arguments about power behaviors signals a structural ambition to the notion of soft power—the ability to act upon perceptions and preferences. Indeed, soft power in this view is arguably skewed toward the structural objectives of credibility and legitimacy.[57] To assume, as Nye does, that soft power is very often operating within a contest of credibility or legitimacy is to assume that agents are embedded in structural relations where these concepts matter as constraining or enabling.

The implications are significant for a foreign policy agenda. Nye writes, "If I can get you to *want* to do what I want, then I do not have to force you to do what you do *not* want to do. If the United States represents values that others want to follow it will cost us less to lead."[58] In this argument, soft power has the potential to obviate other power mechanisms and measures. If the international system is "rigged" toward outcomes desired by an actor wielding soft power—then other forms of power are less pertinent or potentially less viable *as* power.

How does Nye distinguish this kind of power from other forms that an actor can deploy? As presented at the outset of this chapter, Nye's typology of power provides some distinction in the form of what counts as *behaviors* and *resources* of power. "Power behaviors" and "power resources" are terms used to distinguish between "hard" and "soft power."[59] *Behaviors* are ways of exercising power—that fall along a spectrum from "command power" to "co-optive power."[60] As Zahran and Ramos explain: "command power is manifested through acts of coercion and persuasion, and co-optive power can be seen in the attraction exerted by a given agent and his capacity to define political agendas."[61] While Nye has since described persuasion as more *soft*, power in this sense is manifest in what actors *do* as much as through effects.

Nye's emphasis on *behaviors* stems from two principal concerns: a general dissatisfaction with reasoning about power from resources alone, and, with a concept of power that is accessible to practice. Yet behaviors are at times ambiguously categorized in Nye's writings. They are presented as behaviors and behavioral outcomes. For example, "agenda-setting" is discussed as a behavior (a set of actions carried out by an agent) as well as an outcome (the setting of the agenda as an agent's soft power objective).[62] The latter usage inevitably involves both the agent and the subject. The liberal use of the term "behavior" in Nye's writings is indicative of the profoundly relational aspect of power that is explicit across his writings.

Resources are distinct from behaviors implicated in Nye's description of power. Hard power resources typically derive from physical, material quantities, whereas soft power resources are often intangible.[63] Hard power resources are associated with command behavior, while soft power, intangible resources are associated with co-optive behavior. Nye acknowledges this relationship is "imperfect."[64] Since nothing logically prevents one kind of behavior to draw upon either resource, the distinction between tangible and intangible becomes less useful. For example, consider the soft power value of U.S. naval assets used in providing assistance to Indonesia after the 2006 tsunami.

Nevertheless, *co-option* represents the defining conceptual characteristic of power behaviors that can be labeled as typical for soft power. Attraction represents the ideal-typical behavior on the "co-opt" end of Nye's power spectrum. With attraction, the *subjects* of power are co-opted by favorable or at least tolerant attitudes toward the particular aspects of the soft power agent (the actor effectively exerting power over a subject)—aspects that for Nye are typically culture, ideology, and institutions.[65] These, in turn, are the resources that support soft power, but with some caveats.

The resources that support soft power provide favorable conditions for soft power behaviors such as attraction or agenda-setting. Yet these resources are not by their nature effective in a soft power transaction. They must be *converted* or *translated* in appropriate contexts. Nye stresses the "parenthetical conditions" that he attaches to his list of soft power resources as crucial to reaching desired outcomes.[66]

It should be noted that the resources for soft power can also be soft power *ends in themselves* as much as vehicles to be used or cultivated. For example, a shared set of preferences may be the target of a "soft power" initiative, as much as a resource that could be drawn upon to achieve a specific foreign policy outcome. As Janice Bially-Mattern has noted, if an agent's cultural preferences are already shared with a subject, then why are behaviors designed to amplify such values, like public diplomacy, even necessary?[67] Leaving aside such criticism for the moment, Nye acknowledges that there is more room for specification.[68] The idea of soft power rests on the possibility that structural resources work upon behaviors, yet those structures themselves can be acted upon to facilitate soft power. For example, an agent can either work to amplify the value of its cultural heritage, or, it may strive to shape the shared "structures" that make its culture "valuable." This distinction becomes clearer, however, when Nye specifies how soft power "works" via what he calls "approaches" and models of "effects."[69]

Approaches to soft power reflects the way in which an agent relies upon soft power resources—that is, how an actor effectively converts resources into desired outcomes. A *passive* approach would involve an agent relying on resources already established. An *active* approach to soft power—the approach that is the central focus of the cases presented in this book—is one marked by the perceived need to "create attraction and soft power" by programs and initiatives such as public diplomacy, international broadcasting, exchange programs, etc.[70]

Soft power approaches emphasize expected effects that are either *direct* or *indirect*. Direct effects typically manifest in power relations directly between international agents and subjects. In a direct soft power scenario, policymakers in one country might respond to the perceived soft power of another country. Indirect effects involve multiple parties and/or the environment in the outcome. A country might seek influence in another country by reaching out to publics, interests groups, non-governmental organizations, or other key stakeholders that could influence decision-makers.

In *The Future of Power*, Nye makes the straightforward case that power, both in its hard and soft forms, is expressed in how resources are converted into outcomes through behaviors. Therefore, any understanding of soft power has to consider the process of this translation through action: "[w]hether the possession of power resources actually produces favorable behavior depends upon the context and the skills of the agent in converting the resources into behavioral outcomes."[71] Active approaches to soft power work to "frame", "persuade," or "attract"—yet these are ultimately contingent on the ability of the agent to comprehend its strategic situation. While notions like preference setting, credibility, and perception shaping may allude to the ambitions of soft power—it is for Nye the emphasis on the linkage between resources and the behaviors that demands the most scrutiny, rather than continued rumination over power in the abstract.

CONTROVERSIAL ASPECTS

As Bially-Mattern's argument suggests, the soft power concept is not immune to criticism. Watanabe Yasuhi and David McConnell argue that much of the confusion over soft power "stems from misunderstanding, imprecision, distortion, misuse, or in extreme cases, abuse of the concept."[72] This confusion has resulted from underspecification and oversimplification of the agents, processes, and subjects involved in soft power.

How have these elements been underspecified? In short, the ways in which soft power resources are converted into power as represented in specific policy outcomes.[73] If soft power works by the appeal of an actor's ideas, how does this actually happen? Put in Nye's terms, how does "attraction" work? Equally important, how do agents know that attraction is working? As Bially-Mattern succinctly observes: "For actors who aim to deploy soft power, success will ultimately depend on knowing how exactly to make their ideas and themselves attractive to a target population."[74] Yet, as Nye has argued, the successful deployment of soft power is not a simple task.[75]

Equally problematic is the complexity of power relations and resources. For example, Nye does not clearly articulate how particular resources function in conjunction with other more "hard" resources, or perhaps made fungible across different contexts and applications. The term "smart power" has been an attempt to integrate soft power into a more comprehensive depiction of power applied to a foreign policy framework.[76] Yet, it is evident that tangible and intangible resources do not always correspond neatly with command and co-optive "behaviors." We find soft power resources being used in decidedly coercive ways (e.g., rhetoric signaling the impending War on Terror), and hard power resources embodying intangibles that attract and coopt (such as U.S. naval resources used in 2006 for tsunami relief).

For soft power to be more than a term of convenience to justify efforts to augment international credibility or establish legitimacy, analysts needs to disentangle the definitional and logical puzzles that inhere in the concept. Analysts ideally should endeavor to understand how particular intangibles (resources) are *made valuable* in such a way as to elicit particular outcomes (actions, attitude changes, dispositions, etc.). To put the question another way, how do culture, ideas, and values do the work of soft power, and why?

Attraction as Behavior

The three principal *behaviors* involved in soft power provide a rough guide to how soft power is achieved. Two of these behaviors are fairly basic concepts. Agenda-setting/framing operates on the level of perception—influencing how actors, events, or controversies should be understood from a range of possible interpretations. Persuasion is likewise relatively straightforward. As a soft power behavior, persuasion is a means by which agents use arguments to move the beliefs of subjects in some direction. And there may be some in-practice overlap between agenda-setting/framing behaviors and persuasion behaviors, since persuasion most likely involves the selective framing of situations and issues. The idea of "attraction," however, rests on some unelaborated assumptions about how agent characteristics can be translated into soft power outcomes.

Attraction is probably better understood as a form of symbolic, influence-oriented communication that operates in both the passive and active sense of soft power. Thus, attraction can play multiple roles in a soft power relationship—it is a *behavior* in the active approach to soft power, and, a *resource* to be leveraged to achieve an outcome. Attraction thus could be the *outcome*

of active persuasion or advocacy to make resources compelling in some
symbolic way, such as the result of a public diplomacy campaign designed
to promote a political value or cultural asset. Attraction could also reflect the
already existing influence of shared values between subject and agent—a
latent quality of a relationship between agents and subjects.

Attraction is argued by Nye as a crucial mechanism by which soft power
co-opts subjects. Nye claims that attraction is analogous to uses of the term in
relations between individuals. Yet it is unclear whether this analogy translates
directly into the field of political action and influence between international
actors. Attraction instead functions as a generic, covering term—that encompasses the ways in which strategies of appeal facilitate *identification* between
agent and subject.

Nye describes attraction as something "more complex than it first
appears."[77] Attraction implies the magnetic or alluring qualities of an agent—
which can yield both positive and negative attention.[78] Though Nye offers a
number of analogous psychological depictions of attraction, the underlying
logic appears to reflect an Aristotelian sense of "credibility"—which can be
derived from competence, virtue, and good will. Attraction reflects a complex
of attributes—which Nye stresses as only contingently relevant: an agent's
attributes are meaningful only in how they are recognized by the subject of
soft power.

Yet attributes that Nye associates with attraction are not *in themselves*
behaviors—they are qualities, and thus potential resources. To complicate
matters, Nye argues that the "clusters of qualities" that make an agent "attractive" are crucial for converting resources (culture, values, and policies) into
soft power.[79] Presented in this way, attraction appears to rely on resources that
are preconditions for yet other resources.

Given this somewhat circular reasoning, the "conditional resources" of
attraction could just as easily be the resources of soft power. For example,
a nation-states's cultural values could arguably be a basis for demonstrating
credibility *as well as* soft power resources as conceived in Nye's formulation. To be fair, however, Nye's concern with attraction is in the relational
production of shared values and aspirations. As Nye argues, "the production
of soft power by attraction depends on both the qualities of the agent and how
they are perceived by the target."[80] To understand attraction in this way is to
underscore the importance of how specific qualities of the agent are perceived
by "targeted" subjects. In this sense, attraction is probably better understood
as a "behavioral outcome"—where attraction is a *result* of communication or
influence strategies that seek to amplify an agent's resources.

To consider attraction as a behavior in the way Nye uses the term is
to assess how an agent strives to make subjects identify with an agent's

resources. Over the course of his writings on soft power, Nye has presented co-option and attraction as an implicit desire toward emulation.[81] But attraction reflects more than attraction in the individual psychological sense of the term. International actors—especially nation-states—are complex institutional arrangements of social, cultural, and historical traditions. Attraction in the simplest sense of the term assumes the nation-state to be a unitary actor. Thus, a problem with attraction may be in the metaphor itself. *Allure* and *magnetism* are psychological concepts that do not readily scale up to the level of the international actor.

Then how is attraction deployed as a crucial component of soft power? Attraction is presented as a *reaction to compelling attributes*. And there is no singular form that such a reaction might take. Subjects such as states, NGOs, or foreign publics may have positive attitudes that leave them predisposed to accommodate or actively promote the ambitions of the agent in question. In its most compelling form, subjects to attraction have an aspiration to be, in some way, like the agent in question.

To consider attraction as such a range of reactions, a more inclusive reframing is to consider attraction behaviors as those that cultivate "identification." This definition would include attempts to cultivate so-called alluring positive attention as well as attempts to symbolically establish the perception that values, ideas, and cultures are shared in a compelling way. Attraction, *as a soft power behavior*, would be an invitation to recognize a shared experience of being and perspective. Attraction is not persuasion *per se*, but resultant from representational acts that symbolize shared worlds.

Yet attraction, even thusly conceived, operates across such a broad range of engagement that it is impossible to assume that attraction works uniformly. Because attraction isn't easily rendered into neat categories of influence, attraction may be hard for agents to simply conjure up through soft power activities. Attraction may be the product of ingrained historical and cultural perspectives that do not bend easily to purposive "soft power" interventions because attraction (and its opposite) likely has significant inertia. Alternatively, there may be active countervailing efforts to compete over credibility by other agents, making attraction even more difficult to leverage, let alone cultivate. It may be hard to use public diplomacy to enhance attraction, when another actor is aggressively enhancing its own image at the expense of yours. The dramatic narratives of Islamic extremism rely extensively on the presence of a maligned Western antagonist to sustain their own legitimate claim to their political agenda.[82]

Consider the "sources" of attraction between international actors: active soft power initiatives like public diplomacy, cultural resources like entertainment media flows, and the symbolic power of mediated diplomacy. They all operate on different *time frames*, generate different *forms of appeal*, and reflect different *volumes* of communicative exchange. Therefore it is not surprising that what is "attractive" to individuals or small groups may be quite different than how attraction operates on social structures. Attraction, like soft power, is difficult to engineer from a practical perspective because it is very often the consequence of historical experience, social relations, and immersion in ubiquitous cultural and informational flows. Yet attraction remains an essential distinguishing feature of soft power behavior. If "attraction" can occur within such a broad range of contexts and interactions, then how is it *useful* for a workable translation of soft power for policymakers?

Assumptions about Relations and Effects in Soft Power

The lack of specificity in Nye's depiction of attraction is not an analytical problem *per se* if the diversity of possibilities for attraction is understood as a capacity that states can recognize as strategically available to them. Nye's argument for "attraction" is not a rigidly denotative category of power behavior, but rather a statement about how agents and subjects relate to each other in ways that are *constitutive of their identity*. Nye's "attraction" collapses a host of routes to influence under a broader term. This term signifies that symbolic resources can be marshaled to shape constitutive relations in noncoercive ways. Attraction is implicitly presented as a rhetorical tool, something that can be leveraged, cultivated, or otherwise manipulated in the process of influence. Rather than provide a prescriptive *topoi* of recipes for attraction— Nye declares it available to agents among the other tools of power.

This leaves the specifics to be largely determined by context and significantly, *how agents perceive that context*. And as Nye has argued, behaviors like attraction are realized when agents possess good "contextual intelligence," which includes a tacit understanding of which symbolic strategies are expected to "work." The soft power concept generalizes, but does not elaborate, a theoretical vocabulary to describe the available means of persuasion, identification, and perception management. Nor does it specify how soft power might operate differently on individuals, on groups, and on other aggregates of social and political identity.

But soft power doesn't mean *anything* other than force. When soft power gets articulated in policymaker contexts, an implicit set of "working assumptions" for attraction, agenda-setting, or persuasion is lurking in the background. When scholars write about of soft power, the explanatory emphasis can range from a focus on the efficacy of actions like public diplomacy programs to tracing the causal mechanisms of a particular structural quality, such as how a nation-state's political values are *inherently* influential. When the soft power concept encompasses so many routes to influence outside of the "material" and "command" oriented aspects of hard power—it risks being an empty signifier.

The vagaries inherent in the soft power concept are mitigated by Nye's preference to understand soft power as a relational consequence. In Barnett and Duvall's terminology, soft power is not easily reducible to recipes for strategic influence, but a *capacity* for outcomes derived from actions and constitutive relations. Given these relational possibilities, Nye's argues that soft power is both difficult to achieve and realistically only recognized *post hoc* through process tracing. Analysts might count the disparities in military resources or in cultural flows, but recognizing power comes when piecing together the contextual factors of a relationship in particular case of power conversion.

Yet this is not always obvious in Nye's writing. For example, the assumption that "universal" values and norms held in high regard across international subjects will be the most effective for agents suggests that there *are universal values that exist outside of context*. This definition unnecessarily detracts from Nye's emphasis on the practical implication of values for policymakers. Declaring universal values as resources for soft power without clarification confuses the value of "universal" norms with the rhetorical ambition of *making values universal* or at least identifiably common in particular contexts. Can soft power have the objective of value promotion, yet also rely on shared value conventions for persuasion, agenda-setting, and attraction?

For Bially-Mattern, this aspect of soft power is ontologically contradictory.[83] One cannot claim that soft power is about creating intersubjective consonance over ideas and at the same time argue that particular ideas are *a priori* universal in a persuasive way. It is evident in international affairs that ideas and concepts are not necessarily "universal" but rather are made into contingent social facts through communicative and symbolic social acts.[84] Soft power interventions thus presuppose a constructivist understanding of international relations.

When agents actively engage others in "soft power" behaviors, they may affirm or cultivate bonds of value identification across audiences and impact normative guidelines for international behavior. It is *this* process that soft power ultimately alludes to in its set of *prescriptions* for international actors. Soft power involves an intervention in the normative terrain of international relations—to exploit, cultivate, or otherwise transform the social position of an agent on that landscape. For example, when China aims to promote a specific interpretation of sovereignty over other values that constitute the international system, it is directly impacting the status of values that authorize, sanction, and define a legitimate international actor.[85] Distilling soft power in this way brings the notion very close to Peter Van Ham's concept of social power—which locates power in the ability of nation states to determine what is legitimate and normal in international relations.[86]

Understanding soft power as ultimately shaping perceptions of credibility and legitimacy suggests that soft power hews closer to a "power to" capacity, as opposed to "power over." This distinction is suggested in other treatments of soft power. Both Sheng Ding and Stephen Lukes attempt to clarify the different mechanisms of attraction, and note the difference between *changing incentive structures* and the *means by which interests are shaped* that gets glossed over in Nye's earlier writings on soft power.[87] They observe the need to distinguish the various mechanisms by which soft power "works" in practice that can accommodate both direct appeals and through efforts to act upon structures that condition the relation between agent and subject.

Their analysis suggests the prospect of understanding soft power through how particular ideas and values are *made* attractive—both in the intersubjective, systemic sense of constructivist IR scholarship (e.g., why democracy holds particular ideographic value across international actors) and in the policy-initiative sense of actors trying to cultivate some perception of an attractive character attribute (e.g., the perception of Canada standing for multilateral diplomatic solutions). Any soft power catalog of routes to influence for international actors could be *augmented* by assessing how agents act upon their perceptions soft power in ways that anticipate the possibility of outcomes (e.g., norm entrepreneurship, cultural promotion, etc.). Likewise, the explanatory significance of soft power would also be strengthened if such "acts" could be described in ways not reducible to epiphenomenal aspects of hard power.

Yet soft power as analytically and materially distinct from other forms of power is questionable for some scholars. Christopher Layne argues that soft power is a "luxury" of otherwise materially powerful states.[88] For Bially-Mattern, soft power elides what actually counts for influence in world politics. Soft power, in her view, is a euphemism for the "representational force" enacted when one country exerts its power over how political reality itself is described to the subjects of soft power (or, the target audience). This "force" is not the force of *attractive* ideas, but rather competing worldviews that can challenge the very foundation of an audience's sense of "ontological security."[89] Soft power in this sense is counterintuitively *coercive*—threatening the core of a subject's identity by presenting a false choice between cooption and destruction. Supposed soft power tools, like international public address, can be conceived as *weapons* that constrain structures of preference and perception.

Bially-Mattern rightly notes that soft power works fundamentally as a communicative process in shaping the perceived reality of subjects, an idea that resonates with Manual Castells's theory of power emanating from network relations, "programmed" with values and norms, or in Niklas Luhmann's depiction of how communication embodies power effects.[90] However, Bially-Mattern's critique also reflects a very narrow interpretation of the conceptual ambitions of soft power. Following Gramsci, coercion may always be present in some form of cooptation—but that doesn't make coercion the *intended* behavioral outcome of a soft power action. A communication-based power does not have to be coercive.

The concept and practice of *public diplomacy* is instructive for demonstrating the noncoercive possibilities for soft power. Few scholars of public diplomacy would claim that the majority of public diplomacy initiatives—what Nye argues as an emblematic aspect of soft power cultivation—are ultimately charged with crafting a coercive discourse formation to threaten subjects. For example, public diplomacy during the Cold War certainly helped to frame the conflict between the United States and the Soviet Union as a choice between two fundamentally opposed ideological systems.[91] Yet, the arguments embedded in the reporting of the VOA or the charged rhetoric of RFE/RL were not necessarily *coercion*—they were persuasive interventions cast as challenges to a competing ideology. Just because persuasion is manipulative doesn't make it coercive.

This doesn't mean that soft power resources can't be deployed in coercive ways. Bially-Mattern's example of President Bush's "War on Terror" rhetoric illustrate the coercive capacity of international rhetoric quite effectively.[92] But labeling President Bush's rhetoric as indicative of soft power's coercive foundation does not explain the *range* of symbolic activity (from exchanges to development aid) that does not implicitly threaten subjectivity, yet could be argued as a means to soft power. Bially-Mattern's idea of "representational force" could just as easily be categorized as a command behavior under the domain of hard power. While it is certainly true that soft power resources can also be perceived as an ontological threat (e.g., the spread of Western popular culture in China and among Islamic militants)—the overarching intentional logic of soft power (both in resources and behaviors) is less confrontational, at least according to Nye disavowal of coercion.[93]

The act of cultivating influence, through direct appeals of argumentation, through symbolic acts that illustrate identification, or through some demonstration of shared perspective is not by definition coercive—in world politics or otherwise. If a soft power agent questions the ways in which a subject draws linkages between evidence and conclusions about a given issue, this does not necessarily constitute an assault on the ontological security of that subject. When the United States sought to ramp up its public diplomacy presence in the wake of 9/11, it did so under the initial pretext of engaging audiences in order to correct misperceptions in key regional audiences.[94] And something as profoundly ineffective as the U.S. "Shared Values" campaign of brochures and documentaries could not be considered "representational force," even if it was designed to promote the benefits of democracy to the Islamic world.

The Shared Values public diplomacy campaign represents, much like many other public diplomacy programs, an extended exercise of public *argument* that falls somewhere between Nye's notion of persuasion and agenda-setting/framing. Just because argument and exposition can contain elements of threat does not invalidate them as forms of noncoercive communication. Soft power can indeed be soft—even if aspects of it may have the performative effect of coercive "hard power." To read a communication intervention as essentially coercive is an interpretive move to deny the intent and context of its implementation.

Of course, such a "performative" effect reflects a persistent analytical problem for soft power scholars and practitioners. Sheng Ding asks: how do we assess the "conversion" of power resources under the rubric of soft power?[95] As Nye argues, we can't easily disentangle soft power from hard power.[96] Bially-Mattern's important clarification here is to suggest that soft power be examined as a relationship conditioned by communication. By doing so, we can begin to unpack the analytical puzzles contained in the notion of soft power—namely, how resources are realized as a capacity for soft power through analysis of specific programs and actions. When soft power is considered as communication-centric, we can observe qualities and contexts of actors, relationships, messages, and technologies—which then provides a crucial focus to our understanding of attraction through behaviors and resources.

Bially-Mattern's critique (perhaps inadvertently) draws attention to the fact that soft power has an under-articulated conception of rhetorical action at its core. As Lukes observes, "Nye makes no distinction between different ways in which soft power can co-opt, attract and entice those subject to it; between the different ways in which it can induce their acquiescence."[97] Lukes implicitly argues for a rhetoric of soft power as a way to correct the ambiguities of persuasion and identification in soft power. As Lukes indicates, the *persuasion* in soft power can mean a number of things, including "the securing of conviction or inducing of assent by non-rational means. There is a distinction to be drawn between different modes of cooptation, different ways in which preferences can be shaped and 'self-definition.'"[98] For Lukes, we need to further develop the typology of attraction, persuasion, and agenda-setting in soft power.

Thinking beyond Resources and Behaviors

Lukes provides a significant reconsideration of soft power in that he enlarges the analytic lens beyond a focus on resources and behaviors. This move starts with a rejection of probabilistic accounts of power that focus on *vehicles* or *outcomes*—something that Nye gets around by correctly asserting the difficulty and context-dependency of any case of soft power. Yet while Nye strives to rely on straightforward language to demarcate what soft power is really about—such as "getting others to do what you want" with an emphasis on the behavioral outcomes of power, Lukes instead argues we need to look at *both* the agent and the subject.[99] How does soft power operate in the *relationship* between the agent and the subject? Lukes would not have scholars tally up specific soft power assets to understand soft power (for example, the measures of cultural product flows as a proxy for soft power). Nor would he advise, in a Foucauldian mode, examination of how subjects are defined and constrained by discourses of power—which doesn't seem to afford much contingency to the prospect of soft power.

Rather, Lukes suggests that in order to understand soft power, we need to examine

> . . . to what extent, in *what ways* and by what *mechanisms* do powerful agents influence others' conceptions of their own interests? And which *mechanisms* work to widen and which to narrow the scope for "personal reasoning" and "self-definition" of those subject to such power?[100]

Lukes is interested in the structural outcomes of power as a product of agent-driven acts that mobilize resources. Soft power for Lukes is a *capacity* that leverages resources in the context of a particular relationship. There are no soft power assets *per se*, but rather assets that are *realized as assets* in the acts of attraction and other soft power behaviors.

Which is to say, soft power is made visible in its rhetorical action. Nye suggests that careful post-hoc process tracing can reveal the causal mechanisms most likely to be explained as soft power. However, if soft power is so contingent and relation-dependent as Nye suggests, then we might also interpret soft power *as a rhetoric*—a complex of influence strategies deployed in response to the perceived strategic exigencies of a situation, yet ultimately conditioned by history and material forms of power.

As this chapter has indicated, how soft power resources are vested with rhetorical capacity, and indeed, how persuasive arguments should be constructed in interventions like public diplomacy are not elaborated in most depictions of soft power. There is also little specification within the soft power concept on the nature of the agent or importantly, the subject—the *audience* implied in soft power depictions. Soft power "works" within its own logic because of some limited ontological assumptions about the nature of the audience, such as assumed receptiveness to certain messages or its expected influence on decision-making structures (for example, foreign policy elites or extremist groups).

Nye's formulation offers an outline for what counts as the commonplaces for influence (culture, values, institutions, foreign policy motivations), and a somewhat limited measure for such resources (e.g., they are *consistent* or *universal*). As a corrective, Bially-Mattern provides an interpretation of the relation between resources and behaviors—through "representational force." Lukes goes a step further to suggest we look for the range of ways in which soft power reveals itself as actors attempt to use their soft power capacity.

Following Luke's suggestion to assess what agents can do as well as how subjects are affected would entail a conceptual analysis of soft power that links both agents and subjects. This kind of exploration might yield a more robust theory of the audience as *auditor* for soft power activities. Or, it could reframe soft power as irrevocably a *product* of the relation between subject and actor. Indeed, such a relational approach has inspired analysis of public diplomacy that suggests a less instrumental view of how communication works to accomplish foreign policy objectives through social relation building.[101]

A relational focus also provides more practice-oriented reformulation of the concept: as a way to *diagnose* soft power. For example, Edward Lock implies the crucial aspect of rhetorical exigencies *between* agent and subject by arguing that attention be directed to how subjects constrain the soft power of agents, as well as how shared social institutions are made available as soft power resources. He argues that a more robust understanding of soft power would involve a conceptual move toward the *relationship* as the key unit of analysis. A similar argument is echoed in R. S. Zaharna's writing on the strategic imperative of relationships for public diplomacy, and in Robin Brown's argument for networks as the crucial focus of analysis for public diplomacy and strategic communication.[102]

For Edward Lock, Nye's agent-centric focus in soft power obscures the significance of the relationship that forms the power relationship. Like Lukes, Lock argues that power should not be considered as a resource, but rather as a "capacity that must necessarily exist within the context of a relationship between multiple actors."[103] Therefore, soft power is a reflection of the relationship between the agent and the subject, as much as it is the capacity of certain "structures" (e.g., social institutions and ideographs) to shape preferences and alter incentives.

Lock rightly argues we cannot assume in our analysis of soft power that "structures" can be *possessed* by actors. For example, the United States does not "own" democracy or have an explicit monopoly over the value of a pluralist political system. This being the case, the United States can't just invoke these structures in a way that isn't conditioned by the relationship between the United States and its intended audience. Likewise, the rhetorical commonplaces for soft power—those institutions and values that purportedly form the basis of attraction—cannot be assumed as *common*, but rather as contestable and in need of cultivation or amplification. Nye's more recent work has considered the way in which social relationships constrain soft power—it is as much about the agent as it is about the subject.[104] In the wake of the United States' relatively ineffectual public diplomacy efforts during the George W. Bush administration, Nye's assessment is more than justified. Perhaps in reaction to the volume of critical attention, Nye's most recent statement on the subject of soft power squarely situates the concept as a *relational* form of power that acknowledges *both* direct and indirect dimensions.

A METHODOLOGY FOR UNDERSTANDING SOFT POWER

The problem of understanding soft power as something other than just the categorizing of relevant resources and behaviors is not unique to analysis of soft power. This problem also plagues scholarly treatments of *power*. The most common issues identified by Stephen Lukes in social scientific treatments of power are the "exercise" and "vehicle" fallacy.[105] The *exercise fallacy* is expressed by those who understand power solely as the "causing of an observable sequence of events." The *vehicle fallacy* is present in arguments that "power must mean whatever goes into operation when power is activated." As Lukes argues, an understanding of power needs to incorporate both faces of power, its outcomes and its resources, and scholars should be conscious of how they observe and theorize from the available evidence.

Lukes stakes out the limitations of categorical reasoning about power: "In short, observing the exercise of power can give evidence of its possession and counting power resources can be a clue to its distribution, but power is a *capacity*, and neither the exercise nor the vehicle of that capacity"[106] (emphasis added). Therefore, analysts of soft power need to be careful to reason about soft power from the most obvious data outcroppings of resources and actions (e.g., entertainment media flows, public diplomacy expenditures, polling data), because what is observed is as much a reflection of the value commitments of the researcher as much as it is a definitive case of soft power.[107] Understanding soft power as a *capacity* in Lukes's sense of the term conveniently brings together actions and resources, but begs the question of where to look. How do we know soft power when we see it?

To ascertain soft power "capacity" in the sense described by Lukes requires refiguring the ambitions of the researcher *and* what is meaningful as evidence in an anticipated case of soft power. The former requires we abandon the goal of specifying a covering law for soft power or some kind of normative abstraction, such as measuring it against an idealized communication scenario. A

Lukes-inspired approach might start with a focus on the pragmatics of how soft power is translated into actual policies that attempt to draw upon ideal-typical configurations of soft power. Soft power gains meaning in its articulation, both discursively and in material resources put to use with anticipated effect. Soft power effects are circumscribed by the way in which articulations of soft power constitutes the range of possible soft power effects.

The latter point about "evidence" also calls attention to the ways in which power is realized in particular circumstances, linking justificatory appeals to outcomes, and resources to relationships in a way that is non-reductive. Most "cases" of soft power are a constellation of factors: relations, histories, technologies, and inducement strategies. This is not to argue that soft power is an irredeemably relative concept, but a systematic understanding is ultimately ascertained in *relations*, which are likely not static. And thus soft power is ultimately *contingent*—we need to understand how soft power is both understood and identified by actors *as* soft power in particular circumstances, lest its mechanisms work in entirely predictable ways in an uncontroversial explanation or set of expectations.

Stefano Guzzini's argument for a constructivist methodology to study power is instructive to help guide analysis of soft power "capacity" realized in both discourse and practice. He argues that analysis of power should examine the "performative aspects of the concept" by arguing for attention to "what does power do?"[108] A fully exhaustive treatment of soft power outcomes, arguably beyond the scope of this book, would in Guzzini's framework describe *both* what "power" does when it is deployed in discourse and practice but also how the term has "come to mean and be able to do what it does, through a genealogical tracing of the concept—in Western scholarship and in non-Western foreign policy thinking.[109]

Guzzini draws upon Lukes to argue that there is a distinction between a *concept* and its *conceptions*—or how something like "power" is applied and interpreted.[110] Guzzini's analytical move avoids the need to fix soft power in some hierarchy of abstraction about power in traditional positivist conceptual analysis.[111] Instead of parsing the granular mechanics of soft power against other "types," a more useful methodology would be to see how the notion is re-embedded in discourses that lay claim to what soft power does. Guzzini draws inspiration from pragmatic linguistics, which leads him to argue that conceptual analysis of power (or in this case, soft power) "is not so much about what exactly is meant by the concept, but what it achieves in communication."[112]

The distinction is important methodologically, because it directs attention to the ways in which the soft power concept is deployed, rhetorically or otherwise, in discourses that define strategic necessity and expectations of possibility.[113] Guzzini argues we might examine why we call something a phenomenon of power by looking at how the act of attributing power redefines the borders of what can be done. This links power inextricably to "politics" in the sense of the "art of the possible."[114] In other words, attributing a function of power to an issue or case brings it into the public realm where action (or non-action) is compelled to justify itself. Justificatory and explanatory discourse frames the extent of soft power as a tool for statecraft—what argument scholar G. Thomas Goodnight might call the "argument formation" that outlines the strategic significance of soft power.[115]

This approach to the conceptual analysis of power informs the present study by grounding the notion of soft power in its practical application, rather than clarifying soft power as an abstraction or primitive term. Following Guzzini's and Goodnight's insights, any definition of power is a political intervention. It declares the conditions of possibility, attributes praise, blame, causality, efficacy, responsibility, practicality, etc.). Such a working definition also specifies mechanisms, assigns valued qualities and capabilities to actors, etc. The *invoking* and *specification* of soft power refers to an expected ontology of influence and contestation outside the austere geometry of material power—but where global controversy may be located and resolved.

In this sense, the policies of soft power can be read as texts themselves—a complex of policy wisdom, a policy imaginary about political agency in international relations, and contemporary ideas about how audiences (conceived as publics, targets, subjects, etc.) are rendered both susceptible to power and yet crucial to policy objectives. This method is decidedly interpretive—but focuses on concrete elements present in empirically available policies and arguments.

For example: what does it mean when the United States (via official spokespersons and concerned commentators) admits that it must move away from burnishing its own image and move toward a more facilitative role in global communication? Such an argument signals the perception that communication-enabled relationships are crucial points of leverage for the resources of soft power—legitimacy and credibility are sustained through relationships enabled and shaped by a communication environment. The boundaries of soft power discourse suggest larger *constitutive* elements of international politics and the structure of relationships that sustain such a given system.

A RHETORIC OF SOFT POWER:
INSIGHTS AND LIMITATIONS

The present study proposes that soft power can be understood through how international actors make sense of soft power as evidenced in strategic discourse and programs that are justified in the terms of soft power. Discourse and policies represent generative assumptions about the resources and behaviors that make up the soft power concept—contingent sets of policy justifications and worldviews from which programs can be derived. Each nation-state case reflects a different "conversion" process between resources and behaviors. Conversion, as Nye asserts, reflects an actor's "contextual intelligence"—how soft power agents design interventions that reconcile resources and outcomes. How power is anticipated to follow from "conversion" conveys a host of expectations grounded in strategic imperatives. Conversion is assessed on three "levels" of conceptualization: how agents conceptualize the *scope* of soft power (relations among agents and subjects), the *mechanisms* of soft power (what resources are considered available to soft power behaviors), and outcomes (the benefits of an active approach to soft power).

This methodological approach draws inspiration from studies of foreign and public policy in rhetorical studies, and from discourse-focused constructivist research in International relations and political science. While these traditions represent separate disciplinary and methodological trajectories, they yield compatible and indeed complementary insights into the nature of strategic policy analysis. The following section elaborates the methodological perspective that informs the present study.

The notion of soft power "conversion" is argued to be laden with assumptions about how international influence is *possible* and indeed *necessary* given strategic concerns and available resources. To unpack how conversion is loaded with such assumptions, attention to how scope, mechanism, and objective are represented or otherwise argued is required.

A related approach to locating the rhetorical aspect of policy is described by rhetoric and public argument scholar Robert Asen—who makes the case for an invigorated rhetorical approach to public policy analysis.[116] Asen's methodological proposition is targeted toward rhetoric and argumentation scholars, who have historically focused on case-based critical assessments of rhetorical episodes and instances of public address. Asen's call to "investigate the role of rhetoric in public policy and the rhetorical character of the policy text" is applied in this study to justify a focus on the arguments and presumptions that inhere in arguments about soft power programs and in the policies themselves.

Asen states "public policy" is "a mediation of rhetorical and material forces."[117] By this, he suggests that policies both derive from and impact material conditions—yet are also very much the product of deliberative policy discourse. In the present study, "policies" are represented as strategic arguments in support of soft power actions and are packed with assumptions about the nature of agency, proper vehicles of influence, and achievable outcomes.

This approach does not suggest that policies justified under some form of soft power are simply *constructed* artifacts of policy discourse. Rather, as Asen might argue, there is insight to be gained from examining the rhetorical moves contained in debates about policy—where policymakers, strategists, and scholars work within terministic boundaries to argue the best way to deal with very real, material concerns. As Thomas Goodnight argues in his essay on the contributions of argumentation studies to foreign policy analysis, "we examine arguments [everything from public debates to expert discussions] not to theorize about the ends of persuasion, but to see the limits and inventive possibilities of the cultural, social, practical contexts within which actions and judgments are contested."[118] Given this insight—soft power is a provisional way of dealing with perceived strategic exigencies that can be understood through how programs are justified and designed by foreign policy planners.

Asen draws upon the work of political scientist Frank Fischer to illustrate the *constitutive* nature of policymaking and, by extension, talking and debating about policy. He cites Fischer's argument that policymaking is "a constant discursive struggle over the definitions of problems, the boundaries of categories used to describe them, the criteria for their classification and assessment, and the meanings of ideals that guide particular actions."[119] Asen concludes that policies are *representations* of shared meanings, yet also *sustain* such meanings. Policies and strategies are more than rational, calculated adaptations to situations; policy inevitably reflects historical experience and cultural attitudes. If policies are formed from such constitutive elements, then what gets "constituted" in the way that different countries argue for soft power, and what does that tell us about soft power?

One way to approach this question is to link policies and strategies to deeply held cultural formations and practices. Thus, soft power and related programs like public diplomacy and strategic communication derive from the value commitments of policymakers, which inform the reasoning on soft power–inspired public diplomacy programs and reflect historically grounded strategic culture. Following this perspective, policies, strategies, and discourses about international relations can be explained through the sedimentary traces of historical and cultural experiences. Alastair Ian Johnston argues that analysis of *strategic culture* involves understanding the presence of powerful symbols that influence strategic preferences over the course of history, the predominance of strategic texts that inform policies, and prevalent norms and cultural ideas that have shaped strategic thought over time.[120]

Yet soft power and related programs like public diplomacy are reactive to arguably *recent* strategic exigencies and contexts for nation-state decision-makers. This is not to say that soft power never previously figured, implicitly or otherwise, in the formulation of policy. Rather, the work of writers like Nye suggest a transformative *moment*. The preponderance of ICTs, nonstate actors, and networks of identity movements also suggest structural conditions that "traditional" international actors have to contend with, and these factors may not necessarily fit

easily into the expected consequences of "strategic culture" as it has institutional-
ized over time. A historically rich understanding of strategic culture can arguably
provide insight into how soft power is manifest differently across nation-state
contexts. Yet such extensive work is beyond the scope of this comparative study,
which focuses on a contemporary exigency facing policymakers.

Like Johnston, Asen demonstrates the value of historical focus in his
work—which presents policymaking as a subject for rhetorical scholarship
through analysis of debates and deliberation over time. Such analysis of
policymaking debates and representations draw out the implications of how
policymakers "constellate meaning"; how a range of terms, arguments, and
meaning-making assumptions are creatively redeployed over time to frame
the concerns of governance, reinforce the role of publics (or subjects), and
envision idealized futures. Asen's perspective follows from Goodnight's
emphasis on the role of "controversy" to shape public discourse and the conventions of deliberation over specific issues or concerns, through *extended*
argument exchanges engaged by political actors and publics.[121]

In this case of soft power, however, we find a number of arguments and
programs that have chained out from their origins within U.S. discourse to
inform more recent strategic shifts. The strategic orientation toward soft power,
either implicitly or explicitly, across nation-state contexts says something more
significant about the *moment* that policymakers confront. Asen argues that "discourses implicate circulating bodies of rhetoric that serve as publicly articulated
ways of collectively understanding and evaluating our world, and propagate and
enforce social norms with material consequences."[122] Following this assertion,
soft power discourse and policies are a reflection of "collective understanding,"
a barometer of strategic necessity framed within particular nation-state contexts.

But soft power, considered as a "collective understanding," also represents
a set of *meta*-rhetorical positions sketching out the ways in which audiences,
communication forms, and the objectives of influence are available to international policymakers. The *rhetoric* of soft power is a reaction to a strategic
exigency—it presents the necessary forms of statecraft that link resources to
outcomes, in order to enable agents to influence subjects.[123] Put another way,
it is a "rhetoric of a rhetoric"—opening up available routes of influence and
rendering new ways in which power should be realized given the limitations
of hard power. The rhetoric of soft power provides both an *instrumental* set
of prescriptions and a *constitutive* set of assumptions about the role of soft
power in contemporary international politics.

Making Sense of Soft Power "Conversion"

The descriptive task set out for each case considered in this volume is to
outline the strategic emphases reflected in public diplomacy– and strategic

communication–related activities. Each chapter presents an extensive review of the programs *and* related discourse that reflect the country's translation of soft power. Each chapter concludes with a discussion of the conversion process—how the range of public diplomacy related programs and policy statements by government officials and commentators convey the tacit understanding of conversion, even if the term "soft power" is not invoked.

As stated previously, it is argued here that conversion can be ascertained on three levels of conceptualization: the *scope* of soft power the *mechanisms* of soft power, and *outcomes* associated with soft power. Each level reflects the assumptions about soft power that are evident from the policies and discourse. These levels are not intended to be fully discrete levels of analysis, but rather, analytical categories used to organize the explicit and implicit assumptions that sustain the interpretation of soft power in each country considered.

Scope

The level of "scope" is taken directly from Nye's own treatment of soft power, and is used here to draw attention to the actors involved in the soft power concept.[124] Scope signifies how actors are conceived as relevant to the workings of soft power. At the most fundamental level, Nye's notion of soft power assumes that actors other than nation-states are crucial—such as NGOs, civil society, and various forms of foreign publics. But scope can be further elaborated into comparative conceptions of agent and subject. Attention to "scope" reveals how the "targets" of soft power are indeed subject to soft power initiatives like public diplomacy.

Scope is presented as a relational category, that reflects how subjects are articulated to be audiences to direct soft power action by agents and how these audiences are pivotal to subsequent soft power outcomes. Are subjects considered as "dupes" to propagandistic symbolic activities, or, discerning auditors that are empowered to make choices—to resist the levers of soft power? Scope also reveals the significance of the relation: are agents and subjects separate actors, or, they bound together in networks of influence? Put another way, scope considers they way in which actors are considered in purely instrumental terms or alternatively as crucial to the workings of an agent's soft power.

Mechanism

The "mechanisms" of soft power reflect the linkage between what Nye calls "resources" and "behaviors" of soft power, which is further conditioned by the way in which agents prioritize communication vehicles like information technology, cultural flows, and other communication outlets. The term "mechanism" is taken from Luke's own description of soft power, presented as a necessary corrective to the biases found in analysis of power.[125]

To assess mechanisms of soft power is to examine the contingent prioritization of resources, behaviors, and communicative form. Mechanisms represent how these three aspects of soft power are seen as related, linked, and otherwise practical to the agent. Understanding this involves three questions. First, how are resources privileged in a nation-state's conception of soft power? In Nye's terms, these can include culture, political values, and foreign policy legitimacy. Second, how are resources translated into particular behaviors? For Nye, these include agenda-setting, persuasion, and attraction. Finally, what kind of communication outlets or modalities figure most prominently in the translation of resources to outcomes?

None of the nation-states considered in this study rely on one resource or behavior to the exclusion of others. Yet, the array of public diplomacy and strategic influence programs in each case reflect an underlying orientation— a ratio of emphasis where certain resources and behaviors are more salient than other aspects of soft power. "Culture," for example, may signify a range of possible interpretations, and thus be expected to be pertinent to different kinds of influence. While culture plays a significant role in Chinese arguments about its soft power as a kind of globally resonant heritage, culture in the Japanese context reflects a capacity to adapt to shifting global cultural tastes. Culture, in other words, represents different mechanisms for soft power that in turn rely on different communication modalities (media, technologies, etc.)

Outcomes

The level of "outcomes" reveals the ambition of soft power as a strategic option for nation-state agents. This level is admittedly difficult to fully disentangle from the relations between agents and subjects described at the level of *scope*. Indeed, shaping relations is very often the *objective* of soft power actions. Outcomes are presented here as a distinct level of analysis to capture the expected capacity of soft power to achieve influence of some sort; outcomes convey what soft power is supposed to strategically accomplish.

The kind of influence outcomes involved with soft power can be organized into two fundamental categories that roughly map onto Barnett and Duvall's distinction between "interaction" and "constitutive" forms of power. Soft power objectives can manifest as changing relations between two or more actors (interaction power) or on how the structure of relations, which may grant influence of some sort to the agent in question (constitutive power).

A more explicit way to explain these two soft power outcomes is through Arnold Wolfer's distinction between "possession" and "milieu" goals. Agents may conceive of soft power as instrumental in promoting, enhancing, or preserving an asset it deems as valuable; a competitive form of power strategy associated with "possession goals." In the context of soft power, this could be seen as promoting or branding a nation-state quality, or perhaps, to secure specific relational goals like increased negotiating power or policy acquiescence.

Milieu goals, however, aim to "shape . . . the environment in which a nation-state operates."[126] Similar in concept to William Riker's idea of "heresthetics," milieu goals reflect broader structural transformations to the international system that yield greater freedom to act.[127] As a kind of soft power outcome, this typically manifests as a form of structural legitimacy or institutionally sanctioned authority. Such "systemic" flexibility captures what Peter Van Ham describes as social power—which entails how agents work to define and constitute the normative boundaries of international behavior. To engage in constitutive, milieu goals is to strive to shape the normative, eth-nical and institutional aspects of international system. Put another way, this kind of soft power is a form of "rigging the game" of international relations.

The countries compared in this study are not so neatly distinguished along the dimensions of scope, mechanism, and outcome. Meaning, there are some similarities across each context, and the cases are intended to represent arche-typical distinctions of how soft power can be indigenized. Yet the concepts of soft power are different *enough* to merit consideration, and to suggest that there is something more to soft power than as a covering term for noncoercive influence and the purported power of "attraction." Each case tells the story of a different "conversion" process, where nation-states articulate implicitly through programs and explicitly in elite public statements, the outlines of a particular form of soft power. The concept of soft power, considered this way, "stands in" for a variety of configurations of influence tools and ambitions outside the traditional calculus of material, command power.

There are some obvious limitations to the course of study laid out in this book. First, a significant portion of the material scrutinized in each chapter is derived from translated or secondary sources. Second, the descriptive task of representing pragmatic applications of soft power does not yield a transhis-torical conceptual framework for soft power—though such analysis would by definition not be compatible with the methodological framework used in this study. In other words, the comparative analysis provided does not produce a more refined, prescriptive outline of soft power. Nye has *already* provided such a template, if not a theory. Rather, by looking at how soft power is discussed and implemented, explicitly or implicitly, in public discourse and in policy justifications—the analytic objective is focused to illustrate how soft power is discursively embedded in ways that provide refined definitions, conceptual limits, and anticipated effects.

The cases provide a *synchronic* comparison of soft power discourse and public diplomacy initiatives. It is admittedly a first step in a larger project. The cases serve as a starting point for more in-depth discursive and historical analysis to flesh out the likely intersubjective and intertextual diffusion of the concept that has chained out into the practical realm of international politics. Public diplomacy is not the same thing as soft power, but the growth of public diplomacy programs justified in terms of soft power suggests a more significant shift in the relation of communication to international politics is taking place that merits further study.

To complement the explicit focus on the *rhetorical* implications of soft power policies, each case involves an interpretive methodology that takes discursive and practical evidence of soft power as relatively significant (and likely constitutive). This means attention to practice as well as discourse.[128] Public diplomacy and strategic communication programs are read as indicators of broader strategic orientations and assumptions.

The analysis follows the basic constructivist injunction to "observe whether agents take it [in this case, soft power] to be real and to draw the social and political implications that follow."[129] By examining the fundamental assumptions, justifications, and evident logic in soft power programs, these cases offer a constitutive analysis of what matters in the social fact of soft power.[130] The purpose is not to tease out some causal mechanism of influence, but to assess how various aspects of the soft power concept have been expressed and, in the process, to highlight ideal-typical configurations of publics, global communication flows, and the workings of influence that emerge in each case.

The purpose of the case studies presented in this book is to illustrate the politics of definition behind soft power. What kind of idealization of soft power is revealed in how public diplomacy and strategic communication programs are articulated, designed, and argued for in public spaces? What sort of power in the terms articulated by Barnett and Duvall do these programs reflect—do they reveal an emphasis on immediate relationships or structural leverage? Do they suggest impacts on behaviors or in constitutive interests?

Instead of trying to see the ways in which differing international actors "fit" their soft power strategies and programs within Joseph Nye's arguably American-centric formula—the analysis attends to how the concept of soft power emerges in particular contexts and forms. Or, borrowing from Guzzini, the defining question becomes: how do international actors articulate the "art of the possible" with their soft power programs that are more often than not described as "public diplomacy"?

As stated previously, soft power discourse is argued here as a barometer of intention and strategic thinking. Actors decisively moving into communicative programs like public diplomacy reveal a perceived necessity to act in that particular field of international politics. Actions defined as justified by some form of soft power logic are *signals*—demonstrating recognition of the need to engage foreign audiences, to effect perception in some fashion, and to act within communication infrastructures to leverage the so-called "intangible" resources of soft power. More often than not, justifications for soft power actions like public diplomacy are voiced to suggest that more traditional institutions of foreign policy increasingly require soft power instruments to be effective. The impact of soft power in this instance is in transforming the meaning and requirements of institutions like diplomacy and defense.

But while such implications are nominally strategic, they also reveal more fundamental beliefs about the centrality of communication and influence as they relate to the imperatives of foreign policy and international politics. For example, when a nation-state or international actor argues about the requirements of soft power (why it is needed, what counts as soft power, soft power–related programs, etc.) they are also tacitly contributing to the intersubjective practical wisdom of international relations as a field of practice. Actors shift the "rules of the game" by affording particular salience to the discourse about communication and the way it conditions politics.[131] In the process, we may also find evidence of attitude shifts regarding more "traditional" forms of power in relation to soft power—and the struggle to reconcile the inertia of hard power concepts with the perceived necessity of soft power cultivation.

Soft power discourse and practice reveal particular tensions across contexts—where some aspects of power are more salient than others. The differences included the relevance of human agency in international affairs compared to other forms of actorhood, the conception of the "subject" for soft power, the relative capacity of individual versus collective reasoning over soft power interventions, and the cultural specificity of symbolic inducements and other forms of international political rhetoric. Soft power articulations contain a host of not necessarily stable assumptions about politics, agents, and the utility of communication modalities.

In the case of Venezuela's Telesur initiative, soft power is conflated with hard power in the sense that political power is invested heavily in the capacity to communicate and shape images about political reality. Telesur is not an arbitrary investment to craft some kind of Al-Jazeera of Latin America (though the Al-Jazeera analogy did provide some justification)—Telesur reveals sedimentary traces of the historical intersection of media and politics in that country. In Venezuela, mass media communication remains a crucial site of political agency and the demonstration of power. It is the battleground of political contestation, reflecting decades of conflict and controversy between political factions. As such, Telesur's existence as a kind of communication intervention into the regional politics of Latin America is freighted with particular assumptions about what media can accomplish, and how media is implicated in the formation and sustenance of the political subject. Telesur betrays a contextually inflected, particular vision of media reception, subjectivity, and the possibility of political agency through a media communication outlet.

Japan's embrace of its global pop culture as a vehicle for soft power is also laden with particular attitudes toward the ability to shape and indeed, *deny* perception. The idea that popular culture forms can both refashion a historically charged vision of Japan and at the same time deny its own Japanese character seems almost contradictory. The success of Japan's anime and manga products is nearly worldwide, and some of argued that this success is related to the way such products are devoid of particular aspects of Japanese culture. At the same time, the Japanese government has recognized potential in Japanese "cool" for exploitation as a form of soft power. Consumption of such products may predispose foreign audiences to be more interested in Japan, or more accommodating of Japanese foreign policy goals.[132] Again, in this embrace of culture as a soft power tool, we find assumptions about the nature of the audience at work—and assumed linkages between particular cultural resources and anticipated policy outcomes.

China's aggressive promotion of its Confucius Institutes, as well as the expansion of its Xinhua and broadcast television news outlets worldwide reveal an extensive reliance on the soft power concept to justify and frame its rise as a global power. In China, as elsewhere, arguments for soft power conversion are not always explicit or fully articulated. The case of China is interesting because the significance of soft power is very much an open debate among Chinese intellectuals and leadership. Chinese analysts continue to wrestle with the notion that cultural assets will somehow translate into particular foreign policy outcomes. This debate, as well as the kinds of initiatives launched under the rubric of soft power reveal a tacit developing Chinese understanding of soft power at odds with its increasingly restrictive information policies.

The case of the United States is important because the idea of soft power has its origins in Nye's thesis for the continued U.S. domination of world politics. Soft power was not originally voiced as a kind of prescription for any state to achieve soft power, but rather as a means by which a hegemon can retain its power in the international system. Some of the key points that uphold the idea of soft power—such as the value of culture, ideology, and a legitimated foreign policy—have frustrated U.S. foreign policy planners in the wake of 9/11. The U.S. policymakers did not think the United States had to amplify these values and characteristics in order to rely on its soft power. So, the United States has since struggled to implement a revisionist public diplomacy strategy that acknowledges the demands of credibility and legitimacy in a media saturated and fragmented global communication infrastructure—where the struggle is not only to be believed, but to be heard.

The case of the United States, as it moves toward a strategy of engagement via social media platforms and a facilitative (rather than monological) communication strategy, is in the process revising a provisional understanding of soft power in its implementation. R. S. Zaharna has put the issue plainly— U.S. public diplomacy needs to move from information battle to network war.[133] These metaphors contain qualitatively different notions of audiences to be persuaded, what counts as credible messaging, and how relationships are managed between nation-states and foreign publics. As the United States considers ways to diminish negative framing of its intentions and cultivate credibility among skeptical audiences, the idea of soft power is tested and revised in practice.

The point to be stressed here is that soft power is always shaped by the local discursive formations that govern foreign policy thinking. It is not a universal, fully decontextalized concept, but one that is refracted in relation to pivotal defining events, particular vocabularies of policy rhetoric, and the inevitable historical dimension of local foreign policy institutions. For this reason, ratios of emphases within the soft power concept are evident in the way it is locally articulated: Where one actor may emphasize media-based politics, another may aggressively leverage cultural capital. What one state sees as belligerent, the other sees as soft balancing. The rhetoric and practices of soft power shape these opportunities and amplify specific aspects of them. In the process, the anticipated capacity of soft power is made visible

NOTES

1. Joseph S. Nye Jr., *The Future of Power*, 1st ed. (PublicAffairs, 2011).

2. Nancy Snow, "Rethinking Public Diplomacy," in *Routledge Handbook of Public Diplomacy*, eds. Nancy Snow and Phillip Taylor (New York: Routledge, n.d.), 3–11; Jan Melissen, *The New Public Diplomacy: Soft Power in International Relations* (Palgrave Macmillan, 2007); Kathy R. Fitzpatrick, *The Future of U.S. Public Diplomacy: An Uncertain Fate* (Brill, 2010); Joseph S. Nye Jr., "Public Diplomacy and Soft Power," *The ANNALS of the American Academy of Political and Social Science* 616, no. 1 (March 2008):94–109.

3. David Ronfeldt and John Arquilla, "The Promise of Noopolitik," *First Monday* 12, no. 8 (August 6, 2007), http://firstmonday.org/htbin/cgiwrap/bin/ojs/index.php/fm/article/viewArticle/1971/1846%C2%A0%C2%A0; Nye Jr., "Public Diplomacy and Soft Power"; Eytan Gilboa, "Searching for a Theory of Public Diplomacy," *The ANNALS of the American Academy of Political and Social Science* 616, no. 1 (March 1, 2008):55–77.

4. Geraldo Zahran and Leonardo Ramos, "From Hegemony to Soft Power: Implications of a Conceptual Change," in *Soft Power and U.S. Foreign Policy: Theoretical, Historical and Contemporary Perspectives*, eds. Inderjeet Parmar and Michael Cox (New York: Taylor & Francis, 2010), 16; Yasushi Watanabe and David McConnell, "Introduction," in *Soft Power Superpowers: Cultural Assets of Japan and the United States*, eds. Yasushi Watanabe and David McConnell (Armonk, NY: M.E. Sharpe, 2008), xvii; Steven Lukes, "Power and the Battle for Hearts and Minds," *Millennium—Journal of International Studies* 33, no. 3 (June 1, 2005):477–493; Janice Bially Mattern, "Why 'Soft Power' Isn't So Soft: Representational Force and the Sociolinguistic Construction of Attraction in World Politics," *Millennium—Journal of International Studies* 33, no. 3 (June 1, 2005):583–612; Fitzpatrick, *The Future of U.S. Public Diplomacy*; Edward Lock, "Soft Power and Strategy: Developing a 'Strategic' Concept of Power," in *Soft Power and U.S. Foreign Policy: Theoretical, Historical and Contemporary Perspectives*, eds. Inderjeet Parmar and Michael Cox (New York: Taylor & Francis, 2010), 32–50; Peter Van Ham, *Social Power in International Politics* (Taylor & Francis, 2010).

5. Nye Jr., *The Future of Power*, 16.

6. Ibid., 82.

7. Ibid., 83.

8. Joseph S. Nye Jr., "Forward," in *Soft Power Superpowers: Cultural Assets of Japan and the United States*, eds. Yasushi Watanabe and David McConnell (Armonk, NY: M.E. Sharpe, 2008), x.

9. *The Future of Power*, 8.

10. Ibid.

11. Ibid., 10.

12. Ibid.

13. Zahran and Ramos, "From Hegemony to Soft Power: Implications of a Conceptual Change," 13–16.

14. G. Thomas Goodnight, "The Metapolitics of the 2002 Iraq Debate: Public Policy and the Network Imaginary," *Rhetoric and Public Affairs* 13, no. 1 (2010):65–94; Thomas Goodnight, "Public Argument and the Study of Foreign Policy," *American Diplomacy*, January 10, 1998, www.unc.edu/depts/diplomat/AD_Issues/amdipl_8/goodnight.html; Jason A. Edwards, *Navigating the Post–Cold War World: President Clinton's Foreign Policy Rhetoric* (Lexington Books, 2008); Martin J. Medhurst, *Cold War Rhetoric: Strategy, Metaphor, and Ideology* (MSU Press, 1997); Denise M. Bostdorff, *The Presidency and the Rhetoric of Foreign Crisis* (University of South Carolina Press, 1994); Robert Asen, *Visions of Poverty: Welfare Policy and Political Imagination* (Michigan State University Press, 2002); Francis A. Beer and Robert Hariman, *Post-Realism: The Rhetorical Turn in International Relations* (Michigan

State University Press, 1996); Mary E. Stuckey, "Competing Foreign Policy Visions: Rhetorical Hybrids after the Cold War," *Western Journal of Communication* 59, no. 3 (1995):214–227.

15. Stefano Guzzini, "The Concept of Power: A Constructivist Analysis," *Millennium—Journal of International Studies* 33, no. 3 (June 1, 2005):495–521; Friedrich Kratochwil, "Constructing a New Orthodoxy? Wendt's 'Social Theory of International Politics' and the Constructivist Challenge," *Millennium—Journal of International Studies* 29, no. 1 (January 1, 2000):73–101; Vincent Pouliot, "'Sobjectivism': Toward a Constructivist Methodology," *International Studies Quarterly* 51, no. 2 (2007):359–384.

16. Pouliot, "'Sobjectivism': Toward a Constructivist Methodology"; Lene Hansen, *Security as Practice: Discourse Analysis and the Bosnian War* (London: Routledge, 2006); Iver B. Neumann, "Returning Practice to the Linguistic Turn: The Case of Diplomacy," *Millennium—Journal of International Studies* 31, no. 3 (July 1, 2002):627–651.

17. Michael Barnett and Raymond Duvall, "Power in International Politics," *International Organization* 59, no. 1 (2005):40.

18. Peter Morriss, "Steven Lukes on the Concept of Power," *Political Studies Review* 4, no. 2 (May 1, 2006):126; Steven Lukes, *Power: A Radical View* (Palgrave Macmillan, 2005), 65.

19. Barnett and Duvall, "Power in International Politics."

20. Ibid., 42.

21. Van Ham, *Social Power in International Politics*, 1–23.

22. Robert Dahl, "Power," in *International Encyclopedia of the Social Sciences*, ed. David Sills, vol. 12 (New York: Free Press, 1968), 405–415; David Baldwin, "Power and International Relations," in *The Handbook of International Relations*, eds. Walter Carlsnaes, Thomas Risse, and Beth Simmons (Thousand Oaks, CA: Sage, 2002), 177–191; Lukes, *Power*; Thomas C. Schelling, *Arms and Influence* (Yale University Press, 1971), 3.

23. Barnett and Duvall, "Power in International Politics," 45.

24. Ibid., 42.

25. Ibid., 46.

26. Baldwin, "Power and International Relations"; Lukes, *Power*.

27. Barnett and Duvall, "Power in International Politics," 44.

28. Ibid., 55.

29. Nye Jr., *The Future of Power*, 242.

30. Ibid., 95.

31. Ibid., 81.

32. Ibid., 24.

33. Ibid., 5.

34. Lukes, "Power and the Battle for Hearts and Minds," 477.

35. Lock, "Soft Power and Strategy: Developing a 'Strategic' Concept of Power."

36. Joseph S. Nye Jr., "Responding to my critics and concluding thoughts," in *Soft Power and U.S. Foreign Policy: Theoretical, Historical and Contemporary*

Perspectives, eds. Inderjeet Parmar and Michael Cox (New York: Routledge, 2010), 219.

37. Janice Bially Mattern, "Why 'Soft Power' Isn't So Soft: Representational Force and the Sociolinguistic Construction of Attraction in World Politics," *Millennium—Journal of International Studies* 33, no. 3 (June 2005):583–612; Janice Bially Mattern, *Ordering International Politics: Identity, Crisis, and Representational Force* (Psychology Press, 2005); Niall Ferguson, "Think Again: Power," *Foreign Policy* (April 2003):18–24.

38. Steven R. Corman, "Narrowing the Listen–Do Gap in U.S. Public Diplomacy," *COMOPS Journal* (June 18, 2008), http://comops.org/journal/2008/06/18/narrowing-the-listen-do-gap-in-us-public-diplomacy; R. S. Zaharna, "The U.S. Credibility Deficit," *Foreign Policy in Focus* (December 13, 2006).

39. Zahran and Ramos, "From Hegemony to Soft Power: Implications of a Conceptual Change," 18.

40. Joseph S. Nye Jr., *Soft Power: The Means to Success in World Politics* (PublicAffairs, 2004), 111.

41. Watanabe and McConnell, "Introduction," xxiv.

42. Nye Jr., *The Future of Power*, 84.

43. Ibid., 8.

44. Joseph S. Nye Jr., "Soft Power," no. 80 (1990):153–171; Joseph S. Nye Jr., *Bound to Lead: The Changing Nature of American Power* (Basic Books, 1991); Joseph S. Nye Jr., *The Paradox of American Power: Why the World's Only Superpower Can't Go It Alone* (Oxford University Press US, 2002); Nye Jr., *Soft Power*.

45. Paul M. Kennedy, *The Rise and Fall of the Great Powers: Economic Change and Military Conflict from 1500 to 2000* (Random House, Inc., 1989).

46. Nye Jr., *Soft Power*, 5.

47. Robert Owen Keohane and Joseph S. Nye, *Power and Interdependence* (Scott, Foresman, 1989).

48. Nye Jr., *Soft Power*, x.

49. Nye Jr., "Soft Power," 166.

50. Antonio Gramsci, *Selections from the Prison Notebooks* (New York: International Publishers, 1971), 330–331; 348.

51. Louis Althusser, *Ideology and Ideological State Apparatuses* (New York: Montlhy Review Press, 1971).

52. Nye Jr., *The Paradox of American Power*, 9; Nye Jr., *Bound to Lead*, 32; Zahran and Ramos, "From Hegemony to Soft Power: Implications of a Conceptual Change," 14.

53. Zahran and Ramos, "From Hegemony to Soft Power: Implications of a Conceptual Change," 22.

54. Nye Jr., *The Future of Power*.

55. Ibid., 21.

56. Joseph S. Nye Jr., "Limits of American Power," *Political Science Quarterly* 117, no. 4 (2002):554.

57. Nye Jr., *The Future of Power*, 83.

58. Nye Jr., "Limits of American Power," 552.

59. Zahran and Ramos, "From Hegemony to Soft Power: Implications of a Conceptual Change," 17.

60. Nye Jr., *Soft Power*, 7.

61. Zahran and Ramos, "From Hegemony to Soft Power: Implications of a Conceptual Change," 17.

62. Nye Jr., *The Future of Power*, 90–100.

63. Nye Jr., *Soft Power*, 7.

64. Ibid.

65. Nye Jr., "Soft Power."

66. Nye Jr., *The Future of Power*, 84.

67. Bially Mattern, "Why 'Soft Power' Isn't So Soft: Representational Force and the Sociolinguistic Construction of Attraction in World Politics," 591–592.

68. Joseph S. Nye Jr., "Preface," in *Soft Power Superpowers: Cultural Assets of Japan and the United States*, eds. Yasushi Watanabe and David McConnell (Armonk, NY: M.E. Sharpe, 2008), x; Joseph S. Nye Jr., "Notes for a Soft Power Research Agenda," in *Power in World Politics*, eds. Felix Berenskoetter and Dr. Michael J. Williams (New York: Taylor & Francis, 2007), 162–172.

69. Nye Jr., *The Future of Power*, 94.

70. Ibid.

71. Ibid., 22.

72. Watanabe and McConnell, "Introduction," xviii.

73. Sheng Ding, *The Dragon's Hidden Wings: How China Rises with Its Soft Power* (Lexington Books, 2008); Lock, "Soft Power and Strategy: Developing a 'Strategic' Concept of Power."

74. Bially Mattern, "Why 'Soft Power' Isn't So Soft: Representational Force and the Sociolinguistic Construction of Attraction in World Politics," 584.

75. Nye Jr., *The Future of Power*, 101.

76. Richard Lee Armitage et al., *CSIS Commission on Smart Power: A Smarter, More Secure America* (CSIS, 2007).

77. Nye Jr., *The Future of Power*, 91.

78. Ibid., 92.

79. Ibid.

80. Ibid.

81. Nye Jr., *Soft Power*.

82. Jeffry R. Halverson, Steven R. Corman, and H. L. Goodall, *Master Narratives of Islamist Extremism* (Palgrave Macmillan, 2011).

83. Bially Mattern, "Why 'Soft Power' Isn't So Soft: Representational Force and the Sociolinguistic Construction of Attraction in World Politics."

84. Alexander Wendt, "On Constitution and Causation in International Relations," *Review of International Studies* 24, no. 5 (1998):101–118.

85. Joel Wuthnow, "The Concept of Soft Power in China's Soft Power Discourse," *Issues and Studies* 44, no. 2 (June 2008):1–28.

86. Van Ham, *Social Power in International Politics*.

87. Lukes, "Power and the Battle for Hearts and Minds," 487; Ding, *The Dragon's Hidden Wings*, 48–55.

88. Layne, "The Unbearable Lightness of Soft Power."

89. Bially Mattern, "Why 'Soft Power' Isn't So Soft: Representational Force and the Sociolinguistic Construction of Attraction in World Politics," 586.

90. Manuel Castells, *Communication power* (Oxford University Press, 2009); Stefano Guzzini, "Constructivism and International Relations: an Analysis of Niklas Luhmann's Conceptualisation of Power," in *Observing International Relations: Niklas Luhmann and World Politics*, eds. Mathias Albert and Lena Hilkermeier (London: Routledge, 2004).

91. Shawn J. Parry-Giles, *The Rhetorical Presidency, Propaganda, and the Cold War, 1945–1955* (Greenwood Publishing Group, 2002); Nicholas J. Cull, *The Cold War and the United States Information Agency: American Propaganda and Public Diplomacy, 1945–1989* (Cambridge University Press, 2009).

92. Bially Mattern, "Why 'Soft Power' Isn't So Soft: Representational Force and the Sociolinguistic Construction of Attraction in World Politics."

93. Nye Jr., *Soft Power*, x, 94, 139.

94. Jess Ford, *U.S. PUBLIC DIPLOMACY State Department and the Broadcasting Board of Governors Expand Efforts in the Middle East but Face Significant Challenges*, Testimony Before the Subcommittee on National Security, Emerging Threats, and International Relations; Committee on Government Reform; House of Representatives (Washington, DC: General Accounting Office, February 10, 2004).

95. Ding, *The Dragon's Hidden Wings*, 48–55.

96. Nye Jr., *The Future of Power*, 22–24.

97. Lukes, "Power and the Battle for Hearts and Minds," 487.

98. Ibid., 490.

99. Ibid., 492–493.

100. Ibid., 493.

101. R. S. Zaharna, *Battles to Bridges: U.S. Strategic Communication and Public Diplomacy after 9/11* (Palgrave Macmillan, 2009); Fitzpatrick, *The Future of U.S. Public Diplomacy.*

102. R. S. Zaharna, "The Soft Power Differential: Network Communication and Mass Communication in Public Diplomacy," *Hague Journal of Diplomacy* 2, no. 3 (2007):213–228; Robin Brown, "Diplomacy, Public Diplomacy and Social Networks" (presented at the International Studies Association, New Orleans, LA, 2010).

103. Edward Lock, "Soft Power and Strategy: Developing a 'Strategic' Concept of Power," in *Soft Power and U.S. Foreign Policy: Theoretical, Historical and Contemporary Perspectives*, eds. Inderjeet Parmar and Michael Cox (New York: Taylor & Francis, 2010), 38.

104. Joseph S. Nye Jr., *The Powers to Lead* (Oxford University Press US, 2008); Nye Jr., *The Future of Power.*

105. Lukes, "Power and the Battle for Hearts and Minds," 478.

106. Ibid., 479.

107. Patrick Jackson, *The Conduct of Inquiry in International Relations: An Introduction to Philosophy and International Relations* (Taylor & Francis, 2010).

108. Guzzini, "The Concept of Power," 496.

109. Amitav Acharya and Barry Buzan, *Non-Western International Relations Theory: Perspectives on and beyond Asia* (Taylor & Francis, 2009); Arlene B. Tickner and Ole Wæver, *International Relations Scholarship around the World* (Taylor & Francis, 2009).

110. Guzzini, "The Concept of Power," 502–503.

111. Giovanni Sartori, "Concept Misformation in Comparative Politics," *The American Political Science Review* 64, no. 4 (December 1, 1970):1033–1053.

112. Guzzini, "The Concept of Power," 508.

113. K.M. Fierke, "Links across the Abyss: Language and Logic in International Relations," *International Studies Quarterly* 46, no. 3 (September 2002):331–354; Neta C. Crawford, *Argument and Change in World Politics: Ethics, Decolonization, and Humanitarian Intervention* (Cambridge University Press, 2002); David R. Howarth and Jacob Torfing, *Discourse Theory in European Politics: Identity, Policy and Governance* (Palgrave Macmillan, 2005).

114. Guzzini, "The Concept of Power," 511.

115. G. Thomas Goodnight, "The Nuclear Age as Argument Formation" (presented at the Methodologies of Survival, Dubrovnik, Croatia, 1987).

116. Robert Asen, "Reflections on the Role of Rhetoric in Public Policy," *Rhetoric & Public Affairs* 13, no. 1 (2010):121–143.

117. Ibid., 124.

118. Goodnight, "Public Argument and the Study of Foreign Policy."

119. Asen, "Reflections on the Role of Rhetoric in Public Policy," 126.

120. Alaistair Iain Johnston, "Cultural Realism and Strategy in Maoist China," in *The Culture of National Security: Norms and Identity in World Politics*, ed. Peter J. Katzenstein (New York: Columbia University Press, n.d.), 216–268.

121. G. Thomas Goodnight, "Controversy," in *Argument in Controversy: Proceedings of the Seventh SCA/AFA Conference on Argumentation*, ed. Donn W. Pearson, 1991.

122. Asen, "Reflections on the Role of Rhetoric in Public Policy," 134.

123. Lloyd F. Bitzer, "The Rhetorical Situation," *Philosophy and Rhetoric* 1 (1968):6.

124. Nye Jr., *The Future of Power*, 6.

125. Lukes, "Power and the Battle for Hearts and Minds."

126. Arnold Wolfers, *Discord and Collaboration: Essays on International Politics* (Baltimore, MD: Johns Hopkins University Press, 1962), 73–77.

127. William H. Riker, *The Art of Political Manipulation* (Yale University Press, 1986).

128. Neumann, "Returning Practice to the Linguistic Turn."

129. Pouliot, "'Sobjectivism': Toward a Constructivist Methodology," 364.

130. Wendt, "On Constitution and Causation in International Relations."

131. Manuel Castells, "Communication, Power, and Counter-Power in the Network Society," *International Journal of Communication* 1 (2007):238–266.

132. Taro Aso, "Policy Speech by Minister for Foreign Affairs Taro Aso to the 166th Session of the Diet" (Speech, Ministry of Foreign Affairs, Japan, January 26, 2007), www.mofa.go.jp/announce/fm/aso/speech0701.html.

133. Zaharna, *Battles to Bridges*.

REFERENCES

Acharya, Amitav, and Barry Buzan. *Non-Western International Relations Theory: Perspectives on and beyond Asia.* Taylor & Francis, 2009.

Althusser, Louis. *Ideology and Ideological State Apparatuses.* New York: Monthly Review Press, 1971.

Armitage, Richard Lee, Joseph S. Nye, CSIS Commission on Smart Power, and Center for Strategic and International Studies. *CSIS Commission on Smart Power: A Smarter, More Secure America.* CSIS, 2007.

Asen, Robert. "Reflections on the Role of Rhetoric in Public Policy." *Rhetoric & Public Affairs* 13, no. 1 (2010):121–143.

———. *Visions of Poverty: Welfare Policy and Political Imagination.* Michigan State University Press, 2002.

Aso, Taro. "Policy Speech by Minister for Foreign Affairs Taro Aso to the 166th Session of the Diet". Speech, Ministry of Foreign Affairs, Japan, January 26, 2007. www.mofa.go.jp/announce/fm/aso/speech0701.html.

Baldwin, David. "Power and International Relations." In *The Handbook of International Relations*, eds. Walter Carlsnaes, Thomas Risse, and Beth Simmons, 177–191. Thousand Oaks, CA: Sage, 2002.

Barnett, Michael, and Raymond Duvall. "Power in International Politics." *International Organization* 59, no. 1 (2005):39–75.

Beer, Francis A., and Robert Hariman. *Post-Realism: The Rhetorical Turn in International Relations.* Michigan State University press, 1996.

Bially Mattern, Janice. "Why 'Soft Power' Isn't So Soft: Representational Force and the Sociolinguistic Construction of Attraction in World Politics." *Millennium—Journal of International Studies* 33, no. 3 (June 2005):583–612.

Bitzer, Lloyd F. "The Rhetorical Situation." *Philosophy and Rhetoric* 1 (1968):6.

Bostdorff, Denise M. *The Presidency and the Rhetoric of Foreign Crisis.* University of South Carolina Press, 1994.

Brown, Robin. "Diplomacy, Public Diplomacy and Social Networks". New Orleans, 2010.

Castells, Manuel. *Communication Power.* Oxford University Press, 2009.

———. "Communication, Power, and Counter-Power in the Network Society." *International Journal of Communication* 1 (2007):238–266.

Corman, Steven R. "Narrowing the Listen–Do Gap in U.S. public diplomacy." *COMOPS Journal* (June 18, 2008). http://comops.org/journal/2008/06/18/narrowing-the-listen-do-gap-in-us-public-diplomacy/.

Crawford, Neta C. *Argument and Change in World Politics: Ethics, Decolonization, and Humanitarian Intervention.* Cambridge University Press, 2002.

Cull, Nicholas J. *The Cold War and the United States Information Agency: American Propaganda and Public Diplomacy, 1945–1989.* Cambridge University Press, 2009.

Dahl, Robert. "Power." In *International Encylopedia of the Social Sciences*, ed. David Sills, 12:405–415. New York: Free Press, 1968.

Ding, Sheng. *The Dragon's Hidden Wings: How China Rises with Its Soft Power.* Lexington Books, 2008.

Edwards, Jason A. *Navigating the Post–Cold War World: President Clinton's Foreign Policy Rhetoric.* Lexington Books, 2008.

Ferguson, Niall. "Think Again: Power." *Foreign Policy* (April 2003):18–24.

Fierke, K.M. "Links across the Abyss: Language and Logic in International Relations." *International Studies Quarterly* 46, no. 3 (September 2002):331–354.

Fitzpatrick, Kathy R. *The Future of U.S. Public Diplomacy: An Uncertain Fate.* Brill, 2010.

Ford, Jess. *U.S. Public Diplomacy: State Department and the Broadcasting Board of Governors Expand Efforts in the Middle East but Face Significant Challenges.* Testimony before the Subcommittee on National Security, Emerging Threats, and International Relations; Committee on Government Reform; House of Representatives. Washington, DC: General Accounting Office, February 10, 2004.

Gilboa, Eytan. "Searching for a Theory of Public Diplomacy." *The ANNALS of the American Academy of Political and Social Science* 616, no. 1 (March 1, 2008):55–77.

Goodnight, G. Thomas. "Controversy." In *Argument in Controversy: Proceedings of the Seventh SCA/AFA Conference on Argumentation*, ed. Donn W. Pearson, 1991.

———. "The Metapolitics of the 2002 Iraq Debate: Public Policy and the Network Imaginary." *Rhetoric and Public Affairs* 13, no. 1 (2010):65–94.

———. "The Nuclear Age as Argument Formation." Dubrovnik, Croatia, 1987.

Goodnight, Thomas. "Public Argument and the Study of Foreign Policy." *American Diplomacy*, January 10, 1998. www.unc.edu/depts/diplomat/AD_Issues/amdipl_8/goodnight.html.

Gramsci, Antonio. *Selections from the Prison Notebooks.* New York: International Publishers, 1971.

Guzzini, Stefano. "Constructivism and International Relations: An Analysis of Niklas Luhmann's Conceptualisation of Power." In *Observing International Relations: Niklas Luhmann and World Politics*, eds. Mathias Albert and Lena Hilkermeier. London: Routledge, 2004.

———. "The Concept of Power: A Constructivist Analysis." *Millennium—Journal of International Studies* 33, no. 3 (June 1, 2005):495–521.

Halverson, Jeffry R., Steven R. Corman, and H. L. Goodall. *Master Narratives of Islamist Extremism.* Palgrave Macmillan, 2011.

Van Ham, Peter. *Social Power in International Politics.* Taylor & Francis, 2010.

Hansen, Lene. *Security as Practice: Discourse Analysis and the Bosnian War.* London: Routledge, 2006.

Howarth, David R., and Jacob Torfing. *Discourse Theory in European Politics: Identity, Policy and Governance.* Palgrave Macmillan, 2005.

Jackson, Patrick. *The Conduct of Inquiry in International Relations: An Introduction to Philosophy and International Relations.* Taylor & Francis, 2010.

Johnston, Alaistair Iain. "Cultural Realism and Strategy in Maoist China." In *The Culture of National Security: Norms and Identity in World Politics*, ed. Peter J. Katzenstein, 216–268. New York: Columbia University Press, n.d.

Kennedy, Paul M. *The Rise and Fall of the Great Powers: Economic Change and Military Conflict from 1500 to 2000.* Random House, Inc., 1989.

Keohane, Robert Owen, and Joseph S. Nye. *Power and Interdependence*. Scott, Foresman, 1989.

Kratochwil, Friedrich. "Constructing a New Orthodoxy? Wendt's 'Social Theory of International Politics' and the Constructivist Challenge." *Millennium—Journal of International Studies* 29, no. 1 (January 1, 2000):73–101.

Layne, Christopher. "The Unbearable Lightness of Soft Power." In *Soft Power and U.S. Foreign Policy: Theoretical, Historical and Contemporary Perspectives*, eds. Inderjeet Parmar and Michael Cox, 51–82. New York: Taylor & Francis, 2010.

Lock, Edward. "Soft Power and Strategy: Developing a 'Strategic' Concept of Power." In *Soft Power and U.S. Foreign Policy: Theoretical, Historical and Contemporary Perspectives*, eds. Inderjeet Parmar and Michael Cox, 32–50. New York: Taylor & Francis, 2010.

Lukes, Steven. "Power and the Battle for Hearts and Minds." *Millennium—Journal of International Studies* 33, no. 3 (June 1, 2005):477 -493.

———. *Power: A Radical View*. Palgrave Macmillan, 2005.

Mattern, Janice Bially. *Ordering International Politics: Identity, Crisis, and Representational Force*. Psychology Press, 2005.

———. "Why 'Soft Power' Isn't So Soft: Representational Force and the Sociolinguistic Construction of Attraction in World Politics." *Millennium—Journal of International Studies* 33, no. 3 (June 1, 2005):583–612.

Medhurst, Martin J. *Cold War Rhetoric: Strategy, Metaphor, and Ideology*. MSU Press, 1997.

Melissen, Jan. *The New Public Diplomacy: Soft Power in International Relations*. Palgrave Macmillan, 2007.

Morriss, Peter. "Steven Lukes on the Concept of Power." *Political Studies Review* 4, no. 2 (May 1, 2006):124–135.

Neumann, Iver B. "Returning Practice to the Linguistic Turn: The Case of Diplomacy." *Millennium—Journal of International Studies* 31, no. 3 (July 1, 2002):627–651.

Nye Jr., Joseph S. *Bound to Lead: The Changing Nature of American Power*. Basic Books, 1991.

———. "Forward." In *Soft Power Superpowers: Cultural Assets of Japan and the United States*, eds. Yasushi Watanabe and David McConnell, ix–xiv. Armonk, NY: M.E. Sharpe, 2008.

———. "Limits of American Power." *Political Science Quarterly* 117, no. 4 (2002):545–559.

———. "Notes for a Soft Power Research Agenda." In *Power in World Politics*, eds. Felix Berenskoetter and Dr. Michael J. Williams, 162–172. New York: Taylor & Francis, 2007.

———. "Preface." In *Soft Power Superpowers: Cultural Assets of Japan and the United States*, eds. Yasushi Watanabe and David McConnell, ix–xiv. Armonk, NY: M.E. Sharpe, 2008.

———. "Public Diplomacy and Soft Power." *The ANNALS of the American Academy of Political and Social Science* 616, no. 1 (March 2008):94–109.

———. "Responding to My Critics and Concluding Thoughts." In *Soft Power and U.S. Foreign Policy: Theoretical, Historical and Contemporary Perspectives*, eds. Inderjeet Parmar and Michael Cox, 215–227. New York: Routledge, 2010.

———. "Soft Power," no. 80 (1990):153–171.

———. *Soft Power: The Means to Success in World Politics*. PublicAffairs, 2004.

———. *The Future of Power*. 1st ed. PublicAffairs, 2011.

———. *The Paradox of American Power: Why the World's Only Superpower Can't Go It Alone*. Oxford University Press U.S., 2002.

———. *The Powers to Lead*. Oxford University Press U.S., 2008.

Parry-Giles, Shawn J. *The Rhetorical Presidency, Propaganda, and the Cold War, 1945–1955*. Greenwood Publishing Group, 2002.

Pouliot, Vincent. "'Sobjectivism': Toward a Constructivist Methodology." *International Studies Quarterly* 51, no. 2 (2007):359–384.

Riker, William H. *The Art of Political Manipulation*. Yale University Press, 1986.

Ronfeldt, David, and John Arquilla. "The Promise of Noopolitik." *First Monday* 12, no. 8 (August 6, 2007). http://firstmonday.org/htbin/cgiwrap/bin/ojs/index.php/fm/article/viewArticle/1971/1846%C2%A0%C2%A0.

Sartori, Giovanni. "Concept Misformation in Comparative Politics." *The American Political Science Review* 64, no. 4 (December 1, 1970):1033–1053.

Schelling, Thomas C. *Arms and Influence*. Yale University Press, 1971.

Snow, Nancy. "Rethinking Public Diplomacy." In *Routledge Handbook of Public Diplomacy*, eds. Nancy Snow and Phillip Taylor, 3–11. New York: Routledge, 2009.

Stuckey, Mary E. "Competing Foreign Policy Visions: Rhetorical Hybrids after the Cold War." *Western Journal of Communication* 59, no. 3 (1995):214–27.

Tickner, Arlene B., and Ole Wæver. *International Relations Scholarship around the World*. Taylor & Francis, 2009.

Watanabe, Yasushi, and David McConnell, "Introduction." In *Soft Power Superpowers: Cultural Assets of Japan and the United States*, eds. Yasushi Watanabe and David McConnell, xvii–xxxii. Armonk, NY: M.E. Sharpe, 2008.

Wendt, Alexander. "On Constitution and Causation in International Relations." *Review of International Studies* 24, no. 5 (1998):101–118.

Wolfers, Arnold. *Discord and Collaboration: Essays on International Politics*. Baltimore, MD: Johns Hopkins University Press, 1962.

Wuthnow, Joel. "The Concept of Soft Power in China's Soft Power Discourse." *Issues and Studies* 44, no. 2 (June 2008):1–28.

Zaharna, R. S. *Battles to Bridges: U.S. Strategic Communication and Public Diplomacy after 9/11*. Palgrave Macmillan, 2009.

Zaharna, R.S. "The Soft Power Differential: Network Communication and Mass Communication in Public Diplomacy." *Hague Journal of Diplomacy* 2, no. 3 (2007):213–228.

———. "The U.S. Credibility Deficit." *Foreign Policy in Focus* (December 13, 2006).

Zahran, Geraldo, and Leonardo Ramos. "From Hegemony to Soft Power: Implications of a Conceptual Change." In *Soft Power and US Foreign Policy: Theoretical, Historical and Contemporary Perspectives*, eds. Inderjeet Parmar and Michael Cox, 12–31. New York: Taylor & Francis, 2010.

Chapter 3

Japan: Culture, Pop Culture, and the National Brand

The case of Japan represents a significant testing ground for the soft power concept. Japan's efforts to promote its interests abroad through vehicles such as cultural diplomacy, international broadcasting services, and development assistance is suggestive of a nation-state committed to the concept of public diplomacy and soft power as instruments to achieve foreign policy objectives. Yet in Japan's case, soft power is not merely a strategic alternative, but in many respects a *necessity* in light of real constraints on Japan's capacity to project other forms of power in the context of pressing competition for regional influence from neighboring China and South Korea.[1]

Japan's foreign policy options are impacted by a host of material and symbolic constraints. Japan's pacifist constitution limits its ability to deploy military force and, indeed, symbolically works against the perception of an aggressive Japan. Thus, Japan's military posture diminishes the potential of "command" power resources identified by Nye.[2] Japan has also suffered over a decade of economic malaise—making it more difficult for Japan to wield the instruments of economic leverage, especially given the explosive growth of China's economic development.[3]

Compounding the diminishment of Japan's material sources of power is Japan's ambivalent efforts to repair its historical legacy in the wake of World War II, a legacy that continues to complicate its relations with regional partners.[4] The combination of these conditions fuels justifications for Japan's pursuit of soft power as viable strategic recourse.

Yet Japan's embrace of the soft power concept, as is evident in public diplomacy programs and in public discourse, also reflects inherent difficulties in the "conversion" of supposed soft power resources into actual policy objectives. How Japan has adapted soft power certainly reflects its history,

77

its perceived assets, and its strategic ambitions—yet the conversion process evidenced in this adaptation remains an unsettled question about what exactly is expected from using an ambiguously articulated conception of culture to achieve foreign policy objectives. Japan has achieved considerable success in its cultural industries, which has been recognized by a broad spectrum of its foreign policy planners as significant for strategic purposes. Yet can Japan cultivate and promote its cultural assets as a matter of foreign policy—where the state intervenes to cultivate and promote what may already *work* to promote Japan? The conversion of such resources represents a definitive issue in comprehending the case of Japanese soft power.

Japan's consideration of soft power as a strategic compass is not without controversy—as this chapter will explore in further detail. The outlines of internal debate suggest a diversity of views on the value of its soft power resources, and the ability of the state to leverage such resources, through programs such as public and cultural diplomacy, nation-branding, and the expansion of markets and international legal protections for its cultural industries.[5] While there is apparently some consensus in Japan that its culture can be a resource for soft power, and that soft should be pursued as a strategy, there are differences on *why* and *how* a soft power approach to international relations should be developed.[6]

This chapter explores the concept of soft power in the Japanese context, through a review of Japanese policies and programs of public diplomacy (including variant interpretations such as branding and culture industry promotion) that follow from the strategic discourse of soft power. The chapter also examines different perspectives and arguments voiced by Japanese leadership, government spokespersons, and other public figures that relate to the subject of soft power. The analysis reveals notions of idealized publics (or soft power targets), vehicles of delivery, and cultural assets at stake in the Japanese conception of soft power.

The first section of the chapter surveys Japan's public diplomacy programs—considered here to encompass cultural diplomacy, branding, and more formal institutional conceptions of "public diplomacy." The second section draws attention to the key contentions of strategic arguments on soft power. The chapter concludes by identifying how Japanese visions of soft power reflect a particular interpretation of scope, mechanism, and outcome. This configuration of assumptions suggests a particular form of soft power idealized in its public diplomacy policies: the presentation of material and immaterial culture as a means of access—*a gateway*—to Japan, that invites audiences into consideration of Japan. As the analysis concludes, Japanese soft power is presented as deriving from audience interest; soft power is contingent on the potential for foreign publics to identify with the cultural presentation of Japan.

JAPANESE PUBLIC DIPLOMACY PROGRAMS:
A ROUTE TO SOFT POWER

The post–World War II tradition of a Japanese public diplomacy consists of three related activities: developmental aid and investment, administered through the Office of Developmental Assistance, cultural diplomacy–related programs such as language training and cultural exchange programs, and, finally, Japan's international broadcasting services, managed by NHK (Nippon Hoso Kyokai). Of these three areas, the institutions of cultural diplomacy are the most definitive aspects of Japanese public diplomacy.

More recent developments in Japanese public diplomacy involve a focus on the Japanese "brand," a multi-stakeholder effort that draws contributions from Japanese commercial ministries and organizations, as well as from more traditional diplomatic institutions like the Japanese Ministry of Foreign Affairs (MOFA).[7] The emergence of branding as a terministic innovation in Japanese public diplomacy coincides with the increasing popularity of Japanese cultural products.[8]

In the wake of Douglas McGray's provocative 2002 *Foreign Affairs* article "Japan's Gross National Cool," there is a growing sense among Japanese foreign policy and industrial policy-makers that Japanese cultural products are both a route to economic growth after a decade of economic stagnation, as well as a resource to be leveraged for foreign policy.[9] "Japan stands out in terms of its international influence in pop culture, and we need to find a means to enhance this advantage," according to former Democratic Party of Japan lawmaker Yoshikazu Tarui, who headed a group of legislators seeking to promote Japan's video games, animated characters and digital content.[10]

As a tool of *public diplomacy*, the global reach of cultural products such as *anime* (animation), *manga* (graphic novels), toy products (like the "Hello Kitty" franchise), and Japanese television dramas represent a perceived opportunity to promote Japanese cultural values that could translate into other kinds of international influence and have prompted Japanese scholars to connect popular culture with economic, political and diplomatic power.[11]

The rise of Japanese pop culture highlights the relevance of soft power for dealing with Japan's pressing strategic exigencies, and has brought public diplomacy into larger discussions of strategic necessity. The soft power concept has also proven to be an available and adaptable strategic framework to rationalize the potential of cultural industries. Japan is confronted with the need to strengthen economic ties with China and the rest of the ASEAN countries, while overcoming decades of lingering resentment over its imperial past. Soft power provides a discursive frame—a set of reasons and terminology—to articulate policies and programs to deal with its difficult position. Of course soft power is not the *only* perceived strategy. Japan's ties to the United States have provided a strategic counterweight to China's hegemonic status, albeit in a relationship that risks Japan being too closely identified with an increasingly unpopular United States.[12] Yet Japan's lack of significant military resources and a slow-growth economy makes the intangible benefits of soft power an increasingly attractive strategic framework.

In the past, Japan has successfully leveraged its *development aid* as a kind of attributional power, securing Japan's diplomatic objectives while extending the goals of U.S. foreign policy in the region. Yet Japan's economic might and perceived generosity have waned in recent years, along with its willingness to cleave too closely to U.S. policy prescriptions.[13] Soft power thus provides a way to imagine a reconfiguration of strategic possibilities that build upon perceived resource strengths and (at times somewhat hazily sketched out) expected outcomes. Given this context, Japan is an instructive example for the conceptual indigenization of soft power. And the Japanese concept of soft power is profoundly linked to the potency of *culture*.

The relation between culture and statecraft in Japan has evolved considerably since World War II. In particular, Japanese discussion of diplomacy since the 1990s reveals an orientation toward culture as a significant *diplomatic* tool for public diplomacy, coupled with a diminished emphasis on developmental aid.[14] From 2004 through 2009, successive policy claims and strategic arguments from the Japanese "Bluebooks"—official reports on Japanese foreign policy activities—suggest that the Ministry of Foreign Affairs and quasi-autonomous entities such as the Japan Foundation have also placed increased stock in the *public* nature of diplomacy and the significance of nonstate actors for Japanese foreign policy objectives.

However, the use of the term "public diplomacy," much like in the United States, is not consistent. Some MOFA activities are described as "public relations," while others are targeted as "public diplomacy," with little distinction provided.[15] The importance of publics to foreign policy, however, is readily apparent across Japanese MOFA reports as a crucial site of diplomatic activity—as evidenced through arguments that foreign publics are speaking the Japanese language, appreciating Japanese cultural values, and in the consumption of Japanese cultural products.[16] Successive yearly reports claim that foreign audiences who appreciate Japanese cultural products can serve Japanese foreign policy goals by supporting successful cultural industries. And yet, foreign audiences also serve as *subjects* for soft power interventions in their own right—as the *opinions* of foreign audiences are the arbiter of successful diplomatic initiatives. In other words, public opinion is an increasingly central indicator of foreign policy success. In this view, the *audience* for public diplomacy provides the evidence of a successful diplomacy as much as they are conceived as a vehicle for the accomplishment of diplomatic objectives. The most common route to audiences under this view is through culture as a means of both internationalizing the Japanese public and providing means by which foreign audiences can identify with a variety of increasingly globalized cultural expression.

While culture has been a significant vehicle of Japanese public diplomacy since World War II, how it has been conceived in practice has evolved to accommodate a range of foreign policy objectives. Culture—as an implicit soft power resource—figures prominently in programs organized around cultural exchange and language education, the multilateral role of culture amongst ASEAN countries, and in the promotion of culture as a means to dispel uncertainties over its economic dominance during the 1980s.[17] The culture concept took on new significance and meaning during the 1990s as an aspect of Japanese foreign policy, after it became obvious that Japan's cultural industries had achieved considerable popularity across global audiences.[18]

Japanese leaders and intellectuals, such as former Prime Minister Taro Aso and Japan Foundation President Kazuo Ogoura, have since expressed divergent views about the anticipated benefits of cultural promotion, and how these benefits translate into strategic value given the global popularity of Japanese popular culture. As the following sections of this chapter suggest, culture as a resource of soft power is articulated in abstract appeals to perceived international political leverage as much as an obvious material measure of Japanese "power" through the success of its cultural industries abroad. The plurality of the culture concept suggests its currency as a fungible resource to be cultivated and deployed—both for influence and economic gain. Yet culture remains squarely at the core of arguments for renewed attention to Japanese public diplomacy as much as economic growth.

Since 2002, it is evident that the Japanese government has recognized the increased salience of public diplomacy as a set of practical activities to cultivate influence and manage its international relations. Yet the purpose of public diplomacy also reveals concern over the management of effects of global exposure on the *domestic* population.[19] For example, in 2003, the Agency for Cultural Affairs issued the report, "About the Future Promotion of International Cultural Exchange" via the Commissioner's Advisory Group on International Cultural Exchange. The report highlighted how globalization and regional dynamics created a *need* for cultural diplomacy—not only because culture was the recognized vehicle for influence over "hard power," but because the Japanese *themselves* needed to be internationalized. The report argued for

> build[ing] a more attractive society—one that is enriched by greater cultural plurality; that enables the Japanese people to gain a better knowledge of their

own culture and values, while understanding and appreciating those of others; and that ultimately fosters coexistence based on respect for mutual differences.[20]

The report argues for increased structural investment in cultural diplomacy capacity, arguing that Japan cannot rely simply on market forces. Language training is the recommended cornerstone for the new policy direction, as well as developing a more significant network of NGOs and related actors. For Japan to be an effective member of international society, it must be seen as valuing culture for its own sake.[21] Interestingly, the report highlighted how Japanese culture could be promoted as an *international* culture, instead of promoting Japan's distinctiveness. This sentiment would be echoed in subsequent academic assessments of Japan's cultural industry growth in the twenty-first century.[22] Japan leverages culture as a route to influence not simply by promoting culture expression, but through its population and its capacity to create.

The potentiality of culture, what it can be expected to accomplish in relation to foreign policy and economic objectives, remains pivotal in these strategic assessments. The following excerpt from a MOFA report encapsulates this line of reasoning:

> In order for Japan to internationally pursue activities and smoothly enrich communications with people from other countries, it is very important to introduce a wide variety of Japanese culture and senses of value to them and to encourage them to understand Japan well. . . . Furthermore, as a part of diplomatic strategies, the MoFA aims to effectively deepen understandings about Japan in other countries through an intensive exchange, e.g., cooperating with governmental agencies, organizations, and companies and implementing a large-scale comprehensive cultural exchange project in the commemorative year.[23]

Thus, culture is means to "pursue activities," conditioned by the flow of communication and cultural products between Japan and foreign publics. The meaning of culture in the context of cultural diplomacy appears to be changing, however, to accommodate the potential of globally popular media products and to move beyond an emphasis on the traditional aspects of Japan's heritage of cultural expressive forms.[24] Such cultural heritage shares value with contemporary, adaptable forms such as manga or anime.

Yet the impact of Japan's culture—its capacity to be "converted" into soft power gains—might be complicated by the very reason for its success. Japan's globally popular cultural products have become popular because of their cultural accessibility. For some scholars, the local adaptability of Japanese culture products is due to its lack of a strong "cultural odor."[25] Japan's cultural products have gained market share due to their ability to be culturally proximate enough.[26] Anime and manga can be readily dubbed or translated, while their narratives may reflect globally circulating visions of dealing with the consequences of modernity.[27] Thus, Japan's reinvigorated sense of culture as a foundation for public diplomacy rests upon a set of products whose cultural "message" is not as clearly attributed to Japan's cultural heritage; Japan's *traditional* values may not make its pop culture popular. Instead, Japanese pop culture's lack of a clear Japanese referent makes it popular.

Nevertheless, Japan's public diplomacy activities are designed and justified to support a strong linkage between the appeal of *Japanese* cultural products and tangible benefits for Japan in the long-term.[28] Japan's public diplomacy, as directed by MOFA, appears to rely on the assumption that Japanese cultural products can be kind of public good, rather than solely a route to global economic competitiveness. Japan's cultural heritage, both in historical and globally popular forms, is a gift to the Japan's burgeoning global fan cultures. Influence, from cultural identification to the predominance of Japanese cultural industries, can follow.

In 2004 Japan's MOFA established the Public Diplomacy Department, funded by a $400 million budget with the explicit purpose of "establishing a good public image," according to the MOFA website. The Department "combines public relations and cultural exchange in a more systematic way and provides a structure that enables cooperation between the public and private sectors."[29] As the 2005 Bluebook explains:

> The Ministry of Foreign Affairs (MOFA) has introduced the concept of public diplomacy . . . to strengthen its overall ability to communicate information for the purpose of conveying Japan's image, current situation, and policy-related information directly to people in other countries.[30]

The Ministry of Foreign Affairs and the Public Diplomacy Department manage what they call the "public relations" aspect of public diplomacy—to contribute content to international media, work with embassy posts to arrange for speaking engagements, and convene symposia and conferences. The Department's current mission has expanded to coordinate a considerable range of cultural exchange programs and innovative programs like the Japan Creative Center in Singapore, as well as the "Cultural Volunteers Program."[31] As is evident, the Public Diplomacy Department serves as a *hub* in a public diplomacy portfolio largely dominated by cultural concerns.

Promoting Japanese Culture

The central role of culture in the history of Japanese cultural diplomacy reveals an evolving concept of culture's utility in relation to broader foreign policy objectives. Culture has moved from a demonstrative aspect of

Japanese society—a means by which to persuade and shape sentiments—to a more active field of interaction between Japanese and foreign audiences. As Kazuo Ogoura of the Japan Foundation offers, "affirming the common cultural ground shared by different countries leads to the discovery of new creativity, while maintaining each countries ethnicity's uniqueness and discovering differences open up a path to creative endeavors.[32] Culture in this sense is facilitative of relationships, where a focus on culture demonstrates commitments to multilateralism as much as provides a stage for the cultural distinctiveness of Japan. As indicated in the 2003 Agency for Cultural Affairs report, such interaction is crucial not only to Japanese foreign policy objectives, but to the livelihood and cultural vitality of the Japanese people.

Historically, Japan's cultural diplomacy has been "embedded in its general cultural policy."[33] Japan's cultural diplomacy institutions have answered to domestic departments of culture such as the Agency for Cultural Affairs, which was established in 1968. With MOFA taking a greater interest in leveraging cultural products for soft power objectives during the 2000s and with the increased activities of the Japan Foundation, cultural policy has enlarged to include both the management of cultural practice and the promotion of such practice as a route to influence.

The evolution is remarkable given the shifting mandates for Japan's cultural agencies. As the Agency for Cultural Affairs itself became more *internationally* oriented, its emphasis on the preservation of high culture and Japanese exceptionalism as the best strategy for promotion contrasted significantly to the market-oriented approached that has become *de rigueur* in the MOFA.[34] This is likely due to the Agency's primarily domestic orientation—yet it still plays a significant role in the broader field of Japanese cultural policy.[35] As Peter Katzenstein states, the Agency has viewed that "the purpose of international culture exchange is to strengthen Japan's domestic culture."[36] This mandate for exchange seemingly inverts the generic conception of culture as s soft power resource—where culture is leveraged as a resource for influence. If anything, the Agency's approach assumes a wholly other kind of argument—that strategic influence stems from the cultural characteristics of the domestic population.

Yet the Agency is not the primary cultural diplomacy organization. Currently, the most high profile institution of Japanese cultural diplomacy is the Japan Foundation, which was formed in 1972 to "export official culture."[37] The Japan Foundation operates independently, under a mandate from MOFA. It traditionally has organized language teaching and exchange programs, yet it was not initially envisioned as having a "central role in policy implementation, to complete foreign policy objectives."[38] Cultural diplomacy was thus conceived as a necessary component to facilitate larger diplomatic aims.

The origins of the Japan Foundation can be traced to the *Kokusai Bunka Shinkokai* (KBS), established by the Japanese government in 1934 to reinforce the Greater East Asia Prosperity Sphere. The KBS produced books, films and other content to promote Japanese culture and language.[39] After the second World War, culture was downplayed as a diplomatic priority until the 1970s—when concern grew about the perception of Japanese business practices and the impression of Japan as a mature industrial economy.[40] Thus, the perceived need for some form of cultural diplomacy surfaced again as Japan re-entered the global economy, in order to combat a growing sense of isolation. Speaking at the National Diet of Japan in 1972, Kagawa Takaki of the Ministry of Foreign affairs stated:

> if we look at the Foreign Ministries of foreign countries, most of them carry out such cultural exchange activities. Britain, Germany, France and Sweden have set up similar agencies, whereas in the USA and Italy, the foreign ministries carry out such activities directly.[41]

In keeping with the programs of other nation-states, such as the UK's British Council, an organization like the Japan Foundation was deemed a necessary element of statecraft to address "misunderstanding of Japanese foreign policy and Japanese business practices overseas."[42]

Yet, this incarnation of public diplomacy was at least initially a strictly outward-facing proposition. The Japan Foundation was forbidden from introducing foreign culture to the Japanese. While this is no longer policy, the way in which this position has been reversed reflects the enduring trend of Japan's the "theory of internationalization."[43] Katzenstein argues that the management of contact between foreign and domestic publics through diplomacy programs remain bounded by the notion that the distinctiveness of Japan is something to be preserved, even through cultural contact in a time of globalization.

The creation of the Japan Foundation conveyed the sense that a cultural promotion agency was a required tool of international politics and, by extension, that culture was pivotal to Japan's international objectives. In Utpal Vyas's analysis of a 2003 Japan Foundation report, he finds the function of the Japan Foundation has evolved beyond the vague mandate to "increase international understanding" to include the task of ensuring that "people have an interest in Japan."[44] This position underscores an instrumental argument for cultural diplomacy in the foreign policy repertoire.

Put another way, the Japan Foundation sustains the foundations of Japanese soft power which strive to cultivate crucial cultural linkages. The 2003 report positions the Japan Foundation as an institution situated between the government and the "public sector" and that it should play a transparent and accountable role in managing exchanges and informing Japanese citizens. This somewhat ambivalent posture between the management of foreign policy objectives and its status as a mediator between states and publics is not fully articulated in policy documentation. Yet it still remains tied through a special administrative status (*dokuritsu gyōsei hōjin*) to the MOFA and the overarching objectives of Japanese foreign policy.

What the Japan Foundation appears to represent is a tacit conversion process of soft power; a logic of how culture is a crucial vehicle for foreign policy. It provides three primary functions for Japanese cultural diplomacy: the promotion of arts and culture through grants and exchanges, the facilitation of Japanese language instruction programs and testing, and the support of Japanese studies and intellectual exchange programs. These functions balance the promotion of Japan's distinctiveness with the benefits of interaction.[45] As Japan Foundation President Kazuo Ogoura states:

> It has never before been so important to use culture and the arts as a means to respond to these people's interests and enthusiasms as they seek to discover the true spirit of Japan. I believe it is also our mission to foster common sources of creativity around the world, through international exchange activities.[46]

Here, Ogoura locates the facilitative capacities of the Foundation as an implicit mandate for cultural diplomacy to direct international audiences toward the discovery of the "true spirit of Japan." Yet Ogoura also clarifies that culture is also a tool of peace and the protection of cultural assets:

> We will continue to implement cultural programs both to support conflict prevention efforts and to provide comfort to victims of conflict, thereby arousing hope as well as the desire to rebuild communities and countries that have experienced suffering. Also, we will extend cooperation in the protection of cultural assets in developing countries.[47]

The *cooperative* dimension highlighted by Ogoura is suggestive of an incremental shift away from Japanese cultural promotion. The Japan Foundation has developed its portfolio to include more *facilitative* programs of public diplomacy, where the Japan Foundation can use its resources to organize multilateral meetings between other nation-states; the acts of organizing relations and collaboration are demonstrative of the values and culture that Japan seeks to amplify.

For example, the Japan Foundation has experimented with programs geared toward multilateral understanding; promoting understanding of Japan but also of using Japan's soft power and its own reputation to organize meetings between other countries, especially in the East Asia region. The

Japan Foundation has organized "trilateral exchanges" between Thailand and Myannmar, India and Japan, and other inter-ASEAN country programs through its Asia Center resources.[48]

Yet Japanese cultural diplomacy is not limited to the Japan Foundation, as the expanding culture-centric activities of the MOFA indicate. MOFA also manages the principal exchange programs, including the Japan Exchange and Teaching Programme (JET), the Global Youth Exchange program, and the Asia-Europe Young Leaders Symposium. MOFA also maintains support of UNESCO initiatives designed to preserve global cultural heritage, and actively promotes its own artist exchange program.[49]

Japanese cultural diplomacy is also not limited to high-profile official programs. Japan's Center for Global Partnership (CGP) was founded in 1991 to facilitate formal intellectual exchanges and to provide an international forum for the discussion of Japanese foreign policy. The CGP was established without a mandate to promote Japan nor to adhere to the political influence of MOFA.[50] Yet other cultural diplomacy initiatives take place at the post level, where Japanese embassies and consulates sponsor cultural exhibitions, reach out to local educational institutions, and coordinate with local media producers to supplement the activities and communications coming from the Foreign Ministry.[51]

This array of agencies and programs represents a fabric of overlapping institutional agents for public diplomacy. As a whole, they signify more than the policy rhetoric of the administration: an evolving set of priorities that have sustained particular attitudes toward Japanese exceptionalism, stewardship for Japanese domestic culture, and faith in the expected benefits of relationship-building under the pretext of cultural exchange. The culturally focused aspects of Japan's public diplomacy retains elements that emphasize "traditional" components of culture and cultural exchange, yet also appear poised to promote *facilitative* public diplomacy objectives, and to coordinate with other Japanese stakeholders in the private sector and other ministries (such as the Ministry of Economy, Trade, and Industry, the Japan Tourism Agency, and the Agency for Cultural Affairs) that deploy culture through the appeal of the "brand."

Branding as Public Diplomacy?

In the early 2000s, the notion of the nation "brand" and the idea of "Gross National Cool" framed the rising importance of Japan's cultural industries and the prospects of promoting Japan through interagency efforts.[52] The moment signaled the emergent convergence of economic and public diplomacy-related concerns in institutional arguments for policy change. For example, in July 2003, a Ministry of Economics, Trade, and Industry (METI) study group's report emphasized the terms *branding* and *cool* to emphasize the importance of developing content and popular culture industries.[53] As Japan scholar Michal Daliot-Bul observes, this kind of industrial policy (in the form of cultural "contents" promotion) and foreign policy arguments for cultural promotion emerged in response to the decline of its overall economic competitiveness and drew on similar kinds of reasoning. In 2002, the Japanese government proposed the "Intellectual Property Strategic Program" (*Chitekizaisan Suishin Keikakuto*) to protect and promote Japan's intellectual property such as anime, manga, and game software.[54] This policy was framed, in part, as more than an economic policy, but a soft power program designed to protect the brand of Japan.

The utility of culture in branding discourse represents a departure from internationalization and other more domestically oriented justifications for cultural exchange and related cultural diplomacy initiatives. The potential of cultural *products* to improve the image of Japan was recognized by Ichiya Nakamura of the Stanford Japan Research Center, who argued in 2004 that

> [t]he contents industry obviously concerns art and culture, education, and the wellbeing of society. Creativity and the ability of self-expression form the identity and brand value of a country. The contents industry could even become a soft power to enhance diplomatic leverage. Thus, contents policy is something that greatly influences the very form of a country.[55]

Nakamura's argument proposes a strong linkage between cultural product and "image"—a term somewhat confusingly interchangeable in Japanese discourse with "brand." In Nakamura's logic—the creative practice represented in cultural "contents" reflects directly on perceptions of the nation-states, and thus soft power.

Seiichi Kondo, the Commissioner of the Agency for Cultural Affairs and the first Director-General of the Public Diplomacy Department, has similarly argued that "an improved Japanese image will lead to active personal and commodity exchanges."[56] Thus, image cultivation amplifies broader efforts to conduct public diplomacy. The line of reasoning elaborates "image" as a kind of index to more fundamental characteristics of Japanese identity, which in turn has an expected *diplomatic* benefit.

While Japanese cultural products have gained considerable market success in both Asia and the United States since the 1990s, Kondo points to the "explosive" popularity of *Korean* drama as demonstrative of how Japan can proactively "narrow the distance between the world and Japan."[57] The ability of the Korean government to consciously grow a successful global media culture suggests a role for government to intervene in the cultural industries.[58]

If a nation-state can, via government policy, cultivate cultural industries, it may in turn cultivate soft power.[59] The Korean example also frames cultural diplomacy competitively, and suggests a necessary course correction for Japanese policymakers.

It is important to acknowledge that Kondo's position on the relation of image to soft power has changed since 2004. Kondo's subsequent 2008 essay on soft power elaborates a refined logic of soft power, which explains that the content of particular cultural products do not *intrinsically* translate into soft power, but rather depend on particular "subjectivities"—the cultural characteristics of the transmission method as well as the receptivity of the audience.[60] Kondo's nuanced position, taking into account the social dimension of communication forms (how appeals, media outlets, and imagery are in themselves culturally marked and relevant to social ties), reflects an unresolved issue in public diplomacy thinking in Japan—that soft power resources are not *self-evidently* effective as tools.[61]

Despite such concerns, Japan has nevertheless embraced the promotion of cultural products that carry the image or brand, through which soft power assets can be translated into larger foreign policy objectives. As Yoshikazu Tarui explains, "In reality, the competitiveness of a nation's entertainment industry and national power are often proportionate."[62]

But Japanese efforts to promote aspects of its culture as demonstrative of a Japanese brand also reflects domestic as much as foreign policy–related concerns for the role of government in cultural policy—a line of thinking clearly evident in earlier conceptions of cultural diplomacy. One of the recommendations that came out of Prime Minister Koizume's 2005 Council for the Promotion of Cultural Diplomacy identified Japanese popular culture as a means by which foreign publics can access traditional Japanese values such as "harmony," "compassion," and "coexistence."[63] For Daliot-Bul, this statement conceals the motive to rehabilitate and indeed, *control* the politics behind traditional Japanese values. She argues that the international promotion of "good old Japan" serves the dual purpose of promoting particular Japanese values as much as validating more conservative dimensions of Japan culture.[64]

Daliot-Bul's observations are suggestive of the disconnect in Japan's cultural promotion strategy. Japan's brand embodies a global popularity that is *global*, yet promotion activities confront the task of *particularizing* that global popularity. For example, the Japan's METI launched the Japanesque* Modern in 2005 to showcase Japan to the world and thus stimulate the economy through cultural outreach. As the promotional material claimed, "This program has a wide range of focus, covering areas such as art, performance, and craftsmanship, and has as its *core the concept of promoting a*

new national style that embodies modern qualities and the spirit of Japan"
(emphasis added). This initiative provided an opportunity for partnership
with private industry—but also a means by which the definition of a "national
style" could be controlled in its articulation.

The challenge of sustaining a brand made popular through its adaptability
is also exemplified in the Japanese design firm Hirano & Associates' campaign to link nation-branding to economic growth. Their initiative aims to
"utilize the bridge-and-network method to connect the spheres of design, traditional craftsmanship, new technology, and education."[65] As proponents of
the Hirano and Associates project explained, the "ultimate goal of their Brand
Japan project is to go beyond a thin veneer or whiff of the exotic 'other' to
create something that embodies the basic and profound qualities of a special
culture.

What is evident is the pressing need to promote the brand that effectively
renders the compelling aspects of Japanese culture and industry, *as well as*
a desire for a more coherent strategy and support from the government. As
Nakamura argued in 2004,

> There is no guarantee that industrial competitiveness of pop culture continues. A
> mechanism to maintain industrial competitiveness has not been established. Rather,
> Japan faces a crisis because other nations attempt to catch up with Japan.[66]

Mori Yuji, the chief executive officer of THINK, a Japanese media company,
argues that the Japanese government does not fully understand the impact of
its branding strategy through its efforts to promote popular culture industries.
Mori acknowledges that while "high value products" may equate to soft
power, Japan has little empirical knowledge about how its products compete, emergent trends, or how its products create particular media exposure
effects.[67] A "Cool Japan" strategy, for Mori, would be one that acknowledges
the competitive and indeed regional context for a soft power–oriented brand
strategy. Nation-branding in his view is predicated on a strategic contest that
Japan runs the risk of losing.

Japan has nonetheless committed to a nation-brand strategy grounded in
cultural products and the creative industries around these products. In June
2010, Japan's METI launched a "strategic base" in Beijing for the "Cool
Japan Division" to "promote overseas diffusion of Japanese cultural industry,
such as animation, fashion and Japanese food."[68] One of the key aspects of
this new organization is a focus on public–private partnerships. As Japan's
budget for public diplomacy–related programs shrank since 2003, calls for
sharing the costs of branding with the private sector are not surprising.[69]
Speaking in 2009, former prime minister Taro Aso told the Japan National

Press Club: "I would like to develop the cultural industry to be a 20–30 tril-
lion yen–scaled industry until 2020. To do so, we will launch an organization
that works on market cultivation and fundraising comprehensively."[70] Japan's
first director generals of its Public Diplomacy Department, Seichi Kondo
and Kenjiro Monji, have reiterated this call for government assistance, but
not direction, in cultural industry growth as part of Japan's requirements for
global engagement.[71]

Locating Culture Diplomacy in Pop Culture

Two assumptions appear evident in the strategic shift toward linking Japan
to its cultural products—aside from the general observation that cultural
products equate to some form of soft power. First, is that the *material* aspects
of culture are important. The communicative, media-based products represented in cultural expression *represent* Japan and function to cultivate *interest*
among global audiences. This belief is expressed both as arguments about
creative products as well as communication media outlets. A 2008 MOFA
report argues that the "impact of impact of public opinion on diplomatic
policy has been increasing due to the dramatic development of the Internet
and mass media."[72] The necessity for a public diplomacy strategy is amplified by the recognized context of ubiquitous global communication outlets
and connectivity.

The second assumption implicated in the salience of the cultural industry is
the perceived *agency* of nonstate actors that range from NGOs to individual
cultural consumers. Efforts coordinated by the MOFA to use pop culture as
a means to conduct public diplomacy suggest an empowered and crucial role
for publics, rather than just a contextual factor in inter-state relations. Since
2006, the MOFA made the "diffusion of public information" a "policy" *and* a
"structure" priority.[73] As part of this strategic direction, the MOFA promoted
an approach to public diplomacy that emphasized *individuals*: "[W]e should
utilize the increase in Japanese pop culture's popularity[,] and sending volunteers to the other countries would be useful to diffuse Japanese culture and
language among the grassroots level."[74] The logic of Japanese public diplomacy as articulated here signals the significance of individual consumption of
Japanese products and the benefits of interpersonal interaction.

The significance of publics and their relation to communication and media
products is perhaps most explicit in the MOFA programs that promote pop
culture diplomacy—a variant of traditional cultural diplomacy activities (such
as artist exchange programs). In particular, these programs rely upon the centrality of media products as a meaning-making tool for cultural consumers.
This is a significant conceptual move away from equating public diplomacy

more narrowly as information dissemination and propaganda (which has dominated historical perceptions of public diplomacy).[75] Rather, the emphasis on pop culture appears to reflect the ways in which fan cultures make use of media products to understand their world and to manage their own identity.[76] When the Japanese government acknowledges the increasingly global dimension of *otaku* (obsessive fan) and *kawaii* (cute) cultures—they signal the importance of particular communities and their strong relationship to entertainment products. It is this relationship that constitutes an opportunity for leverage.

Hiro Katsumata, a researcher at the Institute of Defense and Strategic Studies in Singapore, offers a blunt justification for this form of culture-based diplomacy: "Cultural diplomacy could be one of the most effective tools of Japanese diplomacy . . . In a decade or two, younger generations in many countries who love Japanese cartoons will start to fill leadership roles."[77] In other words—appreciation of pop culture will translate into some kind of effect later on—yet this argument does not suggest *how* the values and ideals of pop culture products might somehow shape the actions of future leaders—rather, supposed benefits are derived from the affinity toward Japanese products. Japan will accrue power in some from the popularity of its cultural products.

The most high-profile champion of this approach to public diplomacy is former Foreign and Prime Minister Taro Aso, who in 2006 argued for the creation of an International Manga Award to recognize those outside Japan who contributed to the growth of the artform as a shared cultural form.[78] At the announcement of the first Award winners in 2007, Aso declared:

> To the girls in Copenhagen, Denmark, who have grown up together with Tamagotchi, Pokemon, and Sailor Moon, to the Chinese boys who could not have lived a day without Saint Seiya, and to Zinedine Zidane, Francesco Totti, and all the boys who have penned likenesses of Captain Tsubasa, I want all of you to know that you must aim high if you want to become a Manga artist, as you now have a trophy within your reach . . . Manga is about love. Manga is about friendship. Manga is about growing up. Manga is about everything—it knows absolutely no boundaries. Manga, in a word, is the most universal unifier of the hearts and minds that are young or young at heart.[79]

Aso's enthusiasm expresses an unelaborated, implicit logic of influence that is apparent across arguments for Japanese public diplomacy that emphasizes culture—that Japanese culture is unifier and a bridge, a means of universal access to Japan.

The promotion of *anime*, or Japanese animation, is yet another significant dimension of Japan's emphasis on pop culture–based public diplomacy. In March 2008, Japan appointed its first *anime* ambassador, the cartoon cat named Doraemon.[80] During the inaugural ceremony for the position, Japanese foreign minister Masahiko Komoura declared, ""Doraemon, I hope you will travel around the world as an anime ambassador to deepen people's understanding of Japan so they will become friends with Japan." In response, Doraemon the cat announced: "I hope through my cartoons I will be able to convey to people overseas what ordinary Japanese people are thinking, what sort of life we are leading and what sort of future we are trying to create!"[81] Japanese anime's plurality of genres and subject matter have garnered a tremendous global fan community. That anime is argued to symbolize the "future" that Japan is forging reflects a particular faith in the power of the form to accrue larger political leverage.

Building on the global success of its anime, Japan also deployed anime programming in Iraq in support of its 600 soldiers providing noncombat assistance to Coalition forces. Japan painted its water trucks with images from its *Captain Tsubasa*, an animated character from a soccer-focused television series. The Japan Foundation provided the third season of the animated series (*Captain Majed*, in Arabic) for the Iraqi Media Network in 2006, in order to "provide dreams and hopes for the children of Iraq, who will shoulder the future of the country."[82] This effort was complemented by the provision of Japan's long-running television drama, *Oshin*, and the NHK-produced show *Project X* to Iraqi television as part of Japan's contribution to the reconstruction of Iraq.[83]

The case of pop culture usage in Iraq is revealing of pop culture's perceived efficacy as an *immediate* public diplomacy tool, as well a general sense of what such products can accomplish as an enduring point of contact between cultures. Japan's pop cultural promotion expanded considerably during mid-2000s, in conjunction with branding efforts and inter-ministry cooperation efforts to leverage cultural products *as* Japan. In 2002, Japan launched the *Japan Expo* convention to highlight various aspects of Japanese pop culture. The event has grown considerably both in attendance and in stakeholders to include MOFA, METI, and the Japanese Tourism Agency, in conjunction with the French government. Japan Expo is now the largest exhibition of Japanese culture in the world. The recent events drew over 150,000 fans, invited to "share Japan's soft power with the world."[84]

Other efforts reflect awareness of the opportunity to capitalize on the fan community dimension of Japan's pop culture notoriety. MOFA has promoted programs like the World Cosplay Summit, where costumed fans of Japanese anime, manga, and video game characters converge to display their home-made costumes and shared interest in J–pop culture. The purpose of cosplay Summit is argued to: ""contribute to creation of international exchange of youth culture born in Japan through manga and anime."[85] In 2010, the

Summit's tenth year, cosplayers competed for the *Minister of Foreign Affairs Prize*—which was awarded by the Director-General of the Public Diplomacy Department, Kenjiro Monji.

Following the trend in fan community targeting, MOFA also appointed three "Trend Communicators" to promote Japanese pop culture, known as *kawaii* or "cute" Ambassadors in February 2009.[86] Three young women were chosen to represent three aspects of Japan's *kawaii* youth culture and fashion, representing the so-called "Lolita," "Harijuku," and CONOMi school uniform fashion trends. The program was announced to "promote understanding and confidence in Japan" in addition to the "traditional culture and arts" that MOFA has used for public diplomacy efforts.[87] Yet programs like the "Trend Communicators" are not singular efforts at promoting the niche elements of Japanese creative culture—they are presented as a means of access to Japanese culture. Pop culture, as it has been deployed by the Japanese government, represents an invitation to global audiences; to cultivate broader appreciation of Japanese cultural heritage and, by extension, serve the interests of a soft power agenda.[88]

International Broadcasting

In addition to Japan's considerable structural investment in cultural diplomacy and nation-branding related to its cultural products, Japan also maintains a continuing presence as an international broadcaster mainly through the efforts of its NHK broadcasting platforms. The Japanese government also maintains the Japanese Media Communication Center (JAMCO), which is operated by the Ministry of Public Management, Home Affairs, Posts, and Telecommunications to promote Japanese programming by facilitating English, Spanish, and Chinese translations. Since its founding in 1991, JAMCO has translated over 6,500 programs for export to 83 countries.[89] Most of Japan's international broadcasting, however, is the product of its domestic public broadcaster—NHK.

Given Japan's strongly perceived division between NHK and government influence, it is difficult to uncritically classify Japan's international broadcasting as a form of public diplomacy. Despite apparent Japanese reluctance to see NHK as a mouthpiece of the state, arguments in Japan surrounding international broadcasting have come to settle on similar justifications that describe other forms of Japanese public diplomacy. Japanese international broadcasting is seen increasingly as a tool of influence.

Historically, Japan's foreign and English language broadcasting has not received the kind of institutional public diplomacy priority that other aspects of Japan's soft power seem to reflect. Masahiko Ishikuza argues "Japan's

English-language media—electronic and print—have always had a kind of marginalized existence."[90] Early in 2009, however, NHK launched NHK World, a 24-hour-a-day English channel broadcast to over 80 countries via satellite, cable, and Internet. The new format of the channel incorporates both commercially produced content as well as NHK documentaries.[91] Providing content on culture, science, and economics, the channel is intended to "match Al-Jazeera" in terms of its credibility and capacity to provide news about Japan.[92] Koki Matsumoto, a senior director at Japan International Broadcasting Inc., a subsidiary of NHK, describes the value of the content provided by the new NHK offerings: "You don't see these things on CNN. This is a uniqueness we are very proud of. It is something very innovative." Yet the revamped international offerings are not solely justified in terms of improving content, but also in providing a *voice* for Japan.

Hatsuhisa Takashima, the head of Japan International Broadcasting (an NHK distributor), states that the Japan's international broadcasting service contributes to Japan's *leadership* role in international affairs. Specifically, he argues that NHK World can "give the country a global voice to match its economic clout." Tasahima adds, "we would like to put Japan from the rear seat of the plane to the cockpit, and be more active on the global scene."[93] The implicit assumption here is that Japan is outside of a leadership position, and that a communication outlet can propel Japan into such a role.

Takashima's arguments reflect the sentiment that having an international broadcaster is required as a component of power—"economic clout" alone is insufficient. This claim is not the same as China's arguments for international broadcasting, which are primarily justified by the need to combat negative framing by Western news outlets. Takashima equates leadership and agency (the ability to be "active") with broadcasting. Yet such ideas provide little in terms of elaborating *how* such broadcasting works to demonstrate such leadership. In fact, much of the Japanese discussion on international broadcasting in Japan centers more on its relation to the Japanese government and NHK's ability to compete with other international broadcasters.

Japan's international news production remains defined by a thorough form of journalistic objectivity as a core value in its reporting, and not necessarily on flashier kinds of journalism. This form of journalism has been seen as problematic for public diplomacy purposes. As Sakumi Shimizu of Waseda University argues:

> The fact is, unless we create an English-language channel for viewers who are not Japanese, there is no way that this will be a tool for us in our cultural diplomacy. However, it should be pointed out that even NHK would have a difficult time in attracting enough sponsors to produce the "Asian CNN," unless they reform their programming and services in a fundamental way.[94]

Shimizu's observations relate to contemporary proposals to make NHK a commercially driven broadcasting service. Yet debate about the *purpose* of international broadcasting is compounded with concern over the role of government in sponsorship and control of the message. Shimizu also argues for a market-driven, less bureaucratically controlled model for Japan's international broadcasting: "[O]nce such a business model based on commercial sponsorship for overseas broadcasting is established, NHK could produce various important public programs, which would deserve some government subsidies for their merits from the national viewpoint."[95] Yet the political nature of international broadcasting—who gets to decide what gets produced—remains unresolved in Shimizu's recommendation.

Proposals to move NHK to a more commercial, market-driven model appear to conflict with its mandated institutional mission to promote "endeavors focused on international exchange" (expressed not only in the cultural events that it sponsors, but also language training and technical assistance programs).[96] This controversy suggests a moment of redefinition for Japanese international broadcasting and its relation to the government, which was brought into stark relief in a crisis with North Korea.

In November 2006, the Minister of Internal of Affairs and Communications requested that NHK provide content for Japanese citizens abducted by North Korea. This decision touched off public concern that the much vaunted institutional "firewall" between NHK and the Japanese government had been breached. The Japanese government stated that it had no intention of interfering with content, and NHK reaffirmed its autonomy. Yet, the *Mainichi Daily News* reported that the pressure from the government on the NHK amounted to a "danger of administrative guidance spreading to places that can't be seen." Similarly, the Japanese News Agency Kyodo described the scenario as "the first time a minister has issued a detailed and specific order to Japan's public broadcaster, stirring criticism in the media and among experts that it will lead to further government interference with freedom of the press" and worried that "[it] may affect the future of the nation's international broadcasting."[97] The crisis revealed value conflicts that hamper the short-term utilization of NHK as a public diplomacy tool to facilitate political objectives.

Ambiguity in the purpose of NHK, to support longer-term strategic goals while remaining independent from the government suggests that NHK is an ambivalent component of Japan's soft power strategy. Such ambiguity may be on the wane. Shigetaka Komori, the chairman of the board of governors for NHK, argues that foreign audience programming should more aggressively promote "Japan's national interest." Yet, as Ishizuka argues, there is no clear indication of what constitutes the "national interest."[98] Ishizuka suggests that while the content of international broadcasting could be left to the editorial norms of journalists, it's hard for such broadcasters to extricate themselves from their sponsoring institutions—especially during times of crisis. Ishizuka offers that the real concern over the Japanese "firewall" between its broadcasters and the government may be that it is the *domestic public* that is not heard in Japanese broadcasts. In this view, the most disenfranchised actor in Japan's efforts to "speak" to the outside world through broadcasting is the Japanese public.

Office of Development Assistance

Japan's Official Development Assistance (or ODA) deserves some mention as a component of Japanese foreign policy that serves in some capacity as public diplomacy. The ODA is recognized as a significant instrument of Japanese statecraft: a tool of economic leverage to compensate for the lack of overt military power as well as noncommunication-derived source of soft power.[99] Yet ODA has also been criticized as serving Japanese economic interests too narrowly—though this critique could also be leveled at the early years of the Japan Foundation and MOFA's cultural diplomacy.[100] Criticism of ODA reflects the legacy Japan's role as a "nurturing mercantilist" in the years prior to Japan's economic downturn, coupled with its part in Japan's history of supporting U.S. security burdens through so-called checkbook diplomacy.[101]

Evidence of ODA's changing role in Japanese diplomacy became apparent in 1992, with inclusion of "humanitarian," "environmental," "freedom," and "democracy" into its charter of criteria for development assistance.[102] Japan began to focus more on the relation between *soft power* and development aid in the latter half of the 1990s, due in part to the "role of ideas in foreign aid politics" evidenced in the wake of Asian financial crisis.[103] This was reflected in the creation of the IDEA initiative, a program designed to create a forum to gather and share the experiences of Asian countries during the regional financial crisis. The ODA also organized several rounds of the Tokyo International Conference on African Development (TICAD), recognizing the significance of Africa for competing paradigms for development and aid. This program emphasized Japan's focus on the politics of aid and ideas through the "human security" dimension of postwar development and reconstruction efforts.

As Saori Katada observes, the nature of ODA in the 2000s transformed due to both diminished resources (a trend observed across Japan's foreign policy institutions) as well as the supervisory stewardship by MOFA, which began in 2001. Under MOFA, the ODA has since stressed the humanitarian dimension of its mission, and less the *quid-pro-quo* strategy that had defined previous years. Norbert Palanovics argues that the strategic purpose of the

ODA has moved decidedly toward realizing the organization as a tool of diplomatic and international influence.[104] However, as Katada contends, given
the uncertain funding environment, the "indirect benefits" accrued from ODA
activities abroad may make it a less palatable to Japan's domestic constituency. And while the ODA does offer some support to formal Japanese public
diplomacy institutions through exchange program financing, the ODA does
not have a strongly articulated presence within public discourse on Japanese public diplomacy. The ODA is not typically argued as a component of
public diplomacy, even though its soft power benefits have been repeatedly
recognized.[105]

DIMENSIONS OF JAPANESE SOFT POWER DISCOURSE

The programs and institutions surveyed in the previous sections reflect an
emerging set of justifications and adaptations that approximate the outlines
of Japanese soft power discourse. This discourse is not monolithic, and as
the evidence suggests, reveals some disagreements and unresolved questions
about soft power for Japan. While Japan has organizations and programs in
place to conduct public diplomacy like MOFA's Public Diplomacy Department, it is not altogether evident that these reflect a coherent vision for the
"conversion" of soft power resources into policy outcomes.

The context for the evolving discussion of soft power in Japan surely plays
a significant role in shaping the strategic discourse on soft power. As suggested previously, soft power programs may reflect recognition of strategic
opportunity as much as an inevitable recourse to deal with other forms of
perceived power deficiency. Despite Japan's significant economic problems
in the 1990s, exports of Japanese cultural products have enjoyed considerable
growth across both regional and worldwide markets.[106] In 2002 alone, cultural
products exports were estimated to be $12.5 billion.[107] The growth of markets
for Japanese products, such as anime, manga, and fashion expanded globally
and built upon a history of cultural icons coming from the Japanese entertainment industry.[108] As is evident, current Japanese public diplomacy programs
reflect a *tacit* recognition that this form of economic success can be leveraged
for political and related foreign policy objectives—though the explicit logics
of conversion remains somewhat controversial.

Japanese soft power resources—broadly conceived as both material exports
of cultural products and more intangible values and ideals—are perceived to
have application *across* Japan's foreign policy obligations. In a 2004 report
commissioned by Prime Minister Koizume by the Japanese Department of
Defense, soft and hard power are deemed essential to accomplish Japan's

strategy *security* goals: "[I]f Japan is to expand its international cooperation to prevent the emergence of threats around the world, it will need to utilize its soft power more effectively."[109] And as David Leheny observes, the cultivation of soft power through exchanges and developmental aid has been seized upon by commentators who argue that soft power translates into more effective uses of hard power.[110] Leheny argues that the fungibility and indeed "elasticity" of soft power as a resource appeals to a broad swath of domestic political viewpoints within Japan concerning its potential for international affairs.[111] Soft power is conceptually *popular* in Japan.

For example, the METI activities to promote the global competitiveness of the Japanese media content industries explicitly use the language of soft power to frame their actions.[112] This suggests the pervasiveness and indeed, the *normalization* of the soft power concept as it has threaded through strategic justifications. The tenets of soft power is not solely confined to more "traditional" diplomatic and public diplomacy institutions.

Yet there are also critical Japanese perspectives on the soft power. Kazuo Ogoura of the Japan Foundation stands out as a leading voice of moderation, if not outright skepticism of the concept as a strategic justification for cultural diplomacy. Among other concerns, Ogoura questions *who* are the real soft power actors—who is endowed with agency? Is the Japanese government or the creative industries the source of soft power? As he states, there is "confusion over who or what actually exercises this power."[113] Ogoura's criticism conveys discomfort with justifying the practice of organizations like the Japan Foundation within the logics of soft power, and suggest that Japan's public diplomacy is better justified by less obviously self-serving strategic concepts.

Seichi Kondo, the former director general of the Public Diplomacy Department, sees the *state* as the key actor in generating soft power. For Kondo, however, the government is not a direct actor, but an agent responsible for cultivating soft power resources.[114] Given the liberal use of "soft power" across policy justification contexts, the conceptualization of soft power "resources" is also specified in different ways, leading to some ambiguity about how resources might be utilized or converted. Ogoura asks, "[W]hat exactly are the constituent elements that make up 'soft' power and are there any precise indices for quantifying it?"[115] Kondo has argued that measurement is problematic, as it is difficult to reduce the impact of soft power to a relation between output and effect in a manner likely desired by government analysts.[116]

Rather than reduce soft power to balances of resources and effects, Kondo presents soft power in practical orientations that are irrevocably bound by inherent cultural attitudes—both on the "transmission" and on the "reception" end soft power programs like public diplomacy. In other words, soft power is conditioned by how active efforts to persuade, frame, or attract are refracted through policy and cultural attitudes toward the prospects of soft power—a notion akin to what R. S. Zaharna has called the "cultural underbelly" of public diplomacy.[117]

For Kondo, the Japanese state has a particular conception of how resources should be deployed in the effort to influence. He contrasts the United States with Japan, where the United States *projects* its soft power resources while Japan *presents* its assets in the long term. These orientations toward soft power, as they are translated in particular programs or policies, are all too often subject to "cultural constraints" that impact their efficacy—especially when a public diplomacy designed to augment soft power is so inflected with cultural bias that it ultimately fails among its target audience.[118] Put another way, soft power cannot be assumed to follow from the possession of assets, but from the conduct of soft power actions. Kondo's explanation offers a uniquely Japanese conception of how international communication is to work persuasively.

POP CULTURE AS RESOURCE-IN-USE

Despite Kondo's careful delimitation of the utility of soft power resources, others have expressed less cautious faith in the potency of soft power assets. The most vocal, if not fully elaborated, logic of linking soft power actors to resources is in the rhetoric of Taro Aso's strident promotion of popular culture for soft power purposes. Taro Aso, speaking at the time as Japan's foreign minister at the Digital Hollywood University in 2006, hails the virtues of Japanese cultural forms to influence other nation-states:

> We have all grown up nourished by Shakespeare and Beethoven and other forms of culture emerging from the West. Yet we are now at the point where culture made in Japan—whether anime and manga or sumo and Japanese food culture—is equally able to nourish the people of the world, particularly the younger generations. We would be remiss not to utilize these to the fullest.[119]

Aso highlights here the particular utility of *manga* as a representative artform. He also notes the popularity of manga in China:

> If you take a peek in any of the shops in China catering to the young otaku (nerdy)-type manga and anime fans, you will find the shops' walls lined with any and every sort of Japanese anime figurine you can imagine. . . . .We have a grasp on the hearts of the young people in many countries, not the least of which

being China. . . . With all due respect to Mickey and Donald, whether you look at J-pop, J-anime, or J-fashion, the competitiveness of any of these is much more than you might imagine.[120]

Aso's rhetoric envisions culture as both instrumental as well as essential to the competitive nature of international politics. Aso exhorts the observed popularity of Japanese culture as a resource to be utilized beyond the confines of simply promoting a sector of the Japanese economy. Aso's rhetoric also cleaves closely to the Chinese idealization of culture as being a direct site of contest between nation-states, a battleground of credibility and identification.[121]

More specifically, Aso's speech serves as an unqualified justification for the utilization of manga as an instrument of Japanese public diplomacy to capitalize on the global popularity of the cultural form. He also elaborates *why* manga functions as an effective public diplomacy tool:

The more these kinds of positive images pop up in a person's mind, the easier it becomes for Japan to get its views across over the long term. In other words, Japanese diplomacy is able to keep edging forward, bit by bit, and bring about better and better outcomes as a result.[122]

Explicit in this statement is a direct, effectively causal connection between the consumption of a Japanese cultural product and a tangible policy outcome, linked by a partially elaborated conception of how such products cultivate "positive images."

Aso would later argue to the Japanese Diet that "what is important is to be able to induce other countries to listen to Japan. If the use of pop culture or various sub-cultures can be useful in this process, we certainly should make the most of them."[123] Aso's vision is that soft power is rendered in a readily identifiable conversion of cultural resources. Yet Aso's description also implies challenges in the form of active audiences. The consumption of Japanese images translates into an enabling environment for Japanese foreign policy that is implicitly enabled by the preferences of the target audience (the consumers). Japanese power is thus constrained not merely by other governments, but by cultural product consumers.

Aso's agenda setting power as a leader did much to formalize recognition of Japan's pop culture products as a soft power tool. Aso used it as a vehicle for bilateral cultural diplomacy with Russia, in order to highlight the efficacy cultural relations for foreign policy. In December 2008, Japan announced that an individual from Singapore won the second annual International Manga Award.[124] At the ceremony, Kenjiro Monji, then director general of the Department of Public Diplomacy, declared, "To improve your image in the world, you have to make use of all the tools available . . . We can use the attractive power of popular culture as an introduction [to Japan]."[125] Again, the *instrumental* value of culture is emphasized. Monji further clarified that this was demonstrated in significantly increased numbers of people studying in Japan since 2005. As the previously described public diplomacy programs reveal, Aso's enthusiasm for these pop culture vehicles continues to be supported by Japan's foreign policy institutions.

Yet the assumed link between the purported utility of pop culture as a resource for soft power, and its draw as a global entertainment project, remains as much a discursive construction as a proven tool, mainly because there are few metrics of it actually translating into foreign policy gains that one could retroactively attribute to "soft power"–inspired policies. What has stood in for soft power "success" is the popularity of the resource themselves.

For example, in 2005 at the Fifth Annual International Cosplay Summit, thousands descended on Nagoya Japan to celebrate their fandom by dressing up as their favorite manga and anime characters. Michio Oguri, the chairman of the event, declared that "manga is an international language."[126] As YK Heng notes, the global popularity of Japanese popular culture, and not business, has driven more to learn Japanese language in order to consume Japanese products (games, manga, anime, etc.).[127] Yet it is unclear whether the success of such cultural events are demonstrative of soft power or simply that they are resources waiting to be leveraged. Nor is it obvious that the popularity of Japan's cultural output has anything to do with foreign policy decision-makers.

As Japan pop culture scholar Roland Kelts contends, "Japanese pop culture is being pulled into foreign markets far more than it is being pushed."[128] Despite some high-profile government advocacy equating manga to soft power, Kelts argues there is little media recognition that the Japanese government is involved in its success. Seichi Kondo argues that the success of Japanese cultural products is not simply a matter of transmission and reception, but of "sudden amplification" among users, a form of "subjective interaction" among "receivers that make it difficult for analysts to predict."[129] The very adaptability and accessibility of Japanese cultural forms to other cultural audiences may make it popular, but the forces of fan culture may not easily be shaped or prodded by government intervention.

Despite such concerns about the link between popularity and government action, Aso continues to argue for cultural industry support—primarily to promote industry growth. In August 2009, Aso claimed that Japanese cultural "contents" sales abroad represent one-tenth of what the United States sells in the global market in order to make the case for a strong industrial policy for the cultural and entertainment technologies industries and promote successful *global* firms.[130] While Aso has made an explicit connection between such global projection and soft power, Peng Lam's analysis of such discourse on soft power offers that cultural producers themselves did not set out to project soft power for Japan.[131] A working sense of how Japanese power is amplified via such soft power assets remains ambivalent—suspended between justifications for economic gain and the desire to translate such gains into a field of non-military potency.

TOWARD A JAPANESE DEFINITION OF SOFT POWER

Such a "working sense" would outline the tacit assumptions and justifications behind a Japanese strategy of soft power. As stated previously—such a conception is likely strongly tied to the strategic situation facing Japan. The 2005 Bluebook offers that soft power is not easily decomposed into particular assets and actions, nor easily distinguished from hard power:

> One must be careful, however, not to automatically define military and financial strength as hard power and culture as soft power. What is hard power and what is soft power ultimately depends on how the source of that power is used.[132]

This pragmatic sense of the term may be strongly linked to the way in which Japan's strategic discourse must accommodate the growing presence of China. As China also seeks to translate its soft power resources into soft power, Japan is confronted with a soft power competitor. This competition is as much about soft power as it about specifying what *counts* as soft power— the resources for persuasion and building identification between publics. Yoshizaki Tatsuhiko describes this conflict with China as a kind of politics by other means:

> Many of the confrontations in this era will take place through the interchange of words and ideas. It will be an era when the battles among countries are virtual ones. . . . It is necessary to employ as many different routes as possible to create a broad base of Japan fans."[133]

For Seichi Kondo, the route to power can be enhanced by a public diplomacy that facilitates "interactive networks" between the private sector, NGOs, regional governments, and the MOFA. Public diplomacy is a necessary component of foreign policy to reflect fundamentally paradigmatic changes in society, from a hierarchical to a more *network* structure of relations.[134]

Kondo also acknowledges that the public diplomacy concept does not translate readily into Japanese. Various translations of public diplomacy do not imply a notion of "public" while including the government as a key stake-holder. And Kondo adds, "We can't find a proper word in Japanese for soft power, either. Perhaps, we could say *Rinen-Bunka* power (philosophy-culture power)."[135] Kondo notes that the problem with soft power is that it is not nearly as predictably effective as hard power: "The influence of soft power changes depending on diplomatic partners and their situation, as well as either the short or long term."[136] Soft power is more ephemeral than a known index of cultural assets. These assets have to be convertible.

Kondo is also reluctant to draw direct and obvious connections between the sources of soft power and effects. Kondo claims that Japanese soft power cannot be easily compartmentalized into Nye's trinity of values, culture, and a legitimate foreign policy by arguing that "[w]hen considering what is Japan's soft power, we cannot divide clearly culture, philosophy and policy into three."[137] Rather, Kondo suggests that soft power grows in a longer horizon of time and exposure to the way in which Japanese culture is presented by Japanese actions over time. Soft power is in this view is an emergent quality.

Kondo argues that one cannot simply leverage assets in acts of soft power. Soft power accumulates over time, coalescing into perceptions that symbolically link cultural values with practices. He describes the context of soft power as

> "[T]he value of invisible things," i.e. a sense of beauty, a view of nature, a mind of harmony, a sense of moral, and a respect for the others . . . They appear through not only a traditional performance, but also a modern culture, our behavior, ODA, greater regards for the UN, and other diplomatic policies, which gradually but surely generates positive outcomes.[138]

Kondo's claims are a description of Japan's soft power as much as a critique of the pro-active and overt instrumentalization of soft power of the United States. Kondo, arguing at the time as director-general of the Public Diplomacy Department, was not suggesting that Japan's public diplomacy was *unnecessary*—but, rather, that public diplomacy required different forms to contribute to soft power. For Kondo, soft power is located in ideas and institutional values. These are emptied of their "power" when projected too aggressively.

Kondo's concerns are reflected in other venues for public discussion of soft power. One such event on the issue of soft power was the 2009 Fulbright CULCON Joint Symposium, which brought together Japanese and U.S. leaders to discuss challenges in U.S.–Japanese relations, as well as various conceptions of soft power in the Japanese context. The U.S.–Japan Conference on Cultural and Educational Interchange (CULCON) was established in 1961 as a means to improve relations, and comprises binational working groups of government, academic, and private-sector contributors tasked to develop recommendations for the two governments.[139] The 2009 symposium dealt directly with the issue of soft power and featured considerable attention to how Japan has taken advantage of its soft power assets through specific programs, how soft power is conceptualized in the Japanese context, and how it impacts Japan's international relations. Prominent Japanese public figures were given the opportunity to speak candidly about Japan's soft power.

Makato Iokibe, president of the National Defense Academy of Japan, argued that political values can in themselves be a form of soft power: "National power is made up of many aspects such as military power, economic power and population, but the power to express and to project can be regarded as soft power as a whole. . . ."[140] For Iokibe these values represented effective soft power for Japan in the context of its successful economic development after World War II and, importantly, meant that Japan had pursued a policy of cooperation and respect with its regional partners. Soft power, in this sense, is actualized only in relation to other practices that link value to action. Soft power is *demonstrative*; a power to frame the larger context of policies and action.

Hidetoshi Fujisawa of NHK waxed more philosophical, offering that "human beings have the power to realize the future that human beings would like to see. I believe that soft power is indeed such a power."[141] Fukisawa's sentiments portray soft power as a kind of idealized set of social-political arrangements as much as a *capacity* to provide such a template.

The commonly articulated vehicle for this kind of promotion in the Japanese context is "branding." As previously mentioned, branding represents a key aspect of the debate over soft power that draws together the various stakeholders of Japanese foreign policy. And as Lam indicates, there is a perceived *urgency* for a strategy to integrate cultural assets—to translate a "cool Japan brand" into an enduring soft power strategy.[142]

In 2006, Kakutaro Kitashiro, chairman of the Japan Association of Corporate Executives argued that "Japan needs to become a meeting place (hub) of the finest human resources, capital, and information from all over the world in order to further develop and establish a high value-added 'Japanese brand' and promote it to global society."[143] Kakutaro's claim is more than an argument for economic growth. It is an institutional reconfiguration of Japanese foreign policy, to redistribute policy responsibility among public and private actors. Kakutaro states that "[branding] requires not only the effort of the private sector, but also needs to be emphasized as a part of a diplomatic strategy that attaches great importance to 'soft power.'"[144] Branding in this view is a diplomatic imperative as much as an economic policy strategy.

Speaking at the 2009 CULCON symposium, Sadaaki Numata, executive director of the Japan Foundation's Center for Global Partnerships notes that the idea of branding does not provide a readily accessible strategic template for Japan. He argues, "[W]e should be thinking of the national brand of Japan. I do not know how national brand should be translated into Japanese, and when I say national brand, people may associate it with just manga."[145] Numata conveys some skepticism about the faddish elements of Japanese cool, a tenuous soft power resource given the competitive cultural industry policies of South Korea and China.

Numata also recognizes that despite the perceived need for some kind of coordinated industrial and foreign policy focused on the Japanese brand, there is no apparent means by which to link arguments for branding with a vehicle to carry out such a policy. He contends that "when we think about national strategy and national brand, we inevitably come up against the problem that we cannot move without the wherewithal to implement it."[146] Numata's comments appear to acknowledge the context of a shrinking public diplomacy budget.

While Numata argues that branding may not be a sufficient concept from which to promote Japan and cultivate soft power, Yoichi Funabashi, editor-in-chief of the *Asahi Shimbum*, counters by arguing that a more holistic approach to Japanese soft power remains absent: "What is lacking is focus and strategy. For instance in terms of public diplomacy, Japan is now confronted with great difficulties, such as the issue of history. We have no clear memory as to how Japan has properly addressed the issues of history."[147] Funabashi acknowledges the often overlooked element of Japanese discourse on soft power: the ability of Japan to effectively address its imperial past as an impediment to soft power. If soft power reflects competitive credibility, then Japan's historical legacy cannot be ignored.

The other significant issue is that of soft power *conversion*—and the ability the government to facilitate soft power outcomes. Naoyuki Agawa, dean of the faculty of management at Keio University, says, "The so-called Japan 'cool phenomenon' is a great *source* of soft power. But if you think about it, we have not necessarily *projected* that power abroad" (emphasis added).[148] Agawa acknowledges criticism that Japanese soft power may be driven by consumer interest.

Yet Agawa reaches an opposite conclusion: "If the world views Japan as a country of great pop culture, J-pop, but with little more, a nation that has no desire to sit in the driver's seat, . . . that is dangerous for Japan."[149] Agawa warns that Japan must view branding strategies as means to *demonstrate* leadership. Branding therefore must be more than highlighting passive cultural determinants of soft power. Branding is both strategically necessary and symbolic of credible international leadership.

As Daliot Bul argues, this line of reasoning has historical roots in the Japanese rhetoric of domestic cultural policy. In her analysis of Japanese branding policies: "'Culture' (*bunka*) is thus often positioned at the rhetorical core of national renovation projects. Culture is used as a semantic cluster linking ethnicity, aesthetics, citizenship, economic progress, race and the renovation of Japan." For Daliot-Bul, the debate over nation branding strategy and resultant policies to promote Japan are evidence of an overarching concern with domestic cultural policy as much as cultural diplomacy:

> [M]arket driven imagery of Cool Japan is being tamed and appropriated to suit national interests. Through selective appropriation, promotion and combination of cultural products, this strategy aims to construct politically meaningful images of Japan for domestic and international audiences.[150]

Daliot-Bul's analysis reveals multiple motivations embedded in the branding debate in Japan. While branding conceptually renders strategic assets (cultural and creative expression) into concrete and actionable resources that can be promoted or discarded, to do nation-branding is also a means to control what it means to represent Japan—to govern the symbols that express Japanese identity. Daliot-Bul argues that this motive for branding also sustains a kind of Japanese exceptionalism. As Taro Aso argues, "Manga is about everything"—it knows absolutely no boundaries. Manga, in a word, is the most universal unifier of the hearts and minds that are young or young at heart.'[151] Daliot-Bul sees in attempts by Japan to brand itself the intent to build a bridge between Asia and the rest of the world that elides an ambition of *leadership* via a politically governed and distinctive Japanese culture.

THE JAPANESE FUSION OF DIPLOMACY AND PUBLIC DIPLOMACY

Previous stewards of Japanese public diplomacy, figures such as Seichi Kondo and Kenjiro Monji, have articulated far less sweeping ambitions for public diplomacy than the discourse on soft power and branding seem to suggest. They have instead argued about the changing environment for diplomacy that signals the rising importance of public diplomacy and foreign publics for Japanese foreign policy. In the process, they reveal some implicit logics of soft power conversion. Seichi Kondo describes the practice of diplomacy for Japan as involving an expanding range of relevant actors:

> The role of diplomacy expands from working with other countries' governments to directly and indirectly working on other countries' citizens in order to improve overseas understandings and image of our own county, our citizens' security in other countries, and our society and economy through introducing international human resources and investments.[152]

In Kondo's definition, diplomacy converges with public diplomacy. Working "directly and indirectly" suggests a multi-track conception of the business of statecraft that is bound up in the relations and security of citizens, domestically and abroad. In this view, the business of Japanese diplomacy is inseparable from the functions of public diplomacy. This linkage is made explicit in the 2005 Bluebook definition of cultural diplomacy:

> The purpose of cultural exchange and overseas public relations is to enhance understanding and trust of Japan among the public in other countries and to develop an environment conducive to the promotion of foreign policy by broadly publicizing Japan's foreign and other policies and cultural charm to the international community.[153]

While this definition is generic, it foregrounds the promotion of foreign policy in "trust," "understanding," and awareness through "publicizing." Of course there is little explicitly stated here about how public diplomacy could work to *convert* the resources of soft power to the outcomes anticipated. A notion of "conversion" comes closer to being specified in Kenjiro Monji's arguments about the "gateway" function of popular culture.

Monji, director general of Japan's Public Diplomacy Department, builds on Kondo's emphasis on "presentation" as a strategy for public diplomacy, to develop the notion of pop culture as gateway to cultivate interest and identification with Japan. The goals of "understanding" and "image" are achieved in public diplomacy through the provision of cultural *access*. Monji states: "Using pop culture as a gateway, my hope is to broaden people's interests in Japanese culture as a whole and in Japan itself."[154] Public diplomacy can increase the appetite for Japan, where *interests* stand in a kind as a leverage point for soft power.

Monji claims that pop culture serves as a vehicle to yet other soft power objectives. In 2009 Monji states, "I hope to encourage these fans to develop a comprehensive interest in Japan and its culture. In fact, interest in anime and manga has prompted an increasing number of fans to study the Japanese language."[155] Exposure to Japanese culture in this sense also reveals to foreign audiences how Japan has absorbed global influences, while retaining traditional elements of Japanese culture.

Both Kondo and Monji, however, argue that role of public diplomacy as a *government*-driven soft power institution should be limited. While Nye has argued that public diplomacy can be an active and direct approach to cultivate and draw attention to soft power assets, both Kondo and Monji stress the facilitative role that can be played by government (Nye, 2008). Kondo offers that public diplomacy should be the "hub" of a "network" of "cooperative interaction and mutual stimulation."[156] Kondo proposes that "the role of government as a facilitator and network hub may appear to be one of limited influence, but still it is an extremely important role within the new emerging structure of international relations involving a variety of actors connected with each other horizontally." Kondo's assessment links the perceived complexity of contemporary international politics with what diplomacy scholar Andrew Hocking calls the "network model" for diplomacy, which recognizes the interdependent and asymmetric stakeholders of international policy.[157]

Monji elaborates on the idea of facilitation to justify public/private partnerships. "It goes without saying that the wellspring of soft power lies in the private sector, so any attempt to exercise this power at the national level should be premised on working closely with the private sector."[158] Monji echoes Kitashiro and Numata's contentions that soft power cannot be sole-sourced to a public diplomacy institution, but is a larger, societal responsibility for the Japanese.

Monji's vision for public diplomacy within a soft power framework is to coordinate between different branches of government. Keeping with the rhetoric of branding, Monji articulates the holistic view of public diplomacy in relation to soft power. Government-led public diplomacy coordinates among other agencies and domestic actors the responsible stewardship of Japan's comparative advantage in soft power. For Monji, this represents a diverse array of soft power resources:

> Soft power includes not only pop culture but also traditional culture, Japanese values and our way of life, including our reverence for the spirit of harmony and the idea of symbiosis with nature, which are becoming ever more relevant in the globalized world of the 21st century. Indeed, energy conservation and recognition of the need for action to protect the environment could even be considered to embody Japan's traditional values and way of life, with the backing of our leading-edge technology. As Japan's strength lies in soft power, I would like to pursue pop culture diplomacy within the more broadly defined framework of soft power diplomacy.[159]

Much as with Kondo's notion of "invisible things," these *resources* cannot be deployed in some competitive, projecting mode of addressing foreign publics. Monji clarifies, "It is certainly not appropriate . . . to look upon public diplomacy as competition merely for the sake of boosting a country's national image."[160] Rather, Monji would propose a more refined approach whose ultimate objective is to "communicate one's culture" in a manner that acknowledges the cultural characteristics of the recipients. Following Kondo, Monji implicitly argues that soft power emanates from the *act* of communicating responsibility and respectfully.

This understated approach relies on the capacity of public diplomacy's audience to recognize the value and interest of what Japan is presenting. Thus, public diplomacy is not so much persuasive as it is *invitational*—where the global audience can assess the merits of Japan's position and identity in relation to their own without undue coercion or "representational force."

For playwright and commentator Masakuzu Yamazaki, this approach to the strategic promotion of Japan is problematic. Yamazaki argues that the public relations of Japan needs to be more coordinated and requires a "language"—or, a discourse to ground strategic action. As Yamazaki argues, a Japanese conception of something like public diplomacy is lacking:

> [E]ven the term "Cool Japan" was coined by an American journalist. Japan is without an official Information Ministry, with no way of talking about the significance of domestic trends—Kawaii ambassadors in the latest case—as a way of explaining the diverse aspects of Japanese society as well.[161]

The promotion of niche aspects of Japanese popular culture may appeal to certain audiences, but does not say much about what they signify about Japan and how it has adapted to globalizing social and cultural forces.

Yamazaki also argues the international broadcasting outfits like NHK have no role in this kind of promotion, because they are independent from government. Instead of international broadcasting, Yamazaki argues for an empowered government *public relations* institution.

> The bottom line is that PR efforts must convince the rest of the world that Japan shares similar hardships with other countries and will spare no effort to solve them, instead of merely beating its chest and bragging about its superiority and distinctiveness. . . . But its PR stance must remain consistent. The bottom line is that PR efforts must convince the rest of the world that Japan shares similar hardships with other countries and will spare no effort to solve them, instead of merely beating its chest and bragging about its superiority and distinctiveness.[162]

For Yamazaki, the strategic purpose of public diplomacy must be to establish the basis for identification with Japan. Instead of highlighting the Japanese values inherent in its globally popular products, the business of Japanese public diplomacy is in establishing ties that reflect shared priorities, motivations, and experience. In other words, Japanese public diplomacy should not be about promotion of Japan's image, but about attraction.

KAZUO OGOURA: QUESTIONING SOFT POWER

Yamazaki's perspective conveys some concern with the instrumental and overly exceptionalist ideas that lurk within arguments for Japanese soft power promotion. Japan Foundation president Kazuo Ogoura, in marked contrast to more enthusiastic supporters of soft power, argues that the entire concept of soft power may be flawed as *a strategic orientation* for Japan's foreign policy. Ogoura claims that by describing communicative actions as an exercise of soft power masks the implicitly coercive elements that are also present in how nation-states communicate. Ogoura points to the existential rhetoric of the United States' "War on Terror" as presenting a serious implicit element of coercion:

[W]hen forming a multinational force without a resolution from the United Nations, the United States has been known to apply political pressure as a form of "soft" persuasion to "help" other countries decide whether or not to participate in the force. Can it really be said that this is neither coercive nor threatening?[163]

Ogoura's argument here parallels Janice Bially-Mattern's assessment that soft power elides the "representational force" in foreign policy rhetoric. This kind of force, for Janice Bially-Mattern, often speaks louder than the elements of "attraction," the common cultural values that can be amplified in public diplomacy policies.[164] Soft power strategies either are oblivious to the inevitable coercive dimension to international politics or rehabilitate hard power politics through euphemism. Soft power rhetoric adorns the politics of retrospection, as Zahran and Ramos argue in their treatment of soft power as a form of reconstituted American hegemony.[165]

For Ogoura, the prospect of a Japanese soft power is thus questionable. Specifically, Ogoura claims that the application of "soft power" in justifying foreign policy actions, or perhaps in pointing *post hoc* to the success of a foreign policy objectives distracts from what he considers the more likely factors in determining international political outcomes. His assessment is arguably scathing:

[S]oft power as an actual political theory is loaded with ideology and riddled with contradictions and hypocrisy. Religion and ideology, for example, are seen by some as potent examples of soft power. Looking back through history, however, one cannot fail to notice that whenever religion and ideology have spread around the world, they have invariably been accompanied by military might.[166]

Interestingly, Ogoura does not say that a soft power resource such as culture does *not* have an impact on the scenic calculus of international politics. He cautions against uncritical projections of soft power effects, highlighting disjunctures between the role of the subject and the agent in the act of soft power cultural promotion:

No matter how attractive a given country may be, other countries will not accept its attractive power if it obstructs their freedom of action or adversely affects their economic interests. Hollywood movies, for instance, are often cited as a source of American soft power, but in France they have been subject to partial restriction precisely because of their attractiveness.[167]

He highlights that policymakers abstract cultural products into resources for soft power, when their value as an instrument of power to use is debatable. Ogoura's reading of Nye is, admittedly, selective. His 2006 critique of soft power comes amidst the contemporary political fallout from the U.S. invasion of Iraq and its impact on longstanding U.S. allies like Japan. Yet Ogoura does not conceal this context:

> . . . put it another way, we need to be aware that soft power can be a subtle way of rationalizing military action that lacks international legitimacy by bringing into play the concept of good and evil.[168]

Ogoura seems to suggest that the American abuse of soft power has an indelible effect on the ethics of soft power as a strategy. And when Ogoura addresses the idea of Japanese pop culture as a resource for Japanese soft power, he effectively dismantles the utility of appeals to foreign audiences through such means as somehow ethically different from other forms of international politics:

> There is the popular argument, based on the "Japanese cool" concept, that Japanese culture should be thought of as a form of national power, but to remove from the equation the issue of who will use this power and to what ends renders this argument meaningless.[169]

It is not that Ogoura rejects the notion that soft power can be cultivated. Nor is Ogoura rejecting, objectively, that soft power *exists* as a power capacity. Rather, he argues that because it can be co-opted by the state it is inherently flawed. In his final analysis, he offers that the rise of "soft power" as a policy framework or strategic imperative for politics in the twenty-first century is a signal of the diminished significance of the nation-state itself:

> Indeed, we should bear in mind that linking culture to the state carries a high risk of impeding, rather than promoting, the spread of cultural activities around the world . . . The worldwide spread of Japanese culture is a manifestation not of Japanese power but of how the notion of state-based power is gradually losing its meaning in an increasingly globalized world.[170]

Thus, the rise of Cool Japan as a strategic instrument is a signal of larger problem facing the global institution of the nation-state itself, where the state is not an exclusive cultural referent. Underlying Ogoura's argument is a concern over the credibility of the nation-state to leverage cultural attraction. As soon as soft power, through public diplomacy and international broadcasting, becomes an *overt* tool of parochial nation-state objectives, it becomes discredited to global audiences.

The range of arguments of between Taro Aso and Kazuo Ogoura suggest conflicting trajectories for how soft power is imagined in Japanese foreign policy. Rhetorically, they exhort differing visions of the international political milieu. For Aso and, by extension, commentators advocating a stronger "branding" program, culture is a resource untapped, and should be leveraged to achieve foreign policy objectives that involve both economic and soft power outcomes.

Aso's worldview of the political sphere is competitive, while no clear gauge of success is offered other than the successful prosecution of the foreign policy agenda. In contrast, Ogoura's take of soft power is profoundly critical and laced with concern over the kinds of policies it can sanction. For Ogoura, the presence of soft power as a viable policy framework is also a signal for the diminished influence of nation-states like Japan in a complex milieu of international and nonstate actors. Also, the arguments that embrace soft power as justification for branding strategies may also reflect the *convenience* of soft power arguments for domestic cultural policy to justify, as Daliot-Bul claims, the "taming" and appropriation of culture to suit national interests.

POWER CONVERSION AND "THE VALUE OF INVISIBLE THINGS"

Nye's notion of "contextual intelligence" suggests the capacity of soft power agents to recognize the utility of soft power resources in particular situations, where they might translate effectively into soft power outcomes. In the case of Japan, there is clear recognition that soft power is not only a strategic option, but in fact a necessity, given other constraints on the ability of Japan to manage its relations with other international actors. Yet the Japanese interpretation of soft power reveals divergent points of emphasis on the necessary and possible aspects of the conversion process.

The *scope* implied in articulations of Japanese soft power suggests two significant categories of subjects to soft power. Japanese public diplomacy programs and related soft power discourse reflect the notion that foreign publics and other non-governmental actors are important, which is consistent with the generic notions of soft power. These subjects to soft power are predominantly regional publics, who are also targets to other soft power programs, such as South Korean and Chinese efforts to leverage cultural assets in the service of soft power gains. Other subjects are deterritorialized fan communities, the *otaku* and other niche markets to Japanese popular culture and other creative forms of cultural expression.

These relations, however, are consistently *subject*-oriented—meaning that subjects are conceived as having interpretive agency in the soft power transaction. Relations, as evident in the selections of Japanese discourse presented here, do not reflect simply monological efforts to transmit messages and symbols to cultivate soft power, but rather ongoing episodes of cultural appraisal; soft power relations stem from the *choice* made by foreign audiences to identify or otherwise express interest in what Japanese soft power resources offer. Public diplomacy steps in to facilitate the choice, rather than to persuade.

The manner in which Japanese soft power is articulated suggests that foreign subjects have a lot of say in whether Japan actually accrues soft power. Subjects are not "cultural dupes," but discerning auditors of active approaches to soft power such as public diplomacy, as well as the steady stream of cultural flows that represent the global popularity of Japan. Kondo's essay on the distinction between projection and presentation in public diplomacy captures the limitations of soft power in its Japanese form.

This Japanese formulation suggests that messages in themselves don't automatically register effects by virtue of their transmission—in this case, Japanese culture is not a magic bullet, but an invitation to consider more about Japan. There appears to be little place for soft power as a beneficial consequence of propaganda. The implicit logic of communication and selective exposure effects in Japanese soft power discourse tilts strongly toward the interpretive power of the audience, along with the uncertainties that efforts of public diplomacy cannot be so easily predicted.

The ability of the agent is further circumscribed by the role it can institutionally play in cultivating soft power. Across different arguments presented in this study, the government is at best a facilitator, and not the principal agent of soft power. Public diplomacy may augment or organize resources that already function in some sort of soft power capacity, but it is unclear whether it or similar activities like nation-branding can in themselves carry the burden of Japan's soft power requirements. As other nation's move into the credibility game of soft power, Japan's policies are left with shoring up the private sector—the industries and creative capacities that sustain Japan's attractive exposure to foreign publics.

The *mechanisms* of Japanese public diplomacy are clearly reliant on the cache of its cultural industries. The values of Japan's political ideas seem absent from arguments for soft power, and the legitimacy of Japan's foreign policies are overshadowed by the instrumental usage of its development agenda and importantly, the legacy of its imperial past. Culture is thus the remaining pivotal resource in the Japanese concept of soft power—but not an unqualified resource.

The Japanese notion of soft power rests strongly on the perceived benefits derived from *material* sources of culture on the one hand, and on the conduct of communication on the other. A Japanese conception of soft power recognizes the salience of culture over technological form. Put another way, the debate over soft power in Japan is about the implication of culture as an asset and not about the significance of communication technologies and media as a site of cultural or ideational contest—except perhaps on the genre of cultural expression. While culture, broadly considered, is widely viewed as a significant strategic resource, the specific kinds of policies that would translate benefit from perceived soft power resources—the "art of the possible" for Japanese soft power remain uncertain, given Japan's dramatically shrinking budget for public diplomacy.

It is also difficult to disentangle the discourse surrounding Japan's embrace of soft power discourse from the very real economic implications of the success of its cultural industries. Such success has lead Otzmagain to claim that the promotion of its industries is more readily explained by profit imperatives and not the requirements of soft power.[171] As Heng observes, "JETRO figures also indicate that the U.S. market for anime products was $4.35 billion in 2007. Hello Kitty generates $1 billion in global annual sales, while cosplay costumes raked in an estimated 35 billion Yen in 2008."[172] So, while soft power appears as a strategic necessity in arguments for industrial promotion, such arguments cannot be divorced from the economic situation. Indeed, soft power may be a justification of convenience for industrial policy.

While it is evident that culture appears to predominate in Japanese soft power, the *application* of culture, both in public arguments and embodied in programs and initiatives, suggest a marked tendency toward the *objectification* of culture through products, which in turn have a kind of affective power—the ability to convey something about Japan that cultivates interest. Interest, in turn, may to translate into a tangible benefit that somehow contributes Japanese foreign policy objectives. Put simply, the value of culture for soft does not stem from its intrinsic capacity to convey deep-seated values or to establish credibility by demonstrating Japanese policy motives—culture "works" by providing a means of access to further engagement with Japan, as part of a fan community, as a student of language, etc. Culture in this sense reflects the networks of connection. These networks are argued to be sustained and cultivated to further the relations that yield longer term benefits to Japanese foreign policy outcomes.

But how is this objectified culture "converted?" Of the *behaviors* associated with soft power, attraction is the most predominant. Soft power programs are discussed as successful when they point to increased level of attention and interest in Japanese language and cultural expression. Even the most rudimentary expression of soft power–based influence—such as Aso's sense of how pop culture popularity equates unproblematically with foreign policy objectives—relies on attraction more than any other soft power behavior. The salience of Japan's pop culture is *not* argued to dramatically impact Japan's ability to set the international agenda or frame its actions (with the notable exception of Japan's anime exports to Iraq). Nor is Japan leveraging cultural contacts to explicitly persuade foreign publics. Rather, the invitational outcomes of attraction are expected to unfold from the networks of fans, students, and interested demographics—publics who are in turn argued as essential to the practice of statecraft.

The long-term benefits of soft power promotion manifest in increased enrollment in Japanese language programs, more participation in pop culture communities, and increased enrollment in exchange programs. Yet, these *outcomes* are often equated with *justifications* for soft power. Put another way, there is a kind of circular logic to the way in which Japanese discourse conveys the significance of soft power and public diplomacy through the demonstrative impact of its pop culture success.

The mode of influence implied is also *indirect*—both in message and in expected political outcome. While both Monji and Kondo discuss the ways in which popular culture serves as a *gateway* to more traditional forms of Japanese culture, such arguments are laden with assumptions about how global audiences draw inferences and make judgments about a bounded conception of Japanese culture. Exposure to accessible and adaptable cultural products (anime, manga, video games, etc.) provide a means of relating to global audiences—who are assumed to be consumers defined by their cultural context and historical/experiential knowledge of Japan.

Yet as cultural critics such as Allison and Iwabuchi have argued, the global adaptability of Japanese pop culture does not always refer in predictable ways to traditional Japanese culture, which also make up foundational elements of Japanese soft power resources. Nor do Japanese pop cultural exports necessarily speak to the regional anxieties about Japan and its imperial history.

Both the discourse and programs related to soft power convey that Japan is not concerned with shaping the constitutive nature of international relations—but rather at preserving its options given the rising power of China. As such, Japan's overarching soft power objectives are geared toward the *interaction* power identified by Barnett and Duvall.[173] Soft power programs are aimed at securing means of connection to foreign publics in ways that do not alienate via culturally insensitive tactics of projection. In this sense, the Japanese adaptation of soft power is arguably humble in its expected returns. Yet at the same, soft power is also argued as the most significant strategic option available given other material constraints on Japanese power.

The rhetoric of Japanese soft power outlines a set of practices and expectations that derive principally from the conversion of cultural resources into attraction. Yet the specifics of what that kind of power can yield remains somewhat underspecified. Culture is argued to play pivotal role that has yet to take shape. There is a marked ambivalence toward what counts as attractive, as if to promote the global popularity of the Japanese cultural industries as distinctly *Japanese* would diminish their capacity to deliver soft power. As Takeo Miyao offers from his research:

> [T]here seems to be some kind of soft power that one can feel from Japanese pop culture, where soft power can be contrasted to hard power in terms of military power or economic power. Of course, it is not easy to measure that soft power per se, *but there must be something to it.*[174]

Culture is thus represented in the discussion of Japanese soft power as a reconfigurable set of practices and modes of connection, not a stable repertoire of deep cultural traditions that speak for themselves in a universal, transcendently appealing manner.

The tension in culture's role as an instrument of soft power is in *how* it matters, and not *if*. Japan's policy history suggests a strong historical attachment to the idea that culture is a site of interaction that is necessary for responsible statecraft; programs that facilitate exposure to culture are valued components of diplomacy.[175] But in this history, culture is facilitative and not necessarily oriented to promotion. The soft power concept reveals the routes to influence, not that culture is to be promoted *for its own sake.*

The ambivalence to promotion is seen in Kondo's writing, in Ogoura's critique of soft power, and in the ambiguity of implementing a branding campaign. Taro Aso's advocacy stands in marked contrast to this, and goes further to suggest that Japanese cultural forms are something akin to a global public good. Yamazaki offers a middle ground—where Japan is obligated to promote, but in a way that promotes identification. Yamazaki's op-ed, while perhaps not a *definitive* foreign policy document, captures an ethic of soft power toward addressing publics. For Kondo, it is not in projection, but by bringing audiences into a position where they can recognize the value of "invisible things," the intangibles of Japanese culture represented in its actions *and* cultural products. The shift to cultural *products* as a kind of soft power reflects recognition that such material manifestations show culture as a provider of meaning, not simply a marker of Japanese values.

The case of Japan for the study of soft power is in many ways ideal, as Japan has explicitly tried to implement a set of soft power programs in the absence of hard power resources. However, perhaps the most enduring insight is how soft power reflects the power of an analytic concept to make sense of a complicated set of strategic circumstances. As David Leheny states, "[I]f we think of soft power not as a category of power resources but rather as an idea—a component of a cultural and ideological structure of governance—it can affect Japanese policy even if Japan does not really have soft power."[176] Leheny's speculates here on the larger sociopolitical effect of soft power—its capacity to rationalize newly available strategic instruments and otherwise sustain a body of strategic discourse that is reactive to contemporary foreign policy conditions. Leheny states that soft power discourse says something about official intention and "prevailing trends."[177] However, the way interlocutors talk about and justify soft power makes reasoning public. Soft power, as a rhetorical construct, reveals how Japanese strategic discourse makes sense of the situation facing Japan.

NOTES

1. Tsuneo Akaha, "Japan's Diplomacy and Security Policy: Balancing Soft Power and Hard Power," *Politique étrangère* 76, no. 1 (n.d.):115–127; Yul Sohn, "Attracting Neighbors: Soft Power Competition in East Asia" (presented at the Wiseman Roundtable on Soft Power in Northeast Asia, Seoul, Korea: Korea Foundation and East Asia Institute, 2008), 1–14.

2. Joseph S. Nye Jr., *The Future of Power*, 1st ed. (PublicAffairs, 2011), 16–18.

3. "Soft Power: Strive to Be a 'Caring' Nation so as to Help Others That Are Less Fortunate," *Asahi Shimbun*, May 27, 2007.

4. Peng Er Lam, "Japan's Quest for 'Soft Power': Attraction and Limitation," *East Asia* 24, no. 4 (October 2007):349–363.

5. Michal Daliot-Bul, "Japan Brand Strategy: The Taming of 'Cool Japan' and the Challenges of Cultural Planning in a Postmodern Age," *Social Science Japan Journal* 12, no. 2 (December 21, 2009):247–266; Yee-Kuang Heng, "Mirror, Mirror on the Wall, Who Is the Softest of Them All? Evaluating Japanese and Chinese Strategies in the 'Soft' Power Competition Era," *International Relations of the Asia-Pacific* 10, no. 2 (May 1, 2010):275–304; Lam, "Japan's Quest for 'Soft Power'"; Nissim K. Otmazgin, "Contesting Soft Power: Japanese Popular Culture in East and Southeast Asia," *International Relations of the Asia-Pacific* 8, no. 1 (May 2007):73–101.

6. David Leheny, "a Narrow Place to Cross Swords: 'Soft Power' and the Politics of Japanese Popular Culture in East Asia," in *Beyond Japan: The Dynamics of East Asian Regionalism*, eds. Peter Katzenstein and Takashi Shiraishi (Ithaca: Cornell University Press, 2006); Lam, "Japan's Quest for 'Soft Power,'" 357.

7. Daliot-Bul, "Japan Brand Strategy"; Keith Dinnie, "Japan's Nation Branding: Recent Evolution and Potential Future Paths," *Journal of Current Japanese Affairs*, vol. 16, no. 3, 52–65 (2008).

8. Kenjiro Monji, "Japan's Pop Culture Broadens Its Cultural Reach," *Japan Echo*, September 2009; Kenjiro Monji, "Pop Culture Diplomacy," *Public Diplomacy Magazine*, 2010; Christine R. Yano, "Wink on Pink: Interpreting Japanese Cute as It Grabs the Global Headlines," *The Journal of Asian Studies* 68, no. 3 (2009):681–688.

9. Douglas McGray, "Japan's Gross National Cool," *Foreign Policy*, no. 130 (June 2002):44–54; Otmazgin, "Contesting Soft Power: Japanese Popular Culture in East and Southeast Asia"; "Establishment of the Creative Industries Promotion Office," n.d., www.meti.go.jp/english/press/data/20100608_01.html.

10. Alex Martin, "Japan Urged to Exploit Its Tech, Pop Culture," *Japan Times Online*, January 6, 2010, http://search.japantimes.co.jp/cgi-bin/nn20100106f1.html.

11. Heng, "Mirror, Mirror on the Wall, Who Is the Softest of Them All?"; Monji, "Pop Culture Diplomacy"; Takashi Shiraishi, "'Japan's Soft Power: Doraemon Goes Overseas," in *Network Power: Japan and Asia*, eds. Peter J. Katzenstein (Cornell University Press, 1997), 234–274.

12. Gerald Curtis, "Japanese Diplomatic Policies in the Post-Saddam Era RIETI Report No.022: May 15, 2003," May 15, 2003, www.rieti.go.jp/en/rieti_report/022.html.

13. Akitoshi Miyashita, *Limits to Power: Asymmetric Dependence and Japanese Foreign Aid Policy* (Lanham, MD: Lexington Books, 2003).

14. Norbert Palanovics, "Quo Vadis Japanese ODA? New Developments in Japanese Aid Policies," *Asia Europe Journal* 4, no. 3 (May 2006):365–379.

15. Seichi Kondo, *The Front Line of Cultural Diplomacy* (MOFA Public Diplomacy Department, August 1, 2004), www.mofa.go.jp/mofaj/m/pr/staff/bunkagaiko/06/2.html.

16. Tadashi Ogawa, "Origin and Development of Japan's Public Diplomacy," in *Routledge Handbook of Public Diplomacy*, ed. Nancy Snow (Taylor & Francis, 2009), 270–281.

17. Ibid.

18. Koichi Iwabuchi, "Marketing 'Japan': Japanese Cultural Presence under a Global Gaze," *Japanese Studies* 18, no. 2 (September 1998):165–180; Otmazgin, "Contesting Soft Power: Japanese Popular Culture in East and Southeast Asia"; Peter Katzenstein, "Open Regionalism: Cultural Diplomacy and Popular Culture in Europe and Asia" (presented at the American Political Science Association, Boston Marriott Copley Place, Sheraton Boston & Hynes Convention Center, Boston, Massachusetts, 2002), www.allacademic.com/meta/p65437_index.html.

19. Daliot-Bul, "Japan Brand Strategy."

20. Commissioner's Advisory Group on International Cultural Exchange, *About the Future Promotion of International Cultural Exchange* (Agency for Cultural Affairs, Japan, March 24, 2003).

21. Ibid., 17.

22. Heng, "Mirror, Mirror on the Wall, Who Is the Softest of Them All?"; Lam, "Japan's Quest for 'Soft Power'."

23. Ministry of Foreign Affairs, *Diplomatic Bluebook 2008* (Ministry of Foreign Affairs, April 2008).

24. Ibid., 202.

25. Iwabuchi, "Marketing 'Japan': Japanese Cultural Presence under a Global Gaze."

26. Joseph D. Straubhaar, *World Television: From Global to Local* (SAGE, 2007).

27. Anne Allison, "The Attractions of the J-Wave for American Youth," in *Soft Power Superpowers: Cultural Assets of Japan and the United States*, eds. Yasushi Watanabe and David McConnell (Armonk, NY: M.E. Sharpe, 2008), 99–110.

28. Monji, "Japan's Pop Culture Broadens Its Cultural Reach."

29. Ministry of Foreign Affairs, *Diplomatic Bluebook 2005*.

30. Ibid.

31. Japan Creative Centre, "JCC—Japan Creative Centre," n.d., www.sg.emb-japan.go.jp/JCC/about_jcc.html; Ministry of Foreign Affairs, "International Situation and Japanese Diplomacy in 2008," 2009, www.mofa.go.jp/policy/other/bluebook/2009/html/h1/h1_01.html.

32. Kazuo Ogoura, "Culture as a Common Asset," *The Japan Times*, November 30, 2007.

33. Katzenstein, "Open Regionalism: Cultural Diplomacy and Popular Culture in Europe and Asia," 11.

34. Ibid.

35. Ibid., 12.

36. Ibid.

37. Ibid., 13.

38. Ibid., 14.

39. Utpal Vyas, "The Japan Foundation in China: An Agent of Japan's Soft Power?" *Electronic Journal of Contemporary Japanese studies* (August 15, 2008), www.japanesestudies.org.uk/articles/2008/Vyas.html.

40. Katzenstein, "Open Regionalism: Cultural Diplomacy and Popular Culture in Europe and Asia," 11, 14.

41. Vyas, "The Japan Foundation in China."

42. Ibid.

43. Katzenstein, "Open Regionalism: Cultural Diplomacy and Popular Culture in Europe and Asia," 30.

44. Vyas, "The Japan Foundation in China."

45. "The Japan Foundation Organization Chart and Addresses," n.d., www.jpf.go.jp/e/about/outline/org.html.

46. Kazuo Ogoura, "The Japan Foundation President's Message," 2011, www.jpf.go.jp/e/about/president/president.html.

47. Ibid.

48. Vyas, "The Japan Foundation in China."

49. "MOFA: Public Diplomacy/Culture," n.d., www.mofa.go.jp/policy/culture/index.html.

50. Katzenstein, "Open Regionalism: Cultural Diplomacy and Popular Culture in Europe and Asia."

51. "Interview with Consulate of Japan, Los Angeles," February 2008.

52. Otmazgin, "Contesting Soft Power: Japanese Popular Culture in East and Southeast Asia."

53. Daliot-Bul, "Japan Brand Strategy."

54. Strategic Council on Intellectual Property, "Intellectual Property Policy Outline," n.d., www.kantei.go.jp/foreign/policy/titeki/kettei/020703taikou_e.html.

55. Ichiya Nakamura, "Policies on Contents Need to Be Established—A New Strategy for the 'Digital Era,'" *GLOCOM*, January 13, 2004, www.glocom.org/opinions/essays/20040113_nakamura_policies/index.html.

56. Kondo, *The Front Line of Cultural Diplomacy*.

57. Tai Hayashi, "Japan Pushing Cultural Diplomacy," *Kyodo News*, March 2005, http://129.11.188.64/papers/vp01.cfm?outfit=pmt&folder=7&paper=2198.

58. Sohn, "Attracting Neighbors: Soft Power Competition in East Asia."

59. Tomomichi Amano, "How to Promote 'Cool Japan'? — Japan Real Time — WSJ," *Wall Street Journal*, June 14, 2010, http://blogs.wsj.com/japanrealtime/2010/06/14/how-to-promote-cool-japan; Mairi Mackay, "Can Japan Profit from Its National 'Cool'?—CNN," *CNNWorld*, November 19, 2010, http://articles.cnn.com/2010–11–19/world/japan.cool.money_1_japan-s-gdp-fashion-japanese-government?_s=PM:WORLD; "Time to Capitalize on 'Cool Japan' Boom: Editorial," *Daily Yomiuri Online (The Daily Yomiuri)*, August 31, 2010, www.yomiuri.co.jp/dy/editorial/T100830002730.htm.

60. Kondo, "Wielding Soft Power: The Key States of Transmission and Receptions."

61. Kazuo Ogoura, "The Limits of Soft Power," *Center for Global Partnership*, June 2006, www.cgp.org/index.php?option=article&task=default&articleid=341.

62. Martin, "Japan Urged to Exploit Its Tech, Pop Culture."

63. Kondo, "Wielding Soft Power: The Key States of Transmission and Receptions," 200.

64. Daliot-Bul, "Japan Brand Strategy."

65. Tetsuyuki Hirano, "Design and Culture: Developing a Nation's Brand with Design Management," *Design Management Review* 17, no. 1 (winter 2006):15–22.

66. Nakamura, "Policies on Contents Need to Be Established—A New Strategy for the 'Digital Era'."

67. Yuji Mori, "クールジャパンはどこまで真剣なのか—CNET Japan," n.d., http://japan.cnet.com/sp/column_yuji_mori/20392031/.

68. "METI Launched the Cool Japan Division: Throughout the Entire Government, to Diffuse the Japanese Culture overseas," *SankeiBiz*, June 9, 2010, www.sankeibiz.jp/macro/news/100609/mca1006090502008-n1.htm.

69. Monji, "Japan's Pop Culture Broadens Its Cultural Reach."

70. Taro Aso, "For a New Phase of Economic Growth in Japan" (Japan National Press Club, April 9, 2009), www.kantei.go.jp/jp/asospeech/2009/04/09speech.html.

71. Kondo, "Wielding Soft Power: The Key States of Transmission and Receptions."

72. Ministry of Foreign Affairs, *Diplomatic Bluebook 2008* (Ministry of Foreign Affairs, April 2008).

73. Ministry of Foreign Affairs, *Diplomatic Bluebook 2009* (Japan: Ministry of Foreign Affairs, 2009).

74. Ibid.

75. R. S. Zaharna, *Battles to Bridges: U.S. Strategic Communication and Public Diplomacy after 9/11* (Palgrave Macmillan, 2009).

76. Henry Jenkins, *Convergence Culture: Where Old and New Media Collide* (New York: New York University Press, 2006).

77. Hiroko Tabuchi, "SDF Deploys Perky Mascot to Boast Cuddly Image," *Japan Times Online*, February 21, 2007, http://search.japantimes.co.jp/cgi-bin/nn20070221f3.html.

78. Ministry of Foreign Affairs, "MOFA: Establishment of the International MANGA Award," May 24, 2007, www.mofa.go.jp/announce/announce/2007/5/1173601_826.html.

79. Taro Aso, "MOFA: International MANGA Award," n.d., www.mofa.go.jp/policy/culture/exchange/pop/manga/.

80. "MOFA: Inauguration Ceremony of Anime Ambassador," March 19, 2008, www.mofa.go.jp/announce/announce/2008/3/0319-3.html.

81. Ibid.

82. "MOFA: Provision of TV Program 'Captain Majed' to Iraq," March 2, 2006, www.mofa.go.jp/announce/announce/2006/3/0302.html.

83. "Business: Bridges to Babylon; Japanese Television in Iraq," *The Economist* 374, no. 8417 (March 12, 2005):81.

84. "MOFA: Cooperative Project between Three Government Agencies at 'Japan Expo' in Paris, One of the Largest Japanese Pop Culture Events in the World," June 11, 2009, www.mofa.go.jp/announce/event/2009/6/1193058_1160.html.

85. "MOFA: World Cosplay Summit 2010," August 2010, www.mofa.go.jp/policy/culture/exchange/pop/wcs2010.html.

86. Kenjiro Monji, "Working Together to Promote Japan," *Japan Echo*, October 2009; Monji, "Japan's Pop Culture Broadens Its Cultural Reach."

87. "MOFA: Commission of Trend Communicator of Japanese Pop Culture in the Field of Fashion," February 25, 2009, www.mofa.go.jp/announce/event/2009/2/1188515_1152.html.

88. Monji, "Pop Culture Diplomacy."

89. "What We Do," *JAMCO*, n.d., www.jamco.or.jp/english/index.html.

90. Masahiko Ishizuka, "Can NHK Help Japan Speak Its Mind to the World?" *GLOCOM*, May 2, 2008, www.glocom.org/opinions/essays/20080502_ishizuka_nhk.

91. Kim Andrew Elliott, "'Slight Confusion of Intentions' with the New NHK World? (Updated Again)," *Kim Andrew Elliott reporting on International Broadcasting*, February 20, 2009, http://kimelli.nfshost.com/index.php?id=5852.

92. Kim Andrew Elliott, "Revamped NHK World Is on the Air," *Kim Andrew Elliott reporting on International Broadcasting*, February 3, 2009, http://kimelli.nfshost.com/index.php?id=5805.

93. Kim Andrew Elliott, "NHK World Will Relaunch on 2 February, Apparently as 'NHK World,'" *Kim Andrew Elliott reporting on International Broadcasting*, January 29, 2009, http://kimelli.nfshost.com/index.php?id=5768.

94. Sakumi Shimizu, "Comment on Professor Takatoshi Ito's Article 'Bidding for Public Broadcasting Service,'" *Global Communications Platform*, May 10, 2006, www.glocom.org/debates/20060510_shimizu_comment/index.html.

95. Ibid.

96. "NHK International: About Us," n.d., www.nhkint.or.jp/us/index_e.html.

97. "Japan to Launch Radio Channel Targeting N. Korea," *Chosun*, June 7, 2007, http://english.chosun.com/w21data/html/news/200706/200706070017.html.

98. Ishizuka, "Can NHK Help Japan Speak Its Mind to the World?."

99. David Arase, *Japan's Foreign Aid: Old Continuities and New Directions* (Psychology Press, 2005); David Arase and Tsuneo Akaha, *The U.S.–Japan Alliance: Balancing Soft and Hard Power in East Asia* (Routledge, 2009).

100. Yoichiro Sato and Masahiko Asano, "Humanitarian and Democratic Norms in Japan's ODA Distributions," in *Norms, Interests, and Power in Japanese Foreign Policy*, eds. Yoichiro Sato and Keiko Hirata (Macmillan, 2008), 111–128.

101. Saori Katada, *Toward a Mature Aid Donor: Fifty Years of Japanese ODA and the Challenges Ahead*, Asia Program Special Report (Woodrow Wilson International Center, February 2005).

102. Sato and Asano, "Humanitarian and Democratic Norms in Japan's ODA Distributions"; Palanovics, "Quo Vadis Japanese ODA? New Developments in Japanese Aid Policies."

103. Katada, *Toward a Mature Aid Donor: Fifty Years of Japanese ODA and the Challenges Ahead*, 10.

104. Palanovics, "Quo Vadis Japanese ODA? New Developments in Japanese Aid Policies."

105. Akaha, "Japan's Diplomacy and Security Policy: Balancing Soft Power and Hard Power."

106. McGray, "Japan's Gross National Cool."

107. Anthony Faiola, "Japan's Animated Culture of Cool Turns into Biggest Export: Reinvents Itself after Long Slump," *Washington Post* (Washington, DC, January 4, 2004).

108. Leheny, "A Narrow Place to Cross Swords: 'Soft Power' and the Politics of Japanese Popular Culture in East Asia."

109. Rajarum Panda, "Soft Power as a Tool to Foster Cultural Diplomacy in India–Japan Relations," in *Japanese Studies Changing Global Profile*, eds. P. A. George (Northern Book Centre, 2010), 34–62; *The Council on Security and Defense Capabilities Report: Japan's Vision for Future Security and Defense Capabilities* (Japan: Department of Defense, October 2004), www.globalsecurity.org/wmd/library/japan/2004/041000-csdc-report.pdf.

110. Leheny, "A Narrow Place to Cross Swords: 'Soft Power' and the Politics of Japanese Popular Culture in East Asia," 223.

111. Ibid.

112. "Establishment of the Creative Industries Promotion Office," *Ministry of Economy, Trade, and Industry*, June 2010, www.meti.go.jp/english/press/data/20100608_01.html.

113. Ogoura, "The Limits of Soft Power."

114. Kondo, "Wielding Soft Power: The Key States of Transmission and Receptions."

115. Ogoura, "The Limits of Soft Power."

116. Kondo, "Wielding Soft Power: The Key States of Transmission and Receptions."

117. Zaharna, *Battles to Bridges*.

118. Kondo, "Wielding Soft Power: The Key States of Transmission and Receptions," 194.

119. Taro Aso, "A New Look at Cultural Diplomacy: A Call to Japan's Cultural Practitioners" (Speech, Digital Hollywood University, April 28, 2006), www.mofa.go.jp/announce/fm/aso/speech0604-2.html.

120. Ibid.

121. Mingjiang Li, "Soft Power in Chinese Discourse: Popularity and Prospect," in *China's Emerging Strategy in International Politics*, ed. Mingjiang Li (Lanham, MD: Lexington Books, 2009), 21–44.

122. Aso, "A New Look at Cultural Diplomacy: A Call to Japan's Cultural Practitioners."

123. Taro Aso, "Policy Speech by Minister for Foreign Affairs Taro Aso to the 166th Session of the Diet" (Speech, Ministry of Foreign Affairs, Japan, January 26, 2007), www.mofa.go.jp/announce/fm/aso/speech0701.html.

124. Amelia Newcomb, "Japan Cracking U.S. Pop Culture Hegemony," *Christian Science Monitor*, December 15, 2008, www.csmonitor.com/World/Asia-Pacific/2008/1215/p01s04-woap.html.

125. Ibid.

126. "All Dressed Up for Serious Playtime in Cool Japan," *New Zealand Herald*, August 4, 2007, Sec. Videos, www.nzherald.co.nz/videos/news/article.cfm?c_id=354&objectid=10455676.

127. Heng, "Mirror, Mirror on the Wall, Who Is the Softest of Them All?."

128. Roland Kelts, "Japan's Global Power, Soft or Wilted," *Daily Yomiuri*, September 25, 2008.

129. Kondo, "Wielding Soft Power: The Key States of Transmission and Receptions," 197–198.

130. Aso, "For a New Phase of Economic Growth in Japan."

131. Lam, "Japan's Quest for 'Soft Power,'" 351.

132. Ministry of Foreign Affairs, *Diplomatic Bluebook 2005*.

133. Tatsuhiko Yoshizaki, "Japan, The Quiet Genius: Towards a Strategic Public Diplomacy," *Gaiko Forum* 7, no. 1 (2007):27.

134. Kondo, *The Front Line of Cultural Diplomacy*.

135. Ibid.

136. Ibid.

137. Ibid.

138. Ibid.

139. Report of the Fulbright/CULCON Joint Symposium, *Japan & US So_ Power: Addressing Global Challenges* (U.S.–Japan Conference on Cultural and Educational Interchange (CULCON), Fulbright Japan (Japan–U.S. Educational Commission), The Japan Foundation, Japan–U.S. Friendship Commission, June 12, 2009), 175.

140. Ibid., 97.

141. Ibid., 111.

142. Lam, "Japan's Quest for 'Soft Power,'" 355.

143. Ministry of Foreign Affairs, *Diplomatic Bluebook 2006* (Japan: Ministry of Foreign Affairs, 2006), 245.

144. Ibid.

145. Report of the Fulbright/CULCON Joint Symposium, *Japan & US Soft Power: Addressing Global Challenges*, 152.

146. Ibid., 120.

147. Ibid.

148. Ibid., 116.

149. Ibid.

150. Daliot-Bul, "Japan Brand Strategy."

151. Ibid., 14.

152. Kondo, *The Front Line of Cultural Diplomacy.*

153. Ministry of Foreign Affairs, *Diplomatic Bluebook 2005.*

154. Monji, "Pop Culture Diplomacy."

155. Ibid.

156. Kondo, "Wielding Soft Power: The Key States of Transmission and Receptions," 202.

157. Brian Hocking, "Rethinking the 'New' Public Diplomacy," in *The New Public Diplomacy: Soft Power in International Relations*, eds. Jan Melissen and Paul Sharp (Palgrave Macmillan, 2005), 37.

158. Monji, "Working Together to Promote Japan."

159. Monji, "Pop Culture Diplomacy."

160. Monji, "Working Together to Promote Japan."

161. Masakazu Yamazaki, "National PR Strategy Must Be Clear, Informative," *YOMIURI ONLINE (The Daily Yomiuri)*, June 21, 2009, www.yomiuri.co.jp/dy/columns/commentary/20090622dy02.htm.

162. Ibid.

163. Ogoura, "The Limits of Soft Power."

164. Janice Bially Mattern, "Why 'Soft Power' Isn't So Soft: Representational Force and the Sociolinguistic Construction of Attraction in World Politics," *Millennium—Journal of International Studies* 33, no. 3 (June 2005):583–612.

165. Geraldo Zahran, "from Hegemony to Soft Power: Implications of a Conceptual Change," in *Soft Power and U.S. Foreign Policy: Theoretical, Historical and Contemporary Perspectives*, eds. Leonardo Ramos, Inderjeet Parmar, and Michael Cox (New York: Taylor & Francis, 2010), 12–31.

166. Ogoura, "The Limits of Soft Power."

167. Ibid.

168. Ibid.

169. Ibid.

170. Ibid.

171. Otmazgin, "Contesting Soft Power: Japanese Popular Culture in East and Southeast Asia."

172. Heng, "Mirror, Mirror on the Wall, Who Is the Softest of Them All?."

173. Michael Barnett and Raymond Duvall, "Power in International Politics," *International Organization* 59, no. 1 (2005):39–75.

174. Takahiro Miyao, *Japan's Soft Power: Seminar Report* (Japanese Institute of Global Communications, February 24, 2004), www.glocom.org/special_topics/activity_rep/20040224_miyao_soft/index.html.

175. Katzenstein, "Open Regionalism: Cultural Diplomacy and Popular Culture in Europe and Asia"; Vyas, "The Japan Foundation in China."

176. Leheny, "A Narrow Place to Cross Swords: 'Soft Power' and the Politics of Japanese Popular Culture in East Asia," 223.

177. Ibid., 233.

REFERENCES

Akaha, Tsuneo. "Japan's Diplomacy and Security Policy: Balancing Soft Power and Hard Power." *Politique étrangère* 76, no. 1 (n.d.):115–127.

"All Dressed Up for Serious Playtime in Cool Japan." *New Zealand Herald*, August 4, 2007, sec. Videos. www.nzherald.co.nz/videos/news/article.cfm?c_id=354&objectid=10455676.

Amano, Tomomichi. "How to Promote 'Cool Japan'?—Japan Real Time—WSJ." *Wall Street Journal*, June 14, 2010. http://blogs.wsj.com/japanrealtime/2010/06/14/how-to-promote-cool-japan/.

Arase, David. *Japan's Foreign Aid: Old Continuities and New Directions.* Psychology Press, 2005.

Arase, David, and Tsuneo Akaha. *The U.S.–Japan Alliance: Balancing Soft and Hard Power in East Asia.* Routledge, 2009.

Aso, Taro. "A New Look at Cultural Diplomacy: A Call to Japan's Cultural Practitioners." Speech, Digital Hollywood University, April 28, 2006. www.mofa.go.jp/announce/fm/aso/speech0604–2.html.

———. "For a New Phase of Economic Growth in Japan," Japan National Press Club, April 9, 2009. www.kantei.go.jp/jp/asospeech/2009/04/09speech.html.

———. "MOFA: International MANGA Award," n.d. www.mofa.go.jp/policy/culture/exchange/pop/manga/.

———. "Policy Speech by Minister for Foreign Affairs Taro Aso to the 166th Session of the Diet." Speech, Ministry of Foreign Affairs, Japan, January 26, 2007. www.mofa.go.jp/announce/fm/aso/speech0701.html.

Barnett, Michael, and Raymond Duvall. "Power in International Politics." *International Organization* 59, no. 1 (2005):39–75.

Bially Mattern, Janice. "Why 'Soft Power' Isn't So Soft: Representational Force and the Sociolinguistic Construction of Attraction in World Politics." *Millennium—Journal of International Studies* 33, no. 3 (June 2005):583–612.

"Business: Bridges to Babylon; Japanese Television in Iraq." *The Economist* 374, no. 8417 (March 12, 2005):81.

Commissioner's Advisory Group on International Cultural Exchange. *About the Future Promotion of International Cultural Exchange.* Agency for Cultural Affairs, Japan, March 24, 2003.

Curtis, Gerald. "Japanese Diplomatic Policies in the Post-Saddam Era RIETI Report No.022: May 15, 2003," May 15, 2003. www.rieti.go.jp/en/rieti_report/022.html.

Daliot-Bul, Michal. "Japan Brand Strategy: The Taming of 'Cool Japan' and the Challenges of Cultural Planning in a Postmodern Age." *Social Science Japan Journal* 12, no. 2 (December 21, 2009): 247–266.

Dinnie, Keith. "Japan's Nation Branding: Recent Evolution and Potential Future Paths." *Journal of Current Japanese Affairs* (2008) Vol 16 no.3, pp 52-65.

Elliott, Kim Andrew. "NHK World Will Relaunch on 2 February, Apparently as 'NHK World.'" *Kim Andrew Elliott reporting on International Broadcasting*, January 29, 2009. http://kimelli.nfshost.com/index.php?id=5768.

——. "Revamped NHK World Is on the Air." *Kim Andrew Elliott reporting on International Broadcasting*, February 3, 2009. http://kimelli.nfshost.com/index.php?id=5805.

——. "'Slight Confusion of Intentions' with the New NHK World? (Updated Again)." *Kim Andrew Elliott reporting on International Broadcasting*, February 20, 2009. http://kimelli.nfshost.com/index.php?id=5852.

"Establishment of the Creative Industries Promotion Office." *Ministry of Economy, Trade, and Industry*, June 2010. www.meti.go.jp/english/press/data/20100608_01.html.

"Establishment of the Creative Industries Promotion Office," n.d. www.meti.go.jp/english/press/data/20100608_01.html.

Faiola, Anthony. "Japan's Animated Culture of Cool Turns into Biggest Export: Reinvents Itself after Long Slump." *Washington Post*. Washington, DC, January 4, 2004.

Hayashi, Tai. "Japan Pushing Cultural Diplomacy." *Kyodo News*, March 2005. http://129.11.188.64/papers/vp01.cfm?outfit=pmt&folder=7&paper=2198.

Heng, Yee-Kuang. "Mirror, Mirror on the Wall, Who Is the Softest of Them All? Evaluating Japanese and Chinese Strategies in the 'Soft' Power Competition Era." *International Relations of the Asia-Pacific* 10, no. 2 (May 1, 2010):275–304.

Hirano, Tetsuyuki. "Design and Culture: Developing a Nation's Brand with Design Management." *Design Management Review* 17, no. 1 (Winter 2006):15–22.

Hocking, Brian. "Rethinking the 'New' Public Diplomacy." In *The New Public Diplomacy: Soft Power in International Relations*, eds. Jan Melissen and Paul Sharp. Palgrave Macmillan, 2005.

"Interview with Consulate of Japan, Los Angeles," February 2008.

Ishizuka, Masahiko. "Can NHK Help Japan Speak Its Mind to the World?" *GLOCOM*, May 2, 2008. www.glocom.org/opinions/essays/20080502_ishizuka_nhk/.

Iwabuchi, Koichi. "Marketing 'Japan': Japanese Cultural Presence under a Global Gaze." *Japanese Studies* 18, no. 2 (September 1998):165–180.

Japan Creative Centre. "JCC—Japan Creative Centre," n.d. www.sg.emb-japan.go.jp/JCC/about_jcc.html.

"Japan to Launch Radio Channel Targeting N. Korea." *Chosun*, June 7, 2007. http://english.chosun.com/w21data/html/news/200706/200706070017.html.

Jenkins, Henry. *Convergence Culture: Where Old and New Media Collide*. New York: New York University Press, 2006.

Katada, Saori. *Toward a Mature Aid Donor: Fifty Years of Japanese ODA and the Challenges Ahead*. Asia Program Special Report. Woodrow Wilson International Center, February 2005.

Katzenstein, Peter. "Open Regionalism: Cultural Diplomacy and Popular Culture in Europe and Asia." Boston Marriott Copley Place, Sheraton Boston & Hynes

Convention Center, Boston, Massachusetts, 2002. www.allacademic.com/meta/p65437_index.html.

Kelts, Roland. "Japan's Global Power, Soft or Wilted." *Daily Yomiuri*, September 25, 2008.

Kondo, Seichi. *The Front Line of Cultural Diplomacy*. MOFA Public Diplomacy Department, August 1, 2004. www.mofa.go.jp/mofaj/m/pr/staff/bunkagaiko/06/2.html.

———. "Wielding Soft Power: The Key States of Transmission and Receptions." In *Soft Power Superpowers: Cultural Assets of Japan and the United States*, edited by Yasushi Watanabe and David McConnell, 191–206. Armonk, NY: M.E. Sharpe, 2008.

Lam, Peng Er. "Japan's Quest for 'Soft Power': Attraction and Limitation." *East Asia* 24, no. 4 (October 2007):349–363.

Leheny, David. "A Narrow Place to Cross Swords: 'Soft Power' and the Politics of Japanese Popular Culture in East Asia." In *beyond Japan: The Dynamics of East Asian Regionalism*, eds. Peter Katzenstein and Takashi Shiraishi. Ithaca: Cornell University Press, 2006.

Li, Mingjiang. "Soft Power in Chinese Discourse: Popularity and Prospect." In *China's Emerging Strategy in International Polics*, ed. Mingjiang Li, 21–44. Lanham, MD: Lexington Books, 2009.

Mackay, Mairi. "Can Japan Profit from Its National 'Cool'?—CNN." *CNNWorld*, November 19, 2010. http://articles.cnn.com/2010–11–19/world/japan.cool.money_1_japan-s-gdp-fashion-japanese-government?_s=PM:WORLD.

Martin, Alex. "Japan Urged to Exploit Its Tech, Pop Culture." *Japan Times Online*, January 6, 2010. http://search.japantimes.co.jp/cgi-bin/nn20100106f1.html.

McGray, Douglas. "Japan's Gross National Cool." *Foreign Policy*, no. 130 (June 2002):44–54.

"METI Launched the Cool Japan Division: Throughout the Entire Government, to Diffuse the Japanese Culture Overseas." *SankeiBiz*, June 9, 2010. www.sankeibiz.jp/macro/news/100609/mca1006090502008-n1.htm.

Ministry of Foreign Affairs. *Diplomatic Bluebook 2005*. Japan: Ministry of Foreign Affairs, 2005.

———. *Diplomatic Bluebook 2006*. Japan: Ministry of Foreign Affairs, 2006.

———. *Diplomatic Bluebook 2008*. Ministry of Foreign Affairs, April 2008.

———. *Diplomatic Bluebook 2009*. Japan: Ministry of Foreign Affairs, 2009.

———. "International Situation and Japanese Diplomacy in 2008," 2009. www.mofa.go.jp/policy/other/bluebook/2009/html/h1/h1_01.html.

———. "MOFA: Establishment of the International MANGA Award," May 24, 2007. www.mofa.go.jp/announce/announce/2007/5/1173601_826.html.

Miyao, Takahiro. *Japan's Soft Power: Seminar Report*. Japanese Institute of Global Communications, February 24, 2004. www.glocom.org/special_topics/activity_rep/20040224_miyao_soft/index.html.

Miyashita, Akitoshi. *Limits to Power: Asymmetric Dependence and Japanese Foreign Aid Policy*. Lanham, MD: Lexington Books, 2003.

"MOFA: Commission of Trend Communicator of Japanese Pop Culture in the Field of Fashion," February 25, 2009. www.mofa.go.jp/announce/event/2009/2/1188515_1152.html.

"MOFA: Cooperative Project between Three Government Agencies at 'Japan Expo' in Paris, One of the Largest Japanese Pop Culture Events in the World," June 11, 2009. www.mofa.go.jp/announce/event/2009/6/1193058_1160.html.

"MOFA: Inauguration Ceremony of Anime Ambassador," March 19, 2008. www.mofa.go.jp/announce/announce/2008/3/0319–3.html.

"MOFA: Provision of TV Program 'Captain Majed' to Iraq," March 2, 2006. www.mofa.go.jp/announce/announce/2006/3/0302.html.

"MOFA: Public Diplomacy/Culture," n.d. www.mofa.go.jp/policy/culture/index.html.

"MOFA: World Cosplay Summit 2010," August 2010. www.mofa.go.jp/policy/culture/exchange/pop/wcs2010.html.

Monji, Kenjiro. "Japan's Pop Culture Broadens Its Cultural Reach." *Japan Echo*, September 2009.

———. "Pop Culture Diplomacy." *Public Diplomacy Magazine*, 2010.

———. "Working Together to Promote Japan." *Japan Echo*, October 2009.

Mori, Yuji. "クールジャパンはどこまで真剣なのか―CNET Japan," n.d. http://japan.cnet.com/sp/column_yuji_mori/20392031.

Nakamura, Ichiya. "Policies on Contents Need to Be Established—A New Strategy for the 'Digital Era'." *GLOCOM*, January 13, 2004. www.glocom.org/opinions/essays/20040113_nakamura_policies/index.html.

Newcomb, Amelia. "Japan Cracking U.S. Pop Culture Hegemony." *Christian Science Monitor*, December 15, 2008. www.csmonitor.com/World/Asia-Pacific/2008/1215/p01s04-woap.html.

"NHK International: About Us," n.d. www.nhkint.or.jp/us/index_e.html.

Nye, Joseph S. Jr. *The Future of Power*. 1st ed. PublicAffairs, 2011.

Ogawa, Tadashi. "Origin and Development of Japan's Public Diplomacy." In *Routledge Handbook of Public Diplomacy*, ed. Nancy Snow, 270–281. Taylor & Francis, 2009.

Ogoura, Kazuo. "Culture as a Common Asset." *The Japan Times*, November 30, 2007.

———. "The Japan Foundation President's Message," 2011. www.jpf.go.jp/e/about/president/president.html.

———. "The Limits of Soft Power." *Center for Global Partnership*, June 2006. www.cgp.org/index.php?option=article&task=default&articleid=341.

Otmazgin, Nissim K. "Contesting Soft Power: Japanese Popular Culture in East and Southeast Asia." *International Relations of the Asia-Pacific* 8, no. 1 (May 2007):73–101.

Palanovics, Norbert. "Quo Vadis Japanese ODA? New Developments in Japanese Aid Policies." *Asia Europe Journal* 4, no. 3 (May 2006):365–379.

Panda, Rajarum. "Soft Power as a Tool to Foster Cultural Diplomacy in India–Japan Relations." In *Japanese Studies Changing Global Profile*, ed. P. A. George, 34–62. Northern Book Centre, 2010.

Report of the Fulbright/CULCON Joint Symposium. *Japan & US Soft Power: Addressing Global Challenges*. U.S.–Japan Conference on Cultural and Educational Interchange (CULCON), Fulbright Japan (Japan–U.S. Educational Commission), The Japan Foundation, Japan–U.S. Friendship Commission, June 12, 2009.

Sato, Yoichiro, and Masahiko Asano. "Humanitarian and Democratic Norms in Japan's ODA Distributions." In *Norms, Interests, and Power in Japanese Foreign Policy*, eds. Yoichiro Sato and Keiko Hirata, 111–128. Macmillan, 2008.

Shimizu, Sakumi. "Comment on Professor Takatoshi Ito's Article 'Bidding for Public Broadcasting Service.'" *Global Communications Platform*, May 10, 2006. www.glocom.org/debates/20060510_shimizu_comment/index.html.

Shiraishi, Takashi. "'Japan's Soft Power: Doraemon Goes Overseas." In *Network Power: Japan and Asia*, ed. Peter J. Katzenstein, 234–274. Cornell University Press, 1997.

"Soft Power: Strive to Be a 'Caring' Nation so as to Help Others That Are Less Fortunate." *Asahi Shimbun*, May 27, 2007.

Sohn, Yul. "Attracting Neighbors: Soft Power Competition in East Asia." 1–14. Seoul, Korea: Korea Foundation and East Asia Institute, 2008.

Strategic Council on Intellectual Property. "Intellectual Property Policy Outline," July 3, 2002. www.kantei.go.jp/foreign/policy/titeki/kettei/020703taikou_e.html.

Straubhaar, Joseph D. *World Television: From Global to Local*. SAGE, 2007.

Tabuchi, Hiroko. "SDF Deploys Perky Mascot to Boast Cuddly Image." *Japan Times Online*, February 21, 2007. http://search.japantimes.co.jp/cgi-bin/nn20070221f3.html.

The Council on Security and Defense Capabilities Report: Japan's Vision for Future Security and Defense Capabilities. Japan: Department of Defense, October 2004. www.globalsecurity.org/wmd/library/japan/2004/041000-csdc-report.pdf.

"The Japan Foundation Organization Chart and Addresses," n.d. www.jpf.go.jp/e/about/outline/org.html.

"Time to Capitalize on 'Cool Japan' Boom: Editorial." *Daily Yomiuri Online (The Daily Yomiuri)*, August 31, 2010. www.yomiuri.co.jp/dy/editorial/T100830002730.htm.

Vyas, Utpal. "The Japan Foundation in China: An Agent of Japan's Soft Power?" *Electronic Journal of Contemporary Japanese Studies* (August 15, 2008). www.japanesestudies.org.uk/articles/2008/Vyas.html.

"What We Do." *JAMCO*, n.d. www.jamco.or.jp/english/index.html.

Yamazaki, Masakazu. "National PR Strategy Must Be Clear, Informative." *YOMIURI ONLINE (The Daily Yomiuri)*, June 21, 2009. www.yomiuri.co.jp/dy/columns/commentary/20090622dy02.htm.

Yano, Christine R. "Wink on Pink: Interpreting Japanese Cute as It Grabs the Global Headlines." *The Journal of Asian Studies* 68, no. 3 (2009):681–688.

Yoshizaki, Tatsuhiko. "Japan, the Quiet Genius: Towards a Strategic Public Diplomacy." *Gaiko Forum* 7, no. 1 (2007).

Zaharna, R. S. *Battles to Bridges: U.S. Strategic Communication and Public Diplomacy after 9/11*. Palgrave Macmillan, 2009.

Layne, Christopher. "The Unbearable Lightness of Soft Power." In *Soft Power and US Foreign Policy: Theoretical, Historical and Contemporary Perspectives*, eds. Inderjeet Parmar and Michael Cox, 51–82. New York: Taylor & Francis, 2010.

Chapter 4

Venezuela: Telesur and the Artillery of Ideas

Venezuelan strategies of international influence—toward both governments and foreign publics—reflect a profoundly proactive attempt to cultivate soft power through the manipulation of media representation. Venezuela's strategic communication programs reflect two overarching assumptions—that international politics is impacted by mediated communication, and that foreign publics are susceptible to such communication.[1] While not explicitly justified as *public diplomacy*—Venezuela's efforts at influence-oriented outreach constitute a set of communication initiatives that bear some similarity to public diplomacy in other nation-states inspired by soft power.

Venezuela's foreign policy under President Hugo Chavez aims broadly to bring about a multipolar international relations based on opposition to the unipolarity of the United States and the ideological program of capitalism.[2] Venezuela's strategic ambitions are supported through a variety of foreign policy tools, such as the formation of regional, multilateral trade partnerships like the ALBA (Bolivarian Alliance for the Americas), the provision of oil for development, and programs that actively leverage regional media outlets to support foreign policy objectives.[3] Venezuela is argued in this chapter to embody an interpretation of soft power that rests strongly on the expected benefits of political engagement through media that cultivate shared values and a desire for a socialist regional order that counters the influence of the United States.

The Bolivarian Republic of Venezuela is one of the few Latin American countries outside of Cuba and Brazil to embrace a significant strategic program of public diplomacy. Venezuelan efforts are considered here as *public diplomacy* in the sense that they represent programs of influence that leverage communication to nonstate actors in order to facilitate foreign policy objectives, though many Venezuelan diplomatic and development programs could also be described as strategic communication efforts. These descriptive terms are used interchangeably in this chapter. The term "public diplomacy" is used to capture the emphasis on government-to-public *relations* and is intended to signify a range of programs—from cultural exchanges to international broadcasting—as well as *intentions*, from direct influence to relationship building.

Venezuela has been well positioned to develop strategic communication programs, given its oil-related revenues, and has invested considerable resources into a broad program of international broadcasting and other cultural programs designed to amplify the possibilities of the "Bolivaran Revolution" for regional integration and Venezuela's regional leadership. Venezuela's efforts at engagement through strategic communication have evolved considerably since Hugo Chavez became president in 1999, to encompass a more ambitious messaging program that aims to use communication flow dominance for regional integration goals and ideational conflict.[4] What began as Venezuela's more modest attempt to pluralize media content across South America through broadcasting outlets such as Telesur has grown to promote the charismatic presence of Hugo Chavez as an international figure, and to combat alternative media framing strategies in order to present the cultural and ideological voice of the Bolivaran revolution.

The motto for Telesur, Venezuela's international broadcasting service (discussed at length in this chapter) is "the South is our North." This phrase conveys the ambition of Venezuelan strategic communication and, more generally, the orientation of its soft power ambitions. Telesur's statement acknowledges the informational dominance of North America, while suggesting that such dominance need not be the case for South American media consumers. Venezuela lays claim to stewardship of a regional identity in opposition to a perceived ideological antagonist—the United States and media oligopolies.

This ambition is considered in this chapter as strongly evident through Venezuela's international broadcasting policies, which are argued to be "counter-hegemonic."[5] While Venezuela does maintain successful cultural diplomacy initiatives, such as the highly popular youth orchestra program *El Sistema*, and also relies on the symbolic value of its regional development programs, it is Venezuela's media-based programs that illustrate strategic arguments to achieve foreign policy objectives that most readily elaborate conceptual arguments for soft power. Venezuela's efforts to use *media* outlets to achieve its political projects are the primary focus on this chapter; the role of media is an ideal-typification of soft power resource conversion that emphasizes the contested nature of cultural and ideological resources and, significantly, the anticipated power of communication media to achieve the goals of influence over a largely passive audience.

Venezuelan strategic communication policies and programs articulate an implicit interpretation of soft power that describes communication modalities (the communication media, news, journalism) as highly *effective* tools for the practice of international politics that are likewise *necessary* for Venezuelan statecraft.[6] This interpretation also renders the concept of soft power as *competitive*—where international politics is defined by an antagonism between imperialist/capitalist powers and the emergence of socialist solidarity. Soft power is not simply about attraction and nonmaterial means of inducement; soft power in the Venezuelan sense is about competing for legitimacy in a contest of credibility. In this view, the resources of soft power are not simply presented for audience consumption—they are integral to active efforts of persuasion and framing. Venezuela deploys soft power as a tool in the battle over competitive arrangements of political-economic order.

Yet the Venezuelan interpretation of soft power also has implications for how agents and subjects are conceived in international politics. Venezuelan arguments for the utilization of communication outlets such as Venezuela's sponsorship of Telesur suggest not only that media space is a crucial site of international politics, but also that audiences and foreign publics are inherently susceptible to the content of media programming. Media communication, as the rhetoric for Venezuela's broadcasting efforts reveals, is thus a key lever of power, one that operates on publics to counter the perceived hegemonic aspects of Western and capitalist media. Such rhetoric enters the discursive terrain of soft power in policy arguments that capitalist media obfuscate or misrepresent cultural and value orientations, which necessitates intervention by the Venezuelan state.[7]

The chapter first surveys the strategic context behind Venezuela's embrace of international broadcasting as a form of soft power activity, and reviews other programs that reflect Venezuela's *de facto* form of public diplomacy. The chapter then proceeds with an analysis of public arguments surrounding the promotion of Telesur, to elaborate Venezuela's claim toward the goal of "hegemony" over international and domestic communication.[8] This is followed by a consideration of how communication technologies are constructed *as* influential in Venezuelan discourse about strategic communication, in order to illustrate how Venezuelan soft power programs represent a variant of soft power that necessitates a particular *subject* to power in a contested sphere of international communication. The chapter concludes with an assessment of how Venezuela's soft power scope and mechanism translates in particular soft power objectives.

CULTIVATING A BOLIVARAN SOFT POWER

Venezuelan public diplomacy and strategic communication programs bears the indelible influence of Hugo Chavez and the rise to power of his "Bolivaran Revolution." Chavez assumed the role of president in 1999, after decades of discontent over political corruption and poverty.[9] Chavez's ascendency relied heavily on the steady cultivation of the South American political mythology of Simon Bolivar. After being elected, Chavez introduced a new constitution emphasizing democratic socialism, Venezuelan nationalism, and regional integration that was based in a repudiation of neoliberalism, economic dependency, and political corruption.[10] While the politics of Chavez's ascendency were initially local, it is evident that the ambitions of his government's ideological program have a broader, international reach.

As Venezuelan president, Hugo Chavez has been a provocative actor in international relations, and is one of the most outspoken critics of the United States and U.S. hegemony in Latin America.[11] Chavez has repeatedly used a variety of international and domestic platforms to denounce the United States and, through international outreach and promotion of Venezuelan policies, has attempted to counter the foreign policy ambitions of the United States. The Bolivaran Revolution that defines the Chavez government also works to frame Venezuelan foreign policy. Venezuelan foreign policy aims to extend the ideological reach of its own political economic model, an amalgam of quasidemocratic and socialist practices that centralize the authority of the Chavez regime, while offering symbolic resources for democratic participation and expression at the national and local level.[12]

The ideological aspect of Chavez's Bolivaran government animates much of how media outlets have been deployed in the service of Venezuela's international engagement. The historical narratives of resistance and solidarity embedded in Bolivaran political ideals foreground neoliberal and capitalist interference. This defining narrative effectively necessitates outreach to other nation-states. The relation of international communication to ideology here is twofold. The Bolivaran movement, as it has been adapted by the Venezuelan government, assumes the centrality of media flows in the dominance of its adversaries.[13] Yet the political context that gave rise to Chavez's regime is also fundamentally shaped by the historical role of media in Venezuelan politics, where media is seen as a vehicle for forces opposing the Bolivaran revolution and thus a tangible political force in its own right.

The contemporary Bolivaran movement emerged in Venezuela in reaction to the perceived negative influence of private capital, and in particular the politicized media that controlled much of the political reporting and information flows in Venezuela.[14] As a *foreign policy strategy*, Venezuela's Bolivaran agenda has developed to include two primary ambitions: first, to consolidate support among similar ideological movements in South America through a "broad spectrum communication campaign"; second, to provide financial and development aid, in particular through energy-based resources. Venezuela's communication campaign is encouraged in this strategic discourse to articulate support networks and promote the organization of groups and stakeholders who share their ideals and who are willing to carry forward the new political model.[15] Such a program is necessary to promote a new "multipolar system" to counter the perceived aggressive and insidious manipulation by the United States in the region.

But a multipolar system also requires institutions to facilitate regional integration. In addition to development and economic organizations such as Petrocaribe and Banco Del Sur, communication outlets such as Telesur are deemed necessary to facilitate shared identification around principles and values embodied in the Bolivaran revolution.[16] The use of *media* appears essential to evangelizing this model, which is framed by Venezuelan interlocutors as the site of an antagonistic contest with the forces of global capital and the United States.

The significance of media in Venezuela's international influence is very likely tied to Venezuela's own political history.[17] The Chavez government consolidated its control over Venezuelan political institutions in the wake of an unsuccessful coup in 2002, which was portrayed by Chavez supporters as a conspiracy orchestrated by private industry—in particular, by Venezuelan *media*.[18] Since that time, supporters of the Chavez government have articulated a strategic imperative for news and entertainment media against the so-called oligarchic media that serve as the government's principal domestic political scapegoat.[19]

In 2007, government antagonism against non-government media reached a new level, when Chavez declined to renew the broadcasting license of RCTV, one of the main voices of domestic opposition to the Venezuelan government. This signaled a turning point in the increasing politicization of media in Venezuela. In 2009, 34 private radio stations were shut down, in accordance with Venezuelan media laws, to "democratize the airwaves," a move seen by the opposition movement as an attempt to further silence antigovernment voices.[20]

Yet as Chavez moved to silence political opponents, he has also empowered the expressive potential for community-level domestic media by subsidizing community television reporting stations for poor urban environments through programs like CatiaTV.[21] The seemingly contradictory stance toward media pluralism tellingly reveals media as *the* site of political contestation, a site that enables agency for the ideological project of the state. The Chavez government and its supporters' discourse portrays Venezuelan media space as interpenetrated by capitalist and counter-revolutionary forces, with information constrained by the undemocratic practices of corporate media manipulation and the shadowy presence of U.S. media intervention. As media defines political conflict domestically, the perceived force of media representation also appears to inflect Venezuela's strategies of *international* influence.

Venezuelan outreach to other countries, considered here as its tactical repertoire of public diplomacy and strategic communication programs, is framed by rhetoric that represents Venezuela's epic struggle against the insidious influence of the United States. The message that underscores much of the narrative presented in Venezuela's communication emphasizes a form of ideological struggle that exhorts Venezuela's, and, very often, President Hugo Chavez's, role in opposing domination by the United States. Venezuela's policy statements in various international fora aim to demystify what the Venezuelan government considers to be gross manipulation of Venezuela's image in international media, and to demonstrate the inherent hypocrisy of the United States and its political institutions. Venezuelan strategic communication is set to explain the workings of structural domination and amplify the credibility of Venezuela.

It is therefore important to acknowledge that Venezuelan efforts at international influence, including the international broadcaster Telesur, are undeniably influenced by U.S.–Venezuelan relations.[22] According to Javier Corrales, the main strategic aim of Venezuelan foreign policy regarding the United States is "soft balancing," through the effective application of what he calls "social power."[23] Corrales argues that soft balancing is a means to resist and thwart a greater power (in this case, the United States) by working to increase the relative cost of the greater power's ambitions through minor activities that do not merit significant retaliation. Soft balancing defines the objective of what Corrales calls "social power diplomacy."[24]

According to Corrales, Venezuelan "social power" is deployed and cultivated not through efforts to highlight the cultural attractiveness of the Venezuelan state (though that is certainly an aspect of the overarching strategy), but through copious amounts of unconditional monetary aid and oil subsidies that Venezuela distributes to Latin America and Africa. The distribution of such aid carries significant symbolic value, deters other nation-states from criticism of the Chavez government, and offers a ready-made platform to sustain the verbal critiques of the United States. This is demonstrated by Chavez using the aftermath of Hurricane Katrina in the United States to offer aid in the form of mobile health clinics and heating oil to cities impacted in some way by the storm damage, while at the same time sustaining his critique of the U.S. system. Chavez even won the praise of certain U.S. lawmakers, and the Venezuelan oil aid program continued through 2008.[25]

Oil Diplomacy & Humanitarian Aid

While Venezuelan communication programs are argued here as crucial components of Venezuela's implementation of soft power, foreign aid remains a significant aspect in the promotion of Venezuela to foreign publics. By 2007, Venezuela had spent upward of $25 million in foreign aid since Chavez assumed office compared to the smaller sums donated by the United States that went primarily to counter-narcotics efforts in the region.[26] Venezuelan petroleum diplomacy is evident through a variety of regional partnerships and oil-for-development programs such as Petrocaribe, which offer credit incentives for oil imports from Venezuela. The purpose of such initiatives is geared less toward market dominance and more toward the establishing alliances against the interests of the United States government.[27]

Venezuela has also reached out to low-income communities in the United States.[28] Through Citgo, the U.S. affiliate of Venezuela's state-owned Petróleos de Venezuela, S.A., Venezuela has delivered over 170 million gallons of heating oil to the United States through its Venezuela heating program across 25 states.[29] After Hurricane Katrina, Venezuela offered a sizable aid package, including over $5 million in emergency funds and fuel, to the United States.[30] Liza Featherstone, writing in *The Nation* in 2007 notes that "[b]y showing that the richest nation on earth requires foreign 'assistance' to meet its citizens' basic needs, Venezuela reveals our most profound failure as a system."[31] Even token development assistance to the United States serves as a potentially persuasive symbolic act.

Venezuela also deploys medical assistance as a form of public diplomacy. Venezuela provides medical services in South America through Operación Milagro (Operation Miracle). Launched in 2004, this program offers free eye surgery and has completed over 300,000 cataract and other eye operations. Anecdotal accounts suggest that Latin Americans, specifically in Nicaragua and Peru, have more favorable views of Venezuela after benefiting from these kinds of programs—demonstrating the utility of promoting the virtues of the Bolivaran system through direct assistance.[32]

To further demonstrate the benefits of its economic institutions, Venezuela joined the UN Economic and Social Council (ECOSOC) in 2008 to cultivate its standing among international institutions and highlight its successful social policy programs.[33] Venezuela's promotion of the ALBA as an alternative to the U.S.-sponsored Free Trade Agreement of the Americas (FTAA) is also illustrative of this institutional focus. The executive secretary of ALBA, Amenothep Zambrano, declared in 2011 that "the existence of the alliance has provided sorely needed relief to over 70 million people in Latin America and the Caribbean from the predatory and parasitic trade and debt relationships imposed by U.S.-led imperialism."[34] For Zambrano, the alliance represents "[Latin American] solidarity, it is integration, it is unity, it is complementarity, it is cooperation. It is an alliance that promotes equality among our peoples."[35] ALBA provides Venezuela more than an instrumental, coordinating economy body, but is also framed as a compelling symbolic vehicle for regional identification.

Cultural & Citizen Diplomacy

Unlike Japan and China, Venezuela does not possess a significant repertoire of cultural promotion as a form of public diplomacy, although the Chavez government has promoted a variety of initiatives.[36] One way in which Venezuela has sought to promote its Bolivaran social model is through its *misiones*, "public institutions that provide a number of health, education, and other services to neighborhoods and rural areas not thoroughly serviced by traditional state welfare mechanism."[37] International visiting dignitaries are frequently invited to view such programs as exemplars of Bolivaran ideas.

Venezuela has also worked to organize and participate in transnational movements against globalization and neoliberalism, including the provision of a venue for the 2006 World Social Forum. Venezuela has organized efforts in the United States such as the Venezuelan Information Office to advertise the success of its *misiones* and to facilitate the workings of groups sympathetic to the Bolivaran Revolution.[38]

Perhaps the most visible aspect of Venezuela's cultural diplomacy is the success of the *El Sistema* youth orchestra. Founded in 1975 by Jose Abreu as an intervention program in musical education for impoverished children, El Sistema has grown to be an international phenomenon, with programs modeled on El Sistema's success in over 25 countries.[39] The most successful graduate of the program, Maestro Gustavo Dudamel, was chosen to be the new music director of the Los Angeles Philharmonic and is globally recognized as a musical talent. Dudamel has indicated his intention to design a similar program for Los Angeles.[40] El Sistema USA was later established to promote the Venezuelan model of youth education in music in the United States, through the Jose Abreu Fellowship program to train instructors on social change-oriented music education.

Venezuela also engages in other forms of "traditional" cultural diplomacy and citizen outreach, such as through the promotion of music festivals, cinema production.[41] Advocacy groups called "Bolivaran Circles" are supported to promote social democratic practices in other countries. As a whole, Venezuela's engages in a relatively diverse range of public diplomacy activities, even if they are not explicitly justified *as* public diplomacy. The common strand among such programs is the touted benefits of the Bolivarian government, through which aid and cultural program support are demonstrative of the values embodied in the Bolivaran revolution.

Yet, as Michael Bustamante and Julia Sweig observe in their analysis of Venezuelan public diplomacy, Venezuelan soft power programs based on aid runs the risk of the perception of clientelism, in some ways akin to Japan's historical experience with "checkbook diplomacy."[42] Public diplomacy efforts based on humanitarian can be perceived as instrumental and cynical efforts to burnish the Bolivaran brand. But neither development aid nor cultural outreach should be construed as solely representing Venezuelan public diplomacy discourse and practice.

Rather, the development aid endemic to Carrales's definition of "social power" serves a larger symbolic strategy for Venezuelan public diplomacy that is yoked to the twin goals: to assert Venezuelan political ideas as a counter to neoliberalism and to promote regional political institutions to combat the influence of the United States. And media communication provides a demonstrative vehicle for this mission, which is fundamentally dependent on the cultivation of relationships that secure strands of identification between Venezuela and its imagined compatriots. Public diplomacy under this view interpellates Venezuela's partners into the orbit of the Bolivaran narrative of revolution and independence. The ambitions of Venezuela's strategic communication programs foreground an obvious geopolitical set of justifications.

THE ARTILLERY OF IDEAS

The idea that media communication can (and should) be used for the purpose of advancing the Bolivaran agenda is a notion that dates back to the time of Simon Bolivar. According to journalist Eva Golinger, an outspoken critic of U.S. policy in Venezuela and editor of the English language edition of the Venezuelan newspaper *Correo del Orinoco*, Simon Bolivar promoted the practice of journalism during the time of Venezuelan liberation in the early nineteenth century. Bolivar "encouraged writing and reporting as a form of 'artillery,' termed by him as the artillery of ideas."[43] The strategic utilization of communication is rooted in Venezuelan history alongside the emancipatory potential of media outlets.

Yet the contemporary context for Venezuelan international broadcasting reflects a diminishing tolerance for domestic media pluralism in the domestic media space, and an increasingly combative stance toward international news flows. President Chavez has historically attacked the credibility of opposing viewpoints in the domestic media, though he has tolerated some degree of diverse perspectives.[44] This level of tolerance has diminished as Chavez's government attitude toward domestic media space appears to increasingly reflect the concern over the influence of foreign media flows. Chavez's crackdown in domestic media effectively blurs the lines of conflict between domestic and international media.

Domestic media policy reached two pivotal turning points toward diminished tolerance. In 2004, the passage of the Law of Social Responsibility in Radio and Television raised concerns over press freedom. As previously indicated, the 2007 cancellation of the domestic broadcasting license for RCTV, a principal voice of opposition to the Chavez government, signaled further movement away from pluralism toward the politicization of media space.[45]

The climate for media pluralism and journalism also reflects a less tolerant stance on journalistic independence in Venezuela. Guillermo Zuloaga, the head of Globovision, the main Venezuelan private television broadcaster, fled the country in July 2010 for fear of criminal charges issued by the Chavez government.[46] The government has also threatened to seize Globovision's assets.[47] Journalists, in particular, face increased pressure in Venezuela due to state tolerance of physical attacks against journalists and the repression of journalistic freedoms.[48]

The move toward media control is not altogether surprising, given the privileged view of media as defined by ideological fault lines. As Golinger writes in 2010 on the necessity for an English language newspaper from Venezuela,

> Our most important mission is to combat the massive media manipulation and information blockade against Venezuela and to inform the international community about many incredible events taking place daily inside Venezuela that rarely receive attention from the corporate media.[49]

Golinger's justification signals not only the perceived need to get the message of Venezuela out, but also depicts through martial language the strategic significance of media and information flows. Media spaces are, in this sense, already interpenetrated by foreign and capitalism influence and must be seized to promote Bolivaran ideals while combating perceived ideological intrusion. As Chavez has argued, major international broadcasters have devised a strategy of "intrigues" and "lies" whose framing strategies have aimed to "distort the reality" of Venezuela.[50]

The influence strategies that derive from this fundamental view of media are also attuned to the political efficacy of foreign audiences as much as governments. Venezuelan strategic communication to promote a Bolivaran ideal is not simple propaganda, but considered as contingent on the identification of regional publics with Bolivaran ideals.

Speaking on Telesur in 2009, Venezuelan foreign representative Egardo Ramirez described the necessity of Venezuela to cultivate relationships with its neighboring countries and, importantly, argued that its foreign policy must reflect the views of people as much as governments. "Venezuela can not go forward alone . . . A foreign policy today legitimized by the people is a foreign policy that is invincible and can work on any front."[51] Diplomatic outreach, therefore, is more than engagement with specific regimes. It is the cultivation of attraction across regional foreign publics with the ambitions and values of the Venezuelan Bolivaran regime.

Venezuela's strategic communication therefore plays out through the competitive terrain of international *and* domestic media—the scene of mediated international conflict. Carlos Davila, a Venezuelan diplomat in Germany, writes on Aporrea.org (a quasi-governmental website for news and editorials) that Venezuela is engaged in a "mediatic war," and thus requires a "Strategic Communication Plan." Davila elaborates the strategic imperative underlying the need for a communication plan: "We need to transmit the Venezuelan reality to gain allies." Davila suggests that diplomatic institutions aggressively promote the success of Venezuela, and in particular, devise measurements of this kind of communication program. The actual plan amounts to a kind of coordinated nation-branding: "The political and communicational work strategically articulated must represent the central nucleus of tourist, cultural, scientific, sport, consular and military . . ." Davila concludes that Venezuela "must mobilize its emotions and shared . . . common values," with intelligent and truthful messages.[52]

The Venezuelan Information Office engages in this kind of promotion to highlight and amplify the representative power of its development and assistance programs. The office has supported online venues such as www. rethinkvenezuela.com and venezeulaanalys.org, as well as advertising campaigns in international newspapers, and has promoted the linkage of Venezuelan oil profits with its progressive international initiatives.[53] As stated previously, aid provides compelling symbolic ammunition in the "mediatic war" that Venezuela's spokespersons describe as being its strategic situation.

The centrality of media in Venezuelan public diplomacy, however, undoubtedly reflects the historical impact of media on the course of domestic politics as much as it continues the tradition of dependency theory critiques of media in Latin America.[54] Oppositional media were implicated in the 2002 coup attempt against Chavez, an event which further spurred the politicization of media in Venezuela's international interventions. Critical perspectives on the insidious role of outside forces and counter-revolution movements continue to dominate Venezuelan public argument about the role of media as a political force. Former president of Telesur Andrés Izarra, speaking in 2009 at a session of the Organization of American States (OAS) on the right to freedom of thought and expression, argued about the role of private media in Venezuela:

> Venezuelan private media carry out . . . activities of media terrorism. Messages of hatred are broadcasted on TV and radio newscasts. Private media have used subliminal messages and deceptive advertising against the Venezuelan people and government.[55]

As such, the boundaries between a media centric public diplomacy and aggressive media policy in the domestic sphere are likely blurred. Media is at once a domain of the "enemy" as it is valorized as a tool for the socialist ambitions of the Chavez government.

In addition to denouncing the opposition media within his country, however, Chavez has been an avid supporter of community media projects within Venezuela—not (at least initially) as outlets to amplify the popularity of his regime, but to empower local communities to create and report on conditions relevant to specific communities, neighborhoods, and even ethnic voices previously silenced in corporate-dominated Venezuelan media.[56] Broadcast media, in particular, is perceived by the Venezuelan government as a essential aspect of political efficacy and social betterment.

TELESUR

The emancipatory soft power potential of media communication is embodied with the launch of *La Nueva Televisora del Sur* (The New Television Station of the South), or Telesur, in 2005.[57] Telesur was initiated by the Venezuelan government as a collaborative international broadcasting effort with shared ownership among Latin American countries, and was designed to provide an alternative source of news and information programming. Telesur aims to "integrate a region that currently knows other parts of the world better than it knows itself"—a justification that echoes the critiques of international news flows that emerged in the days of the NWICO controversy and the MacBride Commission of the 1970s.[58] According to James Painter, the directors of Telesur are motivated by a concern that Latin American television has been too long dominated by Western programming from outside the region—and that Telsur could be an "antidote" to "information imperialism."[59] Andres Izarra described this need for Telesur:

[Telesur is] a strategic project that was born out of the need to give voice to Latin Americans confronted by an accumulation of thoughts and images transmitted by commercial media[,] and out of the urgency to see ourselves through our own eyes and to discover our own solutions to our problems.[60]

Telesur has since been described as a "subtle public diplomacy tool of the Venezuelan government," that advocates and demonstrates independence from corporate news programming and a pro-social agenda.[61] It achieved a respectable degree of penetration into regional media markets in its first year, including 17 Latin American countries through over-the-air satellite and terrestrial broadcast programming, as well as early plans to expand into North American Hispanic media markets.[62]

The rhetoric of justification and amplification surrounding Telesur is a revealing body of public argument. In particular, it outlines the political implications of the channel to cultivate identification across national boundaries as much as it imagines the transformative potential of satellite news media as a communicative form. The rhetoric is emancipatory in its declaration of independence from Western media news flows.

Yet Telesur is also imbued with a viable social function; Telesur is presented as a crucial force for integration across the Latin American world.[63] To borrow from Janice Bially-Mattern's depiction of soft power, Telesur is argued to be endowed with a particular "representational force."[64] Telesur's strategy of representation signifies a compelling articulation of political and social resources that can cultivate political allegiance and transform the political agency of Latin American publics. While Telesur may effectively function as a mouthpiece for Venezuelan news framing, it is also conceived as an integrative cultural and political resource for an imagined regional community. As Andrés Cañizález and Jairo Lugo claim, Telesur is both an instrument of asymmetric confrontation with the United States and a facilitator of geopolitical integration in the region.[65]

Aram Aharonian, general director of Telesur in 2008, speaks plainly of this instrumental consequence when he argues that the goal of Telesur is "to develop and implement a hemispheric televised communications strategy, of worldwide reach, to promote and consolidate the progression of change and regional integration as a tool in the battle of ideas against the hegemonic process of globalization."[66] Aharonian's argument features media as a crucial aspect of cultural identification, while the dependence on foreign sources equates to vulnerability to exploitation stemming from misrepresentation: "From the North they see us in black and white—mostly in black: we only appear in the news when a calamity occurs—and in reality, we are a continent in Technicolor."[67] Aharonian argues that Telesur can break the constraining bonds of north-dominated media representation by providing coverage that captures the plurality and diversity of South America.

Andrés Izarra also claimed that the channel would both give voice to the diversity of the Latin American region while serving the crucial function of promoting "debate" over the persistent social concerns. The use of media as a tool to promote productive controversy is essential if existing media sources are perceived as an obstacle to progressive political causes. Telesur is pitched as a kind of corrective to imperialist intervention in lieu of military resistance, yet also justified as liberal and deliberative in potential.

Following this logic, Aharonian argues, "In many of our countries today the media dictatorship is out to supplant military dictatorship. It is the large economic groups that use the media, decide who gets to speak and who doesn't, who is the protagonist and who the antagonist."[68] Rather than reiterate the assertions of the NWICO debate about the inequities of the international political economy of communication, Aharonian argues that Telesur's significance reflects the growing demand among *citizen* movements abroad for social justice, human rights, and the democratization of communication. Telesur is presented as responsive to grassroots demand for more representative and participatory communication outlets.

In practice, Telesur has garnered the support of the governments of Argentina, Cuba, Ecuador, Nicaragua, Uruguay, and Bolivia alongside Venezuela's role as the primary sponsor of the network. Yet Telesur continues to face difficulties in gaining access to cable distribution in a number of Latin American countries, and will be facing competition from Brazil, which is launching its own international broadcasting service: TV Brasil.

Despite potential competition and contractual difficulties, Telesur continues to incrementally expand its content sharing and broadcast imprint across Latin America, and has plans for expansion in Africa. In 2009, Venezuelan minister of foreign affairs Reinaldo Bolivar announced plans for Portugese-language broadcasts of Telesur-produced content on Angola public television.[69] Jean Ping, the president of the African Union, met with Hugo Chávez in June 2009 to discuss, among other things, the need for a Telesur-like station to connect nations in the global south. "We become accustomed to listen as the North speaks . . . We must give our countries the opportunity to express themselves, that it be the South–South voice."[70] The "south-south perspective also extends to the Middle East." Telesur announced content sharing agreements with Al-Jazeera in 2006, and while visiting Damascus, Hugo Chavez proposed a Syrian-based branch of Telesur to provide news from the Latin American world.[71]

The Telesur "model" may also function as a compelling public diplomacy resource in its own right. Webster Shamu, the minister of media, information, and publicity for Zimbabwe, applauded the network's ability to foster "integration and unity against U.S. information imperialism," and suggested that "Africa has much to learn from this Latin American venture but U.S. agencies, collaborators and allies will discourage any policies remotely resembling what Bolivia, Cuba and Venezuela have just agreed on."[72] In 2011, the Venezuelan ambassador to Nigeria suggested the formation of an Al-Jazeera–like channel to the Nigerian communication minister, and offered to share the experience of Telesur as a similar tool of regional integration.[73]

Public Diplomacy, Identity Politics and International Broadcasting

On the first anniversary of Telesur, President Chávez proposed to the 53 members of the African Union that they should join the Telesur network to improve integration between Latin America and Africa. It was symbolic of the meshing of his media and foreign policy aims. Telesur fits the pattern of Chávez using petrodollars to spread his message and influence beyond Venezuela.[74]

While Telesur may face competition in a contentious domestic and regional South American media market, it also functions as a platform for diplomatic announcements. During the official announcement of expanding Telesur's signal to Ecuador, the logic of Telesur's transformative potential was made clear. Maria Alisa Alvarez, Telesur's director of distribution and marketing, and Jorge Schwartz, the president of Ecuadorian TV-Cable, issued a joint statement:

> Telesur is a tool that contributes to the process of Latin American integration and consolidation . . . [T]oday is a demonstration that a mass communication project is possible and that the construction of . . . new communication is vital for the development of the peoples of the world.[75]

Telesur, as a form of international broadcasting, is explicitly framed by its advocates as a force for social and cultural integration with the idealized goal of political empowerment. Telesur is argued to be more than a corrective to systemic misinterpretation in international news flows, but also a proactive means to circumvent the obstacles to political reform caused by agenda setting and framing effects perpetuated by "hostile" media companies and their nation-state sponsors. Aharonian makes the case that Telesur is a "tool" to promote a collective awareness:

> The problem in Latin America is that we don't know anything about each other, we are blind to ourselves. We always saw ourselves through the lens of Madrid, London, New York. We begin with the idea that first we must get to know ourselves. Our problems are similar, the expectations are similar. Telesur is merely a tool so that people get to know what's happening in Latin America, and this may spur the process of integration.[76]

Telesur in this view is necessary for both the Venezuelan government and its imagined partners, given the pervasive and corrosive effect of corporate media on the democratic governance of Latin American countries.

An extensive Telesur article in 2009 elaborates this issue, citing public intellectuals and the arguments forwarded by leaders like Chavez and Ecuadorian president Rafael Correa. In the article, Juan Carlos Monedero, a professor of political science at Universidad Complutense de Madrid, proposes that Latin American is in reality a *mediocracy*: "[M]odern media have the ability to apply and remove democratically elected governments, which means that citizens live in a system of mediocracy." [77]

Monedero's Telesur essay depicts a contentious, highly mediated political environment—it constructs a scene where Latin American publics are besieged on a daily basis by private media who relentlessly seeking to sustain hegemonic control over the political landscape by pre-empting news of government assistance to the disadvantaged while being blatantly partisan. The Monedero essay also debunks what it calls the "famous flags of journalism ethics: impartiality, objectivity, freedom of expression" as "nothing more than myths abetting a media business, in the name of freedom, [which] takes daily actions against democratic governments."[78] The majority of corporate media destabilize progressive governments, and therefore an alternative media system is necessary to coordinate and strengthen those governments that resist the pull of private enterprise alone.

The politics of Telesur builds on the assumption that democratically elected governments are held hostage to the increasingly global flows of capital, by working to establish credibility through shared values, perspectives, and importantly, adversity. It foregrounds the shared predicament of media partisanship and the effacement of particular cultural and political groups in corporate media, and suggests that media like Telesur can foster a yet to be realized solidarity. Telesur's promotional slogans tellingly reflect these intentions:

"Finally, we can see each other's faces"
"Getting to know one another"
"There's space here for everyone"[79]

Telesur as a "subtle form of public diplomacy" has a potentially larger ambition than to cultivate positive attitudes toward Venezuela. Looking across the justifications and arguments about Telesur, it is apparent that Telesur aims to subordinate the traditional foundations of the collective social imaginary that upholds the political status quo in Latin America.

As a strategic move, targeting the symbolic resources that sustain the political and social norms of regional international relations would benefit

Venezuelan foreign policy. It is nevertheless striking that broadcast media's social function is so clearly envisioned as a kind of political engineering. Telesur's own promotional text on its website embraces the literalization of Anderson's "imagined community" while explicitly declaring a kind of political instrumentality:

> [Telesur's mission is] to develop a new communication strategy for Latin America. One that promotes the right to information and considers veracity as its main principle. A strategy that stimulates the production and projection of regional content, promoting the recognition of the Latin American imagery. A channel with social vocation that serves as historical memory and cultural expression, a space for meeting and debating ideas, made up of a diverse and plural programming as diverse and plural is the population of Latin America.[80]

As Gentilli and Taveira argue, Telesur is an *innovation* in the use of satellite television for international broadcasting. It represents both a response to media-based cultural and media imperialism as well as an attempt to intervene in the shared memory and history of Latin America—an engineering of the regional imagined community through media communication.[81]

TOWARD AN AGGRESSIVE
SOFT POWER AGENDA FOR TELESUR

The rhetoric surrounding Telesur and Venezuelan international media policy has evolved since the launch of Telesur in 2005 to become more assertive in the strategic intent behind Telesur, as well as the capacity of Telesur to accomplish Venezuela's foreign policy objectives. Andrés Izarra claimed in 2008 that the purpose of the channel was to engage in "ideological struggle on a mass scale . . . . For many years we believed that we had to fight from small radio and small newspapers." Izara indicates that Venezuela was *without* the tools to engage in the kind of ideational conflict that appears dominated by Western and capitalist media owners.

Izarra puts the ultimate agenda of Telesur as a policy instrument in blunt terms: "It is time to stop thinking like dwarfs. The aim of Telesur is fight the battle of mass television." Izarra's rhetoric may be bellicose, but it captures the political language that is inherent in Telesur's institutional identity. As Telesur's own website claims, "[i]f integration is the goal, Telesur is the means."[82]

In a 2007 interview with a Venezuelan domestic news outlet, Izarra explained the logic behind the closure of RCTV and linked this to the conception of Telesur as an instrument of Venezuela's ambitions in international politics. Izarra explains that the Bolivaran agenda of the Chavez government requires what he calls a "communication hegemony."[83] Izarra suggests that the "new strategic landscape" necessitates "communication and information hegemony" that he specifically argues is "Gramscian." Through Gramsci, Izarra explains the need for a direct challenge across levels of society to the values associated with capitalism and implicitly, the foreign powers that support these values. Yet Izarra argues that this struggle is the *responsibility* of the state; it is the strategic mission of Venezuela.

Izarra's call for communication hegemony obscures distinctions between domestic and international contexts for Venezuelan communication policy, to suggest an overarching strategic imperative to promote socialist values across nation-states and regions where other values predominate in media representation. Yet the idea of hegemony, in Izarra's words, is not synonymous with "media dictatorship"—rather, Izarra deploys the term to articulate how media forms work persuasively to solidify commonly held values and worldviews. Izarra explains that hegemony is the "means that we can build capacities to convince, attract, and promote a set of values and ideas about the world." While he acknowledges that he is arguing for a "cultural battle," Izarra is careful not to say that there should be *no* media diversity or dissent.

The strategy Izarra proposes suggests a comprehensive approach to the state-based management of communication policy at the domestic level, to encompass government institutions and civil society actors that can independently produce content. There is also an intertextual element to Izarra's arguments about the requirements of domestic media, that draws upon similar justifications for Venezuelan international efforts like Telesur and the global scene of mediated war. The distinctions between the demands of political competition in the domestic field are blurred with those of international media. Yet embedded in the idealization of media as a space for ideological contest and counterhegemonic struggle are other presumptions about the *capacity* of media and communication technologies to affect outcomes and, in the process, articulate a particular form of agency for both domestic and foreign publics.

Media commentator Joel Hirst describes the international component of this strategy as "a plan to control information access across the hemisphere." The project, which began with Telesur in 2005 under the auspices of the ALBA, has since grown to encompass other information outlets. Hirst argues that the strategic is proving successful, especially in the wake of Telesur's extensive coverage of the coup against Honduran president Zeyala in 2009:

[T]he ALBA has established a series of online services for radio and television such as ALBA-TV, ALBA Ciudad 96.3, the Radio of the South [Radio del Sur], and ALBA Multi-Channel. . . . And the ALBA's propaganda is working. In a recent survey carried out by M&R consulting in Nicaragua, 50% of respondents identified Venezuela as their greatest friend (in terms of cooperation), compared with only 18% for the United States."[84]

Hirst claims that Telesur is but part of a larger effort orchestrated under the auspices of ALBA to build up a comprehensive media outreach strategies across different media platforms—including more traditional mass broadcasting outlets and, now, social media.

The National Character of Technological Interventions

The preceding arguments for Telesur highlight the significance of *mass* media broadcasting as a viable and necessary instrument of political influence and articulate the centrality of media for geopolitical ambitions. Yet Venezuela's promotion of Telesur has not extended to a significant embrace of other communication technologies until 2010. The Chavez government's slow adoption of social network platforms in particular suggests an initial mistrust of the technology and the perception of an implicit ideological bias intrinsic to the media platforms.

Prior to 2010, Venezuela has been outspoken in its opposition to video games and social networking technologies—both technologies considered to be new and innovative outreach tools by digital diplomacy advocates in the United States. For example, the Alliance for Youth Movements, one of the U.S. State Department's efforts to organize pro-democratic advocates around the world, was denounced by Eva Golinger on Telesur during the Alliance Summit in Mexico City in October 2009. The criticism conveyed a profoundly cynical attitude toward the technology itself. Telesur reported that the conference featured representatives from NGOs and corporations, "specializing in the subversion and destabilization of governments." According to Golinger, the "young creators of technologies like Twitter, Facebook, Google, Next Gen, Meetup and YouTube," were present to support the State Department's "new strategy of regime change," signifying "irrefutable evidence of the sinister alliance between Washington and new technologies."[85]

Golinger offered a dramatic appraisal of social networking technology's power: "[The] potential use of these technologies to promote psychological operations and propaganda is unlimited. Its strength is the speed of dissemination of messages and global coverage strategy." Golinger's reporting on Telesur claimed that social networking technologies constitute a massive "destabilization plan" against nation-states that resist the "imperialist" policies of the United States.[86] In 2011, the Venezuelan English-language newspaper *Correo del Orinico* published an essay decrying social networking technologies as effectively compromised by U.S. government attempts to leverage the platforms as propaganda tools and warning readers to beware efforts by the U.S. military to make "fake" social media friends.

Suspicion of popular communication technologies from the United States translated into public announcements and restrictions. In February 2010, President Chavez announced that he considered Twitter and other social networking technologies "terrorist threats."[87] In October 2009, the Venezuelan legislature moved to ban violent video games, a predominantly Western cultural import.[88] President Chavez argued that video games are "poison" on his weekly television show *Alo Presidente*, claiming that "some games teach you to kill. They once put my face on a game, 'you've got to find Chavez to kill him.'"[89] President Chavez declared in 2010 that the "Internet cannot be something open where anything is said and done. Every country has to apply its own rules and norms."[90]

These kinds of public statements represented a sweeping rejection of communication technologies strongly associated with the United States; where the communication technologies themselves are symbolic of the United States. Rather than embrace social networking technologies as part of its international broadcasting strategy, the Venezuelan government instead proceeded to explore other more traditional broadcast technologies. In 2007, planning began for "Radio del Sur"—a 300-station public network designed to promote regional integration that would eventually expand to Africa and other Global south countries.[91] Aside from supporting platforms such as Aporrea.org and Venezuelananalysis.org, the Venezuela until recently has placed significant emphasis on the traditional broadcast media that have historically defined the sites of political struggle in both Venezuela and the Latin American region.

Later in 2010, however, the Chavez government *reversed* its condemnation of new and social media technologies. This move signaled the intent to reclaim the potential of the communication platform, rather than strategically reject social media as tainted by US and Western influence.[92] As part of this shift, Chavez launched a blog and a twitter account to counter what he perceived as lies about his government. Chavez's Twitter account, is http://twitter.com/chavezcandanga, and is purportedly staffed by over 200 people charged with maintaining Mission *ChavezCandanga*.[93] As of June 2011, @chavezcandanga has over 1.6 million followers. Chavez explains the intent of his foray into social media as extending the frontiers of the ideological conflict that already defines Venezuelan strategic communication:

Maybe I'll reach millions, not only in Venezuela but in the world . . . I am going to dig my own trench on the Internet . . . All this is a battle between socialism and capitalism . . . Our Internet—the Bolivarian Internet—has to be an alternative press.[94]

President Chavez evidently deploys the platform to promote the accomplishments of the government and also to continue the mediated conflict with the United States.

For example, in response to proposed U.S. sanctions against Venezuela for alleged support of the Iranian nuclear program, Chavez tweets,

"Sanciones contra la Patria de Bolívar? Impuestas por el gobierno imperialista gringo? Pues: Bienvenidas Mr Obama! No Olvide Q Somos Los Hijos De Bolivar! ("Sanctions against the homeland of Bolivar? Imposed by the Imperialist government gringo? Welcome, Mr. Obama. Don't forget we are the children of Bolivar!") (May 24 http://twitter.com/#!/chavezcandanga)

Chavez also posts messages that exhort broader thematic arguments about Venezuelan values. Here, Chavez promotes socialism's comparative advantages:

En capitalismo nunca habrá solución para el drama de la vivienda. Sólo el Socialismo podrá solucionarlo!!" (In capitalism there will never be [a] solution to the drama of the house. Only socialism can solve it!")

Chavezcandanga represents how social media platforms have been appropriated into a larger messaging strategy. Yet the embrace of this technology is still characterized by previous conceptions of how audiences relate to media in a contest of broadcasted political ideology.

The reversal in Venezuela's stance against social media is also reflected in publicized efforts to train domestic youth through programs like the "Communication Thunder" initiative, which use the Internet to counter attacks on the Bolivaran government and to train citizens to "promote a new way of seeing the world through socialism." Chavez argued that this new strategy would be a form of "guerilla communication," to empower youth to "counter the disinformation of the press."[95]

Diosdado Cabello, a senior member of Chavez's political party and head of Venezuelan telecommunications firm Conatel, described the Communication Thunder project as using "all tools that are available"—including social media platforms.[96] Cabello argues that media are not *intrinsically* the tools of those who oppose the Bolivaran revolution. He states: "The opposition thinks they are the leaders of the social networks. They think that Twitter and Facebook are theirs. We are fighting the battle . . . everyone in the PSUV [Partido Sociolista Unido de Venezuela], let's all have an account."[97] Yet moves to embrace social media as a necessary political tool of influence have also been matched by increased efforts to impose control over such technologies.

Despite the embrace of Internet technologies for international engagement, Venezuela also moved to further restrict information flows. In December 2010, Venezuela expanded the restrictions enacted in the 2004 media reform law to ban Internet content that "promotes social unrest, challenges authority, or condones crime."[98] The law states that it aims "to establish social responsibility in the diffusion and reception of messages, to promote democratic balance between the duties, rights and interests."[99]

Domestic programs like Communication Thunder and President Chavez's personal turn to social media may not constitute a *dramatic* shift in attitudes about strategic communication and Venezuela's international communication policies. Such strategic moves, however, reinforce the observation that there may be significant linkages between the domestic and foreign dimension of the government's strategic objectives—the promotion of widespread identification with Bolivaran ideals and, by extension, the Chavez government. These objectives are conditioned by the salience of media influence as the site of struggle against a multifarious ideological opponent and the perceived susceptibility of media audiences to manipulation and representational strategies.

VENEZUELAN SOFT POWER:
COMMUNICATION HEGEMONY?

A Venezuelan variant of soft power is argued in this chapter to be overwhelmingly defined by political competition through media forms. The centrality of mediated politics is reflected in a variety of public diplomacy-related activities that aim to promote the values, ideals, and accomplishments of Bolivaran government in opposition to an antagonistic and capitalist United States, while also facilitating regional integration through both representational strategies (such as the storytelling of Telesur) and through institutional efforts to strengthen ties like the ALBA.

As a whole, these strategic configurations represent an idealization of soft power that is distinct from other nation-states considered in this volume. The differences are observable across the dimensions of scale, mechanism, and outcomes associated with Venezuelan soft power.

The implied notion of the subject in the scope of relations in Venezuelan soft power is suggestive of a disempowered and manipulated audience. The foreign publics envisioned as the audience for Venezuelan soft power initiatives are not full-agentic, autonomous auditors of political belief. Rather the foreign publics are conceived implicitly as subjects to media imperialism and the deterministic effects of capitalist ideology. The Bolivaran imperative in Venezuelan foreign policy is emancipatory, to provide alternative narratives for coping with conditions of domination and to provide means of solidarity around shared experiences to imagine an alternative form of collective regional identity.

The *scope* of Venezuelan soft power involves the assumption of a regional foreign public waiting to be galvanized into an identity formation that draws inspiration from the Bolivaran narrative. Venezuelan soft power is thus predicated on the implicit attractiveness of the Bolivaran model. The challenge to Venezuelan soft power is not the fickle nature of its audience, but the presence of competing messages and outlets for collective expression. In this conception, the state bears much of the burden in cultivating soft power. More to the point, the breadth of influence initiatives launched by Venezuela expresses a remarkable faith in the prospect of influence through soft power means.

Yet how is this influence supposed to work? The *mechanisms* of Venezuelan soft power involve both media and institutional vehicles that amplify the ideals and values of the Bolivaran republic. Venezuela does not strive to present an ancient culture or represent an enduring universalism, but rather offers a range of political ideals that underscore arguments for a purportedly *legitimate* slate of foreign and domestic policies. In this sense, Venezuelan soft power programs rely more heavily on the latter two of Nye's primary resources for soft power.

Soft power is manifest across the three behaviors of soft power—agenda-setting, persuasion, and attraction—yet the agenda-setting and persuasion behaviors are most prominent. While identification is a goal, the vehicles of Venezuelan public diplomacy and strategic communication strive to redefine the agenda of news and information flows through regionally derived media content, and to persuade regional audiences about the credibility of Venezuela as a regional actor. Of the cases considered in this book, Venezuela is the most explicit in presenting a set of arguments intended to persuade—in order to cultivate soft power.

As is also evident from interventions like Telesur and the later adoption of social media platforms, communication media are considered pivotal to this strategy. As the Telesur English-language brochure says, "To watch us is to know us; to recognise us is to respect us; to respect is to learn to care for each other. These are the first steps toward regional integration. If integration is the end, Telesur is the means."[100]

Assumptions about the role of media in the politics of international influence are not simply idiosyncratic interpretations of Venezuela's political past. While the media is presented as a battleground between Venezuela and meddling capitalist powers, the arguments are not wholly unsubstantiated. Venezuelan journalists seized upon evidence in the Wikileaks trove of diplomatic correspondence that the United States was actively leveraging public diplomacy and Department of Defense–funded strategic communication methods to confront the Chavez government.[101]

The *outcomes* expected from Venezuelan soft power initiatives are relatively straightforward and reflect the behavior mechanisms previously identified. Venezuela public diplomacy seeks to challenge the United States and to strengthen regional credibility. To effectively seek "soft balancing" against the United States, Venezuela must frame its other policy initiatives. This involves transforming the symbolic resources that sustain regional identity and political arrangements. This is not an easily accomplished ambition. As Ahmad Aharonian argues,

> Telesur is only a media service and can't in and of itself make a revolution. We are only a tool for interpretation, and to help integration of the continent. But the real problem in Latin America is to eat every day. It is the same thing throughout the Third World. Our goal is to open the door. We hope in 5–10 years we can have more Latin American television, a real alternative to the mainstream media.[102]

Other media scholars claim that Telesur is fundamentally a counterhegemonic project, providing a truly alternative lens on regional news and political discourse.[103] Telesur in this sense represents a kind of Latin American Al-Jazeera, rather than simply a "vehicle for Venezuelan propaganda."[104] This is not an uncontroversial claim, as others have argued that Telesur is a front for Chavez supporters.[105] Overall, programs like Telesur augur a transformation that will be media-driven, where soft power is actively cultivated and instrumental in the transformation of institutions and political identity in the region.

The rhetoric of Venezuelan soft power implicates the belief that influence can and should be achieved through communicative appeals. The arguments presented also reflect a view of technological effect and significance that is strongly tied to the way in which media have been implicated in that country's tumultuous political history. Telesur is an outgrowth of what the Chavez government believes media can do—grounded in the ideological frameworks of dependency as well as experience of a media-orchestrated coup in 2002. Telesur, in particular, is also justified in very sweeping assumptions about the centrality of media in the fabric of political identification. It is positioned as a tool of political integration. Programs like Telesur indicate that Venezuela may seek to build on the gains made by Al-Jazeera, that a regional satellite network can yield credibility and stature in the geopolitics of media, with consequences that clearly resonate outside the media.[106]

Venezuela is differentiated by other cases addressed in the volume primarily by its emphasis on the perceived utility of communication technology and on the necessity to engage in a kind of communicative struggle that asserts the viability on an alternative ideological project. Unlike China and the United States the cultural resources of soft power are not items that speak for themselves upon presentation. The values of the Bolivaran revolution must be argued for and defended. Like Japan, the *cultural* dimension of Venezuelan soft power—expressed as a kind political culture and ideals—can be actualized through representation and demonstration.

Rather than see soft power as something that exists in latent form, soft power in the cases of Japan and Venezuela is something that states must strive to cultivate. In the case of Japan, public diplomacy strategies seize on the facets of Japanese cultural that present the most readily accessible gateways to "interest" in Japan. For Chavez's Venezuela, the de facto public diplomacy strategy is to leverage strategic communication practices to present Venezuelan ideals and policies in order to project shared experiences that cultivate identification and, ultimately, a shared sense of political destiny. Such identification is a form of attraction that could validate Venezuela's claims to regional leadership.

Yet there are also key differences between Japan and Venezuela. In Japan's soft power strategy, the auditors of public diplomacy and communication are active interpreters—they are ultimately responsible and empowered consumers of communication content. In the case of Venezuela, however, the subjects to "communication hegemony" are far less empowered. Yet despite this conception of audience, the narratives embodied in programming such as Telesur are not intended to be crude propagandistic advertisements.

Rather, the programming represents symbolic equipment to symbolize shared identity with the Venezuelan cause, made common through shared histories. Telesur, like Al-Jazeera, is perceived by policymakers as a significant tool not because it represents Venezuela but because it adheres to a transnational imaginary of South American identity, one constructed against a predominant antagonist. Telesur and the Venezuelan version of soft power that it represents shares some conceptual territory with the U.S. emphasis on facilitation in that Telesur is offered as a shared "voice" for South Americans. The foreign policy benefits of Telesur are inferred and deferred—yet still Venezuelan.

Yet the symbolic linkages between Telesur and Venezuela are perhaps not so significant as to render Telesur a kind of independent voice along the lines

of an Al-Jazeera.[107] Venezuela owns a considerable stake in Telesur's operations—and as evident it is argued as necessary to the ideological imperatives
of Venezuelan long-term strategy. It is not clear that regional audiences perceive Telesur as their own voice, and not simply a mouthpiece for Venezuela.
Yet has the strategy worked?

Despite Chavez's attempts to curtail press freedom, international broadcasting programs like Telesur have indeed yielded soft power benefits. In
March 2011, President Chavez was awarded a "press freedom" award by the
University of La Plata in Argentina in response his efforts to "break media
monopolies" and to promote "popular communication."[108] The dean of the
School of Journalism argued that the award recognized Chavez's attempts to
break the domination of the press by "'the owners of large media corporations." When Chavez received his award, he told a crowd of students that
Venezuela was promoting "a new dynamic of communication and information free from the media dictatorship of the bourgeoisie and the empire."[109]
Recognition of Venezuela's *credibility* to represent regional interests is a
clear indicator of *some* form of soft power.

Yet the term soft power is itself marked as American in Venezuelan discourse. According to James Petras of Venezuelaanalysis.com, the notion of
soft power is a euphemism for the ways in which the United States obfuscates
its intentions to use communication against the Bolivaran regime: "Soft power
is not an end in itself; it is a means of accumulating forces and building the
capacity to launch a violent frontal assault at the Venezuelan government's
'weakest moment.'"[110] While the term soft power may be understood in context as a rhetorical tool of the U.S. government and freighted with symbolic
baggage, the ideas and practices contained in Nye's analytical concept are
clearly evident in Venezuela's considerable attempts to leverage the potential
of international communication to forward its foreign policy objectives.

NOTES

1. Javier Noya, *New Propaganda: The Public Diplomacy of the Authoritarian
Regimes in China and Venezuela* (Madrid: Real Institute Elcano, January 15, 2008), 10.

2. Michael Dodson and Manochehr Dorraj, "Populism and Foreign Policy in
Venezuela and Iran," *Whitehead Journal of Diplomacy and International Relations* 9
(2008):71; Doreen Massey, "Concepts of Space and Power in Theory and in Political
Practice," *Documents d'anàlisi geogràfica* 55, 15–26 January 1, 2009, www.raco.cat/
index.php/DocumentsAnalisi/article/viewArticle/171747/0.

3. Yetzy U. Villarroel, "La Política Exterior de Venezuela: Continuidad y Discontinuidad con el Pasado," *Cuestiones Políticas* 24, no. 41 (n.d.):169–190.

4. Joel Hirst, "The Bolivarian Alliance & the Hugo Chavez Propaganda Machine," *Latin American Herald Tribune*, 2010, www.laht.com/article.asp?ArticleI d=375338&CategoryId=13303.

5. James Painter, *Counter-Hegemonic News: A Case Study of Al-Jazeera English and Telesur*, RISJ Challenges (Oxford, 2006); Claudia Boyd-Barrett and Oliver Boyd-Barrett, "Latin American 24/7 News Battle for Honduras," *Global Media Journal 9*, no. 16 (2010):64.

6. Villarroel, "La Política Exterior de Venezuela: Continuidad y Discontinuidad con el Pasado."

7. James Painter, *The Boom in Counter-Hegemonic News Channels: A Case Study of Telesur* (Oxford: Reuters Institute for the Study of Journalism at Oxford, 2007); Marcelino Bisbal, "Telesur: ¿Concreción de un Proyectocomunicacional-Político Regional?" *Comunicación* (2009):66–75.

8. Marisol Pradas, "Andrés Izarra: El Socialismo Necesita una Hegemonía Comunicacional," *Bolitin Digital Universitario*, 2007, www.boletin.uc.edu.ve/index .php?option=com_content&task=view&id=4990&Itemid=38.

9. Gustavo Coronel, "Corruption, Mismanagement, and Abuse of Power in Hugo Chávez's Venezuela," *Cato Institute: Development Policy Analysis*, November 27, 2006, www.cato.org/pub_display.php?pub_id=6787.

10. Christopher B. Conway, *The Cult of Bolívar in Latin American Literature* (University Press of Florida, 2003); Richard Gott, *In the Shadow of the Liberator: Hugo Chávez and the Transformation of Venezuela* (Verso, 2000).

11. Noya, *New Propaganda: The Public Diplomacy of the Authoritarian Regimes in China and Venezuela*, 8.

12. Robert Duffy and Robert Everton, "Media, Democracy, and the State in Venezuela's Bolivaran Revolution," in *Global Communications: Toward a Transcultural Political Economy*, eds. Paula Chakravartty and Yuezhi Zhao (Lanham, MD: Rowman & Littlefield, 2008).

13. Villarroel, "La Política Exterior de Venezuela: Continuidad y Discontinuidad con el Pasado"; Painter, *The Boom in Counter-Hegemonic News Channels: A Case Study of Telesur.*

14. Alan B. Albarran and Guillermo Gibens, eds., "The Mass Media in Venezuela: History, Politics, Freedom," in *The Handbook of Spanish Language Media* (Taylor & Francis, 2009), 77–87.

15. Leopoldo Colmenares. "La Exportacion de la 'Revolucion Bolivariana' hacia America Latina." *Military Review Enero-Febrero* 2011, 8–23.

16. Villarroel, "La Política Exterior de Venezuela: Continuidad y Discontinuidad con el Pasado."

17. Painter, *The Boom in Counter-Hegemonic News Channels: A Case Study of Telesur*, 11.

18. Gibens, "The Mass Media in Venezuela: History, Politics, Freedom."

19. Kim Andrew Elliott, "Maybe It Should Be Called 'Chávez Siempre Que Él Quiera.'," *Kim Andrew Elliott reporting on International Broadcasting*, February 10, 2010, http://kimelli.nfshost.com/index.php?id=8319.

20. Raymond Colitt and Ana Isabel Martinez, "Venezuela Begins Shutdown of 34 Radio Stations," *Reuters*, August 1, 2009, www.reuters.com/article/2009/08/01/venezuela-media-idUSN0146551720090801.

21. Duffy and Everton, "Media, Democracy, and the State in Venezuela's Bolivaran Revolution."

22. Painter, *Counter-Hegemonic News: A Case Study of Al-Jazeera English and Telesur*, 45.

23. Javier Corrales, "Using Social Power to Balance Soft Power: Venezuela's Foreign Policy," *The Washington Quarterly* 32, no. 4 (October 2009):97–114.

24. Ibid., 97.

25. Michael J. Bustamante and Julia E. Sweig, "Buena Vista Solidarity and the Axis of Aid: Cuban and Venezuelan Public Diplomacy," *Annals of the American Academy of Political and Social Science* 616 (March 2008):223–256.

26. Ibid., 25.

27. "Using Oil to Spread Revolution: Hugo Chávez Is Spending Some of His Country's Oil Windfall on Buying Support Abroad. How Much of a Return Is He Getting?," *The Economist*, June 28, 2005, www.economist.com/node/4232330.

28. Bustamante and Sweig, "Buena Vista Solidarity and the Axis of Aid: Cuban and Venezuelan Public Diplomacy," 28.

29. Juan Reardon, "U.S. Poor to Benefit from 6th Year of Subsidized Venezuelan Heating Oil," Venezuelanalysis.com, January 28, 2011, http://venezuelanalysis.com/news/5965.

30. Bustamante and Sweig, "Buena Vista Solidarity and the Axis of Aid: Cuban and Venezuelan Public Diplomacy."

31. Liza Featherstone, "Chávez's Citizen Diplomacy," *The Nation*, December 17, 2006, www.thenation.com/article/ch%C3%A1vezs-citizen-diplomacy.

32. Bustamante and Sweig, "Buena Vista Solidarity and the Axis of Aid: Cuban and Venezuelan Public Diplomacy."

33. VenWorld, "Venezuela Elected to UN Economic and Social Council « Venezuela World," October 24, 2008, http://venworld.wordpress.com/2008/10/24/venezuela-elected-to-united-nations-economic-and-social-council/.

34. venezuealaanalysis.com, "The Fundamentals of ALBA: Interview with Executive Secretary Amenothep Zambrano," Venezuelanalysis.com, February 11, 2011, http://venezuelanalysis.com/analysis/6025.

35. Ibid.

36. Bustamante and Sweig, "Buena Vista Solidarity and the Axis of Aid: Cuban and Venezuelan Public Diplomacy," 246.

37. Ibid., 233.

38. Ibid.

39. John Terauds, "Venezuela's Winning System for Saving Children through Music," Venezuelanalysis.com, October 18, 2009, http://venezuelanalysis.com/analysis/4872.

40. Neal Rosendor, "Maestro Dudamel, Venezuelan Soft Power and Lessons for America," *USC Center for Public Diplomacy*, March 6, 2008, http://uscpublic

diplomacy.org/index.php/newsroom/pdblog_detail/maestro_dudamel_venezuelan_ soft_power_and_lessons_for_america/.

41. See note 35.

42. Saori Katada, *Toward a Mature Aid Donor: Fifty Years of Japanese ODA and the Challenges Ahead*, Asia Program Special Report (Woodrow Wilson International Center, February 2005).

43. Eva Golinger, "Announcing Venezuela's First and Only English Language Newspaper, Correo del Orinoco International," venezuelanalysis.com, January 22, 2010, http://venezuelanalysis.com/news/5093.

44. Gibens, "The Mass Media in Venezuela: History, Politics, Freedom."

45. Ibid.

46. VOA News, "Head of Venezuela's Globovision Considering Asylum in U.S.," *Voice of America*, n.d., www.voanews.com/english/news/americas/Head-of-Venezualas-Globovision-Considering-Asylum-in-US-98558144.html.

47. Ingrid Bachman, "Chávez Issues New Warning to Opposition Channel Globovisión," *Knight Center for Journalism in the Americas*, July 5, 2010, http://knight-center.utexas.edu/blog/chavez-issues-new-warning-opposition-channel-globovision.

48. Monica Medel, "Study: Government Supporters Responsible for One in Four Attacks on the Press in Venezuela," *Knight Center for Journalism in the Americas*, April 29, 2011, http://knightcenter.utexas.edu/blog/study-government-supporters -responsible-one-four-attacks-press-venezuela.

49. Golinger, "Announcing Venezuela's First and Only English Language Newspaper, Correo del Orinoco International."

50. Ingrid Bachman, "Venezuelan President Denounces International Media Campaign against His Administration," *Knight Center for Journalism in the Americas*, August 31, 2010, http://knightcenter.utexas.edu/blog/venezuelan-president-denounces-international-media-campaign-against-his-administration.

51. Edgar Ramirez, "Política Exterior de Chávez Se Aprecia en Proyecto Simón Bolívar," TeleSURtv.net, February 2, 2009, www.telesurtv.net/secciones/noticias/41926-NN/politica-exterior-de-chavez-se-aprecia-en-proyecto-simon-bolivar/.

52. Carlos Davila, "Enfrentar la Guerra Mediática Internacional, a Través de un Plan Estratégico de Comunicación," *Aporrea*, June 14, 2008, www.aporrea.org/medios/a58833.html.

53. Juan Forero, "Venezuela's New Campaign," *The New York Times*, September 30, 2004, sec. Business / Media & Advertising, Www.nytimes.com/2004/09/30/business/Media/30adco.html; Bustamante and Sweig, "buena Vista Solidarity and The axis of Aid: Cuban and Venezuelan public Diplomacy," 232.

54. Daya Thussu, "Mapping Global Media Flow and Contra-Flow," in *Media on the Move: Global Flow and Contra-Flow* (London, New York: Routledge, 2007), 10–29.

55. Kim Andrew Elliott, "Head of Venezuelan International Broadcaster Turns His Attention to Venezuelan Domestic Broadcasting," *Kim Andrew Elliott reporting on International Broadcasting*, April 26, 2009, http://kimelli.nfshost.com/index .php?id=6399.

56. Duffy and Everton, "Media, Democracy, and the State in Venezuela's Bolivaran Revolution."

57. Fernando Buen Abad Domínguez, "Aporrea: Algunos Aportes de TeleSur en Su Cumpleaños," Apporrea.org, n.d., www.aporrea.org/medios/a104708.html.

58. Jens Erik Gould, "Latin Governments Launching a Competitor for CNN," *Cox News Service*, June 23, 2005, sec. Financial Pages, www.lexisnexis.com.proxyau .wrlc.org/hottopics/lnacademic/.

59. Painter, *The Boom in Counter-Hegemonic News Channels: A Case Study of Telesur.*

60. Blanche Petrich, "Telesur: A Counter-Hegemonic Project to Compete with CNN and Univisión," *Agencia Latinoamericana de Información y Análisis-Dos (ALIA2)* (March 2, 2005), www.alia2.net/article4055.html.

61. Bustamante and Sweig, "Buena Vista Solidarity and the Axis of Aid: Cuban and Venezuelan Public Diplomacy."

62. Natalie Obiko Pearson, "Venezuela's Chávez-Backed TV Station Eyes U.S. Markets," *Associated Press*, July 27, 2006; Vinod Sreeharsha, "Telesur Tested by Chávez Video," *Christian Science Monitor*, November 22, 2005.

63. Andrés Cañizález and Jairo Lugo, "Telesur: Estrategia Geopolítica con Fines Integracionistas," *CONFines* (n.d.):53–64.

64. Janice Bially Mattern, "Why 'Soft Power' Isn't So Soft: Representational Force and the Sociolinguistic Construction of Attraction in World Politics," *Millennium—Journal of International Studies* 33, no. 3 (June 2005):583–612.

65. Cañizález and Lugo, "Telesur: Estrategia Geopolítica con Fines Integracionistas."

66. Sally Burch, "Telesur and the New Agenda for Latin American Integration," *Global Media and Communication* 3, no. 2 (August 2007):227–232.

67. Ibid.

68. Ibid.

69. Kim Andrew Elliott, "Zimbabwe Official: Africa Has 'Much to Learn' from Latin American Telesur Agreement," *Kim Andrew Elliott reporting on International Broadcasting*, November 19, 2009, http://kimelli.nfshost.com/index.php?id=7792.

70. James Suggett, "Presidents of Venezuela and African Union Discuss Upcoming Africa–South America Summit," Venezuelanalysis.com, June 10, 2009, http://venezuelanalysis.com/news/4509.

71. Ibid.

72. Elliott, "Zimbabwe Official: Africa Has 'Much to Learn' from Latin American Telesur Agreement."

73. Kim Andrew Elliott, "Venezuelan Ambassador to Nigeria Suggests an Al Jazeera–Like, Telesur-Like Channel for West Africa," *Kim Andrew Elliott reporting on International Broadcasting*, March 20, 2011, http://kimelli.nfshost.com/index.php?id=10924.

74. Painter, *The Boom in Counter-Hegemonic News Channels: A Case Study of Telesur*, 16.

75. "Aporrea: Desde el Próximo Miércoles Telesur Abrirá Su Señal a Todo Ecuador," *Aporrea*, April 10, 2009, www.aporrea.org/medios/n143359.html.

76. Nikolas Kozloff, "Telesur's Program Aram Aharonian with Nikolas Kozloff," *The Brooklyn Rail*, April 2007, www.brooklynrail.org/2007/4/express/telesurs-program.

77. "Democracy vs. Mediacracy," TeleSURtv.net, 2009, www.telesurtv.net/noticias/entrev-reportajes/listado.php?class=Reportaje.

78. Ibid.

79. "Telusur Promotional Brochure" (Telesur, 2008).

80. "TelesurTV", n.d., www.telesurtv.net.

81. Davi Gentilli and Vitor Rocha, "Telesur: Televisão E Comunidade Imaginada Latino-Americana," *Revista Extraprensa* 1, no. 1(4) (December 3, 2010), www.usp.br/celacc/ojs/index.php/extraprensa/article/viewArticle/s-ses2–4.

82. Noya, *New Propaganda: The Public Diplomacy of the Authoritarian Regimes in China and Venezuela*, Noya.

83. Pradas, "Andrés Izarra: El Socialismo Necesita una Hegemonía Comunicacional."

84. Hirst, "The Bolivarian Alliance and the Hugo Chavez Propaganda Machine."

85. Eva Golinger, "Goicochea and Clinton Plan 'Revolution' in Venezuela in Twitter," TeleSURtv.net, October 16, 2009, www.telesurtv.net/noticias/opinion/1385/goicochea-y-clinton-planifican-la-revolucion-twitter-en-venezuela/.

86. Ibid.

87. Xeni Jardin, "Venezuela: Chavez Equates Twitter with Terrorism," *Boing Boing*, February 4, 2010, www.boingboing.net/2010/02/04/venezuela-chavez-equ .html?utm_source=feedburner&utm_medium=feed&utm_campaign=Feed%3A +boingboing%2FiBag+%28Boing+Boing%29; Mariana Gonzalez Insua, "Hugo Chávez: Taking the Battle to the Internet," www.MountainRunner.us, April 30, 2010, http://mountainrunner.us/2010/04/chavez.html?utm_source=feedburner&utm _medium=feed&utm_campaign=Feed%3A+Mountainrunner+%28Mountain Runner%29.

88. Christopher Toothaker, "Venezuela to Outlaw Violent Video Games, Toys," MSNBC.com, October 4, 2009, www.msnbc.msn.com/id/33165079/ns/technology_and_science-games/wid/7468326/6.a10984/6.a10984/6.b10984/5??cm =WaterCooler-SC.

89. Luke Plunkett, "Venezuelan President Says Games Are 'Poison,'" *Kotaku*, January 18, 2010, http://kotaku.com/5450754/venezuelan-president-says-games-are-poison?utm _source=feedburner&utm_medium=feed&utm_campaign=Feed%3A+kotaku %2Ffull+%28Kotaku%29.

90. Frank Jack Daniel and Eyanir Chinea, "Venezuela's Chavez Calls for Internet Controls," *Reuters*, March 13, 2010, www.reuters.com/article/2010/03/14/us-venezuela-chavez-idUSTRE62D05I20100314.

91. Kim Andrew Elliott. "Venezuela's Radio del Sur Signs on, Claims Affiliates in 18 Countries." kimelli.nfshost.com/index.php?id=7437.

92. "In Chavez's Venezuela, the Revolution Will Be Blogged," *AFP*, March 23, 2010, www.google.com/hostednews/afp/article/ALeqM5hOYZWPVlVlUZ dOZgEOxccVw41Fow.

93. Kiraz Janicke, "Venezuela's Chavez Launches Interactive Blog," venezuela-nalysis.com, May 25, 2010, http://venezuelanalysis.com/news/5386.

94. "Hugo Chavez: The Blogging President I," PinoyGigs.com, March 24, 2010, www.pinoygigs.com/blog/technology/hugo-chavez-the-blogging-president/.

95. "Chávez Ahora Tiene una 'Guerrilla contra la Mentira,'" Lanacion.com, April 13, 2010, www.lanacion.com.ar/1253623; Marianne Diaz, "President Chávez and His 'Communicational Guerrilla,'" *Global Voices Advocacy*, April 16, 2010, http://advocacy.globalvoicesonline.org/2010/04/16/president-chavez-and-his-communicational-guerrilla/.

96. "Chávez Ahora Tiene una 'Guerrilla contra la Mentira.'"

97. Tamara Pearson, "Venezuela's Chavez Takes the Media War to Twitter," venezuelanalysis.com, April 28, 2010, http://venezuelanalysis.com/news/5315.

98. "Venezuela Passes Media, Internet-Muzzling Law," *AF:*, December 20, 2010, www.google.com/hostednews/afp/article/ALeqM5hX8P0LZnd4XSj92ygla5HV0raX WA?docId=CNG.5e300c93ec9b464f061edc2145035df7.2a1).

99. Ibid.

100. "Telusur Promotional Brochure."

101. Eva Golinger, "Wikileaks in Venezuela: Espionage, Propaganda and Disinformation," ZCommunications, December 10, 2010, www.zcommunications.org/wikileaks-in-venezuela-espionage-propaganda-and-disinformation-by-eva-golinger.

102. Jim Mcilroy and Coral Wynter, "Telesur: 'Another Television Is Possible'," venezuelanalysis.com, February 15, 2006, http://venezuelanalysis.com/analysis/1618.

103. Boyd-Barrett and Boyd-Barrett, "Latin American 24/7 News Battle for Honduras."

104. Cañizález and Lugo, "Telesur: Estrategia Geopolítica con Fines Integracionistas."

105. Coronel, "Corruption, Mismanagement, and Abuse of Power in Hugo Chávez's Venezuela I Gustavo Coronel I Cato Institute: Development Policy Analysis."

106. Shawn Powers, "The Geopolitics of the News: The Case of the Al-Jazeera Network" (Unpublished dissertation, Los Angeles: University of Southern California, Annenberg School for Communication and Journalism, 2009).

107. Painter, *Counter-Hegemonic News: A Case Study of Al-Jazeera English and Telesur.*

108. "Argentina Gives Hugo Chavez Press Freedom Award," *BBC News*, March 29, 2011, www.bbc.co.uk/news/world-latin-america-12902155.

109. Ibid.

110. James Petras, "Venezuela: Democracy, Socialism and Imperialism," venezuelanalysis.com, April 18, 2008, http://venezuelanalysis.com/analysis/3367.

REFERENCES

"Aporrea: Desde el Próximo Miércoles Telesur Abrirá Su Señal a Todo Ecuador." *Aporrea*, April 10, 2009. www.aporrea.org/medios/n143359.html.

"Argentina Gives Hugo Chavez Press Freedom Award." *BBC News*, March 29, 2011. www.bbc.co.uk/news/world-latin-america-12902155.

Bachman, Ingrid. "Chávez Issues New Warning to Opposition Channel Globovisión." *Knight Center for Journalism in the Americas*, July 5, 2010. http://knightcenter .utexas.edu/blog/chavez-issues-new-warning-opposition-channel-globovision.

———. "Venezuelan President Denounces International Media Campaign against His Administration." *Knight Center for Journalism in the Americas*, August 31, 2010. http://knightcenter.utexas.edu/blog/venezuelan-president-denounces-international -media-campaign-against-his-administration.

Bially Mattern, Janice. "Why 'Soft Power' Isn't So Soft: Representational Force and the Sociolinguistic Construction of Attraction in World Politics." *Millennium— Journal of International Studies* 33, no. 3 (June 2005):583–612.

Bisbal, Marcelino. "Telesur:¿Concreción de un Proyectocomunicacional-Político Regional?" *Comunicación* (2009):66–75.

Boyd-Barrett, Claudia, and Oliver Boyd-Barrett. "Latin American 24/7 News Battle for Honduras." *Global Media Journal* 9, no. 16 (2010):64.

Burch, Sally. "Telesur and the New Agenda for Latin American Integration." *Global Media and Communication* 3, no. 2 (August 2007):227–232.

Bustamante, Michael J., and Julia E. Sweig. "Buena Vista Solidarity and the Axis of Aid: Cuban and Venezuelan Public Diplomacy." *Annals of the American Academy of Political and Social Science* 616 (March 2008):223–256.

Cañizález, Andrés, and Jairo Lugo. "Telesur: Estrategia Geopolítica con Fines Inte-gracionistas." *CONFines* (2007):53–64.

"Chávez Ahora Tiene una 'Guerrilla contra La Mentira.'" lanacion.com, April 13, 2010. www.lanacion.com.ar/1253623,.

Colitt, Raymond, and Ana Isabel Martinez. "Venezuela Begins Shutdown of 34 Radio Stations." *Reuters*, August 1, 2009. www.reuters.com/article/2009/08/01/ venezuela-media-idUSN0146551720090801.

Conway, Christopher B. *The Cult of Bolívar in Latin American Literature*. University Press of Florida, 2003.

Coronel, Gustavo. "Corruption, Mismanagement, and Abuse of Power in Hugo Chávez's Venezuela | Gustavo Coronel | Cato Institute: Development Policy Analysis." *Cato Institute: Development Policy Analysis*, November 27, 2006. www.cato .org/pub_display.php?pub_id=6787.

Corrales, Javier. "Using Social Power to Balance Soft Power: Venezuela's Foreign Policy." *The Washington Quarterly* 32, no. 4 (October 2009):97–114.

Daniel, Frank Jack, and Eyanir Chinea. "Venezuela's Chavez Calls for Internet Controls." *Reuters*, March 13, 2010. www.reuters.com/article/2010/03/14/us-venezuela-chavez-idUSTRE62D05I20100314.

Davila, Carlos. "Enfrentar la Guerra Mediática Internacional, a Través de un Plan Estra-tégico de Comunicación." *Aporrea*, June 14, 2008. www.aporrea.org/medios/a58833 .html.

"Democracy vs. Mediacracy." TeleSURtv.net, 2009. www.telesurtv.net/noticias/ entrev-reportajes/listado.php?class=Reportaje.

Diaz, Marianne. "President Chávez and His 'Communicational Guerrilla.'" *Global Voices Advocacy*, April 16, 2010. http://advocacy.globalvoicesonline. org/2010/04/16/president-chavez-and-his-communicational-guerrilla/.

Dodson, Michael, and Manochehr Dorraj. "Populism and Foreign Policy in Venezuela and Iran." *Whitehead Journal of Diplomacy and International Relations* 9 (2008):71.

Domínguez, Fernando Buen Abad. "Aporrea: Algunos Aportes de TeleSur en Su Cumpleaños." Apporrea.org, n.d. www.aporrea.org/medios/a104708.html.

Duffy, Robert, and Robert Everton. "Media, Democracy, and the State in Venezuela's Bolivaran Revolution." In *Global Communications: Toward a Transcultural Political Economy*, eds. Paula Chakravartty and Yuezhi Zhao. Lanham, MD: Rowman & Littlefield, 2008.

Elliott, Kim Andrew. "Head of Venezuelan International Broadcaster Turns His Attention to Venezuelan Domestic Broadcasting." *Kim Andrew Elliott reporting on International Broadcasting*, April 26, 2009. http://kimelli.nfshost.com/index. php?id=6399.

——. "Maybe It Should Be Called 'Chávez Siempre Que Él Quiera.'" *Kim Andrew Elliott reporting on International Broadcasting*, February 10, 2010. http://kimelli .nfshost.com/index.php?id=8319.

——. "Venezuelan Ambassador to Nigeria Suggests an Al Jazeera–Like, Telesur-Like Channel for West Africa." *Kim Andrew Elliott reporting on International Broadcasting*, March 20, 2011. http://kimelli.nfshost.com/index.php?id=10924.

——. "Zimbabwe Official: Africa Has 'Much to Learn' from Latin American Telesur Agreement." *Kim Andrew Elliott reporting on International Broadcasting*, November 19, 2009. http://kimelli.nfshost.com/index.php?id=7792.

Featherstone, Liza. "Chávez's Citizen Diplomacy." *The Nation*, December 17, 2006. www.thenation.com/article/ch%C3%A1vezs-citizen-diplomacy.

Forero, Juan. "Venezuela's New Campaign." *New York Times*, September 30, 2004, sec. Business / Media & Advertising. www.nytimes.com/2004/09/30/business/media/30adco.html.

Gentilli, Davi, and Vitor Rocha. "Telesur: Televisão e Comunidade Imaginada Latino-Americana." *Revista Extraprensa* 1, no. 1(4) (December 3, 2010). www.usp .br/celacc/ojs/index.php/extraprensa/article/viewArticle/s-ses2–4.

Gibens, Guillermo. "The Mass Media in Venezuela: History, Politics, Freedom." In *The Handbook of Spanish Language Media*, ed. Alan B. Albarran, 77–87. Taylor & Francis, 2009.

Golinger, Eva. "Announcing Venezuela's First and Only English Language Newspaper, Correo del Orinoco International." venezuelanalysis.com, January 22, 2010. http://venezuelanalysis.com/news/5093.

——. "Goicochea and Clinton Plan 'Revolution' in Venezuela in Twitter." TeleSURtv. net, October 16, 2009. www.telesurtv.net/noticias/opinion/1385/goicochea-y -clinton-planifican-la-revolucion-twitter-en-venezuela.

——. "Wikileaks in Venezuela: Espionage, Propaganda and Disinformation." *ZCommunications*, December 10, 2010. www.zcommunications.org/wikileaks-in -venezuela-espionage-propaganda-and-disinformation-by-eva-golinger.

Gott, Richard. *In the Shadow of the Liberator: Hugo Chávez and the Transformation of Venezuela*. Verso, 2000.

Gould, Jens Erik. "Latin Governments Launching a Competitor for CNN." *Cox News Service*, June 23, 2005, sec. Financial Pages. www.lexisnexis.com.proxyau.wrlc. org/hottopics/lnacademic.

Hirst, Joel. "The Bolivarian Alliance and the Hugo Chavez Propaganda Machine." *Latin American Herald Tribune*, 2010. www.laht.com/article.asp?ArticleId=3753 38&CategoryId=13303.

"Hugo Chavez: The Blogging President I." PinoyGigs.com, March 24, 2010. www .pinoygigs.com/blog/technology/hugo-chavez-the-blogging-president.

"In Chavez's Venezuela, the Revolution Will Be Blogged." *AFP*, March 23, 2010. www.google.com/hostednews/afp/article/ALeqM5hOYZWPVlV1UZdOZgEOxcc Vw41Fow.

Insua, Mariana Gonzalez. "Hugo Chávez: Taking the Battle to the Internet." www. MountainRunner.us, April 30, 2010. http://mountainrunner.us/2010/04/chavez .html?utm_source=feedburner&utm_medium=feed&utm_campaign=Feed%3A +Mountainrunner+%28MountainRunner%29.

Janicke, Kiraz. "Venezuela's Chavez Launches Interactive Blog." venezuelanalysis .com, May 25, 2010. http://venezuelanalysis.com/news/5386.

Jardin, Xeni. "Venezuela: Chavez Equates Twitter with Terrorism." *Boing Boing*, February 4, 2010. www.boingboing.net/2010/02/04/venezuela-chavez-equ .html?utm_source=feedburner&utm_medium=feed&utm_campaign=Feed%3A+ boingboing%2FiBag+%28Boing+Boing%29.

Katada, Saori. *Toward a Mature Aid Donor: Fifty Years of Japanese ODA and the Challenges Ahead*. Asia Program Special Report. Woodrow Wilson International Center, February 2005.

Kozloff, Nikolas. "Telesur's Program Aram Aharonian with Nikolas Kozloff." *The Brooklyn Rail*, April 2007. www.brooklynrail.org/2007/4/express/telesurs-program.

Massey, Doreen. "Concepts of Space and Power in Theory and in Political Practice." *Documents d'anàlisi geogràfica* 55, 15–26 January 1, 2009. www .raco.cat/index.php/DocumentsAnalisi/article/viewArticle/171747/0.

Mcilroy, Jim, and Coral Wynter. "Telesur: 'Another Television is Possible.'" venezuelanalysis.com, February 15, 2006. http://venezuelanalysis.com/analysis/1618.

Medel, Monica. "Study: Government Supporters Responsible for One in Four Attacks on the Press in Venezuela." *Knight Center for Journalism in the Americas*, April 29, 2011. http://knightcenter.utexas.edu/blog/study-government-supporters -responsible-one-four-attacks-press-venezuela.

VOA News. "Head of Venezuela's Globovision Considering Asylum in U.S.." *Voice of America*, n.d. www.voanews.com/english/news/americas/Head-of-Venezualas -Globovision-Considering-Asylum-in-US-98558144.html.

Noya, Javier. *New Propaganda: The Public Diplomacy of the Authoritarian Regimes in China and Venezuela*. Madrid: Real Institute Elcano, January 15, 2008.

Painter, James. *Counter-Hegemonic News: A Case Study of Al-Jazeera English and Telesur*. RISJ Challenges. Oxford, 2006.

———. *The Boom in Counter-Hegemonic News Channels: A Case Study of Telesur*. Oxford: Reuters Institute for the Study of Journalism at Oxford, 2007.

Pearson, Natalie Obiko. "Venezuela's Chávez-Backed TV Station Eyes U.S. Markets." *Associated Press*, July 27, 2006.

Pearson, Tamara. "Venezuela's Chavez Takes the Media War to Twitter." venezuel analysis.com, April 28, 2010. http://venezuelanalysis.com/news/5315.

Petras, James. "Venezuela: Democracy, Socialism and Imperialism." venezuel analysis.com, April 18, 2008. http://venezuelanalysis.com/analysis/3367.

Petrich, Blanche. "Telesur: A Counter-Hegemonic Project to Compete with CNN and Univisión." *Agencia Latinoamericana de Información y Análisis-Dos (ALIA2)* (March 2, 2005). www.alia2.net/article4055.html.

Plunkett, Luke. "Venezuelan President Says Games Are 'Poison.'" *Kotaku*, January 18, 2010. http://kotaku.com/5450754/venezuelan-president-says-games-are-poison?utm_source=feedburner&utm_medium=feed&utm_campaign=Feed%3A+kotaku%2Ffull+%28Kotaku%29.

Powers, Shawn. "The Geopolitics of the News: The Case of the Al-Jazeera Network." Unpublished dissertation, Los Angeles: University of Southern California, Annenberg School for Communication and Journalism, 2009.

Pradas, Marisol. "Andrés Izarra: El Socialismo Necesita una Hegemonía Comunicacional." *Bolitin Digial Universitario*, 2007. www.boletin.uc.edu.ve/index.php?option=com_content&task=view&id=4990&Itemid=38.

Ramirez, Edgar. "Política Exterior de Chávez Se Aprecia en Proyecto Simón Bolívar." TeleSURtv.net, February 2, 2009. www.telesurtv.net/secciones/noticias/41926-NN/politica-exterior-de-chavez-se-aprecia-en-proyecto-simon-bolivar/.

Reardon, Juan. "U.S. Poor to Benefit from 6th Year of Subsidized Venezuelan Heating Oil." Venezuelanalysis.com, January 28, 2011. http://venezuelanalysis.com/news/5965.

Rosendorf, Neal. "Maestro Dudamel, Venezuelan Soft Power and Lessons for America." *USC Center for Public Diplomacy*, March 6, 2008. http://uscpublic-diplomacy.org/index.php/newsroom/pdblog_detail/maestro_dudamel_venezuelan_soft_power_and_lessons_for_america.

Sreeharsha, Vinod. "Telesur Tested by Chávez Video." *Christian Science Monitor*, November 22, 2005.

Suggett, James. "Presidents of Venezuela and African Union Discuss Upcoming Africa–South America Summit." Venezuelanalysis.com, June 10, 2009. http://venezuelanalysis.com/news/4509.

"TelesurTV," n.d. www.telesurtv.net.

"Telusur Promotional Brochure." Telesur, 2008.

Terauds, John. "Venezuela's Winning System for Saving Children through Music." venezuelanalysis.com, October 18, 2009. http://venezuelanalysis.com/analysis/4872.

Thussu, Daya. "Mapping Global Media Flow and Contra-Flow." In *Media on the Move: Global Flow and Contra-Flow*, 10–29. London; New York: Routledge, 2007.

Toothaker, Christopher. "Venezuela to Outlaw Violent Video Games, Toys." MSNBC.com, October 4, 2009. www.msnbc.msn.com/id/33165079/ns/technology_and_

science-games/wid/7468326/6.a10984/6.a10984/6.b10984/5??cm=WaterCooler -SC.

"Using Oil to Spread Revolution: Hugo Chávez Is Spending Some of His Country's Oil Windfall on Buying Support Abroad. How Much of a Return Is He Getting?" *The Economist*, June 28, 2005. www.economist.com/node/4232330.

venezuealaanalysis.com. "The Fundamentals of ALBA: Interview with Executive Secretary Amenothep Zambrano." Venezuelanalysis.com, February 11, 2011. http://venezuelanalysis.com/analysis/6025.

"Venezuela Passes Media, Internet-Muzzling Law." *AF:*, December 20, 2010. www .google.com/hostednews/afp/article/ALeqM5hX8P0LZnd4XSj92ygla5HV0raXW A?docId=CNG.5e300c93ec9b464f061edc2145035df7.2a1).

VenWorld. "Venezuela Elected to UN Economic and Social Council," *Venezuela World*, October 24, 2008. http://venworld.wordpress.com/2008/10/24/venezuela-elected-to-united-nations-economic-and-social-council.

Villarroel, Yetzy U. "La Política Exterior de Venezuela: Continuidad y Discontinuidad con el Pasado." *Cuestiones Políticas* 24, no. 41 (n.d.):169–190.

Chapter 5

China: Cultivating a Global Soft Power

The case of China offers the most explicit demonstration of the soft power concept in foreign policy discourse. It has been the subject of considerable debate among Chinese academics and policymakers, has been featured in journalistic coverage, and is increasingly central to foreign policy speeches and statements by government leadership.[1] Put simply, China has devoted significant resources and rhetoric to the concept of soft power, both to inform a strategic framework to guide China's rise as a global power and to justify policies, programs, and institutions of public diplomacy designed to amplify and cultivate China's influence.

As China analyst Shanthi Kalathil argues, China's ascendency is broadly recognized as aided by a sophisticated and comprehensive soft power strategy. China is, "expanding its soft power through strategically deploying cultural, media, and economic resources and amplifying these efforts in the global networked information space."[2] In this view, China's efforts to cultivate soft power reflect a strategic *awareness* that soft power resources and mechanisms are crucial to the larger effort of managing China's rise, addressing challenges, and leveraging a highly mediated and increasingly transparent environment for international politics. Yet analysis of what China's leaders and scholars argue about soft power, in the context of what China has done to manage its presence in international communication, suggests a more complicated history of adapting the notion of soft power to China's perceived strategic requirements and its linkages with the strategic importance of managing information flows.

What the soft power concept does provide the Chinese leadership is a convenient set of claims and prescriptions to address the Chinese government's desire to temper fears abroad of its growing material power, as well as to shape global opinion by highlighting cultural strengths. While it is true that Chinese accomplishments—its developmental strategy and its considerable structural investments in African countries—may function as a soft power resource, soft power (*ruanshili*) is also argued to justify sizeable intervention in international communication for the purpose of agenda-setting, persuasion, and attraction.

China has translated its emphasis on soft power into a multimodal approach to public diplomacy that leverages cultural and education-based assets like the Confucius Institutes, considerable investment in international broadcasting, and attention to the structure of information flows that inevitably frame foreign perceptions about China. And perhaps unique to China, the soft power concept has been appropriated to justify the authority of the state and, by extension, the Chinese Communist Party.[3] Overall, the case of China represents the most comprehensive utilization of resources to cultivate soft power by an international actor other than the United States.

The chapter begins with an exploration of China's embrace of soft power as a strategic compass for its steady rise to global preeminence. The chapter draws on statements and analysis of the significant level of public attention to soft power from academics and policymakers in China. The first section of this chapter deals directly with different strategic arguments that represent Chinese's turn toward a soft power strategy. Unlike the other cases addressed in this book, there is abundant evidence of Chinese public discussion of the soft power concept and the arguments that elaborate its strategic significance.

The chapter then turns toward the subject of public diplomacy, and how China has steadily grown its capacity to cultivate or amplify soft power through strategies of international communication and cross-cultural engagement. The section focuses on the institutional capacities that reveal strategic concerns about China's vulnerabilities to foreign media framing, its ability to project an undistorted vision of its image to foreign audiences, and to cultivate enduring respect and understanding of Chinese cultural institutions and history around the world. The chapter's focus on public diplomacy deals primarily with its cultural and media-centric interventions in international communication, as representative of the turn to soft power.

The focus here on international communication is not to suggest that other strategic activities and foreign policies are not significant aspects of China's investment in the soft power concept. As stated previously, the volume of Chinese foreign direct investment in Africa, especially the symbolic power of pervasive infrastructure projects and cultural outreach efforts, constitutes a substantial aspect of China's soft power strategy.[4] Chinese attention to Africa and the staging of global media spectacles like the 2008 Beijing Olympics and the 2010 World Expo in Shanghai can be argued as contributing to soft power outcomes.[5] The emphasis in this chapter, however, is on influence-oriented institutional commitments justified primarily under the terms of soft power—public and cultural diplomacy programs and international broadcasting efforts. The chapter concludes with an overview of the dominant themes present in the Chinese idealization of soft power and how Chinese public diplomacy programs reveal specific logics of "conversion"; how Chinese strategic arguments anticipate the conversion of soft power resources into outcomes in a highly mediated and interconnected global communication environment.

TOWARD A CHINESE SOFT POWER

Soft power represents a popular subject in the Chinese policymaker and academic community. Unlike its somewhat lukewarm treatment in American academia, Joseph Nye's notion of soft power is arguably a "major issue" in Chinese foreign policy discourse and media.[6] It also explicitly informs broader strategic frameworks as articulated in speeches by the Chinese leadership.[7]

The idea of soft power has antecedents in the history of Chinese thinking on international relations. The conception of international politics as a "harmonious community" rather than a competition goes back thousands of years.[8] Classical Chinese thinkers such as Confucius, Mencius, and Sun Tsu articulated means by which China could manage its relations with foreign powers in war and peace without recourse to war. More recently, Chinese analysts have compared soft power to Sun Tsu's praise for the ability to subdue an opponent without war (bu zhan er qu ren zhi bing).[9] Wang and Lu observe that some Chinese commentators have compared the idea of soft power to what Mencius called the "kingly way" (wang dao), rather then the "hegemon's way" (ba dao).[10]

This is not to suggest that China has abandoned so-called "hard" or "command" power options. As Qingquo Jia explains, the Chinese slogan "guojia zunyan shi da chulai de" (national respect can only be obtained through fighting) frames China's historical struggle to achieve sovereignty and economic gains.[11] He contends that a Chinese conception of power has come to include the "power to persuade other nations through attraction to one's policies, performance, identity, and culture."[12] While soft power may be a peripheral strategic concept in the United States, as Cho and Jeong observe, "Chinese leaders at the center [are] beginning to pursue the strengthening of China's soft power from a strategic point of view."[13]

Given that the soft power concept resonates with strategic thinking in Chinese history, it is not surprising that China has engaged in a significant public discussion about the necessity of soft power as a potential strategic framework to justify and guide China's growing prominence over other aspects of state power.[14] Well-publicized accounts in the West of China's "charm offensive" indicate that China seeks to *frame* its rise in global power and prestige through communication and symbolic acts. In the twenty-first century, Chinese strategic thought—expressed in both formal government statements and in academic circles—has emphasized the necessity of *explaining* and *communicating* China as a form of power.[15]

This imperative to communicate and to manage China's image involves promoting a Chinese voice to frame China's rise in power, as well as an ideological alternative to the universalizing ambitions of Western international relations and values.[16] Soft power has become a salient strategic term, deployed both to *promote* the image of China and to *react* to the perceived soft power of other countries like the United States.[17] To cultivate such power, much of the Chinese discourse on soft power claims that it derives from both the intrinsic value of its culture, the promotion of harmony without suppressing differences among nation-states and cultures and from the credibility of its development and foreign policies.[18]

Yet what soft power means in Nye's terms of resources and behaviors remains unsettled in internal Chinese treatments of soft power. Meaning, there is no obvious focal point from which Chinese thinkers and policymakers argue that soft power can and should be derived through specific policies and programs. For example, despite the tremendous growth of the Chinese economy, there is a marked reluctance to promote its own model of economic development—the so-called "Beijing Consensus"—as a centerpiece its soft power strategy, and there is evident uncertainty whether other aspects of its social, political, and cultural institutions can suffice as a form of soft power in comparison to its perceived soft power competitors.[19]

And despite China's commitment to soft power as a component of comprehensive national power, China's embrace of soft power very often appears self-limiting—like China's negative reaction to the Liu Xiaobo Nobel prize award, or the increasingly strict information control policies that limit free speech in China. As global information transparency forces other states to reconsider the role of publics in their foreign policy formulation, China continues to maintain a firm grip on internal communications and connections with global telecommunications.[20] China may have embraced soft power, but the concept is still irrevocably filtered through the perceived exigencies of an authoritarian state faced with the prospect of explaining itself to a discerning and informed global audience.[21]

An overview of China's soft power actions

The rise of China as a global power presents a variety of challenges that can be addressed through soft power mechanisms—to frame its intentions, establish legitimacy as a responsible state, and to influence the agenda of the international system that constrains its actions. Soft power, as an "analytical concept," provides China with a set of noncoercive mechanisms through which to translate resources into desired outcomes. Yet while the idea of soft power has been popularized, there is by no means a consensus that China has successfully sustained the potential of its soft power. Qingquo Jia argues:

> If Chinese are not satisfied with China's soft power resources, they are even less content with China's ability to utilize those resources; one often hears criticism of Chinese public relations efforts. Consequently, China has made increasing efforts to enhance its soft power utilization capabilities in recent years.[22]

According to the comprehensive 2009 report by Center for Strategic and International Studies on Chinese soft power, China has engaged in a variety of programs and policies that have contributed to its soft power. Roughly summarized, these include foreign aid and foreign direct investment, participation in peacekeeping and humanitarian missions, cultural exchange programs like the Confucius Institutes, reinvigorated diplomacy initiatives, and increased involvement in multilateral governance.[23]

Yet China has also dramatically increased its investment in its international communication capabilities, such as its international broadcasting outlets and its news services (e.g., China Radio International, CNC World, Xinhua). It has also made public diplomacy a significant foreign policy priority. Through staged events like the Beijing Olympics, the Shanghai World Expo, and the 2010 Guangzhou Asian games, China has crafted global spectacles to make itself "attractive to foreigners."[24] Such events are complemented by high-profile diplomatic outreach initiatives like the Boao Forum for Asia, which hosts events that bring together regional Asian government, corporate, and social stakeholders to facilitate discussion, insights, and the exchanges of ideas.

Chinese diplomatic discourse also feature new conceptual terms to frame its intentions in international relations. These concepts are presented in international fora to foster what Van Ham might call China's "social power" in international politics—the ability to effectively shape the normative and discursive boundaries that define "legitimate" international politics.[25] These conceptual terms include "new security concept," "democratization of international relations," "responsible power," and "harmonious world."[26]

Possibilities for a Chinese Soft Power

Public commentary among Chinese intellectuals and policymakers reflects a degree of consensus that China does possess soft power resources—in its cultural traditions, domestic governance structure, and its foreign policies.[27] And these concepts map onto Nye's own formulation of the primary sources of soft power. The major fault lines in Chinese thinking about soft power, however, appear to be on what is the most readily available resource: culture or political institutions.[28] Culture is the resource viewed by the Chinese leadership as the "core" of its soft power strategic thinking.[29]

The tremendous volume of Chinese reports, papers, and conferences on the subject over the past decade indicate that soft power is increasingly central to Chinese strategic formulations.[30] However, there is no consensus on the possibilities of converting resources into outcomes. For example, some analysts define soft power as intangible, nonquantifiable, nonmaterial, or spiritual power, while others emphasize it as a capacity to persuade others with reason and to convince others with moral principles (rather than simply a consequence of soft power assets being deployed effectively).[31] Such conceptual diversity suggests that while there is a general agreement that soft power is *important*, how it should translate into specific programs and strategic intention is far from obvious. Chinese conceptions of soft power alternatively emphasizes cultural, political, and economic routes toward global influence—all of which are either conceived in policy-related discourse as available to China, or are qualities possessed by its adversaries.

The strategic significance of soft power as a form of influence is further complicated by the ultimate *purpose* for the outcomes that soft power can generate. Bonnie Glaser and Melissa Murphy argue in the 2009 CSIS report that debate within China has focused on whether or not soft power serves the imperatives of sustaining particular foreign policy objectives, or that it should support the goals of development.[32] Cho and Jeong's analysis lead them to conclude, "[D]iscussions of soft power in China broadly fall under one of two categories—soft power theory as national development strategy and soft power theory as foreign policy."[33] Glaser and Murphy claim that the "debate" has largely been resolved to the extant that the "internal" and "external environments are inextricably linked."[34] Soft power can support China both directly and indirectly, by providing support for particular foreign policies or by creating an environment among foreign publics that make Chinese actions more acceptable.

Yet, as in the case of Japan, there is also a sense of urgency about *doing something* about soft power in China. According to Li Mingiang's analysis of soft power discourse, soft power is being elevated to a new level of importance because of a perception that China's soft power is weak relative to other Western powers.[35] That this urgency surrounding soft power is surfacing now may be an accident of history. Nye's theory arrived in Chinese strategic discussions at a time when it was seeking an alternative fate to the one that befell the Soviet Union after the Cold War. It was introduced at a time when strategic thinkers were seeking a framework to build and justify China's newly significant status as a global power.[36] Soft power's significance may very well be explained by its *convenience* as a strategic set of arguments that do not telegraph hostile intentions or propose potentially threatening "hard power" investments.

Soft power in the Chinese context is often articulated in terms of a *lack* as much as recognition of *potential*. Meaning, many soft power commentators suggest that Chinese soft power is wanting, and resources should be more actively cultivated.[37] As Qinqquo Jia states, "Chinese are not satisfied with China's soft power resources. In general, they share the view that China is still backward in many ways.[38] Arguments that follow from this perspective suggest that China's soft power would benefit from greater exposure—in particular from more favorable media coverage of Chinese culture, society, and politics. If foreign publics *knew* about China's cultural traditions and motivations, they would recognize China's credibility as an international actor, and China's soft power would grow.

What remains unarticulated is the translation of exposure to something resembling power. The 2006 Five-Year Plan for Cultural Development, including its "go global" strategy of cultural promotion, provides some sort of elaboration. As the plan indicates, China's soft power is not just based on *attraction*, but on "whether it possesses strong propaganda methods and strong propaganda capabilities . . . to form public opinion powers commensurate with China's international status."[39] In this logic, a great power must have the communicative capacity to actively shape public sentiment and not just possess cultural and ideation assets that may or may not be able to speak for themselves.

The sheer volume of Chinese discourse about soft power and its considerable investment in broadcasting and public relations conveys much about the relation of exposure and transmission in Chinese strategic communication, yet how particular actions or policies generate soft power remains somewhat underspecified. The most commonly articulated *benefit* of soft power in the case of China is increased agency, or, the ability to act internationally.[40] China's lack of soft power, most commonly reflected by foreign publics' knowledge of China's cultural and historical assets, can hamper China's ability to act on a global stage. As China scholar Ingrid d'Hooge claims:

> Chinese leaders realize that more understanding of Chinese culture and ideas are an absolute prerequisite for acceptance by the international community. They feel that the negative views are mainly the result of lack of knowledge or misunderstanding of Chinese values and of the difficulties confronting China.[41]

So how have Chinese leaders presented the notion of soft power in foreign policy discourse? And what do they expect from its accumulation and exercise? Li Mingiang's extensive discursive analysis suggests that soft power is perceived as a defensive strategy—an instrument to create a better image for China, to influence perceptions, and to defend China from Western culture and ideology.[42] Li notes the striking increase in reports, speeches, and even conferences convened on the topic of soft power, as well as the range of actors (from President Hu Jintao to lesser ministers, functionaries, and journalists) who describe the significance of soft power for China's evolving strategic priorities.[43] Soft power is not just significant, it is a *necessary* prerequisite for statecraft. But unlike other cases of soft power discussed in this book, this necessity is explicitly stated—it is not a hypothetical strategic alternative, but part of a larger understanding of power in the Chinese view of international relations. More importantly, soft power dovetails with the existing Chinese preoccupation with "comprehensive national power" (CNP), or *zonghe guoli*.[44]

Chinese soft power thinking reflects Nye's claims that it enables a kind of leverage and a capacity to effect political objectives, with the added dimension that soft power both is *derived from* and *contributes to* domestic stability and the strength of the state. At the level of specific programs and interventions, arguments for soft power are explicitly used to justify a burgeoning set of public diplomacy activities and research in China.[45]

Noncoercive Strategies of Chinese Soft Power

What kind of "power" does soft power give China? Contemporary discourse on soft power in China reflects what Joel Wuthnow calls three "noncoercive" strategies of soft power: the transmission of culture, the success of Chinese development and its assistance in developing countries, and the significance of China's acting responsibly given its rising prominence in global affairs.[46] Culture, as in the case of Japan, is arguably the most prominent subject of soft power discussion—and is broadly interpreted to include both the cultural heritage of China as well as the values and ideals that underpin the normative terrain of international relations. Culture often represents both the tangible legacy of Chinese cultural expression as well as a defining carrier of credibility and legitimacy in international relations.

Arguments about culture in Chinese discussion of soft power, in particular, illuminate international politics as a competitive field, where culture represents a key asset that potentially shapes relations between state actors, as much as assigning meaning to the importance of nonstate actors. As Xan Yutong argues, "During a period of globalization, the sphere of competition is no longer about land, resources, or markets but rule-making, setting regulations, norms, or customs."[47] In this view, international politics is a proving ground for soft power, marked by the capacity of culture to shape preferences, assign value to actions, and afford legitimacy to international actors. The Chinese promotion of its cultural legacy would in turn translate to a kind of social power to define the normative contours of international politics in its favor.

Chinese president Hu Jintao has framed the significance of culture within international relations on several occasions. In a January 2006 speech to the Chinese Communist Party's Foreign Affairs Leading Small Group [zhong-yang waishi gongzuo lingdao xiaozu] Hu stated, "The increase in our nation's international status and influence will have to be demonstrated in hard power such as the economy, science and technology, and defense, as well as in soft power such as culture."[48] Hu declares that soft power, via culture, is a crucial pillar of Chinese standing and capabilities. It is not a dispensable concept.

Hu's position on soft power was clarified in a high-profile and oft-cited speech to the 17th CPC Congress in October 2007, in which he argued that China should "enhance the country's cultural soft power [wenhua ruanshili]." Hu explains that "culture has increasingly become an important source of national cohesion and creativity and an important factor in the competition of overall national strength."[49] In this speech, Hu articulates a distinctly Chinese conception of soft power, where power emanates from *unity* and the distinction between the foreign and domestic faces of soft power begins to blur. Chinese soft power can derive from the responsible stewardship of a strong state, poised to demonstrate the virtues of Chinese culture as embodied in the state and its rising international preeminence.

Yet Hu also presents soft power as a kind of responsibility for great powers; soft power is demonstrated in the *conduct* of international affairs. Chinese scholar Zhang Tuosheng, drawing on Hu's call for increased soft power, argues that "China is playing an active part in international affairs with emphasis on gaining 'soft strength' and acting as a responsible big country as it should be."[50] In this sense, soft power is as much a manner of action as a capacity or asset.

The Culture Concept: From Asset to Strategy

As indicated previously, the discussion of culture in Chinese discourse about soft power manifests on various levels of abstraction, from the implication of Chinese culture for international relations to the significance of cultural products and ideas in a competitive vision of soft power. Culture is a soft power resource that aids in the competitive distinction of China.

For example, Wu Jianmin, the president of the China Foreign Affairs University and former Chinese ambassador to France, argues that China's cultural history demonstrates a compelling legacy of values to define international politics in opposition to the implicitly Western norms of competition and conflict:

China's greatest contribution to the world in the 21st century is not its manufacturing, but the Chinese culture. . . . As a matter of fact, Chinese civilization
never had a fight in history, there was not any religious war in Eastern Asia,
and the reason was what Confucius said more than two thousand years ago,
"harmony but not sameness." . . ."Harmony but not sameness" should be the
world's path in the 21st century.[51]

Chinese thinking on the relation of soft power to culture, while by no means
homogenous, is suggestive of culture as a tangible asset to be leveraged, as
well as a *measure* of state power in relation to other nation-states. In other
words: culture is a power as much as a resource for power. In 1993, Wang
Huning, now a member of the CCP Central Committee secretariat, declared
that "culture is the main source of a state's power." [52] Yet the significance
of culture carries two distinct implications across Chinese public discourse
about culture and soft power. It is both a necessary component of China's rise
as much as it is a defining aspect of international competition.

To illustrate the former, Hu Jintao stated in 2007 that "the great rejuvena-
tion of the Chinese nation will definitely be accompanied by the thriving of
Chinese culture."[53] China's rise is not simply a reflection of material gains,
but also derived from cultural strengths. If the ideas that drive Chinese success are found within culture, then culture can be a compelling resource for
influence abroad. Culture in this view carries a Chinese developmental ideology, blurring the lines between culture, political ideals, and policy legitimacy
found in Nye's conception of soft power resources. Yu Xintian, director
emeritus of the Shanghai Institute of International Studies, offers that "the
more fashionable the ideology, the more people will accept it and the greater
the possibility to build the country's soft power."[54] Culture is *demonstrative*
of greatness and *embodied* in political ideals.

The latter view, that culture is a currency of competition, underscores the
centrality of culture to the Chinese soft power concept as vital to foreign policy
strategy. Li Haijuan argues that "the competition of cultural power is the core
of soft power contention."[55] These arguments frame culture as a competitive
tool of statecraft, instrumental in shaping the context of international action. As
Li Shulei of the Central Party School claims: "[P]owerful foreign nations wish
to use culture as a weapon against other nations, and for this reason we must
work hard to raise our country's 'soft power.'"[56] Similarly, He Chuanqi, director of the China Center for Modernization Research under the CAS, claims that
"the ascent of China's cultural influence reflects clearly the rise of China's soft
power."[57] For He, culture stands in as a measure for soft power.

Wu Jianmin offers that soft power is a concept already dominated by the
West. He offers "cultural power" as a concept to better account for the conflation of culture with soft power and its potential for China:

Speaking of "soft power," I prefer the term "cultural power." The reason why China does not have strong soft power or the power of discourse is because of the contextual background. The Western civilization played the dominant role for last hundreds years, they did not have much understanding about Eastern civilization. But we have to understand that things are changing. Asia is rising, and the core of international affairs is shifting toward the East, the Asia Pacific region. The world is showing more interest in Eastern civilization, and Asia wants to introduce Eastern civilization to the world.[58]

But what does "culture" signify in terms of power in these arguments? Arguments for a Chinese form of *cultural power* range from the potential draw of historical artifacts for foreign audiences to the ability to transform values and normative behavior in international relations. Cultural power is very often presented enythematically—where the key premise that links the power of cultural expression to the ability of China to shape the international relations is not fully elaborated.

Culture power is, instead, often *inferred*. One of the most prominent figures in public argumentation about soft power and public diplomacy, Zhao Qizheng, explains culture is a crucial medium through which power can derive:

The way to learn about a nation is not from the skin colors, appearances, or wealth, but starts from the culture. The culture itself is abstract. It has to be expressed through languages, behaviors, and products, such as value of filial obligation, value of study, ways of thinking, ways of living, etc. Soft power is disseminated through carriers like media, cultural performance (for example, paintings, dramas, and novels).[59]

Zhao Qizheng is the former minister of China's State Council Information Office (SCIO) and in 2011 was the spokesman for the National Committee of the Chinese People's Political Consultative Conference (CPPCC). He is one of the most outspoken advocates for public diplomacy and strategic communication in China and has argued for a Chinese interpretation of soft power as part of its strategic thinking. Zhao's emphasis on culture reflects a common deference to the expected impact of China's cultural history.

Like Zhao, Wang Huning's writing on soft power in 1993 links power to the principle elements of Chinese culture, including historical texts and ideas related to Confucian, Taoist, and Buddhist thought. For Wang, these represent the Chinese conceptions of winning respect through virtue (yi de fu ren), benevolent governance (wang dao), peace and harmony (he), and harmony without suppressing differences (he er bu tong).[60]

A working definition of culture is often found in specific policy or program proposals. Premier Wen Jiabao argues that "[w]e should expand cultural exchanges with other countries. Cultural exchanges are a bridge connecting the hearts and minds of people . . . an important way to project a country's image." For Wen, it is necessary for China "to promote Chinese culture and its appeal overseas" through exposure to cultural *practices*.[61]

Culture as promotional vehicle is also presented in the form of objects, ideas, and history. Cai Wu, the head of the Chinese Ministry of Culture argues in 2010 that "China should step up efforts and apply to list its cultural relics as world cultural heritage. China boasts a very rich cultural heritage."[62] Cai Wu's statement suggests an *intrinsic* quality to the objects of culture that translate into power.

Li Changchun, member of the Chinese politburo and chief of public relations, draws a direction connection between cultural inventories and power— both domestically and abroad. Li argues, "[The] protection and promotion of cultural heritage is important to China's overall development, ethnic unity and social stability, and is much needed in enhancing China's soft power globally."[63] Cai Wu, likewise, calls for a comprehensive approach to cultural policy in order to boost the cultural influence of China:

> Facts have proven that China must adhere to diverse means to implement the 'going global' cultural strategy" . . . . The government should lead cultural exchanges; pay the same attention to the official and private sectors and mobilize non-governmental sectors to participate in cultural exchanges; and attach great importance to expanding the overseas cultural market and cultivate competitive national cultural brands. If China makes good achievements in these areas, and the third one in particular, the "going global" cultural strategy will play a considerable role in improving the influences and affinity of Chinese culture.[64]

Cai's recipe presents sites of culture that can be leveraged for influence, and suggests the particular role of the state as the key actor in coordinating the deployment of culture for influence. The strategic significance of culture is not simply the potential influence of China's heritage, but also the potential of its cultural industries. Along these lines, the Chinese Communist Party's program of *zuoqiang zuoda* ("Making media big and strong") was initiated in 2002 to create powerful media organizations that can compete globally.[65] As Li Changchung argues, Chinese cultural producers need to "go global" in order to "expand the export of cultural products and services and enhance the nation's 'soft power.'"[66] Li Changchung argues that culture is readily translatable into a power capacity that merits the active intervention of the state in promoting cultural exposure.

Hu Jintao made a similar case in a political report on the benefits of China's socialist culture in 2007, in order to "stimulate cultural innovation" to both boost cultural development and increase China's relative soft power. Hu emphasized the production and transmission of culture as crucial: "The only way to invigorate culture . . . is to promote innovation in its content and form, its structure and mechanism, and its means of dissemination . . ." Hu made the case for "vigorously develop[ing] the cultural industry" and "creat[ing] a thriving cultural market and enhanc[ing] the industry's international competitiveness." Hu's arguments for cultural investment appear justified as both a domestic cultural policy and an intervention in global cultural flows.[67] As analyst Shanthi Kalathi observed in 2010, the "go global strategy" resulted in significant increases in "culture-related exports" and Chinese sponsorship and involvement in international film festivals, according to China's State Administration of Radio, Film and TV.[68]

Culture and State Institutions

China's "go global" strategy appears to lay out a mandate for leveraging cultural output for soft power gain that bears some similarity to the Japanese and Korean emphasis on their contents industries.[69] Yet China's emphasis on translating cultural resources into overarching soft power gains relies on a broad spectrum of assets. To explain the "conversion" of culture resources and capacities to a soft power outcome, the Chinese leadership has pushed a variety of outreach mechanisms across communication platforms, cultural industries, and media systems. Culture is argued to contribute to "image." Yet the image of China is not by itself a resource of power, but rather something that requires cultivation through forms of cultural diplomacy as well as direction intervention into international media systems. Image is an *end*, not a means.[70] Culture therefore figures prominently as a pivotal dimension for a variety of public diplomacy programs.

Li Changhung has argued that *dissemination* is the key component of cultural soft power; China must compete in the space of international media flows: "Preventing giant foreign media agencies from monopolizing the right of voice, enabling foreign people to hear the voice of China and popularizing actual and outstanding Chinese culture[,] is of vital importance in enhancing China's soft power."[71] Cultivating Chinese soft power under this view is dependent on addressing the perceived imbalance of cultural flows through media products.

Yet while global media flows remains an significant target of Chinese public diplomacy interventions (like its considerable international broadcasting efforts), soft power remains a responsibility of the *state* and its institutions that ultimately convey soft power—it is not a quality independent of cultural assets in themselves. To cultivate soft power is to address the way in which

China's image is portrayed as much as to reform those institutions that are framed in media. As Yan Xueton claims, soft power stems from the inherent credibility of Chinese institutions.[72] In this argument, soft power is bound up in the ways in which speakers discuss the state itself—in addition to broad appeals to "culture."

This expansive interpretation of soft power grounds Chinese soft power strategy in both representation (public diplomacy) and institutional reform. What the state does with its structural advantages (i.e., domestic economic development) and international policies both reflects *and* generates 'soft power.'[73] This conception goes beyond Nye's notion of foreign policy legitimacy to suggest that legitimacy is conveyed by state strength. The state *as an institution of Chinese society* is a significant soft power resource.

Such logic was expressed at the 16th CPC Congress in 2002, when China's cultural system reform (CSR) was introduced. The 2009 CSIS analysis of Chinese soft power cites propaganda minister Liu Yunshan as making the case for culture and the state as strongly linked—the state conveys the influential value of Chinese culture. Liu claims, "[T]he strategic position of the building of culture in the documents of the Party's guiding principles" justified the "extreme importance of building culture."[74] He argues that culture is "becoming an important component in integrating national power and international competitiveness." Liu's assessment entails how the development of Chinese political and social culture can be a vital source for attraction: an implicit call for the strengthening of state institutions.

Chinese president Hu Jintao makes the case bluntly: culture is "an important source of national cohesion."[75] Cohesion, in this view, can effectively demonstrate soft power. As Ingrid d'Hooge observes, Chinese analysts also argue that governments require the support of the population in order to demonstrate soft power—so that a strong state is thus essential to soft power. She also notes, however, that it is therefore the state's responsibility to be responsive to its citizens, by emphasizing social justice and equality.[76] Cho and Jeong argue that a report introduced by Zhang Youwen and Huang Renwei in 2004 provides the basis to link the growth of national power to soft power through institution building, such as "revising the Constitution to protect private property, enhancing the ruling capacity of the CCP, and construction of the legal system."[77]

As Yu Keping argues, soft power in China is fundamentally conditioned by the domestic context, where national cohesion, education, and social morality are bound together as determinants of such power.[78] Following this reasoning, if soft power is fundamentally based on good institutions, then Chinese soft power blurs the line between domestic and foreign policy. As Men Honghua clarifies, "the construction of national image is not entirely a type of international behavior; a country's image in international society is even more an extension of its internal politics and affairs."[79] As Li Mingiang has argued, the wealth of discourse on soft power in China is as much about the necessity of *competing* with other nation-states as much as a justification for the consolidation of state power in China.[80] Arguments for soft power project the demands of the ruling party onto the calculus of China's strategic worldview.

The Limitations of Culture as Soft Power

The common emphasis on *culture* in Chinese discourse on soft power has lead some to consider it an altogether distinct form of Chinese power. Zhao Qizhen argues that "cultural power" and "soft power" should *not* be conflated, since they imply different dynamics of influence:

> "[C]ultural power" [. . .] is not completely equal to soft power, because soft power and hard power contain expansion, commanding position, and the sense of threat. Whereas cultural power is equal, no high and low. The problem is that, how do we express China's cultural power?[81]

Zhao's argument attempts to distinguish the concept of soft power as somehow marked, representative of a Western-derived international relations that China seeks to change. Yet while Zhao argues for an invigorated "cultural power"—others note that Chinese promotion of its cultural is inadequate compared to the output of the United States and requires innovation.

Innovation in cultural promotion may be required because China simply does not possess the brands and media products that would signify a strong cultural base for soft power. Yet other scholars question whether culture can be something deployable for Chinese strategic interests. Wuthnow cites Luo Jianbo of the Central Party School, who recognize the significant challenges facing a culture-based approach to soft power for China. Luo argues that many cultural attitudes are not easily susceptible to interventions; it may difficult to promote Confucian values where Islamic and Christian ideas predominate.[82] The entrenched presence of other cultural perspectives may diminish the prospects for soft power cultivation through culture-based strategies. Culture, as an inventory of expressive forms or a legacy of values and traditions, may not be so readily convertible a resource for international politics.

China's cultural presence abroad is also recognized as limited due to the dominance of Western culture and the China's cultural products abroad, leading some to argue for more rigorous cultural policies to deal with this disparity.[83] As Xie Xue-peng claims, cultural soft power is critical means to promote national image, which therefore requires China to improve its "international cultural communication."[84] Such arguments serve as principal justifications for programs like the Confucius Institutes and other cultural programs tasked with long-term relation building.[85] They also fuel concerns for increased investment in the cultural industries and in particular, global film promotion.[86]

For others, *direct* overtures to foreign audiences (like increased international broadcasting and public relations activity) can revitalize the potential of Chinese culture for the purposes of soft power. In other words, culture can function as a resource for soft power so long as it is helped along by specific programs and policies, such as public diplomacy. In this perspective, the "power" of culture is *augmented* by overcoming negative framing of Chinese political institutions by the West, building appreciation and knowledge of Chinese culture in foreign audiences, and building up international communication capacity to promote Chinese culture and to reach out to the Chinese diaspora.

The aforementioned critiques of Chinese culture as a resource for soft power do not suggest that culture is somehow *intrinsically* insufficient. Rather, the implications of the discourse seem to suggest that culture is in fact quite determinative of China's relative power—Chinese culture merely requires a more focused strategy of promotion. Hu Jintao's notion of "cultural soft power" discussed in his 2007 address illustrates this, in that he argues for a form of *cultural security*—where culture provides the freedom to self determine outside of foreign influence. Thus, China requires a kind of cultural policy to bolster its traditional resources, amplify their presence abroad, and work to cultivate soft power more generally. This view builds upon previously articulated policy toward culture in the National Planning Guidelines for Cultural Development in the Eleventh Five-Year Period and is used to justify renewed attention to cultural resources that bring together domestic and external justifications for soft power.

As Hu's 2007 address on Chinese soft power suggests, China is not without assets—rather, they are waiting to be translated for soft power purposes, to strengthen the perceived linkage between a strong "cohesive" state and soft power abroad. Cultural security in this sense implies a link between the development of domestic "institutions" and the promotion of China through enhanced modes of outreach. Li Changchung argues in 2008 on the creation of new international television broadcasters that China must "strengthen both domestic and international communication capability to promote China's influence in the international society, to promote China's cultural soft power, and to modernize the social constructions."[87] Culture, under this view, is the lynchpin of soft power.

Following Yan Xuetong's reasoning, however, political institutions may be *more* significant than culture. Zhu Feng highlights the importance of policies and choices in foreign policy as more important than culture in soft power.[88] The promotion of China's cultural assets and heritage to a broader foreign audience cannot in this view be a guarantor of China's soft power. Other resources and institutions may be better suited to amplify China's power—such as its tremendous economic growth.

The Chinese development model as soft power?

Any treatment of Chinese discussion of soft power would be incomplete without some reference to the symbolic value of China's development model. Joshua Cooper Ramo's notion of the "Beijing Consensus" provides an example of how China' development policies could be translated into tangible soft power effects.[89] The "Beijing Consensus" term represents a model for economic development embodied by China's successful growth into an economic superpower.

While some Western analysts highlight China's successful development that did not embrace Western norms of economic growth, it is far from certain that the *Chinese government* views its development model as a source of soft power.[90] Rather, Chinese politics scholar Shogo Suzuki notes Zhang Jianjing's claim: "[I]f there is a consensus in Beijing, then it is that China's reforms are by no means complete."[91] There is a noticeable reluctance in public statements about soft power in China to draw a direct linkage between China's economic power and soft power.[92] As Cho and Jeong claim, the Beijing Consensus isn't so much a rhetorical tool of Chinese soft power discourse as much as a "proxy measure to propagate China's official stance."[93] The Beijing Consensus may not have been a focal point for Chinese soft power because it offered nothing substantively "new" in terms of foreign policy, and was limited by the implication of a serious challenge to the West.

This does not mean that the Chinese development model cannot serve in some capacity as part of China's soft power, as Xiao Yong-Ming and Zhang Tian-Jie argue in their assessment of soft power strengths for China.[94] Chen Yugang notes the values embodied in the Chinese development model—coordinated "scientific development" that has minimal impact on the environment or society, social stability, and harmonious relations between individuals, society, the environment, and states—to suggest a coherent set of themes for developing countries, even if the conditions of Chinese development cannot be emulated in their entirety in the various contexts of the developing world.[95]

While China has not aggressively promoted the "Beijing Consensus" as part of its effort to cultivate soft power, its economic success and minimal conditions attached to its bilateral economic agreements arguably remain a soft power resource. China's domestic economic strategy and its policy of "win–win" agreements may provide leverage in the construction and direction of international political economy norms and negotiations. To use Li Mingiang's terms, the soft power of Chinese development may manifest in its *institutional* power to "propose new arrangements or international agreements. It may also work as a kind of *assimilating* power, by providing an example to demonstrate the attraction of China's cultural values, ideology and social system.[96] Li's notions of institutional and assimilating power, however, locate soft power as an *outcome*—a residual benefit of economic gains rather than an active approach to soft power cultivation, such as through aggressive public diplomacy.

This more modest tact toward the promotion of the development model is evidenced in Zhao Qizheng's disclaimer about Chinese developmental policy as a persuasive tool. He has stressed that China does not intend to export any "Chinese model." Rather than promote a model, Zhao Qizheng suggests that China represents a successful *case* with unique conditions.

> Case means a fact. But when you say model, it's more or less like a sample or example. Then others may think China is propagating, or competing with other country's models . . . How can other countries emulate the Chinese model directly without adapting it to its own national condition?[97]

Others are less sanguine about the potential for translating economic growth into soft power. Shen Xin, director of the Chinese People's Association for Friendship with Foreign Countries, argues that the "Chinese fast-growing economy and the advancement of overall power have provided Chinese public diplomacy a solid foundation. From the ardent discussion about 'Chinese Model' and 'Beijing Consensus,' the growing trend of Chinese soft power can be easily observed." The recognized significance of Chinese cultural and, increasingly, economic accomplishments are symbols waiting to be translated into effective aspects of soft power through programs such as public diplomacy.

Implications of the Soft Power Discourse

Looking across depictions and arguments for soft power, the clearest *justification* for the pursuit of soft power appears to be, as Wuthnow describes, the "ability to foster an external environment conducive to China's rise as an economic and military power."[98] Soft power is thus a fungible *means to multiple ends*.[99] It is both a marker of global status, indicative of cultural, political, and other institutional strengths, as it is a way to affect an idealized geopolitical landscape for China. Hu Jintao calls this landscape the "four environments"—a stable international and regional environment for China to operate within as well as a cooperative environment marked by an objective media climate toward China.[100]

Soft power in the Chinese context is pointedly an instrumental concept; a framework to enhance its options in the international sphere. As Foreign Minister Shen Guofang states, soft power must yield some benefits in the ability to claim authority in international politics and to achieve a "moral high ground."[101] Yet despite such ambitions of normative and policy agenda-setting, Chinese discussion of soft power is often tempered by its own often tentative and hedging language. Wuthnow identifies that Chinese soft power discourse is articulated in such a way as to diminish fears of an unpredictable rising power.

Therefore, it is not surprising to find the terms *harmonious* and *peaceful* as key descriptors in China's diplomatic language of passive and non-threatening terms.[102] This aspect of the discourse is suggestive of China's desire to portray itself as a responsible power. It reflects Li Mingiang's aforementioned *identifying* power—the ability to influence based on others recognizing your ability to lead.[103] Soft power is a marker of credibility and accomplishment.

Li argues that China "downplays or neglects the function of soft power to aggressively influence others."[104] Unlike U.S. international messaging tactics that elaborate how cultural values are universally shared, China's soft power strategy is less obviously concerned with the movement of foreign opinion toward a specific conclusion than with the construction of a favorable information environment.

Overall, Chinese soft power discourse highlights comparative advantages along with challenges; the strategic rhetoric depicts a moment of crisis. The international environment is a scene of *competition*, where Western powers hold asymmetric advantages over China that impede its cultivation of soft power. And since Chinese discourse about soft power is often articulated in conjunction with claims about material (hard) power capacities—it follows then that this logic would justify strengthening hard power resources as well. In this regard, arguments about soft power ultimately articulate the interests of the state.[105]

The scenic depiction of politics as competition extends into the conception of soft power itself. As Zhang Jianjing states:

> The competition among nation-states appears to be a rivalry of hard power, but behind such rivalry is the competition between institutions, civilizations, and strategies, which are essentially the rivalry of soft power.[106]

In 2006, the *People's Daily* declared, "We cannot be soft on soft power" with the scene of competition fundamentally about culture—not manufacturing prowess or developmental success:

> Just as experts have said, [despite China's being] a cultural fountainhead with more than 5,000 years of civilization, we only export television sets and don't export content to be televised. We have become an "assembly plant." Actually, culture is a key integral part of a country's overall national strength, what people have called "soft power," and it has become a point of competition between national powers.[107]

As a result, China is compelled to respond to the cultural hegemony that is perceived as cultivated by the United States and its asymmetric predominance in global cultural flows/industries. The salience of soft power for China, even when couched in terms that exhort harmonious cooperation, convey the perceived necessity of competing in the plane of ideas and culture. Given this depiction of international relations as competitive, coupled with the perception that the global media environment negatively frames news and information about China, suggests the pervasive, implicit argument that China's soft power imperative is ultimately *communicative*.

As Wuthnow explains, Chinese strategic discourse indicates that soft power derived from communication (symbolic or otherwise) is necessary because China must be able to convey the legitimacy and credibility given its ascendance on the global stage. To adequately contend with how China is framed, how it can demonstrate credibility as a global power, and to portray itself as a responsible regional partner—China needs to *convert* some of its success into soft power outcomes.[108] These demands are not confined to one form of soft power behavior (agenda-setting, persuasion, attraction)—but a variety of strategic communicative actions to allay fears, demand respect, and cultivate attraction. The timing of China's growing power makes the case for such active soft power cultivation increasingly expedient. Vice Foreign Minister Fu Ying makes the case plainly: "We have been doing well on the development front, and we are facing an even better new decade. Now we need to talk better, to make our messages clearer to the world. That can not only help form a better environment, but also boost the nation's confidence."[109]

The ability to communicate is thus crucial to connecting the resources of soft power to anticipated returns. Zhao Qizheng argues that *public diplomacy* is therefore necessary because China's soft power is insufficient—it must be amplified. He contends that there are not enough people speaking Mandarin, and that there aren't enough visitors to China in order to cultivate a broader global understanding. But Zhao also suggests that China does not possess enough "hard" communicative power—in the form of media broadcasters like CNN or services like the Associated Press. For Zhao, there remains ideological differences with other major powers that may impact China's future leadership role, implying that more efforts to clarify and explain China's position against perceived misrepresentation is necessary.[110]

As Zhao would later explain as justification for public diplomacy, "China cannot always be the gentleman who works more but talks less in the present world flooded with information." China must instead strive for "national rhetorical competence" in the form of a robust public diplomacy.[111]

CHINESE PUBLIC DIPLOMACY

Given the considerable attention to soft power in Chinese foreign policy and strategic discourse, it is not surprising that public diplomacy is an increasingly significant aspect of China's foreign relations. The highly publicized accounts of a Chinese public diplomacy "charm offensive" including the immense global spectacles of the 2008 Olympic games in Beijing, the 2010 World Expo, as well as the Confucius Institutes established around the world—represent the continuation of a longer tradition of what could ostensibly be called a Chinese "public diplomacy" strategy of image management and strategic communication.[112] China's public diplomacy efforts comprise a sweeping array of cultural and mediacentric initiatives; a multifront concern for *image cultivation, information sovereignty*, and, increasingly, *network authoritarianism* to cultivate power for the Chinese state.[113] Chinese public diplomacy reflects both a marked preoccupation with soft power as much as particular attitudes toward the expected efficacy of persuasive strategic communication.

Zhang Zhexin argues that China's "international cultural communications" and "international information communication" programs are more significant for China's public diplomacy in both "scale and effect" than China's foreign assistance and involvement in peace-keeping operations.[114] According to Zhang, public diplomacy has become one of the "topmost concerns of central leaders since the beginning of New China history" (sic).[115] Chinese public diplomacy has also evolved in response to a changing international communication environment and the growing perception that its soft power is tied to communication flows that condition its image. This transformation is marked by a change in communication strategies, both in terms of message framing and in the reliance on different kinds of communication outlets.

China provides an important and instructive case for the consideration of a comprehensive, multimodal public diplomacy strategy. It has announced its intentions to improve its image, advertise its success, and correct or counter representation in Western media outlets. China's state-run media strategy (both domestic and international) is also represented in official discourse as embedded within a competitive global message environment, which is reflected in its strict domestic controls on media content and ownership. Overall, China's public diplomacy strategy as described here represents a synthesis of domestic and international communication strategy, defined by message management, advocacy, and the ability to leverage global and domestic communication infrastructure.

China's public diplomacy tactics are both justified and constrained by prevalent assumptions in Chinese formulations of soft power. Zheng argues that China's attention to communication strategy and public diplomacy differs from the United States' in that China's public diplomacy is not a "global strategy" of persuasion as much as a means to achieve development ends.[116] As such China's public diplomacy is not *necessarily* a competition with the United States, but an instrument to carve out credibility for its broader foreign policy objectives.

Zheng's characterization of Chinese public diplomacy is not entirely representative of both its history and indeed, the diversity of conceptions of soft power among Chinese leaders and experts. Zheng's arguments do, however, reflect how China has changed its tactics of strategic representation (both diplomatically and through other communicative outlets).

For example, China embraced Zheng Bijian's notion of *heping jueqi* (peaceful rise) earlier in the 2000s, to characterize its growing power earlier, only to abandon the rhetoric in favor of the less assertive term "peaceful development," after concerns from policymakers and academic community.[117] China's public diplomacy over the past decade suggests the steady adaptation of a domestically-inspired framework of strategic communication to an invitational public diplomacy mandate. As Cho and Jeong describe, the "peaceful rise theory symbolically declares that China's global strategy has transformed from internal to external orientation rise."[118] Defining its diplomatic message as *development* instead of *rise* defuses the potential that China is actively promoting as shift in the global balance of power.

Chinese Public Diplomacy in Transition Away from Domestic Focus

How China has developed its public diplomacy capacity to cultivate themes and messages about its relative "rise" in power represents the growing institutionalization of public diplomacy. According to Yiweih Wang, *public diplomacy* historically is a term that has no direct translation in Chinese (though one could argue the term suffers from definitional problems in the United States). It is often referred to as *dui wai xuan chuan* or *wai xuan*, or external propaganda and image promotion, though it is also termed *minjian waijiao*, or people-to-people diplomacy.[119] And there are yet other translations of the term, which further underscores a lack of definitional clarity. Yet China has moved to a definition of public diplomacy that is not significantly different from how it is defined in the West. Kejin Zhao identifies public diplomacy as "the process by which direct exchanges and communications with people in a country are conducted to advance the image and extend the values of those being represented."[120] Zhao Qizheng describes the *scope* of public diplomacy and its role among the other institutions of Chinese foreign policy:

> Public diplomacy occurs between nations and aims to explain a foreign country's conditions and policies. It generally takes the form of cultural dissemination. It plays a significant role and supports government diplomacy. The main players in public diplomacy include various government departments, but also non-government organizations, such as civil societies, universities, research institutions, media, religious organizations and specific persons of standing. These parties and individuals are able to get involved in international exchanges and explain a nation's conditions and foreign polices from a different perspectives to foreign NGOs, the general public and even government institutions. It plays a wider role than the more familiar civil diplomacy.[121]

Zhao Qizheng's definition establishes the scene and the actors relevant to the over-arching objectives for Chinese public diplomacy. These are, broadly speaking, the communication of (1) understanding of the Chinese political system, (2) depiction of China as a "developing country" (to reduce expectations for political reform), (3) the elaboration of Chinese policies (through whitepapers, magazines, and scholarly exchanges), and (4) cultivating an image of China as a stably, trustworthy, and responsible nation-state.[122] These objectives also mirror the discourse surrounding soft power in the Chinese context.

China's public diplomacy history has its origins in the practice of "foreign propaganda" that aimed to "glorify China."[123] In the 1950s, strategic information activities were coordinated through committees established by the CPC Central Committee and included a variety of offices and departments across China's foreign policy and domestic communication bureaus, as well as news outlets such as the *People's Daily*, Xinhua, and the Central People's Broadcasting system. As Zhang Zehxin explains, this early phase of Chinese public diplomacy was dominated by concerns over information propagation, rather than more long-term programs such as educational and cultural exchange. The consequence of this emphasis, according to Zhang, is that most of the news about China during much of the twentieth century pertained to its political development, rather than its "economic, social, and cultural aspects."[124]

More recent history of Chinese public diplomacy can be traced through a series of pivotal decisions by government and Chinese Communist Party (CCP) officials that clarified an integrated strategic communication strategy. In the aftermath of the 1989 Tiananmen Square uprising, the CCP formed the Overseas Propaganda Department under the Party Central Committee (which was renamed the External Publicity Department in 1998) and oversaw the formation of the State Council Foreign Propaganda Office in 1991.[125] This period was a turning point for Chinese public diplomacy. Instead of "glorifying China," these new institutions were charged with "publicizing China in an authentic, colorful, lively, and timely way" to effectively deal with growing fears of China's rise in power in the 1990s.[126]

In 1998, Zhao Qizheng assumed the role of minister of the Information Office of the State Council, and announced a series of new directives for Chinese propaganda work—including that foreign audiences required different kinds of propaganda and that important foreign audiences must be identified. Not surprisingly, the Chinese diaspora (with over 2.5 million living in the United States alone) was identified as significant to Chinese public diplomacy efforts. Pro-Chinese associations and organizations were also identified as potent recruits for a united network of advocacy.

In addition to a concern for audiences, Zhao's reforms highlighted the foreign media. For Zhao, the Chinese government should manage how China is perceived by through outreach to the foreign media and countering negative representation. This would be accomplished by leveraging international media, using press releases, and engaging in more direct outreach by officials on state visits. In 2000, the Chinese minister of foreign affairs announced the formation of a media center to deal with the foreign press, an institutional effort in parallel to the Information and Foreign Publicity office.

The concern for media during this period necessitated more knowledge about media effects on audiences. Audiences, both foreign and domestic, were crucial for promoting China's development. At the National Conference on Foreign Propaganda in 2001, Zhao Qizheng announced a new direction for Chinese public diplomacy—with an emphasis not only on providing information to foreign audiences, but also on a concerted effort to *understand* audiences. The emphasis on awareness of Chinese economic development, growth, and achievements was argued as part of the strategy of general development. Public diplomacy, in other words, was linked to the strategic ambitions of national development.[127]

According to Chinese affairs scholar Rumi Aoyami, the subsequent directives issued by the Chinese government amounted to calls for a series of techniques related to the task of publicity:

> (1) boosting external publicity through the Internet; (2) expanding external cultural exchanges by unifying exchanges and external publicity; (3) making the external cultural industry more competitive and influential, thereby making cultural publicity more attractive; (4) adopting a more positive attitude toward foreign media and reporters; (5) strengthening external publicity activities by studying the market mechanism for external publicity items, and promoting moves abroad by Chinese media; and (6) making concentrated efforts to publicize important issues on a priority basis.[128]

While China has since embraced the notion that Chinese officials and statesman can and should engage the foreign press to "explain China" and its position on controversial issues, China's use of the media as a vehicle for advocacy and information sovereignty remain a central facet of its public diplomacy strategy.[129]

Chinese discourse about public diplomacy reflects much of the soft power discourse preoccupation with representation and the consequences of foreign media framing. Zhao Qizheng explains in 2004 the imperatives behind this focus on global media and representation:

> More than 80 percent of international news is now supplied by news agencies of advanced countries. It is indispensable for China to explain itself to counter the image shaped by these media of advanced countries. It is especially important for us to give high priority to offering explanations to the international community about matters such as the human rights issue, the Tibetan and Taiwanese questions, the issue of religion, the Falun Gong cult question, and the theory of a "China threat."[130]

In March of 2004, a Division of Public Diplomacy was established as part of the Information Department of the Ministry of Foreign Affairs, which coincided with a high-profile academic seminar on public diplomacy. While this conference highlighted the importance of public diplomacy to the Chinese community of foreign policy scholars, the claims made apparent the linkages between internal and external propagandistic communication. During the seminar, Foreign Minister Li Zhaoxing stated: "We have actively conducted public diplomacy by publicizing China's foreign policies and activities to the

Chinese public, thus winning their understanding and support."[131] The conflation of public diplomacy with domestic communication strategies illustrates perceived significance of information management across domestic and foreign boundaries, and also suggests a concern over China's vulnerability to foreign public diplomacy and media flows. In this view, the *audience* of public diplomacy represents both foreign and domestic auditors. Yet this also suggests the potential agency of publics as significant actors in the service of Chinese diplomacy.

At the time of the Shanghai Expo in 2010, Zhao Qizheng explains why *publics* are significant:

> Public diplomacy is an integral part of a nation's overall diplomacy. People meeting people of different nationalities and cultures exchange something very personal. Prejudices and misunderstandings melt away. In essence, public diplomacy is an exchange of information and opinions. In today's world, the development of any country is not only determined by its national conditions but also by global circumstances.[132]

Zhao's efforts to subsequently explain China's increased investment in public diplomacy acknowledges the evolution of China's attitude toward communicating to foreign publics through public diplomacy. "In most cases, we are doing the propaganda thing, instead of cross-cultural communication . . . . And the result is, unfortunately, low credibility."[133]

During the meeting of the CPPCC in 2011, Zhao signaled that China's public diplomacy was moving away from a propagandistic model of communication:

> [S]ome big countries taking very aggressive and hegemonic postures to disseminate their ideologies throughout the world and even to interfere in the internal affairs of other countries . . . Instead, China tries to explain to the world its cultural traditions, social development, and internal and external policies, and to answer foreigners' questions about the country.[134]

Zhao articulates here a path toward a Chinese public diplomacy strategy— that appears to abandon the goal of simply amplifying Chinese soft power resources. It is a pointedly modest communication position—that shares the criticism of overtly projecting public diplomacy practices that Japanese public diplomat Seichi Kondo levied against U.S. efforts. More importantly, Zhao's statement reflects a particularly Chinese stance on the basic requirements of international persuasion that seems at odds with some of the more overtly competitive assertions about the requirements of soft power articulated elsewhere by the Chinese leadership.

IMPLEMENTING PUBLIC DIPLOMACY:
ATTITUDES TOWARD COMMUNICATION

The organizational strategy behind Chinese public diplomacy has been to incorporate a public diplomacy mandate into the ways in which various levels of the government communicates to their foreign and domestic constituencies. Aoyami observes the growth of China's focus on public diplomacy has translated into "publicity activities" and "disclosure" that are evident in Chinese government at a number of levels (such as local and regional authorities).[135] This has manifested in a series of organizational changes, broadcasting and cultural diplomacy initiatives, which contribute in some fashion toward an articulated goal of enhancing China's soft power in a global environment. In particular, Chinese public diplomacy strategy is reiterated in official Chinese news media, as well as in official statements made by the leadership—where Chinese news outlets explicitly talk about the necessity of public diplomacy. The foregrounding of such efforts suggests that public diplomacy is not a peripheral component of Chinese foreign policy, but a defining element of its strategy.

A central element to the strategic shift is the attitude toward *messaging*. As Zhao Qizheng's public arguments suggest, Chinese attitudes toward messaging at some level reflects increased recognition of *credibility*—as opposed to more monolithic messaging strategies from China's previous propaganda efforts. From a strategic perspective, Zhao's remarks indicate that Chinese propaganda, public diplomacy, or press relations, needs to contain an element of authenticity—and that earlier methods of addressing foreign audiences may no longer be viable. Chinese communication to foreign entities and publics needs to reference known difficulties and problems, as well as highlight successes. This sentiment is expressed by Wu Zheng, who argued in *China's Need for a Strategy of International Communication*, a scholarly volume on international relations published in China in 2001, that the previous Chinese tactic of not addressing internal problems would result in failed communications with external audiences.[136]

Wu Zheng's commentary is revealing in that it recognizes no significant difference between "internal" and "external" propaganda: *the only significant difference is in how audiences are addressed*. Wu Zheng implicitly argues for a kind of message strategy that is made more persuasive by acknowledging the characteristics and context of the audience. "Just carrying domestic propaganda into international communications is ignoring the audience and is not practical." This kind of audience adaptation reflects a kind of pragmatic approach to public diplomacy and overall messaging strategy, and how that might be at odds with the burdens of promoting China through a strict attention to message management. Wu Zheng draws attention to the kind of news that comes from Chinese outlets that are read by foreign publics and ethnic Chinese living abroad:

> By my calculation, 70 percent of the *People's Daily* Foreign Edition and 50 percent of the English-language *China Daily* consists of politics, economic achievements and commentaries from the New China Press Agency. Regardless of the intention behind that, it gives people the impression that they are being force-fed and they reject it. What good is communication if people won't accept it? Moreover that strict political approach will not win the people of the world over to a more positive view of China. Entertainment and historical information without a strong political message won't achieve an overnight effect. But over the long term it will build friendly feelings towards China. So from a practical point of view, I believe that there should be a suitable reduction in political content and an increase in non-political material.[137]

Two distinct attitudes toward communication are apparent. First, Wu Zheng suggests that Chinese communication can rely upon the strength of its cultural and historical capital as a legitimate and trust-building message strategy. This is effectively an argument for accruing soft power. Second, Wu Zheng reorients strategic communications away from the tactical, short-term time horizon, and toward thinking about communication from a "strategic," long-term dimension.

Yet is unclear whether this kind of criticism has permeated into other forms of public diplomacy, aside from Zhao's ubiquitous public statements. For example, in 2003 China released its *Practical Manual for Party Propaganda Work, New Edition*, with a forward by Hu Jintao, which was intended as a guide for dealing with foreigners and the press.[138] The "practical manual" advised officials to "speak simply" and "oversimplify if necessary," yet rely on facts so that foreigners could draw their own conclusions. The *Manual* also advised officials in contact with foreigners to arrange for articles by Chinese officials to be published in foreign media, and to engage with television programs that foreigners watch in order to give a good impression of China. This sensitivity to foreign communication preferences is nonetheless tempered by the need for *message management*, as the manual also suggests that tour guides and interpreters subscribe to PRC foreign language publications.[139]

The previous example is illustrative of how historically-grounded attitudes toward domestic persuasion inhere in contemporary strategies of foreign engagement. Yet it is also apparent that Chinese public diplomacy in its various forms—cultural or media-based—is not conceived as just a euphemism for propagandistic message transmission but as a necessary component of statecraft that requires the development of practical knowledge to inform the building of public diplomacy institutions. In a 2011 interview Zhao Qizheng contends: "From the perspective of the Chinese government, we are not trying to be high-profile. We can further explain through public diplomacy. And the task of public diplomacy is disambiguation, stating clearly our national conditions and policies."[140] Zhao characterizes the continued challenge for public diplomacy is the practice of better communication.

In September of 2010, the Beijing Foreign Studies University opened the first Center on Public Diplomacy in China. The Center's purpose is to "provide intellectual support for the practice of the government's public diplomacy and a platform for the public to participate in public diplomacy."[141] The Chinese Vice Foreign Minister Fu Ying explained the necessity of public diplomacy for China: "Having public diplomacy is like playing a football match. Playing a game is good even when you don't care about winning or losing. One gets the chance to present his side and allow others to feel his existence. But one will definitely lose if he doesn't play at all."[142] Fu's comments state plainly that public diplomacy is a *requirement* for credible foreign policy. It is a competency that must be institutionally cultivated alongside traditional elements of diplomacy and statecraft. Fu claims that, "We have made much progress in negotiating with foreign governments, congressmen, and military officers, but lack experience in dealing with the public and media agencies."[143] Chinese institutional knowledge about public diplomacy is therefore in need of further development.

MAJOR CHINESE PUBLIC DIPLOMACY PROGRAMS

Chinese public diplomacy over the past decade is defined by considerable investments in international broadcasting and high-profile cultural relations efforts like the Confucius Institutes. The following sections survey these programs, and how they reflect broader thematic elements in Chinese soft power discourse.

International Broadcasting

International broadcasting represents a key aspect of Chinese public diplomacy practice, and this is reflected in the multimedia international broadcasting presence that China maintains around the world. Chinese international broadcasting efforts also reflects China's frequently articulated concern over its relative inability to control how it is portrayed in Western media flows. China reportedly spent nearly $9 billion for international broadcasting and publicity efforts between 2009 and 2010 for what is arguably a global effort to reach audiences across a range of media technology platforms.[144] The majority of China's boost in investment went to the most prominent aspects of China's international broadcasting efforts: China Radio International (CRI), China Central Television (CCTV), the Xinhua news agency, and the *China Daily* newspaper.[145]

China's emphasis on international broadcasting as a mediated form of public diplomacy is clearly justified by the perceived significance of communication capacity to larger strategic objectives. Just as Western powers like the United States control a preponderance of media and information flows, Chinese leaders argue that its own material communication assets can help to translate the resources of Chinese soft power into soft power outcomes. Li Changchun, speaking in 2008 at the commemoration of the television industry in China and the fiftieth anniversary of the creation of China Central Television, described the crucial role that "capacity" can play in the cultivation of soft power:

> Communication capacity determines influence. In the modern age, whichever nation's communication methods are most advanced, whichever nation's communication capacity is strongest, it is that nation whose culture and core values are able to spread far and wide, and that nation that has the most power to influence the world. Enhancing our communication capacity domestically and internationally is of direct consequence to our nation's international influence and international position, of direct consequence to the raising of our nation's cultural soft power, and of direct consequence to the function and role of our nation's media within the international public opinion structure.[146]

Li Changchun's statements plainly articulate the equation: power is derived from the ability to transmit or disseminate messages, images, and culture. China media analyst Sophie Yu notes the coherence of such arguments in support of China's broadcasting capabilities. Yu cites Xinhua president Li Congjun: a Chinese global network can break the "monopoly and verbal hegemony of the West."[147] Yu also quotes at length communication scholar Tian Zhihui, who describes the context for the recent push to expand information operations.

> The torch relay ahead of the Beijing 2008 Olympics was a trigger point. As the relay wound its way around the globe, it was dogged in many cities by protesters against China's polices in Tibet and other human-rights issues. The Olympics was supposed to be China's moment to shine, but Beijing felt its side of the story was drowned out . . . The torch was resisted from London to Paris to the Americas . . . Beijing was taught a lesson on the importance of being heard.[148]

As Yu concludes, China has moved to enlarge its global media presence in large part because its economic development has not been matched by a concurrent rise of favorable public opinion around the world.[149] President Hu Jintao frames the situation as "an increasingly fierce struggle in the domain of news and opinion."[150] While China's soft power discourse may be framed to diminish the sense of conflict with other nation-states like the United States, discussion about the exigencies facing Chinese public diplomacy are often striking depictions of competition and struggle.

One of China's principal tools in establishing a global media footprint is China Radio International (CRI). According to its website, CRI is the only state-run radio network, and transmits programs worldwide in 38 foreign languages, Mandarin, and four Chinese dialects (Cantonese, Chaozhou, Fujian, and Hakka). CRI also maintains bureaus in 27 countries, as well as across China itself. Its daily radio programs total over 1,500 hours.[151] CRI provides a significant backbone of communication infrastructure for Chinese international broadcasting and public diplomacy. Beginning in 1998, China launched the online CRI service (www.cri.com.cn), a comprehensive set of news, streaming video, and cultural content, and has subsequently added the following offerings: Chinese News Network, Overseas Chinese Network, and a CRI TV Network, as well as other networks in English, Spanish, French, German, Japanese, Portuguese, Russian, and Korean.

CRI is also being used in conjunction with cultural diplomacy objectives. Chinese language training (through the Confucius Institutes) has been expanded via a cooperation between the Office of Chinese Language Council International, the State Administration of Radio, Film and Television (SARFT), and CRI to establish a wireless language training program, with plans to create a television-based language training service and a more robust online library of Chinese language education materials.[152]

More recent efforts to revamp CRI's offerings have included the purchase of AM and FM radio transmitters in the United States and Europe, as well as direct transmission capabilities in the Middle East, China, and Africa. CRI's growth is marked by organizational moves to establish global media corporations, such as the formation of the China International Broadcasting Network (CIBN), based on CRI's extensive online presence. CIBN will purportedly offer broadcasting services in over 61 languages online, via TV, and mobile platforms. In addition, CRI also announced a "Global GO" professional shopping channel focused on "high end items."[153]

In addition to CRI, China seeks to build its satellite media capacity with two other satellite news networks, Xinhua TV's China News Network and CCTV News. Xinhua, in particular, is well positioned to have an impact on news flows. China's news service has a newsgathering network of 140 bureaus outside China, and provides wire news services at a far discounted rate compared to other global news services.[154] Xinhua TV's China News

Network (CNC), is operated out of Times Square in New York City, and offers 24 hours of English-language programming. It is purportedly modeled on the success of Qatar's Al-Jazeera network.[155]

Li Congjun stated at CNC World's launch in July of 2010 that "CNC will present an international vision with a China perspective. It will broadcast news reports in a timely way and objectively and be a new source of information for global audiences."[156] CNC promotional materials claim that Xinhua TV news will cover nearly 100 countries and regions by 2014 and aims to have "global influence" by 2020. Mi Ligong, director general of CNC's English TV, claimed that CNC would purchase overseas stations to carry CNC content.[157]

CNC World joins an existing English-language service, CCTV News (formerly CCTV-9), which broadcasts six international channels in five languages and claims a total global audience of 125 million. To complement this offering, China Central Television has also launched CNTV, which provides content from 20 Chinese content providers and other online video platforms. In addition to Xinhua and CCTV, the ostensibly private Blue Ocean Network was launched in 2006 as yet another English language content provider for satellite networks worldwide.[158]

Despite the global reach of China's multiple international broadcasting outlets, it is also evident that China is targeting regions and audiences that are significant to its foreign policy concerns. For example, in January 2008, China announced a full-service television channel available to all countries within the Commonwealth of Independent States, including Russia. The new service would provide a focus on Sino-Russian relations, doing business with China, and Chinese culture and history.[159]

This move reflects a developing momentum for China to deploy its public diplomacy resources to augment soft power objectives. In 2006, China launched CRI services in Nairobi, Kenya, with over 19 hours of programming per day in English, Kiswahili, and Chinese.[160] This was supplemented in 2007 by the addition of CCTV broadcasting via Kenya Broadcasting Corporation and CitizenTV.[161] Perhaps not surprisingly, China in 2008 announced the launch of three CCT channels in Cuba, with exposure to 45,000 hotel rooms as well as "health, education, and diplomatic centers."[162] In Southeast Asia, CRI broadcasts in English 24 hours a day, according to CRI online.

The sweeping reach of China's international broadcasting programs suggest an *ecological* approach to communication-based influence. Meaning, China is investing in both transmission capabilities and the communication infrastructure that sustains the social fabric in developing regions identified as significant to China's interests abroad. A 2010 Center for Media Assistance report highlights this key media strategy, as employed in Africa,

Latin America, and Southeast Asia.[163] These include the support for state-run media, the provision of content for cash-strapped regional partner governments, memoranda for the sharing of news content, and training programs in China for journalists in developing countries.

China's media-based partnerships also signal interest in *new media* platforms. For example, extensive agreements with media technology developers in Singapore have yielded new social media platforms and influence metrics, game development, and the digitization of Chinese television content. Speaking at an ASEAN meeting of editors in 2010, Qian Xiaogan, Vice Minister at the State Council Information Office, declared that new media "will bring new vigour and vitality to traditional media, and it will make us more influential than ever before through multimedia and new technologies."[164]

Cultural Diplomacy: Confucius Centers and Beyond

Chinese public diplomacy is not solely characterized by a focus on producing media content to combat foreign representation. China's Confucius Institutes represent a wholly different form of public diplomacy intervention, with a less overt mandate to influence foreign publics. The Confucius Institute program comprises a network of partnerships between the institutions of higher education and the Chinese government, in order to provide language instruction and exposure to Chinese cultural heritage.

The program originated in 2004, with a mandate from the State Council for the Leading Small Group for Foreign Language education to launch 100 "Confucius Institutes"—designed to offer instruction in Chinese language and culture in partnership with local educational institutions in host countries.[165] The program is managed by the Chinese Language Council International (also known as Hanban). Over 322 Confucius Institutes and 369 Confucius classroom programs were established in over 66 countries by the end of 2010.[166] At least 64 such programs exist in the United States as of 2011.[167]

The Institutes are not, however, justified as distinctly public diplomacy initiatives, but rather as cooperative partnerships to further education about Chinese language and culture. The implication that the Confucius Institutes serve a strategic communication purpose is rejected by Americans citizens in the employ of the institute.[168] Yet the Confucius Institutes are not without controversy. The program has been accused of serving a "propaganda function" in the United States and in Israel.[169]

The rapid expansion of the Confucius Institutes signifies a considerable investment in long-term cultural diplomacy and the estimated value of Chinese culture as a strategic asset for public diplomacy. Aside from the obvious opportunity for cultural diplomacy embodied in the 2008 Beijing Olympics and the 2010 Shanghai Expo, China has also engaged in targeted bilateral cultural exchanges to bolster its image with foreign populations. High-profile events such as the 2003–2004 "Cultural Year" of exchanges and expositions in France, the China–Russian National Year in 2005, and the China–Indian Friend Year in 2006 all demonstrate the implicit importance of cultural diplomacy to overall public diplomacy thinking.

Nevertheless, media remains a vehicle for cultural diplomacy—especially in the field of professional exchanges related to the media industry. For example, China announced via the *People's Daily Online* that it has received requests from Arab countries for more Chinese content. Jordanian Minister of Culture Adel Tweisi is quoted as stating that media play an important role for cultural exchanges between China and the Arab world. The article announcing this relationship framed the exchanges between the Arab world and China as an alternative to the "violent" content of Western programming. It also indicated that China Central Television is currently broadcasting an Egyptian-produced program called Arabesque, and anticipates more Arab programming. This was announced around the 2006 anniversary of 50 years of diplomatic relations with the League of Arab States, and a concurrent three-week Arab cultural festival in China.[170]

THE DOMESTIC SPHERE OF CHINESE PUBLIC DIPLOMACY

The notion of soft power carries implications for domestic political institutions as well as China's efforts to communicate to foreign audiences. Likewise, Chinese public diplomacy initiatives are impacted and potentially contingent on prevailing domestic communication policies. China maintains strict guidelines for media ownership, content, and flow across its borders. These restrictions have implications beyond the regulation of online content. China's "great firewall" is symbolic of its strategic thinking on information flow and the relationship between mediated information and political control. The management of opinion via a controlled information environment is the essence of information sovereignty, and is suggestive of an overarching view on the potential of public diplomacy as a persuasive tool.[171]

Attention to communication "infrastructure" in China is forward-looking. In December 2007, China announced the launch of the China Direct Broadcast Satellite Company, which "owns all direct all civil and direct broadcasting satellites of the country." This is a significant public diplomacy development in that it represents a consolidation of state control over global media news and entertainment content that was previously available via semilegal communication equipment.[172] By controlling the influx of communication, it can likewise sustain greater control of content "outflow."

This concern also reflects a pervasive strategic doctrine of information management, codified in a 2001 Communist Party memo that called for the consolidation of information and media control. According to media scholar Wei Yongzheng, the principle of "the party governs the media" (*dangguan meiti*) has resulted in the increased centralization of the media industries to fall under government control, ostensibly to ensure "national unity" and promote "harmony" (terms also deployed to justify investment in soft power amplification).[173]

Information sovereignty is most obviously apparent in China's considerable Internet firewalls that block or filter Internet content, which undoubtedly reflects the Chinese government's particular attitude toward information technology as a strategic concern as much as means to manage the domestic population. The "Great Firewall of China" represents a complex arrangement of state-sponsored and private industry coordination to maintain a controlled information sphere—what China scholar Rebecca McKinnon calls *networked authoritarianism*—that shields China from communication interventions and upholds state authority.[174] As a Chinese official argued in 2007, the United States, among other Western countries, uses technology against China

> to create an information hegemony and ha[s]made the Internet a very important channel to infiltrate our politics, strengthening the delivery of Western democracy and values . . . . More and more frequently, they organize writers to create bad information, exaggerating things that are inharmonious with our development and raise the specter of the China threat on the international scene.[175]

In 2009, Google accused the Chinese government of sponsoring a hacking attack that yielded the names of Chinese dissidents, and subsequently pulled out of China. In 2011, the Chinese government moved to clamp down on the domestic use of Virtual Private Network access to Internet sites outside of China, and purportedly blocked access to Google email services as a warning. In March 2011, the *People's Daily* described Google as a tool of the United States government, and accused Google of playing a role in manufacturing social disorder by intervening in the politics of other countries. During the Arab political uprisings, the Chinese government stepped up domestic surveillance efforts—and reportedly developed methods to censor mobile phone conversations that included the word "protest."[176]

Yet despite such aggressive moves to manage China's domestic information environment and its linkages with the outside world, China has also brokered deals with major international broadcasters to obtain media feeds. China therefore has managed to sustain its internal media sovereignty while remaining connected to the global flow of information via content delivered to outlets such as CCTV from material provided by the BBC.[177]

The tight relationship between media and social control, however, betrays some assumptions about the effectiveness of media messaging to persuade. Inherent in China's media policies are implicit assumptions about the relationship between media and audience. How the Chinese government considers the sustained persuasive impact of its media on Chinese living abroad is illustrative of intrinsic beliefs about strategic media effects. This is exemplified in the experience of the Chinese diaspora, which is identified as an important component of Chinese public diplomacy and, more generally, soft power initiatives.[178] In this case, international broadcasting becomes an instrument of sustaining media sovereignty objectives, and cultivating communities of support across geographic highlights the need to project some sort of *distributed* control of media messaging. Former Chinese reporter Fan Huiqiang argued in November 2007 that this is evident in places like Australia, with a considerable Chinese population. According to Ming Dai,

> While keeping a tight control on media at home the CCP still tries to force Chinese people living outside China to follow the Party line. It reprints the Party's newspaper the *People's Daily* here in Australia, which is given away free of charge and it has also been distributed to all the Chinese language schools, Chinese shops and restaurants. CCTV has also landed here in Australia. The tragedy is a lot of Chinese people who've fled their country and have settled down in Australia still read the *People's Daily* and watch CCTV. Therefore, their mindset is still in line with the Party.[179]

China's media representation of its *own* media policy remains a case for how press coverage of Chinese politics remain tightly managed, despite claims of increased "transparency" to foreign news outlets. A recent analysis of the tightly controlled access to the 17th Chinese Communist Party Conference in 2007 observed the official Chinese news outlets tout transparency and access. China's media outlets reported unsubstantiated polling of foreign news correspondents who praised the Chinese External Propaganda Department for its handling of press access to the conference. However, Ming Dai, the researcher who conducted the analysis of coverage of this event, cautioned that the CCP continues to assert media transparency alongside more considerable attempts to manipulate perception of Chinese politics.[180]

China's tight control of information and news flows makes for a complicated public diplomacy strategy that balances the recognized power of social connections with the perceived demand to maintain message control. Media scholar Monroe Price observes the tension in China's stated policies to reform international communication flows with its own attempts at domestic information control. He cites Li Congjun of Xinhua:

The rules governing the international media order lag behind the times, especially compared to changes in politics and economics. The gap is seen, first and foremost, in the extremely uneven pattern of international communication. The flow of information is basically one-way: from West to East, North to South, and from developed to developing countries.[181]

Li Congjun proposes a series of principles to sustain a new balance of communication flows and regulations to ensure access. International media organizations, in Li's words, "should provide comprehensive, objective, fair, balanced and accurate coverage to minimize discrimination and prejudice." To ensure such a fair environment for communication, Li seeks a "media UN" to ""keep to rational and constructive rules so as to turn mass communication into an active force for promoting social progress."[182] As Price observes, Congjun is proposing a soft power "gambit" that draws upon memories of a decades-old debate within the UN over the ill-fated NWICO (New World Information and Communication Order) that sought to redress imbalances of news and media flows which distorted representation of the developing world, to propose a governance initiative that reflects China's values. For Price, this attempt seems tenuous given China's well-publicized attempts to frame Internet governance as a matter for states to preserve their own information sovereignty.

As *public diplomacy*, Li's op-ed telegraphs a broader objective—to establish China as a responsible stakeholder on global governance issues that directly impact its strategic orientation toward information and media. Li's arguments also reflect the larger body of discourse on soft power, whereby soft power can translate China's resources into structural and institutional changes that facilitate China's developmental goals.

CHINESE SOFT POWER: IMPLICIT, EXPLICIT, AND CRITICAL DIMENSIONS

In 2010, China faced a significant amount of international scrutiny as it launched a vociferous protest against the nomination of Chinese political dissident Liu Xiaobo for the Nobel Peace Prize. The Chinese leadership lashed out against Western media portrayal of Liu, who eventually won the award in November 2010, and embargoed the story in Chinese press outlets. The Chinese government even created an alternative "Confucius Prize" to "promote peace from an Eastern perspective."[183] The story of Liu Xiaobo and the Chinese reaction is illustrative of the limitations facing Chinese soft power, as much as validation for Chinese arguments that its soft power must be cultivated with greater urgency.

Joseph Nye has argued in multiple venues that China's soft power is potentially limited by its own actions, and is skeptical of a preponderance of Chinese soft power.[184] Despite well-documented Chinese investments in developing regions, the conversion of these assets into durable soft power outcomes appears uncertain, because despite efforts to convert soft power resources toward outcomes, these attempts do not take place in a vacuum. China's pronounced focus on particular form of cultural soft power and heavy intervention into communication flows appears at odds with the ubiquity of communication technologies that make China's actions transparent. China's indigenous soft power concept betrays certain peculiar qualities that illustrate potential strategic communication impediments.

On the level of *scope*—Chinese discourse on soft power and subsequent investment in public diplomacy and strategic communication programs bear the indelible mark of China's historical attitude toward communication, which very often takes the uncritical reception of persuasive messages for granted. Put another way, communication and media effects in Chinese soft power discourse are assumed to be powerful and not mitigated by the critical capacities of the audience itself. Aside from Zhao Qizheng's calls for further communication research, the notion of *audience*—the role of global audiences as auditors of supposed soft power-derived policies—is not elaborated. Rather, foreign publics reflect vulnerabilities as much as objects of opportunity for the promotion of China's image.

The circumscribed view of communication audiences is matched by an overwhelming emphasis on media and communication technologies as key to soft power strategy. Through arguments for public diplomacy and soft power—communication and influence are profoundly linked. Media and media organizations are inherently powerful, or are powerful tools of adversaries intent on framing China negatively. As such, the soft power and public diplomacy discourse places a significant amount of faith in the potency of media communication tools for soft power and international influence. Media is presented as a strategic exigency that must be redressed through increased investment in the capacity to communicate across the scope of China's soft power ambitions. Foreign audiences are seen as vulnerable to the "prejudiced" views of non-Chinese media.[185]

As is evident, media and information also represent crucial *mechanisms* of soft power. What makes the case of China distinct in this regard is the level of expected gains from such mechanisms, and how the terrain of mediated communication is so central to competition in international politics. It is also clear that *culture*, in its varied interpretations, represents the most potent resource in China's soft power inventory. But much like Venezuela's strident narratives to broadcast its Bolivaran institutions, the compelling and persuasive aspects of Chinese culture are not fully elaborated within strategic arguments. Rather, Chinese culture must be presented and disseminated.

Put another way, there is a pervasive sense that soft power mechanisms will *follow* from exposure to Chinese culture. If people are more interested in Chinese culture through study at a Confucius Institute, then this will somehow accrue soft power benefits. While some of have argued that Chinese culture can impact international relations by providing an alternative set of values based around *harmony*, there is no clear set of reasoning about how such values can displace Western norms for international relations.

The outcomes of Chinese soft power, however, seem readily apparent from the discourse. China seeks short and long term mechanisms through which it can more readily accomplish its "development goals." In a 2011 report by the office of U.S. Senator Richard Lugar, Chinese soft power ambitions are straightforward—China seeks access to resources and markets that put China at odds with other nation-states.[186] Thus, Chinese strategy involves both possession and milieu goals, to secure material resources and to alter the institutional frameworks that would make China's rise to power more legitimate and acceptable to the global community.

But how soft power is argued *within* China, as Li Mingjiang claims, adds another dimension to both the scope and expected outcomes of soft power. By reinforcing soft power as a reflection of institutional strength—the sweeping cultural heritage of China embodied in its state government—Chinese policy rhetoric provides justification toward maintaining the status quo more than it inspires specific policy prescriptions that are outwardly responsive to the demands of global audiences. This means that Chinese soft power is not driven solely by attention to the communicative realities of foreign publics, but is yet another tool to strengthen the state. While there is indeed recognition of culture as a resource for political agency in international politics, the consequences of the rhetoric stop short of a template for significant domestic policy changes or messaging strategies that address concerns over Chinese human rights violations. Rather, China has opted for structural and technological objectives: the construction of alternative media networks, Internet tools, and social media platforms. Democratizing technologies are being co-opted to construct authoritarian alternatives, with surveilled virtual communities subject to monitored communication.

The significant concern that China has for information control and consolidation suggests that it has not accepted the tenets of Nye's soft power concept wholesale. Instead, China's *managed* program of soft power and public diplomacy aim not at demonstrative universal values, but at shifting the boundaries of norms, values, and the markers of legitimacy for a rising global power. As a recent academic summary of Chinese soft power proposes, soft power is a *U.S. concept* that reflects U.S. conditions and interests.[187] China must balance its hard power concerns with the long term benefits that ultimately demand attention to soft power. Qingguo Jia argues that "[o]ne may debate the strength of Chinese soft power resources, but most Chinese would agree that a nation can only maximize its soft power through smart use of both 'hard' soft power resources and 'soft' soft power resources."[188]

The result is a set of soft power strategies that may be ultimately self-defeating. China launched a publicity campaign in advance of President Hu Jintao's visit to the United States in 2011. As part of the campaign, China featured the video "Experience China," featuring prominent Chinese personalities such as basketball player Yiao Ming, on several video screens in New York's Times Square. As PBS reports, however, the persuasive impact is questionable. PBS noted U.S. media outlets as criticizing the video for being "out of touch with its American audience" and "more scary than friendly."[189]

Given the context of China's rising power set against global financial and employment concerns, China's attempts to deploy public diplomacy to cultivate soft power may, using Zhao Qizheng's words, require more "rhetorical competency." According to Gill and Huang, an authoritarian political system, a questionable human rights record, and the rise of concern over China as a threat, pose serious challenges to lasting attempts to reframe China's motivations and intentions.[190]

Shanthi Kalathi provides a sweeping critique of China's emphasis on soft power. She argues that China has "fundamentally misread the nature of the relationship between soft power and the globally networked, information-rich environment, thus misunderstanding how soft power is accumulated." In other words, Chinese strategic discourse does not account for how soft power resources are ultimately converted into soft power outcomes. The deployment of soft power mechanisms is by no means a guarantee of success. As journalist Andy Yee argues,

> Dazzling public relations is no substitute for credibility, which is key to winning influence in a critical global audience. . . . As China is spending billions of dollars to make its media go global, it also needs to rethink its heavy-handed approach on media control and suppression of free speech. The world welcomes a diversity of voices, including that of China, but not one which is distorted, censored and sanitized.[191]

The previous passage illustrates the disconnect in the way in which foreign publics are conceived in Chinese strategic discourse as audiences subject to soft power initiatives. If transmission matters more than content, then the mechanisms of persuasion, let alone attraction, becomes more difficult to leverage. Kim Andrew Elliott argues, "China's international broadcasting efforts won't have much impact unless it provides a useful news service."[192]

Yet China's launch of its Public Diplomacy Institute in 2010 and the reiteration of soft power as a strategic priority in the 2011 CPPCC conference suggest the continued enthusiasm for soft power and public diplomacy. Speaking at the CPPCC, Huang Youui claimed that "[t]he public overseas is gradually beginning to understand that China is not on a path of achieving hegemony but cherishes equality. The Chinese people value kindness, patience, wisdom and virtue."[193] In an interview with Zhao Qizheng in 2011, Zhao explains the principle difficulty facing Chinese public diplomacy: "The campaign is not big enough."[194]

NOTES

1. Sheng Ding, *The Dragon's Hidden Wings: How China Rises with Its Soft Power* (Lexington Books, 2008); Mingjiang Li, "Soft Power: Nurture Not Nature," in *Soft Power: China's Emerging Strategy in International Politics,* ed. Mingjiang Li (Lanham, MD: Lexington Books, 2009), 1–18; Li Mingjiang, "China Debates Soft Power," *The Chinese Journal of International Politics* 2, no. 2 (December 21, 2008):287–308.

2. Shanthi Kalathil, *China's Soft Power in the Information Age: Think Again*, ISD Working Papers in Diplomacy (Washington, D.C.: Georgetown University, May 2011), 1, http://isd.georgetown.edu/files/Kalathil_Chinas_Soft_Power.pdf.

3. Mingjiang, "China Debates Soft Power."

4. Deborah Brautigam, *The Dragon's Gift: The Real Story of China in Africa* (Oxford University Press U.S., 2009); Joshua Kurlantzick, *Charm Offensive: How China's Soft Power Is Transforming the World* (Yale University Press, 2007); Douglas Farah and Andy Mosher, *Winds from the East: How the People's Republic of China Seeks to Influence the Media in Africa, Latin America, and Southeast Asia* (Washington, D.C.: Center for International Media Assistance, September 8, 2010).

5. Zhongying Pang, *The Beijing Olympics and China's Soft Power* (Washington, D.C.: Brookings Institution, Winter 2008), www.brookings.edu/opinions/2008/0904_olympics_pang.aspx.

6. Young Nam Cho and Jong Ho Jeong, "China's Soft Power: Discussions, Resources, and Prospects," *Asian Survey* 48, no. 3 (June 1, 2008):335.

7. Joel Wuthnow, "The Concept of Soft Power in China's Soft Power Discourse," *Issues and Studies* 44, no. 2 (June 2008):1–28.

8. Ding, *The Dragon's Hidden Wings*, 24.

9. Hongying Wang and Yeh-Chung Lu, "The Conception of Soft Power and Its Policy Implications: A Comparative Study of China and Taiwan," *Journal of Contemporary China* 17 (August 2008):427.

10. Ibid.

11. Jia Qingguo, *Continuity and Change: China's Attitude toward Hard Power and Soft Power* (Washington, D.C.: Brookings Institution, December 2010), www.brookings.edu/opinions/2010/12_china_soft_power_jia.aspx.

12. Ibid.

13. Cho and Jeong, "China's Soft Power," 457.

14. Mingjiang, "China Debates Soft Power."

15. "How China Deals with the U.S. Strategy to Contain China," *Qiushi Journal* (December 10, 2010), http://chinascope.org/main/content/view/3291/92/.

16. Shogo Suzuki, "Chinese Soft Power, Insecurity Studies, Myopia and Fantasy," *Third World Quarterly* 30, no. 4 (June 2009):779–793; Kurlantzick, *Charm Offensive*.

17. Zhexin Zhang, "China's Public Diplomacy Institution: Its Development, Challenges, and Prospects of Its Practice," *IO Journal* 1, no. 3 (2009):12–17.

18. Mingjiang Li, *Soft Power: China's Emerging Strategy in International Politics* (Lexington Books, 2009), 30.

19. Suzuki, "Chinese Soft Power, Insecurity Studies, Myopia and Fantasy."

20. Rebecca MacKinnon, "China's Internet White Paper: Networked Authoritarianism in Action," rconversation.blogs.com, June 10, 2010, http://rconversation.blogs.com/rconversation/2010/06/chinas-internet-white-paper-networked-authoritarianism.html.

21. Kalathil, *China's Soft Power in the Information Age: Think Again.*

22. Qingguo, *Continuity and Change: China's Attitude toward Hard Power and Soft Power.*

23. Carola McGiffert, ed., *Chinese Soft Power and Its Implications for the United States: Competition and Cooperation in the Developing World: A Report of the CSIS Smart Power Initiative* (Washington D.C.: CSIS, 2009), 3–5.

24. Qingguo, *Continuity and Change: China's Attitude toward Hard Power and Soft Power.*

25. Peter Van Ham, *Social Power in International Politics* (Taylor & Francis, 2010).

26. Yul Sohn, "Attracting Neighbors: Soft Power Competition in East Asia" (presented at the Wiseman Roundtable on Soft Power in Northeast Asia, Seoul, Korea: Korea Foundation and East Asia Institute, 2008), 3–4; Qingguo, *Continuity and Change: China's Attitude toward Hard Power and Soft Power.*

27. Wang and Lu, "The Conception of Soft Power and Its Policy Implications."

28. Bonnie S. Glaser and Melissa Murphy, "Soft Power with Chinese Characteristics: The Ongoing Debate," in *Chinese Soft Power and Its Implications for the United States: Competition and Cooperation in the Developing World: A Report of the CSIS Smart Power Initiative* (Washington D.C.: CSIS, 2009), 13.

29. Ibid., 15.

30. Li, "Soft Power: Nurture Not Nature."

31. Wang and Lu, "The Conception of Soft Power and Its Policy Implications," 427.

32. Glaser and Murphy, "Soft Power with Chinese Characteristics: The Ongoing Debate."

33. Cho and Jeong, "China's Soft Power," 458.

34. Glaser and Murphy, "Soft Power with Chinese Characteristics: The Ongoing Debate," 19.

35. Mingjiang Li, "Soft Power in Chinese Discourse: Popularity and Prospect," in *China's Emerging Strategy in International Polics*, eds. Mingjiang Li (Lanham, MD: Lexington Books, 2009), 26.

36. Glaser and Murphy, "Soft Power with Chinese Characteristics: The Ongoing Debate."

37. Li, "Soft Power in Chinese Discourse: Popularity and Prospect."

38. Qingguo, *Continuity and Change: China's Attitude toward Hard Power and Soft Power*.

39. Glaser and Murphy, "Soft Power with Chinese Characteristics: The Ongoing Debate," 15.

40. Zhang, "China's Public Diplomacy Institution: Its Development, Challenges, and Prospects of Its Practice."

41. Ingrid D'Hooge, *The Limits of China's Soft Power in Europe: Beijing's Public Diplomacy Puzzle*, Clingendael Diplomacy Papers (Netherlands Institute of International Relations: Clingendael, January 2010), 8.

42. Li, "Soft Power in Chinese Discourse: Popularity and Prospect."

43. Mingjiang, "China Debates Soft Power."

44. Li, "Soft Power in Chinese Discourse: Popularity and Prospect," 28.

45. "China's First Public Diplomacy Research Center Established in Beijing," *People's Daily Online* (Beijing, China, August 27, 2010), http://english.peopledaily.com.cn/90001/90776/90883/7120534.html.

46. Wuthnow, "The Concept of Soft Power in China's Soft Power Discourse."

47. D'Hooge, *The Limits of China's Soft Power in Europe: Beijing's Public Diplomacy Puzzle*, 4.

48. Lisi Ma, "'Guanyu Woguo Jiaqiang Ruan Shili Jianshe De Chubu Sikao (Preliminary Thoughts on Accelerating China's Soft Power Building)," *Dang De Wenxian (Literature of Chinese Communist Party)*, no. 7 (n.d.):35–38.

49. Glaser and Murphy, "Soft Power with Chinese Characteristics: The Ongoing Debate," 16.

50. Tuosheng Zhang, "China in New Phase of World Integration," *China Daily*, October 17, 2007, sec. Commentary, www.chinadaily.com.cn/opinion/2007–10/17/content_6182330.htm.

51. "Interview with Wu Jianmin (President of China Foreign Affairs University, former Chinese ambassador to France, on riots in Tibet)," September 27, 2010, www.want-daily.com/NEWs/Content.aspx?id=0&yyyymmdd=20100927&k=17915aed7bb9a81196139f84ceafb832&h=c6f057b86584942e415435ffb1fa93d4&nid=K@20100927@N0010.001.

52. Li, "Soft Power in Chinese Discourse: Popularity and Prospect," 25.

53. "Hu Jintao Calls for Enhancing 'Soft Power' of Chinese Culture," *People's Daily Online*, October 17, 2007, http://english.peopledaily.com.cn/90002/92169/92187/6283148.html.

54. Glaser and Murphy, "Soft Power with Chinese Characteristics: The Ongoing Debate," 13.

55. Ibid., 14.

56. David Bandurski, "Hitting Hard with 'Soft Power': China Explores Macro-Measures to Bolster Its Global Cultural Prowess," December 19, 2007, http://cmp .hku.hk/2007/12/19/797/.

57. "How to Improve China's Soft Power?" *People's Daily Online*, March 11, 2010, http://english.peopledaily.com.cn/90001/90776/90785/6916487.html.

58. "Interview with Wu Jianmin (President of China Foreign Affairs University, former Chinese ambassador to France, on riots in Tibet)."

59. "Interview with Zhao Qizheng (chairman of the Foreign Affairs Committee of the Chinese People's Political Consultative Conference and dean of the School of Journalism and Communication, Renmin University of China)," September 27, 2010, www. want-daily.com/NEWs/Content.aspx?id=0&yyyymmdd=20100927&k=17915aed 7bb9a81196139f84ceafb832&h=c6f057b86584942e415435ffb1fa93d4&nid=K@2010 0927@N0010.001.

60. Huning Wang, "Zuowei Guojia Shili De Wenhua: Ruan Quanli (Culture as National Power: Soft Power)," *Fuda Daxue Xuebao (Journal of Fudan University)*, no. 3 (1993):23–28.

61. Glaser and Murphy, "Soft Power with Chinese Characteristics: The Ongoing Debate," 19.

62. "The Whole World Moved by China," *People's Daily Online*, n.d., sec. Opinion, http://english.people.com.cn/90001/90780/91342/6761629.html.

63. "Senior Chinese Leader Stresses Protection of Cultural Heritage," *News of the Communist Party of China*, June 13, 2010, sec. News, http://english.cpc.people.com .cn/66102/7024799.html.

64. "The Whole World Moved by China."

65. David Bandurski, "Propaganda Head Liu Yunshan Promotes Commercialization of Media to Strengthen China's 'Cultural Soft Power,'" *China Media Project*, April 7, 2007, http://cmp.hku.hk/2007/04/10/225.

66. "Senior Party Official: Enhance Cohesion, Appeal of Socialist Ideology," November 30, 2007, http://english.cpc.people.com.cn/66102/6312736.html.

67. Bandurski, "Hitting Hard with 'Soft Power': China Explores Macro-Measures to Bolster Its Global Cultural Prowess."

68. Kalathil, *China's Soft Power in the Information Age: Think Again*, 7.

69. Sohn, "Attracting Neighbors: Soft Power Competition in East Asia."

70. Wuthnow, "The Concept of Soft Power in China's Soft Power Discourse."

71. "How to Improve China's Soft Power?"

72. Yuetong Yan, "Ruan Shili De Hexin Shi Zhengzhi Shili ('The Core of Soft Power Is Political Power)," *Huanqiu Shibao (Global Times)*, May 22, 2007.

73. Majie Zhu and Xintian Yu, "Ruan Guoli Jianshe: Bu Rong Hushi De Wuxing Yingxiang (Soft Power Construction: Invisible Influence Not to Be Ignored)," in *Proceedings of Annual Meeting of Shanghai Social Sciences Circle*, 2004.

74. Glaser and Murphy, "Soft Power with Chinese Characteristics: The Ongoing Debate," 15.

75. "Hu Jintao Calls for Enhancing 'Soft Power' of Chinese Culture."

76. Wang and Lu, "The Conception of Soft Power and Its Policy Implications," 430.

77. Cho and Jeong, "China's Soft Power," 458–459.

78. Li, "Soft Power in Chinese Discourse: Popularity and Prospect," 28.

79. Wuthnow, "The Concept of Soft Power in China's Soft Power Discourse," 21.

80. Li, "Soft Power in Chinese Discourse: Popularity and Prospect."

81. "Interview with Zhao Qizheng (chairman of the Foreign Affairs Committee of the Chinese People's Political Consultative Conference and dean of the School of Journalism and Communication, Renmin University of China)."

82. Wuthnow, "The Concept of Soft Power in China's Soft Power Discourse," 12.

83. "The Promotion of Soft Power and the Strategies of Chinese Peaceful Development," *Maozedong Thought Study* 27, no. 2 (March 2010).

84. Xue-Peng Xie, "The Cultural Soft Power and the Shaping of China's National Image," *Journal of Shanxi Normal University* 36, no. 5 (September 2009).

85. Zhang, "China's Public Diplomacy Institution: Its Development, Challenges, and Prospects of Its Practice."

86. Sanden Totten, "China Invests in Filmmaking, for Image and Profit: NPR," n.d., www.npr.org/2011/06/19/137253607/china-invests-in-filmmaking-for-image-and-profit?sc=17&f=1001.

87. Li Changchun, "Li Changchun's (China's Top Media Control Official) Speech on Celebration Marking the Foundation of the Chinese Television Affairs and 50th Anniversary of China Central Television (CCTV)," China.com, December 23, 2008, http://news.china.com/zh_cn/news100/11038989/20081223/15248144.html.

88. Li, "Soft Power in Chinese Discourse: Popularity and Prospect."

89. Joshua Cooper Ramo, *The Beijing Consensus* (Foreign Policy Centre, 2004).

90. Suzuki, "Chinese Soft Power, Insecurity Studies, Myopia and Fantasy."

91. Ibid., 788.

92. Bonnie S. Glaser and Evan S Medeiros, "The Changing Ecology of Foreign Policy-Making in China: The Ascension and Demise of the Theory of 'Peaceful Rise,'" *The China Quarterly* 190 (2007):291–310.

93. Cho and Jeong, "China's Soft Power," 463.

94. Yong-ming Xiao and Tian-Jie Zhang, "The Retrospection and Prospect to the Research of Chinese Cultural Soft Power," *Journal of Hunan University (Social Science)* 24, no. 1 (January 2010).

95. Wuthnow, "The Concept of Soft Power in China's Soft Power Discourse," 15.

96. Li, "Soft Power in Chinese Discourse: Popularity and Prospect," 27.

97. Haizhou Zhang, "China Needs More Public Diplomacy, Zhao Says," March 11, 2010, www.chinadaily.com.cn/china/2010npc/2010–03/11/content_9570697.htm.

98. Wuthnow, "The Concept of Soft Power in China's Soft Power Discourse," 7.

99. Li, "Soft Power in Chinese Discourse: Popularity and Prospect," 30.

100. Ibid., 31–32.

101. Yong Deng, "The New Hard Realities: 'Soft Power' and China in Transition," in *Soft Power: China's Emerging Strategy in International Politics*, ed. Mingjiang Li (Lanham, MD: Lexington Books, 2009), 72.

102. Li, "Soft Power in Chinese Discourse: Popularity and Prospect," 24.

103. Ibid., 27.

104. Ibid., 37.

105. Mingjiang, "China Debates Soft Power," 301–302.

106. Ibid.

107. Bandurski, "Hitting Hard with 'Soft Power': China Explores Macro-Measures to Bolster Its Global Cultural Prowess."

108. Wuthnow, "The Concept of Soft Power in China's Soft Power Discourse," 19–22.

109. "Strong Public Diplomacy Vital for China," *People's Daily Online*, April 8, 2011, http://english.peopledaily.com.cn/90001/90776/90883/7343844.html.

110. "Interview with Zhao Qizheng (chairman of the Foreign Affairs Committee of the Chinese People's Political Consultative Conference and dean of the School of Journalism and Communication, Renmin University of China)."

111. "Strong Public Diplomacy Vital for China," *People's Daily Online*.

112. Kurlantzick, *Charm Offensive*.

113. MacKinnon, "China's Internet White Paper: Networked Authoritarianism in Action."

114. Zhang, "China's Public Diplomacy Institution: Its Development, Challenges, and Prospects of Its Practice," 13.

115. Ibid.

116. Ibid., 17.

117. Robert Seuttinger, "The Rise and Descent of 'Peaceful Rise,'" *China Leadership Monitor* 12 (n.d.):1–10.

118. Cho and Jeong, "China's Soft Power," 468.

119. Yiwei Wang, "Public Diplomacy and the Rise of Chinese Soft Power," *The ANNALS of the American Academy of Political and Social Science* 616, no. 1 (March 1, 2008):257–273.

120. Keijn Zhao, *Theory and Practice of Public Diplomacy* (Shanghai: Shanghai Dictionary Press, 2007), 21.

121. Qizheng Zhao, "People's Daily Online—Better Public Diplomacy to Present a Truer Picture of China," March 30, 2007, http://english.people.com.cn/200703/30/eng20070330_362496.html.

122. Ingrid D'Hooge, "Public Diplomacy in the People's Republic of China," in *The New Public Diplomacy: Soft Power in International Relations*, ed. Jan Melissen (New York: Palgrave Macmillan, 2007).

123. Zhang, "China's Public Diplomacy Institution: Its Development, Challenges, and Prospects of Its Practice."

124. Ibid., 14.

125. Hongying Wang, "National Image Building and Chinese Foreign Policy," *China: An International Journal* 1, no. 1 (2003):46–72.

126. Zhang, "China's Public Diplomacy Institution: Its Development, Challenges, and Prospects of Its Practice," 14.

127. Rumi Aoyama, "Chinese Diplomacy in the Multimedia Age: Public Diplomacy and Civil Diplomacy" (Waseda University Working Paper: Center of Excellence Contemporary Asian Studies, 2004), 11.

128. Ibid., 13.

129. Rumi Aoyama, "Chinese Public Diplomacy" (Waseda University Working Paper: Center of Excellence Contemporary Asian Studies, 2007).

130. Qizheng Zhao, "'To Formulate a Favorable Public Opinion in the World,'" *(Nuli Jianshe Youliyu Woguode Guoji Yulun Huanjing)*, *Journal of Foreign Affairs College*, no. third quarter (2004):3.

131. Wang, "Public Diplomacy and the Rise of Chinese Soft Power."

132. Qizheng Zhao, "Zhao Qizheng: Mobilizing Public Diplomacy" *Shanghai World Expo*, April 29, 2010, http://en.expo2010.cn/a/20100429/000005.htm.

133. "'Public Diplomat' Wants Foreigners to See the 'True China,'" *GLobal Times*, May 19, 2011, http://news.cultural-china.com/20110519094031.html.

134. "'Public Diplomacy at Early Stage'—China.org.cn," *NPC & CPPCC 2011*, March 3, 2011, www.china.org.cn/china/NPC_CPPCC_2011/2011–03/03/content_22042058.htm.

135. Aoyama, "Chinese Diplomacy in the Multimedia Age: Public Diplomacy and Civil Diplomacy."

136. Zheng Wu, *Zhongguo De Da Guo De Wei Yu Guo Ji Chuan Bo Zhan Lüe (China's Need for a Strategy of International Communication)*, Di 1 Ban. (Beijing: Chang Zheng Chu Ban She, 2001).

137. Ibid.

138. David Cowhig, "How to Do Propaganda Work with Foreigners," *China Digital Times*, December 2, 2007, http://chinadigitaltimes.net/2007/12/how-to-do-propaganda-work-with-foreigners-david-cowhig/.

139. Ibid.

140. "Exclusive Interview with Zhao Qizheng on China's Diplomacy," *CCTV—CNTV News*, March 2, 2011, http://english.cntv.cn/program/newsupdate/20110302/115431.shtml.

141. "China's First Public Diplomacy Research Center Established in Beijing."

142. "Public Diplomacy Gains Ground," *Global Times*, n.d., http://china.globaltimes.cn/diplomacy/2010–09/573212.html.

143. Ibid.

144. David Shambaugh, "China Flexes Its Soft Power," *New York Times*, June 7, 2010, sec. Op-Ed, www.nytimes.com/2010/06/08/opinion/08iht-edshambaugh.html; Sophie Yu, "China's Voice Is About to Get Louder All around the World," *Center for International Media Assistance*, November 1, 2010, http://cima.ned.org/chinas-voice-about-get-louder-all-around-world.

145. Ananth Krishnan, "China to Give a Fillip to International Relations," *The Hindu*, February 11, 2011, sec. International, www.thehindu.com/news/international/article1487217.ece; Shambaugh, "China Flexes Its Soft Power."

146. David Bandurski, "Li Changchun on the Media and China's 'Global Influence,'" *China Media Project*, December 19, 2009, http://cmp.hku.hk/2009/01/19/1457/.

147. Yu, "China's Voice Is About to Get Louder All around the World."

148. Ibid.

149. Ibid.

150. Andy Yee, "China Makes Global Media Push, but Skeptics Abound," *PBS MEDIASHIFT*, April 19, 2011, www.pbs.org/mediashift/2011/04/china-makes-global -media-push-but-skeptics-abound109.html.

151. "CRI's 70th Anniversary Contest," June 22, 2011, http://english.cri.cn/8706/ 2011/06/22/1461s644144.htm.

152. "China Opens First Confucius Institute on Air," *English Xinhua*, December 6, 2007, http://news.xinhuanet.com/english/2007–12/06/content_7211620.htm.

153. "CRI Launches New Media Broadcasting Network," January 18, 2011, http:// english.cri.cn/6909/2011/01/18/2742s616142.htm.

154. Yu, "China's Voice Is About to Get Louder All around the World."

155. Nathanael Massey, "CCTV—The Voice of China's 'Soft Power,'" *Global Media Wars*, 2011, http://globalmediawars.com/?page_id=61.

156. "Xinhua Launches CNC World English Channel," English.news.cn, July 1, 2010, http://news.xinhuanet.com/english2010/china/2010–07/01/c_13378575.htm.

157. Yu, "China's Voice Is About to Get Louder All around the World."

158. Massey, "CCTV—The Voice of China's 'Soft Power.'"

159. "First 'Channel of China' to Open in Russia," *Xinhua*, January 17, 2008, http://news.xinhuanet.com/english/2008–01/17/content_7434371.htm.

160. Ted Fackler, "Kenya: The Chinese Make a Home Away from Home," AllAfrica.com, July 3, 2007, http://allafrica.com/stories/200707021725.html.

161. Beatrice Gachenge, "Kenyans Flock to Chinese Classes," *Business Daily– Nairobi*, June 28, 2007.

162. Andy Sennitt, "China's CCTV Opens Three Channels in Cuba," *Radio Netherlands Worldwide*, February 20, 2008, http://blogs.rnw.nl/medianetwork/chinas -cctv-opens-three-channels-in-cuba.

163. Farah and Mosher, *Winds from the East: How the People's Republic of China Seeks to Influence the Media in Africa, Latin America, and Southeast Asia*.

164. Ibid.

165. Cho and Jeong, "China's Soft Power."

166. "Introduction to the Confucius Institutes," August 29, 2009, http://college .chinese.cn/en/article/2009–08/29/content_22308.htm.

167. Matthew Armstrong, "China and American Public Diplomacy: Another U.S. Deficit," www.MountainRunner.us, n.d., http://mountainrunner.us/2011/02/ Senator_Lugar_China_and_US_Public_Diplomacy_Another_Deficit.html?utm _source=feedburner&utm_medium=feed&utm_campaign=Feed%3A+Mountainru nner+%28MountainRunner%29; Chen Chen, "Finding Support for the Confucius Institutes," April 27, 2010, http://uscpublicdiplomacy.org/index.php/newswire/ cpdblog_detail/finding_support_for_the_confucius_institutes/.

168. "Interview with University of Maryland Confucius Institute," April 12, 2010.

169. Peter Schmidt, "At U.S. Colleges, Chinese-Financed Centers Prompt Worries about Academic Freedom," *The Chronicle of Higher Education*, October 22, 2010, http://chronicle.texterity.com/chronicle/20101022a?pg=8#pg8.

170. "Arab Officials Ask for More Chinese TV Programs," *People's Daily Online*, June 26, 2006, http://english.people.com.cn/200606/26/eng20060626_277329.html.

171. Monroe Edwin Price, *Media and Sovereignty: The Global Information Revolution and Its Challenge to State Power* (MIT Press, 2004).

172. Kim Andrew Elliott, "China: Satellite Television Becomes Official," *Kim Andrew Elliott reporting on International Broadcasting*, n.d., http://kimelli.nfshost .com/index.php?id=3003.

173. Yuen-Ying Chan, "A Scholar's View: The State Media Have an Iron Grip and Grand Plans," June 2010, www.globalasia.org/V5N2_Summer_2010/Chan_Yuen_Ying. html.

174. MacKinnon, "China's Internet White Paper: Networked Authoritarianism in Action."

175. Edward Cody, "Chinese Official Accuses Nations of Hacking," *Washington Post*, September 13, 2007, www.washingtonpost.com/wp-dyn/content/article/2007/09/12/AR2007091200791.html.

176. Sharon LaFraniere and David Barboza, "China Tightens Electronic Censorship," Nytimes.com, March 21, 2011, www.nytimes.com/2011/03/22/world/asia/22china.html?_r=1.

177. "BBC Worldwide Strikes Another Deal with China," *BBC Press Office*, April 23, 2007, www.bbc.co.uk/pressoffice/bbcworldwide/worldwidestories/pressreleases/2007/04_april/motion_cctv.shtml.

178. Kurlantzick, *Charm Offensive.*

179. Ming Dai, "Beijing Hones Media Manipulation," *Asia Times*, November 17, 2007, www.atimes.com/atimes/China/IK15Ad01.html.

180. Ibid.

181. Monroe Price, "Xinhua, China's Soft Power Initiative and the Return of the New World Information Order," *Huffington Post*, June 7, 2011, www.huffingtonpost.com/monroe-price/xinhua-chinas-soft-power-_b_872578.html.

182. Ibid.

183. Steven Jiang, "Winner a No-Show as China Hands Out Its First Peace Prize," *CNNWorld*, December 9, 2010, http://articles.cnn.com/2010–12–09/world/china .confucius.peace_1_prize-committee-norwegian-nobel-prize-jury?_s=PM:WORLD.

184. Joseph S. Nye, "China's Century Is Not yet upon Us," *Financial Times*, May 18, 2010, http://cachef.ft.com/cms/s/0/649e807a-62aa-11df-b1d1–00144feab49a .html#axzz1S0gtvQGE; Joseph S. Nye Jr., *The Future of Power*, 1st ed. (Public Affairs, 2011).

185. Qingguo, *Continuity and Change: China's Attitude toward Hard Power and Soft Power.*

186. Richard G. Lugar and Paul Foldi, *Another U.S. Deficit—China and America— Public Diplomacy in the Age of the Internet*, Committee on Foreign Relations, U.S. Senate (Washington D.C., February 15, 2011).

187. "Re-Understand Soft Power," *Journal of Nanjing University; Philosophy, Humanities and Social Sciences*, no. 1 (2010).

188. Qingguo, *Continuity and Change: China's Attitude toward Hard Power and Soft Power.*

189. Yee, "China Makes Global Media Push, but Skeptics Abound."

190. Bates Gill and Yanzhong Huang, "Sources and Limits of Chinese 'Soft Power,'" *Survival* 48, no. 2 (June 2006):17–36.

191. Yee, "China Makes Global Media Push, but Skeptics Abound."

192. Kim Andrew Elliott, "Perhaps Too Much Sleep Is Lost over the 'Seduction, Prestige, and Omnipresence' of China's International Media Campaign," *Kim Andrew Elliott reporting on International Broadcasting*, April 14, 2011, http://kimelli.nfshost.com/index.php?id=11080.

193. Ke Wang, "China Slowly Learning Public Diplomacy: Huang Youyi," China.org.cn, March 5, 2011, www.china.org.cn/china/NPC_CPPCC_2011/2011–03/05/content_22064456.htm.

194. Zhang, "China Needs More Public Diplomacy, Zhao Says."

REFERENCES

Aoyama, Rumi. "Chinese Diplomacy in the Multimedia Age: Public Diplomacy and Civil Diplomacy." Waseda University Working Paper: Center of Excellence Contemporary Asian Studies, 2004.
———. "Chinese Public Diplomacy." Waseda University Working Paper: Center of Excellence Contemporary Asian Studies, 2007.
"Arab Officials Ask for More Chinese TV Programs." *People's Daily Online*, June 26, 2006. http://english.people.com.cn/200606/26/eng20060626_277329.html.
Armstrong, Matthew. "China and American Public Diplomacy: Another U.S. Deficit S." www.MountainRunner.us, n.d. http://mountainrunner.us/2011/02/Senator_Lugar_China_and_US_Public_Diplomacy_Another_Deficit.html?utm_source=feedburner&utm_medium=feed&utm_campaign=Feed%3A+Mountainrunner+%28MountainRunner%29.
Bandurski, David. "Hitting Hard with 'Soft Power': China Explores Macro-Measures to Bolster Its Global Cultural Prowess," December 19, 2007. http://cmp.hku.hk/2007/12/19/797/.
———. "Li Changchun on the Media and China's 'Global Influence.'" *China Media Project*, December 19, 2009. http://cmp.hku.hk/2009/01/19/1457/.
———. "Propaganda Head Liu Yunshan Promotes Commercialization of Media to Strengthen China's 'Cultural Soft Power'—China Media Project," April 7, 2007. http://cmp.hku.hk/2007/04/10/225/.
"BBC Worldwide Strikes Another Deal with China." *BBC Press Office*, April 23, 2007. www.bbc.co.uk/pressoffice/bbcworldwide/worldwidestories/pressreleases/2007/04_april/motion_cctv.shtml.
Brautigam, Deborah. *The Dragon's Gift: The Real Story of China in Africa.* Oxford University Press U.S., 2009.
Chan, Yuen-Ying. "A Scholar's View: The State Media Have an Iron Grip and Grand Plans." *Global Asia*, June 2010. www.globalasia.org/V5N2_Summer_2010/Chan_Yuen_Ying.html.
Changchun, Li. "Li Changchun's (China's Top Media Control Official) Speech on Celebration Marking the Foundation of the Chinese Television Affairs and 50Th

Anniversary of China Central Television (CCTV)." China.com, December 23, 2008. http://news.china.com/zh_cn/news100/11038989/20081223/15248144.html.

Chen, Chen. "Finding Support for the Confucius Institutes," April 27, 2010. http://uscpublicdiplomacy.org/index.php/newswire/cpdblog_detail/finding_support_for_the_confucius_institutes/.

"China Opens First Confucius Institute on Air." *English Xinhua*, December 6, 2007. http://news.xinhuanet.com/english/2007–12/06/content_7211620.htm.

"China's First Public Diplomacy Research Center Established in Beijing." *People's Daily Online*. Beijing, China, August 27, 2010. http://english.peopledaily.com.cn/90001/90776/90883/7120534.html.

Cho, Young Nam, and Jong Ho Jeong. "China's Soft Power: Discussions, Resources, and Prospects." *Asian Survey* 48, no. 3 (June 1, 2008):453–472.

Cody, Edward. "Chinese Official Accuses Nations of Hacking." *Washington Post*, September 13, 2007. www.washingtonpost.com/wp-dyn/content/article/2007/09/12/AR2007091200791.html.

Cowhig, David. "How to Do Propaganda Work with Foreigners." *China Digital Times*, December 2, 2007. http://chinadigitaltimes.net/2007/12/how-to-do-propaganda-work-with-foreigners-david-cowhig/.

"CRI Launches New Media Broadcasting Network," January 18, 2011. http://english.cri.cn/6909/2011/01/18/2742s616142.htm.

"CRI's 70th Anniversary Contest," June 22, 2011. http://english.cri.cn/8706/2011/06/22/1461s644144.htm.

D'Hooge, Ingrid. "Public Diplomacy in the People's Republic of China." In *The New Public Diplomacy: Soft Power in International Relations*, ed. Jan Melissen. New York: Palgrave Macmillan, 2007.

———. *The Limits of China's Soft Power in Europe:Beijing's Public Diplomacy Puzzle*. Clingendael Diplomacy Papers. Netherlands Institute of International Relations: Clingendael, January 2010.

Dai, Ming. "Beijing Hones Media Manipulation." *Asia Times*, November 17, 2007. www.atimes.com/atimes/China/IK15Ad01.html.

Deng, Yong. "The New Hard Realities: 'Soft Power' and China in Transition." In *Soft Power: China's Emerging Strategy in International Politics*, ed. Mingjiang Li, 63–81. Lanham, MD: Lexington Books, 2009.

Ding, Sheng. *The Dragon's Hidden Wings: How China Rises with Its Soft Power*. Lexington Books, 2008.

Elliott, Kim Andrew. "China: Satellite Television Becomes Official." *Kim Andrew Elliott Reporting on International Broadcasting*, n.d. http://kimelli.nfshost.com/index.php?id=3003.

———. "Perhaps Too Much Sleep Is Lost over the 'Seduction, Prestige, and Omnipresence' of China's International Media Campaign." *Kim Andrew Elliott reporting on International Broadcasting*, April 14, 2011. http://kimelli.nfshost.com/index.php?id=11080.

"Exclusive Interview with Zhao Qizheng on China's Diplomacy." *CCTV—CNTV News*, March 2, 2011. http://english.cntv.cn/program/newsupdate/20110302/115431.shtml.

Fackler, Ted. "Kenya: The Chinese Make a Home Away from Home." AllAfrica. com, July 3, 2007. http://allafrica.com/stories/200707021725.html.

Farah, Douglas, and Andy Mosher. *Winds from the East: How the People's Republic of China Seeks to Influence the Media in Africa, Latin America, and Southeast Asia.* Washington, D.C.: Center for International Media Assistance, September 8, 2010.

"First 'Channel of China' to Open in Russia." *Xinhua*, January 17, 2008. http://news .xinhuanet.com/english/2008–01/17/content_7434371.htm.

Gachenge, Beatrice. "Kenyans Flock to Chinese Classes." *Business Daily–Nairobi*, June 28, 2007.

Gill, Bates, and Yanzhong Huang. "Sources and Limits of Chinese 'Soft Power.'" *Survival* 48, no. 2 (June 2006):17–36.

Glaser, Bonnie S., and Evan S Medeiros. "The Changing Ecology of Foreign Policy-Making in China: The Ascension and Demise of the Theory of 'Peaceful Rise,'" *The China Quarterly* 190 (2007):291–310.

Glaser, Bonnie S., and Melissa Murphy. "Soft Power with Chinese Characteristics: The Ongoing Debate." In *Chinese Soft Power and Its Implications for the United States: Competition and Cooperation in the Developing World: A Report of the CSIS Smart Power Initiative*, 10–26. Washington D.C.: CSIS, 2009.

Van Ham, Peter. *Social Power in International Politics.* Taylor & Francis, 2010.

"How China Deals with the U.S. Strategy to Contain China." *Qiushi Journal* (December 10, 2010). http://chinascope.org/main/content/view/3291/92/.

"How to Improve China's Soft Power?" *People's Daily Online*, March 11, 2010. http://english.peopledaily.com.cn/90001/90776/90785/6916487.html.

"Hu Jintao Calls for Enhancing 'Soft Power' of Chinese Culture." *People's Daily Online*, October 17, 2007. http://english.peopledaily.com.cn/90002/92169/92187/6283148 .html.

"Interview with University of Maryland Confucius Institute," April 12, 2010.

"Interview with Wu Jianmin (president of China Foreign Affairs University, former Chinese ambassador to France, on riots in Tibet)," September 27, 2010. www .want-daily.com/NEWs/Content.aspx?id=0&yyyymmdd=20100927&k=17915ae d7bb9a81196139f84ceafb832&h=c6f057b86584942e415435ffb1fa93d4&ni d=K@20100927@N0010.001.

"Interview with Zhao Qizheng (chairman of the Foreign Affairs Committee of the Chinese People's Political Consultative Conference and dean of the School of Journalism and Communication, Renmin University of China)," September 27, 2010. www.want-daily.com/NEWs/Content.aspx?id=0&yyyymmdd=20100927&k =17915aed7bb9a81196139f84ceafb832&h=c6f057b86584942e415435ffb1fa93d4 &nid=K@20100927@N0010.001.

"Introduction to the Confucius Institutes," August 29, 2009. http://college.chinese.cn/ en/article/2009–08/29/content_22308.htm.

Jiang, Steven. "Winner a No-Show as China Hands Out Its First Peace Prize." *CNNWorld*, December 9, 2010. http://articles.cnn.com/2010–12–09/world/china .confucius.peace_1_prize-committee-norwegian-nobel-prize-jury?_s=PM:WORLD.

Kalathil, Shanthi. *China's Soft Power in the Information Age: Think Again.* ISD Working Papers in Diplomacy. Washington, D.C.: Georgetown University, May 2011. http://isd.georgetown.edu/files/Kalathil_Chinas_Soft_Power.pdf.

Krishnan, Ananth. "China to Give a Fillip to International Relations." *The Hindu,* February 11, 2011, sec. International. www.thehindu.com/news/international/article1487217.ece.

Kurlantzick, Joshua. *Charm Offensive: How China's Soft Power Is Transforming the World.* Yale University Press, 2007.

LaFraniere, Sharon, and David Barboza. "China Tightens Electronic Censorship—NYTimes.com." Nytimes.com, March 21, 2011. www.nytimes.com/2011/03/22/world/asia/22china.html?_r=1.

Li, Mingjiang. "Soft Power in Chinese Discourse: Popularity and Prospect." In *China's Emerging Strategy in International Polics*, ed. Mingjiang Li, 21–44. Lanham, MD: Lexington Books, 2009.

———. *Soft Power: China's Emerging Strategy in International Politics.* Lexington Books, 2009.

———. "Soft Power: Nurture Not Nature." In *Soft Power: China's Emerging Strategy in International Politics*, ed. Mingjiang Li, 1–18. Lanham, MD: Lexington Books, 2009.

Lugar, Richard G., and Paul Foldi. *Another U.S. Deficit—China and America—Public Diplomacy in the Age of the Internet.* Committee on Foreign Relations, U. S. Senate. Washington D.C., February 15, 2011.

Ma, Lisi. "Guanyu Woguo Jiaqiang Ruan Shili Jianshe De Chubu Sikao (Preliminary Thoughts on Accelerating China's Soft Power Building)." *Dang De Wenxian (Literature of Chinese Communist Party)*, no. 7 (n.d.):35–38.

MacKinnon, Rebecca. "China's Internet White Paper: Networked Authoritarianism in Action." rconversation.blogs.com, June 10, 2010. http://rconversation.blogs.com/rconversation/2010/06/chinas-internet-white-paper-networked-authoritarianism.html.

Massey, Nathanael. "CCTV—The Voice of China's 'Soft Power.'" *Global Media Wars*, 2011. http://globalmediawars.com/?page_id=61.

McGiffert, Carola, ed. *Chinese Soft Power and Its Implications for the United States: Competition and Cooperation in the Developing World: A Report of the CSIS Smart Power Initiative.* Washington D.C.: CSIS, 2009.

Li, Mingjiang. "China Debates Soft Power." *The Chinese Journal of International Politics* 2, no. 2 (December 21, 2008):287–308.

Nye, Joseph S. "China's Century Is Not yet upon Us." *Financial Times*, May 18, 2010. http://cachef.ft.com/cms/s/0/649e807a-62aa-11df-b1d1-00144feab49a.html#axzz1S0gtvQGE.

Nye, Joseph S. Jr. *The Future of Power.* 1st ed. PublicAffairs, 2011.

Pang, Zhongying. *The Beijing Olympics and China's Soft Power.* Washington, D.C.: Brookings Institution, Winter 2008. www.brookings.edu/opinions/2008/0904_olympics_pang.aspx.

Price, Monroe Edwin. *Media and Sovereignty: The Global Information Revolution and Its Challenge to State Power.* MIT Press, 2004.

Price, Monroe. "Xinhua, China's Soft Power Initiative and the Return of the New World Information Order." *Huffington Post*, June 7, 2011. www.huffingtonpost. com/monroe-price/xinhua-chinas-soft-power-_b_872578.html.

"'Public Diplomacy at Early Stage'—China.org.cn." *NPC & CPPCC 2011*, March 3, 2011. www.china.org.cn/china/NPC_CPPCC_2011/2011–03/03/content _22042058.htm.

"Public Diplomacy Gains Ground," *Global Times*," n.d. http://china.globaltimes.cn/ diplomacy/2010–09/573212.html.

"'Public Diplomat' Wants Foreigners to See the 'True China.'" *Global Times*, May 19, 2011. http://news.cultural-china.com/20110519094031.html.

Qingguo, Jia. *Continuity and Change: China's Attitude toward Hard Power and Soft Power.* Washington, D.C.: Brookings Institution, December 2010. www.brookings.edu/ opinions/2010/12_china_soft_power_jia.aspx.

Ramo, Joshua Cooper. *The Beijing Consensus*. Foreign Policy Centre, 2004.

"Re-Understand Soft Power." *Journal of Nanjing University; Philosophy, Humanities and Social Sciences*, no. 1 (2010).

Schmidt, Peter. "At U.S. Colleges, Chinese-Financed Centers Prompt Worries about Academic Freedom." *The Chronicle of Higher Education*, October 22, 2010. http:// chronicle.texterity.com/chronicle/20101022a?pg=8#pg8.

"Senior Chinese Leader Stresses Protection of Cultural Heritage." *News of the Communist Party of China*, June 13, 2010, sec. News. http://english.cpc.people.com. cn/66102/7024799.html.

"Senior Party Official: Enhance Cohesion, Appeal of Socialist Ideology," November 30, 2007. http://english.cpc.people.com.cn/66102/6312736.html.

Sennitt, Andy. "China's CCTV Opens Three Channels in Cuba." *Radio Netherlands Worldwide*, February 20, 2008. http://blogs.rnw.nl/medianetwork/chinas-cctv -opens-three-channels-in-cuba.

Seuttinger, Robert. "The Rise and Descent of 'Peaceful Rise.'" *China Leadership Monitor* 12 (n.d.):1–10.

Shambaugh, David. "China Flexes Its Soft Power." *New York Times*, June 7, 2010, sec. Op-Ed. www.nytimes.com/2010/06/08/opinion/08iht-edshambaugh.html.

Sohn, Yul. "Attracting Neighbors: Soft Power Competition in East Asia." 1–14. Seoul, Korea: Korea Foundation and East Asia Institute, 2008.

"Strong Public Diplomacy Vital for China" *People's Daily Online*, April 8, 2011. http://english.peopledaily.com.cn/90001/90776/90883/7343844.html.

Suzuki, Shogo. "Chinese Soft Power, Insecurity Studies, Myopia and Fantasy." *Third World Quarterly* 30, no. 4 (June 2009):779–793.

"The Promotion of Soft Power and the Strategies of Chinese Peaceful Development." *Maozedong Thought Study* 27, no. 2 (March 2010).

"The Whole World Moved by China." *People's Daily Online*, n.d., sec. Opinion. http://english.people.com.cn/90001/90780/91342/6761629.html.

Totten, Sanden. "China Invests in Filmmaking, for Image and Profit: NPR," n.d. www.npr.org/2011/06/19/137253607/china-invests-in-filmmaking-for-image-and -profit?sc=17&f=1001.

Wang, Hongying. "National Image Building and Chinese Foreign Policy." *China: An International Journal* 1, no. 1 (2003):46–72.

Wang, Hongying, and Yeh-Chung Lu. "The Conception of Soft Power and Its Policy Implications: A Comparative Study of China and Taiwan." *Journal of Contemporary China* 17 (August 2008):425–447.

Wang, Huning. "Zuowei Guojia Shili De Wenhua: Ruan Quanli' (Culture as National Power: Soft Power)." *Fuda Daxue Xuebao (Journal of Fudan University)*, no. 3 (1993):23–28.

Wang, Ke. "China Slowly Learning Public Diplomacy: Huang Youyi." China.org. cn, March 5, 2011. www.china.org.cn/china/NPC_CPPCC_2011/2011–03/05/ content_22064456.htm.

Wang, Yiwei. "Public Diplomacy and the Rise of Chinese Soft Power." *The ANNALS of the American Academy of Political and Social Science* 616, no. 1 (March 1, 2008):257–273.

Wu, Zheng. *Zhongguo De Da Guo De Wei Yu Guo Ji Chuan Bo Zhan Lüe (China's Need for a Strategy of International Communication)*. Di 1 Ban. Beijing: Chang Zheng Chu Ban She, 2001.

Wuthnow, Joel. "The Concept of Soft Power in China's Soft Power Discourse." *Issues and Studies* 44, no. 2 (June 2008):1–28.

Xiao, Yong-Ming, and Tian-Jie Zhang. "The Retrospection and Prospect to the Research of Chinese Cultural Soft Power." *Journal of Hunan University (Social Science)* 24, no. 1 (January 2010).

Xie, Xue-Peng. "The Cultural Soft Power and the Shaping of China's National Image." *Journal of Shanxi Normal University* 36, no. 5 (September 2009).

"Xinhua Launches CNC World English Channel." English.news.cn, July 1, 2010. http://news.xinhuanet.com/english2010/china/2010–07/01/c_13378575.htm.

Yan, Yuetong. "Ruan Shili De Hexin Shi Zhengzhi Shili (The Core of Soft Power Is Political Power)," *Huanqiu Shibao (Global Times)*, May 22, 2007.

Yee, Andy. "China Makes Global Media Push, but Skeptics Abound." *PBS MEDIASHIFT*, April 19, 2011. www.pbs.org/mediashift/2011/04/china-makes-global -media-push-but-skeptics-abound109.html.

Yu, Sophie. "China's Voice Is About to Get Louder All around the World." *Center for International Media Assistance*, November 1, 2010. http://cima.ned.org/chinas -voice-about-get-louder-all-around-world.

Zhang, Haizhou. "China Needs More Public Diplomacy, Zhao Says," March 11, 2010. www.chinadaily.com.cn/china/2010npc/2010–03/11/content_9570697 .htm.

Zhang, Tuosheng. "China in New Phase of World Integration." *China Daily*, October 17, 2007, sec. Commentary. www.chinadaily.com.cn/opinion/2007–10/17/content _6182330.htm.

Zhang, Zhexin. "China's Public Diplomacy Institution: Its Development, Challenges, and Prospects of Its Practice." *IO Journal* 1, no. 3 (2009):12–17.

Zhao, Keijn. *Theory and Practice of Public Diplomacy*. Shanghai: Shanghai Dictionary Press, 2007.

Zhao, Qizheng. "People's Daily Online—Better Public Diplomacy to Present a Truer Picture of China," March 30, 2007. http://english.people.com.cn/200703/30/eng20070330_362496.html.

———. "'To Formulate a Favorable Public Opinion in the World.'" *Nuli Jianshe Youliyu Woguode Guoji Yulun Huanjing), Journal of Foreign Affairs College*, no. Third Quarter (2004).

———. "Zhao Qizheng: Mobilizing Public Diplomacy," *Shanghai World Expo*, April 29, 2010. http://en.expo2010.cn/a/20100429/000005.htm.

Zhu, Majie, and Xintian Yu. "Ruan Guoli Jianshe: Bu Rong Hushi De Wuxing Yingxiang (Soft Power Construction: Invisible Influence Not to Be Ignored)." In *Proceedings of Annual Meeting of Shanghai Social Sciences Circle*, 2004.

Chapter 6

The United States of America

Public Diplomacy 2.0 and
Twenty-First Century Statecraft

Joseph Nye's assessment of the post Cold War environment for U.S. foreign policy yielded an "analytical concept" that provided a reasonable argument to justify the continued primacy of the United States.[1] Yet as subsequent iterations of soft power, notions like "smart power" or "sticky power" in U.S. strategic discourse suggest the soft power concept has never been a primary strategic concept contributing to U.S. foreign policy thinking. While soft power may be American in origin, it has not fit easily into U.S. foreign policy and its attendant rhetoric; soft power is rarely presented as an objective as much as it is as a given.[2] This chapter aims to chart, through official statements and policy programs of public diplomacy, an evolving U.S. interpretation of soft power that emphasizes the particular benefits of *technological* platforms for outreach that demonstrate, rather than elaborate on, the resources of U.S. soft power. The chapter examines the strategic communication policies and discourse surrounding U.S. public diplomacy in the twenty-first century, to arrive at a working sense of how soft power is tacitly understood as a strategic orientation to communication as a foreign policy tool and context.

What constitutes American soft power? The question is posed here not to invite speculation on what specific resources of an ideological program should be included in a catalog of U.S. power assets—but to investigate how such resources are *made valuable* under a rhetoric of soft power. The U.S. interpretation of soft power in the aftermath of 9/11 remains closely bound up with debates over the necessity and improvement of public diplomacy, yet, as Brian Hocking argues, this has complicated the two concepts, and may have led "to the danger of misunderstanding the significance of public diplomacy and confusing its role as a mode of exercising power with the changing environments in which power is projected."[3] Hocking points to the difficulty in disentangling the conceptual threads of soft power from public diplomacy. Yet soft power remains an underlying justificatory framework from which to argue for public diplomacy.

Equating soft power and public diplomacy raises more basic questions about what counts as public diplomacy in ways that are relevant to the discussion of soft power: is public diplomacy a *context*—the volume of potentially influential communication flows between publics (e.g., popular culture that "speaks" for the United States), or is soft power primarily located in the institutions of government that do strategic communication of some sort? If public diplomacy supposedly cultivates soft power or redirects foreign public attention to soft power (a somewhat ambiguous claim that Nye makes for the necessity of public diplomacy) then a distinction of soft power is necessary.[4]

Nancy Snow argues that there remains a considerable amount of confusing overlap between soft power and public diplomacy—particularly in U.S. public discourse.[5] And, as Kathy Fitzpatrick notes in her analysis of U.S. public diplomacy, "there has been virtually no serious debate about whether soft power provides a sound conceptual foundation for public diplomacy."[6] Yet *some* set of assumptions about soft power appear to shape discourse about public diplomacy, which in turn has ramifications for the imagination of an ideal strategy of international influence, the definition of the strategic "problem" at hand, and how policymakers recognize resources and practices as contributing to soft power.

U.S. public diplomacy represents a broad range of actors and organizations with competing inertias of strategic significance. American public diplomacy comprises an extensive legacy of international broadcasting programs, cultural and educational exchange programs, and a variety of information programs designed to inform, educate, and influence foreign audiences.[7] Responsibilities for these programs are also distributed between diplomatic, military, and non-governmental organizations. Yet these programs rely on different conceptions of what counts for influence.

An American conception of soft power is undoubtedly reflective of likely competing visions for soft power—the role of values embodied in the objectivity of international broadcasting or, for example, the benefits of identification fostered through culture and educational exchange programs. Put simply, U.S. public diplomacy is a *big* enterprise, and not easily reducible to a set of idealizations drawn from analyzing programs in their entirety. Therefore, the analysis presented here draws from public arguments about the requirements of diplomacy, public diplomacy, and strategic communication for the United States going forward that describes a strategic role for public diplomacy in the broader field of U.S. foreign policy. Specifically, this chapter argues that the shift toward *technological interventions*, begun during the latter half of the Bush administration, suggest a strategy to *facilitate* the ability of foreign publics to communicate. This shift represents a fundamental move away from the transmission-oriented paradigms of Cold War public diplomacy and strategic communication. There are a number of insights that can be drawn from this transformation.

First, the move toward *facilitation* and *engagement* that define public diplomacy strategy in the Obama administration suggest the continuation of a historical trend of ambivalence toward the necessity of persuasion—the need to elaborate the attractiveness of U.S. political culture, institutions, and values.[8] Facilitation displaces the persuasive burden onto policies and technologies that *stand in* as persuasive in themselves, and demonstrate soft power values rather than explain them.

Second, the move toward facilitation and engagement suggests a more robust conception of the *audience* for public diplomacy that not only acknowledges a perceived potency for nonstate actors like NGOs and other transnational groups, but in which citizens themselves possess the power to judge and act within networks that have impact on the power of the United States. The shift away from transmission models for communication strategy means both that nonstate actors matter and that such actors consume information critically—they are not dupes to propaganda campaigns. *How* the U.S. communicates matters as much as *what* is communicated in the cultivation of soft power.

Various academic treatments of this evolution in the practice of public diplomacy, such as the "new public diplomacy" and "network diplomacy," do explain some aspects of U.S. strategic discourse after 9/11.[9] The focus here is on how the United States has interpreted the requirements of soft power for its own foreign policy objectives. The development is labeled here as "public diplomacy 2.0," a term coined by James Glassman, former Undersecretary of State for Public Diplomacy and Public Affairs, mainly to describe a distinctly U.S. version of new public diplomacy thinking that relies heavily on the modes of communication for the burdens of influence.[10] While other terms have emerged with successive U.S. foreign policy leadership, such as "transformational diplomacy," "network diplomacy," and "twenty-first century statecraft," public diplomacy 2.0 provides a convenient term to mark historical changes in the communication assumptions behind public diplomacy and an evolving understanding of what soft power means for diplomatic practice.

The case of the United States presented here offers a view of soft power that assumes the intrinsic power of values, ideas, and culture alongside the capacity of material communicative forms to express these values. As with China, the U.S. version of soft power assumes an arguably exceptionalist stance toward its soft power resources. And as with Japan, the forms of communication (in particular, the material aspects of communication technology) carry an intrinsic argument about such values—communication forms represent attractive values. To explain the U.S. idealization of soft power, this chapter focuses extensively on programs that elaborate evidence for a soft power embedded in technology and, to borrow from James Carey, in the "rituals" or practices of international communication.[11] It also examines the discourse of a profoundly exceptionalist set of arguments for public diplomacy to a set of claims that conflate the compelling aspects of U.S. values with the deployment of technologies that are perceived to be demonstrative of these values.

There are other excellent historical and contemporary treatments of U.S. public diplomacy that explain in greater detail the breadth of U.S. public diplomacy activities carried out by a wide range of institutional actors in the U.S. federal government and supporting organizations.[12] Rather than reiterate their observations, this chapter focuses on activities that reflect a strategic shift in the conception of soft power when leaders and policies convey a kind of exigency in the strategic environment. Public argument and programs that appear inspired or associated with the notion of "public diplomacy 2.0" in U.S. public diplomacy are presented as indicative of a discursive shift—a new frame of public discourse through which traditional public diplomacy is argued for and understood within the field of U.S. foreign policy strategic reasoning.

HISTORY OF AMERICAN SOFT POWER CULTIVATION: A VERY BRIEF OVERVIEW

Central assumptions about soft power have been present in U.S. reasoning on public diplomacy and strategic communication throughout the twentieth century. The formative period of what would later become the formal institutions of U.S. public diplomacy (the term would not be invented until 1965) are discussed here to provide contextual insight into how influence was perceived as possible through strategic communication and public diplomacy programs. The expressed strategic necessity of public diplomacy-related activities, especially during the Cold War, reveal some enduring strategic assumptions about information and communication that are implicated in U.S. perceptions of international politics.

The origins of U.S. public diplomacy can be traced to the activities of the Committee on Public Information (CPI), set up by President Woodrow Wilson during World War I. The CPI, also known as the Creel Commission after its chairman, George Creel, was instrumental in promoting support, both domestically and among foreign publics, for the U.S. cause during the Great War. The U.S. proto–"public diplomacy" of this time period was an integrated effort incorporating news, film, and public address—and was widely recognized as instrumental in swaying newspaper opinion around the world for President Wilson's programs.[13] The CPI is unusual compared to more contemporary U.S. efforts at public diplomacy in that the lines between domestic and foreign were less clearly demarcated in its efforts.[14] The CPI was dissolved after World War I.

The Office of War Information was set up during World War II to assist the U.S. war efforts, and again featured programs that targeted both domestic and foreign environments through the USIS.[15] The OWI, like the CPI, used a broad spectrum of media to support its propaganda efforts—including film, magazines, books, and newsreels.[16] In addition to these programs, the State Department engaged in educational and cultural exchange programs through its Division of Cultural Relations. Yet, as Wilson Dizard claims in his history of U.S. public diplomacy, there was concern at this time over the efforts of other nations to draw the United States into the war—a concern that would continue to manifest in a lingering suspicion of propaganda that impacted subsequent efforts to defend public diplomacy operations during the Cold War. Implicit in this anxiety is the presumption of audience vulnerability—strategic communication interventions represented a kind of power over audiences that had little recourse but to be persuaded.

At the dawn of the Cold War, the U.S. public diplomacy apparatus developed with the passage of key legislation—the Fulbright Act of 1946 and the Smith–Mundt Act of 1948. The Fulbright Act established a mandate for exchange programs that still reflect part of U.S. cultural and educational diplomacy. The Smith–Mundt Act, or the United States Information and Education and Exchange Act of 1948, established international communication capacities within the State Department to "promote the better understanding of the United States among peoples of the world and to strengthen cooperative international relations."[17] The Smith–Mundt Act is the foundational legislation for a formalized U.S. public diplomacy, providing both a mandate to create international communication institutions and a set of strategic justifications for peacetime "information efforts."[18]

The Smith–Mundt Act did more than create institutional capacity. It was also a turning point in strategic thinking. Following George Kennan's influential observations that the Soviets were engaged in psychological and ideological warfare with the United States, the Smith–Mundt act represented a formal strategic response. The Smith–Mundt Act authorized the U.S. Secretary of State to prepare and disseminate "information about the United States, its people, and its policies, through press, publications, radio, motion pictures, and other information media, and through information centers and instructors abroad."[19] This institutional capability to engage foreign audiences through communicative means (in particular, international broadcasting) was later formalized with the creation of the United States Information Agency in 1953 by President Eisenhower. In 1961, the Fulbright-Hays Act established the institutional mandate to promote "mutual understanding" through cultural and educational exchange."[20]

The post-war legislation was also significant in that it articulated a set of durable strategic reasons for public diplomacy—justificatory arguments that reflected how U.S. policymakers saw what was required for foreign policy and what counted as necessary for international persuasion. This is not to suggest that there was a widespread consensus on the intent and ethics of public diplomacy. The 1981 Zorinsky amendment to the Smith–Mundt Act, which expanded the prohibitions on domestic dissemination of USIA-produced material, reflected lingering ambivalence toward government-produced communication.[21] Yet the body of legislative discourse since the Cold War betrays an overarching logic and set of strategic assumptions that anticipate a kind of soft power.

U.S. attention to international communication revealed the strategic recognition that power was inherent in competitive persuasive activities, and that the relevant actors in international relations had expanded beyond just nation-states. As early as 1945, government officials framed international relations in ways not dissimilar to those in the twenty-first century. Speaking to the House Foreign Affairs Committee, Assistant Secretary of State William Benton stated that

> Relations between nations have constantly been broadened to include not merely governments but also peoples. The peoples of the world are exercising an ever larger influence upon decisions of foreign policy. That is as it should be. . . . The people themselves, as well as their ideas, are moving about the world farther and faster.[22]

Benton's arguments seem prescient, anticipating the transformative thinking about communication and international relations that appeared at the end of the Cold War.[23] Nonstate actors are depicted here as politically significant in their own right, due in no small part to the capacities of communication systems. Thus a robust communicative capacity to engage foreign audiences would be required, especially in the face of a considerable campaign of propaganda from the Soviet Union.[24]

Communication argued as necessary to U.S. foreign policy objectives at the dawn of the Cold War was defined by the volume and reach of the platforms involved and less in terms of message and argument strategy.[25] What remained underdeveloped during the Truman administration was a working logic of persuasion. How could soft power assets be presented in such a way as to combat the Soviet message? The course of persuasion involved in U.S. communication strategy during the Truman administration was largely based on exposure. To *know* the United States would accrue influence.

Secretary of State George Marshall, speaking in 1947 before a subcommittee of the House Appropriations Committee on the issue of the Department of State Appropriation Bill for 1948, explained the need for more communication:

> One effective way to promote peace is to dispel misunderstanding, fear, and ignorance. Foreign peoples should know the nature and objectives of our foreign policy. They should have a true understanding of American life. This is the purpose of the information and cultural relations program.[26]

Marshall's appeal to the U.S. legislature provides a straightforward mandate for strategic communication: to provide an "understanding of American life." Of course, left out of this argument is *how* such understanding would translate into the kind of leverage and influence desired. Would American life by its very nature be compelling and attractive? One of the reasons for this lack of elaboration may have been political—it was difficult to argue to Congress that the United States needed to explain *why* its values needed to be amplified and explained.[27] Here again, Marshall tries to distinguish an ostensibly American form of communication from the "propaganda" of others:

> I think the whole matter is an offset to the type of propaganda, newspaper articles, and so forth, that appear in various countries. We have to do something about it. If propaganda is fire, I do not think it is advisable that we fight fire with fire in this particular case, because it is not in accord with our traditions.[28]

Marshall's appears to argue for a different kind of persuasive practice—that would not reflect the manipulative practices of Soviet propaganda—and embody the political ideals of the United States. The tacit logic of U.S. soft power at the dawn of the Cold War was inherently based in exceptionalism, which was translated into the very assumptions about what was persuasive for foreign audiences.[29] Along these lines, Shawn Parry-Giles's analysis implicates the exceptionalist tenor of policy argumentation in hampering Truman's initial efforts to implement an effective propaganda strategy. She argues that Truman-era arguments for propaganda "assumed that democracy could be exported with ease."[30] Early attempts to persuade and attract international audiences at the dawn of the Cold war were assumed to work through awareness and through broadcasting the purportedly universal qualities of American institutions. As Parry-Giles observes, "justificatory arguments and America's propaganda were . . . driven by a belief in the inherent naturalness of democracy."[31] The persuasion of this early form of U.S. public diplomacy was assumed to be inherent in the subject of the message itself.

During the early stages of the Cold War, the communication transaction—the process by which messages were sent and consumed—was perceived to be relatively straightforward. Audiences did not need to be *convinced* so much as they needed to be *aware* of democracy and the United States. In a 1953 address to the United States Information Agency, Eisenhower claimed that when given a choice between governments, the American system had "greater appeal to the human soul."[32] As Parry-Giles interprets, under this logic "foreign audiences would naturally believe the "truth" disseminated by America and naturally reject the principals of Communism."[33] In his own historical account, former Assistant Secretary of State Edward Barrett reflected that the United States was well positioned to be effective in a propaganda war with the Soviets because "in the contest for men's minds . . . truth can be a peculiarly American weapon."[34] Yet the "truth" involved in this conception of U.S. soft power assets was assumed to be effectively self-evident.

By the 1960s, U.S. public diplomacy was entrenched as a significant component of U.S. foreign policy institutions. The term "public diplomacy" was also introduced by Edward Gullion, the dean of the newly formed Edward R. Murrow School of public diplomacy at Tufts University. In the inaugural speech, Gullion laid out the strategic significance of public diplomacy:

> Public diplomacy . . . deals with the influence of public attitudes on the formation and execution of foreign policies. It encompasses dimensions of international relations beyond traditional diplomacy; the cultivation by governments of public opinion in other countries; the interaction of private groups and interests in one country with those of another; the reporting of foreign affairs and its impact on policy; communication between those whose job is communication, as between diplomats and foreign correspondents; and the processes of intercultural communications.[35]

In the decades after the start of the Cold War, the USIA public diplomacy activities grew to include stewardship of a publications bureau, educational and cultural exchanges, international broadcasting outlets such as the Voice of America and, eventually, the surrogate radios (e.g., Radio Free Europe, Radio Free Liberty), and the United States Information Service (USIS). By

1999, the year the USIA was dismantled and folded into the State Department, the USIS maintained over 190 posts in 142 countries—staffing U.S. embassies with public affairs officers, information officers, and cultural affairs officers to "study and absorb the political and cultural climate of the host country, the better to craft messages and offer insights about America which can be coherently read in the local context."[36]

After end of the Cold War, domestic cost-cutting politics contributed to the end of the USIA and the perceived need for a permanent organization dedicated to communicating U.S. interests abroad. The global preponderance of U.S. cultural and news flows led lawmakers and policymakers to suggest that the United States no longer needed the USIA, while others argued that the State Department could be better positioned to integrate the implementation of foreign policy with the requirement to communicate about such policy.[37] In 1999, the USIA was formally dismantled. Its international broadcasting efforts were given to the Broadcasting Board of Governors, while its other information, education, and cultural exchange activities were folded into the State Department.[38]

PUBLIC DIPLOMACY AFTER 9/11:
CONTINUITY AND CHANGE

In the wake of the 9/11 attacks, public diplomacy and soft power resurfaced as crucial priorities for United States foreign policy and national security.[39] Numerous reports and legislative hearings after the attacks highlighted the failures of U.S. communication efforts abroad along with the precipitous rise of anti-American sentiment. In particular, the state of opinion about the United States was positioned as a public diplomacy *problem* and a measure of the decline of U.S. soft power. As such, public diplomacy was argued as a government-led instrument to remedy the decline.

Pivotal documents, such as the Djerejian report on U.S. relations with the Arab world, the 9/11 Commission reports, and the 2004 Defense Science Board's evaluation of U.S. strategic communication, yielded observations that would be echoed in over 85 reports, white papers, and policy–position papers on how to improve U.S. public diplomacy and strategic communication efforts.[40] Yet despite numerous calls for reform and increased investment in public diplomacy capacity since the events of 9/11, much of U.S. public diplomacy reflects the legacy of the presumptive value of U.S. ideals and policy legitimacy; U.S. public diplomacy has operated on the assumption that its soft power resources can be *converted*; that exposing foreign audiences to U.S. values will illuminate a shared identification with U.S. motives and policies. In this view, public diplomacy provides a kind of revelatory function—pointing foreign audiences toward the belief that American values and institutions are in fact their values.

As the United States debated reforms shortly after 9/11, Undersecretary of State for Public Diplomacy Charlotte Beers, a successful U.S. advertising industry executive, told the House Committee on International Relations that foreign audiences may not *know* about United States and its values:

> The burden is on us to act as if no one has ever understood the identity of the United States, to redefine it for audiences who are, at best, cynical. It is a war about the way of life and fundamental beliefs and values. We did not expect to ever have to explain and defend concepts like freedom and tolerance.[41]

Beers's comments reflect the tone of U.S. foreign policy rhetoric at the time regarding the emergent global war on terror. If the United States was engaged in an existential battle of ideological narratives—it needed to explain itself.

The aftermath of a widely unpopular war in Iraq complicated U.S. public diplomacy efforts, with the U.S. administration appearing increasingly tone-deaf to the complaints of the Arab and Muslim world. Though President Bush signaled increased attention to the requirements of persuading foreign publics by appointing his campaign advisor, Karen Hughes, to the post of Undersecretary of State for Public Diplomacy and Public affairs in 2005, there was little substantial strategic reform to public diplomacy. In 2005, U.S. Secretary of State Condoleezza Rice seemed to acknowledge the predicament of the United States in arguing for its policies and values with audiences skeptical or hostile.

> I know that sometimes it is difficult to see that this is a history that is moving in the right direction but I think as long as we remain true to our values and true to our belief that democracy and freedom and liberty are the birthright of every living human being, that we will one day stand here and see that the world has been transformed, indeed, for the better.[42]

Secretary Rice's comments reveal a persistent belief that American soft power need not be explained or cultivated. This was echoed across the political spectrum. For example, Anne-Marie Slaughter, who later served in the Obama administration, argues in 2004:

> Our shared values are essential because they link America to the world. The belief that American values are universal values—that all men and women are created equal, that all are entitled to life, liberty, and the pursuit of happiness, regardless of race, creed, or nationality—connects us to other nations.[43]

Slaughter presupposes that influence is accomplished in the revelation of shared values and, in particular, that the United States embodies universal values. Despite such attitudes, public diplomacy strategy did begin to change as evidence of public diplomacy's inability to address U.S. unpopularity continued to increase.

Public Diplomacy in Transition: Toward Technology, Networks, and Influence

In the wake of persistent negative attitudes toward the United States among audiences considered crucial to U.S. foreign policy objectives—such as youth demographics in Arab and Muslim countries—as well as widespread disapproval of U.S. intervention in Iraq, U.S. public diplomacy strategy began to change toward the end of the Bush administration. This transition was part of a broader effort to reframe U.S. diplomatic practice and deal with the perception that under President George W. Bush, the United States engaged in so-called "cowboy diplomacy." Secretary of State Condoleezza Rice claimed that in the post-9/11 world, traditional practices of state-to-state diplomacy reflected an inadequate strategic orientation.[44]

The idea of "transformational diplomacy" signaled that the strategic culture behind U.S. diplomatic institutions needed to change, in response to new threats and opportunities that challenged existing diplomatic organizations—such as global terrorism, failed states, environmental security, law enforcement, and democracy promotion. These challenges were complicated by profound changes in the communication environment, which enabled and empowered nonstate actors while offering unprecedented transparent scrutiny of nation-state actions.

Criticism of U.S. public diplomacy accumulated since the 9/11 attacks figured prominently in the proposals suggested under Secretary Rice's "transformational diplomacy." Under the supervision of Karen Hughes, a number of initiatives were launched to align U.S. public diplomacy practice with the perceived context for strategic communication. These included the establishment of a Rapid Response Unit to monitor open-source media messages about the United States, an "Echo Chamber" program to allow for common messaging practices across U.S. representatives abroad, and the easing of clearance procedures to allow for greater flexibility among such representatives. Hughes explains the context demanding changes in U.S. public diplomacy practice:

> [T]here is an information explosion and no one is hungry for information. We are now competing for attention and for credibility in a time when rumors can

spark riots, and information, whether it's true or false, quickly spreads across the world, across the Internet, in literally instants.[45]

Hughes articulates a different view of the global communication ecology, where soft power cannot be derived simply from the provision of objective information as a public good. This reflects R. S. Zaharna's incisive analysis of the deficiencies in U.S. public diplomacy after the 9/11 attacks—that the United States was waging an "information battle" akin to the strategies of the Cold War, while contemporary public diplomacy requires, in her analysis, more attention to networks and relation-building.[46] At the very least, the public diplomacy reforms proposed during Hughes's tenure and during her successor, James Glassman, suggest the recognition that the communication environment may be more significant than the transmission of the message. The social context of communication matters for the cultivation of influence.

Yet the latter Bush-era public diplomacy policies retained significant bias toward the crafting of a more perfect message. The "Echo Chamber" program, in particular, is illustrative of this approach: that influence can be garnered by strategic communication that is consistent across spokespersons.[47] Only after the "public diplomacy 2.0" era proposals—such as the Digital Outreach Team efforts described later in this chapter—would the shift in public diplomacy strategy move emphasis away from message management and toward a facilitative paradigm of diplomacy and the provision of communication as basis for establishing relations. Strategic shifts in public diplomacy strategy at end of the George W. Bush presidency revealed a critical consensus that messaging-based persuasion could not be *the* defining mechanism of a successful public diplomacy strategy.

The focus on *relationships* repositions the significance of persuasion within public diplomacy, where the outcomes of facilitating democratic practices and civil society are goals that become the expected public diplomacy benefit. In other words—influence accrues not in the elaboration of arguments about the United States, but in the symbolic significance of diplomatic practices that aid, facilitate and connect. Central to this shift in public diplomacy is the potential for information and communication technologies (ICTs) that enable network relations and empower nonstate actors in such a way as to bring about U.S. foreign policy objectives.

Yet how are such technologies conceived as significant for the objectives of public diplomacy? Programs such as the Digital Outreach team of State Department bloggers and the @america Center in Indonesia, reflect the growing significance of new and social media technologies—as both means of engagement *and* foreign policy ends in their own right. The capacities of new and social media technologies to facilitate democratic participation, build a robust civil society, and otherwise empower political agency are conceived as crucial to the public diplomacy objectives of the United States. As the initiatives pursued under the Obama administration suggest, influence is not necessarily to persuade, but to enable democratic practices through increasingly networked, technological contexts.

U.S. public diplomacy transitioned under the supervision of Secretary of State Hillary Clinton and Undersecretary of State for Public Diplomacy and Public Affairs Judith McHale in two significant ways. First, communication technologies came to signify an increasingly high-profile aspect of what the State Department was doing to practice public diplomacy, and second, these technologies also *embodied* an attitude toward the prospect of strategic influence that rejected direct persuasion as a central objective. While information and communication technologies are not necessarily "new" to the practice of public diplomacy, how they define the practice and indeed, the strategic context for public diplomacy is a more recent development.[48] Their significance can, in part, be traced to recognition of how audiences crucial to U.S. foreign policy goals actually use and access such technologies.

There also appeared to be a growing relationship between the modalities of communication and the kinds of strategies they would support. Traditional technologies of public diplomacy prior to the George W. Bush administration were mostly mass communication–oriented, such as the international broadcasting of the Voice of America and Radio Liberty/Radio Free Europe. The controversial Al-Hurra Arab language satellite network continued this emphasis on mass media. While these services have since taken advantage of Internet-based delivery methods, other programs have emerged, such as the Digital Outreach Teams, the DipNote blog, and the Democracy Video Challenge, to capitalize on the affordances of networked, relation-oriented communication technologies.

The rise of social networking and new media technologies within public diplomacy indicates not only the increasing significance of technology in its own right, but also a related recognition of the importance of nonstate actors, global governance, and social relations that have encroached on the terrain of traditionally state-centric international politics—a strategic shift that increasingly collapses the distinction between "public" and "traditional" diplomacy. The policy discourse and programs in the wake of the "public diplomacy 2.0" turn are suggestive of both the increased adoption of technology for public diplomacy and, implicitly, the salience of the *network form* on the practices of international engagement.[49]

As the arguments presented under the "transformative diplomacy" turn suggests, the predominance of various and overlapping networks that define relations among the diverse range of actors within international politics requires a different kind of outreach to diplomatic stakeholders—and is suggestive of the *structural* significance of the network form itself.[50] This development, coupled with the enduring legacy of public diplomacy-as-persuasion, has driven continued criticism of the concept. Kristin Lord and March Lynch have proposed that "engagement" better describes the obligatory communication stance required by U.S. soft power strategy.[51]

The term "engagement," however, replaces a historically charged concept with an ambiguous one. Lord and Lynch deploy the term to distinguish strategic influence and communication attempts from a kind of sermonizing, monological stance behind U.S. *diplomacy* as much as public diplomacy. Engagement, as used by public diplomacy advocates and practitioners, suggests technological tools as crucial mediators that enable the United States to operate among the circuits of relations within audiences critical to foreign policy goals. Yet to "engage" in environments such as blogs, Twitter, or Facebook does little to clarify the practice of public diplomacy, nor does it distinguish public diplomacy from other forms of outreach that downplay the asymmetries of power between citizens and the nation-state.

As it is argued here, the implications of ubiquitous *networks* (both social and technological) have forced a transformation on the ambitions of U.S. public diplomacy; an uneasy transition that may yet be fraught with contradictions. The body of public arguments suggestive of a technological approach stand out in the many reports and white papers on U.S. public diplomacy course corrections. In particular, awareness of the global communication infrastructure appears as a common theme.* The evolution of U.S. position papers and official policy discourse on public diplomacy underscores the opportunity represented in media technologies and the communities (or networks) that rely upon them, rather than elaborating strong linkages between media content and political identification. A U.S. Government Accountability Office report in 2009 captures the concern that this "environment" of networked global communication is crucial, while previous public diplomacy efforts were slow to adapt:

> [T]he current information suggests a failure to adapt in this dynamic communications environment could significantly raise the risk that U.S. public diplomacy efforts could become increasingly irrelevant, particularly among younger audiences that represent a key focus of U.S. strategic communication efforts.[52]

Such concerns track with growing scholarly recognition that communication and media flows constitute significant challenges for nation-state action. Joseph Nye argues that publics important to foreign policy objectives are subject to a "paradox of plenty," as they are inundated with multiple channels of information, news, and perspectives.[53] Individuals immersed in the global communication infrastructure are at the same time *empowered* by what Manual Castells calls "mass-self-communication" to articulate shared interests and organize political projects and communities.[54] This context for foreign policy has fueled increased attention to technology as a solution to policy objectives. The attention to technology also highlights the increased importance of public diplomacy as a strategic orientation, an idea at least in part justified by the stream of scholarly writing about the significance of media and information technologies for the practice of international politics.[55] The convergence of technology, diplomacy, and practice has lead to a reconsideration of "statecraft" for U.S. policymakers and foreign policy commentators.

Twenty-First Century U.S. Statecraft and the need for "Public Diplomacy 2.0"

The perceived need for technologies of engagement reflects a qualitatively new kind of justification for public diplomacy as an instrument of foreign policy. Rather than emphasizing the penetration of the global communication infrastructure with messages that exhort the common values and motives of the United States, contemporary arguments for public diplomacy and diplomatic messaging make the case for actions to demonstrate the role of the United States as a respectful global partner. Donna Oglsby, a former U.S. diplomat, describes this as requiring "an understanding of what is credible and politically viable in the context of other societies who interpret messages sent to them in terms of their own realities."[56]

Oglsby offers that a "mediated diplomacy" would not highlight the identity of the United States as a messaging objective, but rather emphasize what the United States does to recognize the particular context of those it is engaging.[57] This kind of diplomacy also requires a degree of reflexivity and attentiveness. Monroe Price suggests that U.S. public diplomacy should move from "primarily a means of projecting perceptions of the U.S . . . to one which would be a platform for cooperation, mediation, and reception—a mode of being informed as well as informing."[58]

This ethic reorients public diplomacy to a facilitative and symbolic role, as opposed to being directly concerned with image management. Public diplomacy "works," in this view, by performing, rather than declaring, the values and ethics that messaging cannot by itself do in a pluralistic and complex global media environment. It is *facilitative* in the sense that public diplomacy programs offer communicative and deliberative provisions for foreign stakeholders to empower them in some way. It is *symbolic* in that public diplomacy should not be obviously self-referential, but rather should demonstrate credibility through how its actions enable identification with the United States in some fashion.

The pivotal expression of this perspective on U.S. public diplomacy was elaborated by James Glassman, the last Undersecretary of State for Public Diplomacy and Public Affairs under the Bush administration. Speaking in December 2008, Glassman made the case for technology as the route to effective statecraft:

> We have arrived at the view that the best way to achieve our goals in public diplomacy is through a new approach to communicating, an approach that is made far easier because of the emergence of Web 2.0, or social networking, technologies. We call our new approach Public Diplomacy 2.0. PD 2.0 is an approach, not a technology.[59]

The key to this new strategy articulated by Glassman is to embrace the possibilities afforded by information and communication technologies as social and political technology, and the ways in which these technologies are used in the process of opinion formation and political action. Put simply, Glassman is arguing for a kind of communication intervention which targets *where* communication is most significant in the social fabric of important demographics. Glassman also argues to deprioritize message management and the preoccupation with message consistency:

> Don't we want to maintain control of our message? Perhaps. But in this new world of communications, any government that resists new Internet techniques faces a greater risk: being ignored. Our major target audiences—especially the young—don't want to listen to us lecture them or tell them what to think or how wonderful we are . . . But our broad mandate in public diplomacy is to understand, inform, engage, and influence foreign publics. All of these activities work best by conversation rather than dictation.[60]

Glassman's arguments also signal the developing sense public diplomacy's instrumental role in delivering foreign policy goals directly is in fact an end in itself. In other words, the practice of public diplomacy—the acts of communication that sustain "engagement" with foreign publics—matter as symbolically charged objectives for the practice of diplomacy. For example, Alec Ross, a senior advisor to Secretary of State Hillary Clinton and staunch advocate of technology as a policy tool for the State Department, argues that "the goal is to move beyond just government-to-government relationships and enhance government-to-people and people-to-people relationships around the world."[61] Such relationships are conceived here as strategic ends.

The practice of "statecraft" suggests more than an increasing reliance on technological platforms to influence. Rather, it means that strategically mandated outcomes have changed. This strategic reformulation means that the United States would facilitate dialogue via social and new media network platforms to bring about the kinds of changes it could otherwise not achieve just by trying to bolster its own image. For example, if the goal of U.S. foreign policy is to reduce the incentives for audiences to engage in violent extremism, then those who have the credibility to effect this change should be empowered and connected via available communication technology resources. Public diplomacy in this view works not by persuading per se, but by providing contexts wherein foreign publics act of their own volition to create environments ultimately desired by the United States (e.g., a more accountable democratic society).

Judith McHale's public discourse on public diplomacy elaborates much of the intrinsic logic behind this strategic shift, and telegraphs a number of assumptions about the expected political agency of foreign publics, their relevance to U.S. foreign policy objectives, and the necessary means by which public diplomacy can effectively engage these audiences. As the principal spokesperson for U.S. public diplomacy, her explanations for U.S. public diplomacy also do much to illustrate the tacit working assumptions behind a U.S. conception of soft power.

In a speech to the Council on Foreign Relations in June 2011, McHale laid out a series of positions on why an invigorated public diplomacy is necessary as a strategic priority. McHale's arguments do not draw on previous narratives that have animated much of U.S. discourse on public diplomacy—such as that the failure to engage in public diplomacy is a kind of disarmament in the global war of ideas, or that foreign publics are simply unaware of U.S. values. Rather, McHale's commentary says something more abstract about the nature of foreign publics as actors in their own right, with a historically unprecedented kind of power. Here, McHale references the tumultuous political upheavals in the Arab world in 2011 as indicative of this change:

> For most of human history, power has been held by the privileged few sitting atop an ever-widening base of people in a pyramid of systematic social control. In Bono's conception, and that of the New York Times' art department, that pyramid has been upended: Wide tiers of people, their arms raised in active participation, narrowed to a point. And together, they bear into the bent back of a strongman, straining to hold up under the weight of the empowered masses.[62]

By itself, this statement declares a kind of political efficacy for nonstate actors. Yet McHale argues that this is a distinct concern for the practice of public diplomacy. The so-called *power* she describes is implicitly linked to a capacity to communicate.

In a world where power and influence truly belongs to the many, we must engage with more people in more places. That is the essential truth of public diplomacy in the Internet age. . . . The pyramid of power flipped because people all around the world are clamoring to be heard, and demanding to shape their own futures. They are having important conversations right now — in chatrooms and classrooms and boardrooms—and they aren't waiting for us.[63]

McHale's depiction of a world characterized by an increasingly pluralized and diffused distribution of power is fundamentally based on the *agency* of foreign publics, empowered and enabled by the ability to articulate, argue, and associate via communication technologies. She states: "Citizens around the world are increasingly driving political, social, and economic trends, and we must adapt." For McHale, the United States is not the indispensible actor in this dramatic scenario. McHale's warning is that the United States risks irrelevance.

Much like the arguments for public diplomacy during the "transformative diplomacy" period under the Bush administration, McHale argues that the United States must be *present* in global communication circuits that increasingly challenge hierarchies of power and influence. Just as Glassman argued in his call for a "public diplomacy 2.0"—McHale explains, in rather straightforward terms, that the United States must be a credible contributor to communication and information flows:

How do we stand out and respond in such a crowded and complex environment? Our answer is simple: By taking our public diplomacy into the marketplace of ideas. . . . Being in the marketplace of ideas means using the same venues and platforms that communities and activists use.[64]

McHale's use of the term "marketplace of ideas" conjures a vision of global relations as contentious; a place of competing claims to legitimacy and credibility. More important, this "marketplace" is *the politically significant* locus of nonstate communicative action. In other words, to persuade or otherwise influence, the United States must communicate within the most pertinent and salient spaces of those acting internationally that could directly impact the foreign policy concerns of the United States. If foreign publics, citizens, and nonstate organizations increasingly operate and organize within such technological platforms, then the United States must intervene in such communicative spaces.

Yet McHale's comments also fall short of saying that communication and network relations demand a different kind of public diplomacy *message* or form of persuasive intent. Rather, McHale seems to indicate that the ubiquitous new media spaces are an opportunity to *listen* as much as an opportunity for influence:

> Just as Tunisia ignited a wider trend in the Middle East, it is a bellwether of what is happening globally. In this rapidly evolving landscape, as we seek to advance our foreign policy and enhance the security and prosperity of our world, our approach must have public diplomacy—and the citizens it seeks to engage—at its core.[65]

For McHale, communication technologies that facilitate meaningful relations among global actors are both key indicators and a necessary field for the practice of statecraft. More important, McHale makes the bold case that public diplomacy is the essential response to the condition she identifies. If nonstate actors are so empowered, and if these actors are so enabled by network-sustaining communication technologies, public diplomacy is the obvious strategic response.

Technology as Mediated Diplomacy

McHale's statement on the essential quality of public diplomacy for statecraft three years after the advent of public diplomacy 2.0 is by no means idiosyncratic. Rather, it describes an ongoing period during which arguments for a reinvigorated U.S. public diplomacy call for the most influential media of influence (a form of contextual intelligence) and assert that such technology is incredibly transformative. Public diplomacy is not merely a tool for persuasion, but also a means by which to engineer foreign publics toward more democratic societies amenable to U.S. interests.

The reformulation of public diplomacy as a "2.0" form of statecraft is framed within a rhetoric of urgency as much as a celebration of technological capability. The scenic depiction of international relations appears as populated with subjects waiting to be enabled by technological assistance—that a liberal, pluralistic public sphere is waiting to be catalyzed by a more robust technological intervention: something the United States can provide. Here, U.S. senator Richard Lugar explains the logic:

> The adroit use of social networking sites, such as Twitter, Facebook, and others, coupled with text messages and increasingly widespread mobile-phone technology, can help lend support to existing grassroots movements for freedom and civil rights, connect people to information, and help those in closed societies communicate with the outside world.[66]

Yet the communication context is *also* the terrain of conflict, which requires an appropriate technological response to America's opponents:

Terrorists and other anti-American propagandists have for some time been using the Internet and other techniques to communicate and recruit. America needs to beat them at their own game, especially since we invented most of the technology.[67]

Lugar warns here that technology *as a national security asset* has been co-opted by the enemy. The United States must not only use the appropriate tools to combat the enemy—in a public diplomacy reconceptualized as symbolic conflict—but also to reclaim a kind of culturally defined technological dominance. To do this requires the fusion of both technology and a new kind of diplomatic practice: "I would encourage the administration and our diplomats to be *nimble, flexible*, and *innovative* as they pursue a wide range of foreign-policy initiatives that use these new communication and connection techniques."[68]

Lugar's statements represent part of a larger (if perhaps belated) acknowledgement among U.S. foreign policy planners of the global communication infrastructure—how communication media platforms feature as meaningful aspects of everyday social and political life. Michael Doran, assistant secretary of defense for public diplomacy under the Bush administration, has described how the United States sensed the development of audience engagement with ICTs and its ramifications for U.S. public diplomacy. Speaking in January 2009, Doran described how during the Cold War era, audiences were "deferential" to information and media messaging. Since that time, however, there has been a steady delegitimizing of authority for information received through mass media outlets. Whereas at one time international audiences were *deferential* to mass communication, they are now *referential*.[69] Articulated in theoretical terms, Doran's argument justifies a U.S. presence in the networks that cultivate and sustain credibility—to be a peer in the networks that constitute the media dependency of foreign audiences.[70]

In his 2010 essay, Senator Lugar explicitly calls for the use of ICTs as symbolic of twenty-first-century statecraft. In particular, he points to the ways in which the State Department has paid for social network services in Pakistan, and the new mobile phone–based social network Humari Awaz, or "Our Voice."[71] Yet Lugar frames such actions as instrumental to "winning the hearts and minds" of audiences abroad, as if the provision of communication technology is both a charitable demonstration of U.S. goodwill as much as a persuasive action to lead audiences toward the conclusion that U.S. policies are at lease acceptable. The emphasis on *facilitative* technological engagement is defined by this tension. Yet influence remains at the core of arguments for so-called "twenty-first-century statecraft."[72]

Jared Cohen, one of the principal of evangelists of technology and diplomacy in the State Department, has been an outspoken advocate of technological innovation for diplomatic ends. During his tenure as part of the State Department's policy planning staff, Cohen was responsible for a number of so-called "digital" initiatives and, in his words, worked with the State Department to develop "out of the box ideas" and to "think long-term."[73] His explanation of the Alliance for Youth Movement of 2009 summit reveals fundamental assumptions about the requirements of international political action as transformed by ICTs: "So it's not about how many people have access today, it's about how many people have access tomorrow and a year from now."[74] Here, *access* constitutes a crucial goal for U.S. diplomacy.

For Cohen, *civil society* also represents the range of actors that U.S. public diplomacy must engage and empower to promote the objectives of U.S. foreign policy. U.S. public diplomacy must locate and encourage such political actors that share some aspect of the value-orientation that U.S. foreign policy seeks to encourage. Yet even Cohen's argument for facilitation is interspersed with the (increasingly anachronistic) impulse to *control* the technological sphere:

> And at the end of the day, we have two options: We can recognize that nobody can control these technologies—bad people will continue to use them, but that's all the more reason to engage in these spaces. And the other option is to be fearful that hostile actors might use it and shy away from it.[75]

Thus, for Cohen, ICTs are a means to amplify the agency of actors that represent U.S. interests, even in a loosely coordinated fashion that diminishes the imprint of U.S. action. This represents a rudimentary logic of influence through ICTs. But Cohen demurs when asked about why the Iranian Twitter revolution, a potential "proof of concept" for Cohen's social network–based diplomacy, failed to overturn the results of the Iranian election in 2009. He points to the *potential* of technologies rather than the demonstrative evidence that such social technologies were exploited by an authoritarian regime to diminish the pro-democratic potential of Twitter: "That just even putting the use of these technologies out on the public domain, that showcasing the power of these technologies as a tool to organize and express oneself, is in and of itself a victory."[76]

Cohen would later leave the State Department to join Google, as the director of the Google Ideas research organization in 2010, though he would continue to argue for more technologically sophisticated means to practice statecraft. Cohen, along with Google CEO Eric Schmidt, argued in 2010 that the preponderance of information and communication technologies would fundamentally transform the arena of competition between global actors—as a way to describe the challenges of twenty-first-century statecraft:

> For the world's most powerful states, the rise of the interconnected estate will create new opportunities for growth and development, as well as huge challenges to established ways of governing. Connection technologies will carve out spaces for democracy as well as autocracy and empower individuals for both good and ill. States will vie to control the impact of technologies on their political and economic power.[77]

Cohen and Schmidt's claims present technology as the crucial context for politics and, by implication, the terrain for soft power. While Cohen distinguishes a focus on statecraft from public diplomacy, similar arguments are deployed to justify an increasing range of public diplomacy 2.0 style initiatives.

Former communication executive and journalist Walter Isaacson, promoted to chairman of the Broadcast Board of Governors in 2011, claims that "[d]igital technology is doing more to shape our politics than anything since Gutenberg's introduction of the printing press helped Europe usher in the Protestant Reformation."[78] The "digital disruption" that Cohen and Schmidt describe creates a pressing exigency in U.S. strategy that must be addressed. Similarly, Judith McHale offers: "To put it bluntly: The world has changed, and if we do not change the way we interact with people, we risk being marginalized or made obsolete."[79] McHale's arguments offer that the sweeping strategic implications identified by Cohen, Schmidt, and Lugar impel the United States to develop more innovative public diplomacy practices. McHale argues that the "immediate and widespread access to information has fundamentally changed the way we do business . . . from mobile messaging to Facebook and Twitter feeds to Smartphone apps."[80] McHale suggests that these technologies are not substitutes for traditional methods of public diplomacy personal contact:

> "Instead, using technology, we are moving the work of diplomacy into new arenas and connecting directly to new audiences. We launched new Twitter feeds in Arabic and Farsi last month that allow us to share our messages directly with populations across the Middle East and see their unfiltered, uncensored responses. . . . We see every message, positive and negative."[81]

McHale's arguments present the necessity of technologies as a pragmatic solution—a necessary precondition to the prospect of influence and also, that influence requires the ability to "see every message"—to be receptive to the complex of communication flows among critical audiences.

Yet McHale also offers that the technological context is something that requires the United States to present itself as something other than on over-whelming asymmetric power—and that this is characteristic of all nation-states that seek to leverage the capacity of communication technologies. "We engage as equals. And sometimes it presents challenges. But they are challenges we welcome, and they are challenges we share with nations around the world."[82] Similarly, public diplomacy and strategic communication scholar Ali Fisher observes that the horizontal and peer-to-peer aspect of social media and contemporary internet communities necessitate a kind of "open source" attitude toward the prospect of strategic influence online. For Fisher, this entails not merely inserting a U.S. presence into peer-based social networks, but also being meaningful contributors to the conservations and community building that take place with these spaces.[83]

Kambiz Hosseini, the host of Voice of America's Persian satire program "Parazit," claims, "Without Facebook, nothing is possible these days."[84] Hosseini's remarks reflect attention to technological platforms that create social relations—as opposed to simply messaging media. Instead of attention to the volume of messaging or the quality of content, situating the U.S. perspective within existing meaningful conversations becomes paramount—and this involves both a concern for the most socially prevalent technologies as much as the conventions of communicating. For example, Brian Conniff, the president of the U.S. Middle East Broadcasting Network announced in 2011 that it would be launching mobile device applications to deliver its international broadcasting content. As Conniff argues, "It is extremely important to employ modern communication technologies and techniques to meet the needs of our audiences around the world."[85]

Concern for the "audience" of U.S. public diplomacy efforts also manifests in the kind of communication and message strategies delivered across the media platforms that are most frequented and useful to the "target audiences." Senior public diplomacy official Duncan McGuiness described how public diplomacy messages coming out of the State Department's International Information Programs (IIP) are increasingly modified to fit the messaging norms of the medium. "We'll produce an article, we'll reduce that to a 200-word piece that can be used for a Facebook page and three or four tweets that can be used on a Twitter feed and instant messaging."[86] In a related move, the State Department's IIP division closed down its America.gov web project in April 2011 in favor of less static social media initiatives in order to appear more responsive to local audience media and information needs. Yet the concerns articulated by McHale and subsequent moves to implement social media initiatives comes after a series of experiments in facilitative, public diplomacy 2.0–related efforts.

PUBLIC DIPLOMACY 2.0 INITIATIVES

The Digital Outreach Team

One of the definitive public diplomacy 2.0 efforts launched by the U.S. State Department is the U.S. Digital Outreach Team (DOT). The DOT represents an approach to online engagement with audiences who are at best skeptical of U.S. intentions and policies. The DOT originated as a three-person project out of the International Information Programs (IIP) office of the U.S. Department of State, and was originally conceived as a means to directly engage Arab Muslims in dialogue over U.S. policies in online forums and chat rooms. Rather than serve as a mouthpiece to reiterate U.S. positions, members of the team would forward the mission established by then Undersecretary of State for Public Diplomacy and Public Affairs, Karen Hughes, "to prevent mistakes and speculation about the United States from being accepted as truth."[87] To accomplish this, members of the team respond to comments or initiate threads about U.S. foreign policy in online forums—so that the U.S. perspective can be discussed and elaborated.[88]

By 2009, the program grew to 11 full-time members, of which six are Arabic speakers. The manner in which they address their online audience is intended to be respectful and knowledgeable of the communication going on in these forums. Duncan McGuiness of IPP claims that the team members "speak the language and idiom of the region, know the culture reference points and are often able to converse informally and frankly, rather than adopt the usually more formal persona of a U.S. government spokesperson."[89] DOT members enter online forums, identify themselves as members of the U.S. government, and attempt to engage participants who might otherwise be sympathetic to Islamic extremist and/or anti-U.S. sentiments.

The DOT was not, however, intended as an counter-terrorist measure, but primarily as a means to converse with mostly Muslim audiences around the world and to clarify points about U.S. foreign policy. The DOT targets news websites, discussion forums, and blogs that have high traffic, and thus a high likelihood of exposure. The DOT does not currently engage in English-language forums and explicitly Al-Qaida–affiliated or extremist websites.

Brent Blaschke, the DOT coordinator in 2009, estimates that the DOT visits between 25 and 30 websites and produces between 60 and 100 comments and responses a week. After two-and-a-half years of operation, the team was only denied access to a forum a few times, and some of these occasions sparked protest from other forum users demanding that U.S. access rights be restored.[90] While there are no internal benchmarks for how effective the DOT has been at improving opinions about the United States in the broader Muslim community online, as Blaschke argues, "[I]f we're not there, then we know we're not going to change a single opinion".[91]

Given the immensity of global internet traffic and the relatively small nature of this program, it is clear that the impact of this kind of program is difficult to ascertain in its early stages. Yet the United States continues to develop online initiatives as part of its recent attempts to leverage ICTs, and specifically social networking technologies.

Democracy Video Challenge

The *Democracy Video Challenge* represents another take on the "public diplomacy 2.0" concept by inviting participants rather than disseminating content promoting U.S. perspectives. The *Democracy Video Challenge* was launched online September 15, 2008, United Nations International Democracy Day. The State Department, working in partnership with NGOs and various private media corporations, sponsored the contest—which involved participants submitting via *YouTube* short films answering the question "Democracy is . . ." The program concluded with over 900 applicants, and the winners were rewarded with "time on television/film sets, meetings with film professionals, democracy advocates, the media, government officials, and special screenings of their videos."[92] A similar initiative was sponsored by the State Department's Bureau of Educational and Cultural Affairs, which invited participants to submit short films on the subject of *My Culture + Your Culture = ? Share Your Story*. According to the U.S. Department of State press release, the contest was part of an effort to "encourage cross-cultural community building and mutual understanding via the Web and social media platforms."[93]

The perceived success of these initiatives encouraged the Department of State to continue pursuing the potential of the ICT platforms. A second *Democracy Video Challenge* was announced in September 2009 via the State Department's own *Dipnote* blog. Speaking at the awards ceremony in 2010 for the second competition, Secretary of State Hillary Clinton indicated the facilitative logic inherent in this kind of public diplomacy:

> . . . the prompt for this challenge, as you know, is "Democracy is . . ." It's open ended. It is meant to provoke thought and to spur ideas. It truly is a challenge that builds on the freedom that democracy provides for individuals to pursue their own dreams. Each of these young winners has captured six different visions of democracy—some satirical and lighthearted, some poignant and haunting—but each shaped by their own experiences and expressed through their own unique artistic lens.[94]

Clinton's remarks, while clearly supportive of democracy as a foreign policy objective, does not explicitly tie the notion of democracy, or the values and practices that the concept entails, to the United States. Rather, the video challenge is *demonstrative* of democracy in itself. The program encourages consideration of democracy, by linking the affordances of new and social media technology with their capacity to support democratic ideals. Following the success of its early forays into new and social media technologies, further technology-based interventions were launched around such platforms.

As of July 2010, the State Department maintains over 230 Facebook accounts, 80 Twitter feeds (50 at overseas posts), 55 YouTube channels, 40 Flickr (photo-sharing) sites, and 25 blogs.[95] The Facebook accounts include roughly 80 embassy accounts, as well as cross-posted material from *eJournal USA*, which involves input from members (or "fans") from around the world. As of July 2009, the Twitter account for *Dipnote* had 6,624 followers, and the Twitter account for America.gov had 2, 260 followers While these numbers are significant given their recent implementation, it is important to recognize that Twitter has 370 million daily page views and 50 million daily visitors[96]—putting the scale of the U.S. foray into social networking into perspective.

Much of U.S. social media–focused public diplomacy activity is managed by embassy staff, though such programs are also coordinated by the State Department's Bureau of International Information Programs (IIP) and the Office of eDiplomacy. According to U.S. government reports on the implementation of these programs, there remain significant challenges, such as training of staff members, updating antiquated State Department equipment, and balancing the use of this technology with other aspects of diplomacy.

The State Department also maintains 62 Virtual Presence Posts (VPPs), developed "as a means to provide diplomatic engagement to an important city or region without the use of a physical facility."[97] These Web-based platforms target particular demographic groups, such as indigenous peoples in Central America, and involve a team of foreign service officers, as well as media and travel appearances to better facilitate "engagement" when conditions for an actual embassy are not optimal.[98] There were 39 planned VPPs as of July 2010, which may be more viable given restrictive budget conditions within the U.S. federal government.[99]

Another program suggestive of a *strategic* shift is the @america Center in Jakarta, Indonesia. The @america Center is the result of focus group testing of Indonesian youth, and provides a facility built and staffed by contractors in a shopping mall, and features communication and entertainment technology facilities provided in partnership with major U.S. corporations such as Microsoft and Google. The center, which opened in December 2010, provides thematic educational content about global issues such as the environment, as well as the ability to use video-conferencing solutions to connect Indonesians with American citizens. While there is an obvious promotional aspect to this facility, the intended usage suggests a different strategic justification.

Judith McHale articulates some of this logic in her opening remarks for the @america Center. She claims: "We believe that, at a time where citizens everywhere are more connected and more informed, governments acting alone cannot solve the problems which confront us or seize the opportunities which surround us." Here she foregrounds the role of *individuals* as relevant and empowered by the technological, networked context of contemporary international politics. She explains the facilitative emphasis represented by the model facility in Jakarta:

> We are working hard to find new and innovative ways to expand and strengthen the relations between the people of the United States and people all over the world. @america has been designed to engage young Indonesians and their families. Although the United States and Indonesia are separated by the vast Pacific Ocean, @america will use modern technology to bring our young people together to learn and cooperate on issues of importance to our nations and the world.[100]

This speech is suggestive of more than the involvement of public–private partnerships in the promotion of the U.S. image abroad. It is also reveals some of the strategic undercurrents in the calculus of diplomacy introduced during the Obama administration. The @america center is audience-centric, focused on the affordances of technology to provide services and feedback from the local constituency, and is conceived as empowering this constituency. This position reflects an emergent trajectory where the practices of public and traditional diplomacy coverage around the provision of communicative tools to enable foreign audiences to better govern themselves.

Tech@State and the "Freedom to Connect" Agenda

In 2009 in Morocco, Secretary Clinton announced the "Civil Society 2.0" initiative, a set of diplomatic programs to encourage democratic institutions, economic growth, and cultivate the involvement of civil society actors. The initiative is articulated as a developmental diplomacy initiative, yet it appears to reflect similar arguments for a facilitative public diplomacy. Clinton states, "[W]e will seek to work with all of you in government and in civil society to try and build local capacity and empower local organizations and individuals to create sustainable change."[101] The ambitions for diplomacy expressed here are development-oriented, yet inevitably framed as targeting public, nonstate stakeholders.

Subsequent state-sponsored initiatives, while not public diplomacy in the strictest sense of the term, such as the "Tech@State" programs, use social networking, streaming technologies, and other facilitative methods to bring together stakeholders in the development community. The description on the State Department website suggests the inextricable nature of technology with diplomatic methods *and* objectives:

> Tech@State connects technologists to targeted goals of the U.S. diplomacy and development agenda via networking events that combine physical and virtual presence. As part of Secretary Clinton's 21st Century Statecraft initiative, Tech@State connects established leaders, new innovators, government personnel, and others to work together on 21st century technology solutions to improve the education, health, and welfare of the world's population.[102]

The Tech@State program held its "Civil Society 2.0" conference in November 2010, where it convened a meeting of its stakeholders to "explore applications of technology to ensure civil society organizations operate more effectively and collaboratively." First among its listed objectives was to encourage technologically enabled means to promote "democratic transparency and civic engagement." Diplomacy in this case is geared toward the provision of democratic practices, and delivered in the manner of a public diplomacy intervention.

The impetus for this kind of democracy-oriented diplomacy is found in pivotal policy statements, such as Secretary Clinton's "Freedom to Connect" speech of January 2010, where she outlined a significant clarification of strategic direction for U.S. diplomacy:

> [T]oday I'm announcing that over the next year, we will work with partners in industry, academia, and nongovernmental organizations to establish a standing effort that will harness the power of connection technologies and apply them to our diplomatic goals. By relying on mobile phones, mapping applications, and other new tools, we can empower citizens and leverage our traditional diplomacy.[103]

The strategic reorientation outlined here does not suggest that technology amplifies the traditional objectives of diplomacy. Rather, the statement indicates that technological contexts necessitate new imperatives for diplomatic practice and indeed, foreign policy formulation. The technological context is an opportunity for diplomatic reinvention.

The "Freedom to Connect" agenda, however, also reflects a profound statement about the justification for diplomatic intervention as much as diplomatic practice. Clinton's rhetoric depicts the ability to communicate—to connect via the global communication infrastructure of new and social technologies—as a *human right* supported by the United States. As Clinton explains: "We stand for a single Internet where all of humanity has equal access to knowledge and ideas."[104]

Implicit in Clinton's moral rhetoric is a notion of power. If communication is so central to the conduct of everyday life, then it can be exploited and therefore should be protected. Clinton explains the U.S. position in a 2011 address on the Freedom to Connect policy:

> Two billion people are now online, nearly a third of humankind. We hail from every corner of the world, live under every form of government, and subscribe to every system of beliefs. And increasingly, we are turning to the Internet to conduct important aspects of our lives.[105]

While the Freedom to Connect agenda may not be a formal *public diplomacy* program, it does function *as* public diplomacy, and it conveys a set of value commitments about the significance of international communication—the crucial context for public diplomacy. Clinton states the U.S. position:

> For the United States, the choice is clear. On the spectrum of Internet freedom, we place ourselves on the side of openness. . . . We realize that in order to be meaningful, online freedoms must carry over into real-world activism. That's why we are working through our Civil Society 2.0 initiative to connect NGOs and advocates with technology and training that will magnify their impact.[106]

The ethic behind this declaration shares much with the Glassman speech in 2008. The United States can and should seek diplomatic objectives through facilitation of foreign publics and NGO actors, rather than through direct, monological promotion of U.S. interests. In this sense, the Freedom to Connect policy underscores the soft power concern with shaping the norms and values that legitimize state action. By advocating for a universalizing norm of communication, the United States can aim to secure the "milieu" goals identified in Arnold Wolfer's concept of power.[107]

TOWARD A COHESIVE STRATEGY

Despite declared commitments to unfettered international communication infrastructure, U.S. public diplomacy has still vacillated between the perceived need to promote the United States through messaging and the indirect cultivation of soft power through facilitation and relationship building. These unresolved tensions in U.S. public diplomacy were left unaddressed in official strategy statements about strategic communication that emerged in 2009, which declared that *relationships* enabled by technologies of engagement are strategic ends in their own right—without thoroughly elaborating the connection. The National Framework for Strategic Communication of 2009 outlines specific expected outcomes for U.S. engagement abroad:

> Foreign audiences recognize areas of mutual interest with the United States; Foreign audiences believe the United States plays a constructive role in global affairs; and *Foreign audiences see the United States as a respectful partner in efforts to meet complex global challenges*" (emphasis added)[108]

The overarching emphasis in the document ultimately settles on the promotion of the United States as a credible actor. To accomplish this goal, the document calls for two specific approaches—the *synchronization* of public diplomacy and strategic communication practice, and "deliberate communication and engagement."[109] Synchronization reflects the perceived need to link "words and deeds," while "deliberate communication" appears to call for a declarative agenda. Specifically, "[p]rograms and activities focused on communicating and engaging with the public need to be strategic and long-term, not just reactive and tactical. They should also focus on articulating what the United States is for, not just what we are against."[110] So, despite the previously discussed trend toward *facilitation* present in other public diplomacy initiatives and discourse, the National Framework remains grounded firmly in the possibility of image and message promotion, with effective influence stemming from the alignment of resources in order bring about *intentional* communication.

The National Framework is indicative of a persistent ambivalence toward public diplomacy and strategic communication among policymakers in the United States, which appears at once focused on adaptation to the ramifications of a globalized social media sphere, while at the same time persistent on the possibility of message management. Very often, a "solution" to U.S. public diplomacy issues has been pegged to possibilities of a "whole of government approach"—if the United States could only coordinate the various organizations that speak for the United States, it could implement a more effective strategy of engagement.[111]

One possible outcome of this "coordination" line of reasoning is the increasingly convergent conceptions of diplomacy and public diplomacy in official discourse and programs, which can be facilitated by technologies of engagement to better organize diplomacy's stakeholders.[112] Put simply, the real significance of technological deployment across the State Department is the changing mission of diplomacy itself. Speaking at a December 2009 briefing on diplomacy in the Western Hemisphere, Secretary of State Clinton outlined a broad mandate for technological integration:

We have, more than ever in today's world, the chance to cooperate, collaborate, and innovate. It's why the United States is committed to building what I've called a new architecture of cooperation, one where we leverage all the tools at our disposal, our diplomacy, our development efforts, civil society, the private sector, through crosscutting partnerships that are really necessary if we're going to address and hopefully solve the complex problems we confront."[113]

Clinton blurs the lines between public and "traditional" diplomacy here, by declaring the "cooperation" theme as both means *and* ends to U.S. foreign policy. Alec Ross, Clinton's top technology advisor, speaking at the Brookings Institute in December 2009, explains this logic and its technological basis, with some caveats about technology:

I don't take a utopian view of technology. I don't believe you can just sprinkle the Internet on a foreign policy challenge and get a good outcome. That point of view is naïve and it's wrong. . . . What is clear, however, is that this technology and the global connectedness it creates is at the core of the exercise of power in today's world. And while these technologies are new, the correlation between access to information and power is not.[114]

Ross also elaborates how the State Department used the "new connection technologies to engage and empower our interlocutors in new and different ways that are consistent with our foreign policy goals." He describes how the State Department developed a program by which individuals in poor areas of Mexico can provide free text messages to local NGOs that then can pass information along to public authorities about drug-trafficking and crime activities.

Ross also describes the case of Iran and exploitation of Twitter against the pro-democracy protesters as a demonstrative case of the media as a space for conflict, as an argument for *more* technology-based intervention, not less:

So we clearly can't take a sort of kumbaya approach to connection technologies. They can and are being used by our enemies, like al-Qaeda, and by authoritarian regimes . . . . Times have changed and those changes require pivots in our statecraft.[115]

For Ross, the embrace of technology is a matter of *urgency* as much as it is a *practical response* to the strategic realities that constrain the United States in the twenty-first century. "Look, if Paul Revere were alive today, he wouldn't have taken a Midnight ride from Boston to Lexington, he would have just used Twitter. And the lantern hangers would have helped make it viral by re-tweeting."[116] Ross appeals to the historic narrative of the American revolution to emphasize the immanent significance of technology for contemporary diplomacy. To not embrace technology is tantamount to obsolescence—foreign policy objectives are simply out of reach without technology.

Secretary Clinton has not been sanguine about the strategic and conceptual ramifications of a new communications environment for diplomacy. After the release of the first Quadrennial Diplomacy and Development Review report in 2010, Clinton wrote in *Foreign Affairs* about the transformation at the State Department:

> [T]he department is broadening the way it conceives of diplomacy as well as the roles and responsibilities of its practitioners . . . . But increasing global interconnectedness now necessitates reaching beyond governments to citizens directly and broadening the U.S. foreign policy portfolio to include issues once confined to the domestic sphere, such as economic and environmental regulation, drugs and disease, organized crime, and world hunger.[117]

Clinton carries forward the thematic arguments behind "transformative diplomacy" by noting the imposition of context on the practice of diplomacy. Specifically, other fields that were once the domain of sovereign governments now become transnational concerns, with governance implications for publics, non-governmental organizations, and traditional state governments.

To effectively deal with this context, no less than a strategic revisioning of diplomacy and its institutions is required. Clinton identifies the defining practice of this new form of diplomacy, the conceptually ambiguous term *engagement*:

> Engagement must go far beyond government-to-government interactions. In this information age, public opinion takes on added importance even in authoritarian states and as non-state actors are more able to influence current events. Today, a U.S. ambassador creates ties not only with the host nation's government but also with its people.[118]

Clinton's mandate for engagement signifies a potentially dramatic realignment for the conceptualization of diplomacy and, by extension, the viability of soft power as an actionable strategic concern. Yet U.S. public diplomacy in practice remains divided among potentially competing justifications for increasing institutional investment in public diplomacy—on the cutting edge of new media technologies and in revamping traditional practices of exchange diplomacy.

For example, Walter Isaacson of the Broadcast Board of Governors makes the seemingly anachronistic case for more investment in public diplomacy that "America cannot be outcommunicated by its enemies."[119] Yet Isaacson attempts to reconcile this concern for transmission with relation-building and facilitation by declaring that U.S. international broadcasting (perhaps the most traditionally monological of U.S. public diplomacy efforts) can also demonstratively promote the possibilities of community- building. Speaking in 2010, Isaacson explained:

> Our traditional role of delivering the news top down needs to be complimented by a new approach that catalyzes social networks . . . . By creating peer-to-peer global communities, we help guarantee the universal human right of access to the free flow of information.[120]

Curiously, Isaacson also counters scholarly criticism of previous eras of international broadcasting. Public diplomacy during the Cold War was described as "information battle" by R. S. Zaharna, an outmoded approach that emphasized the volume of content delivered.[121] Yet Isaacson asserts that the purpose and intent of U.S. international communication remains the same:

> Our media tools have changed. In the 1950s, we floated weather balloons containing leaflets with news from the outside world over the Iron Curtain and into Poland, Hungary, and Czechoslovakia. Today, we help information flow freely using sophisticated anti-censorship tools including satellite transmissions, web encryptions, and proxy servers to evade Internet firewalls. . . . Whatever the media platform, and whatever the era, the idea is the same. Free media works. Accurate information empowers citizens to build a more hopeful, democratic world.[122]

Isaacson makes the provocative claim that U.S. public diplomacy has *always* been facilitative in some sense. When the United States provides communication in the form of information and news services, or, in the *capacity* to communicate as suggested in the Freedom to Connect agenda and in Glassman's "public diplomacy 2.0," it succeeds in bringing about desired foreign policy ends for the United States. The crucial caveat, of course, is that U.S. public diplomacy is effective when it provides information that is needed, relevant, or otherwise significant to the audience and its media consumption habits.

AMERICAN SOFT POWER: RECONCILING TWENTY-FIRST CENTURY STATECRAFT AND PUBLIC DIPLOMACY 2.0

Advocates for transforming U.S. diplomacy like Jared Cohen have expressed some concern that the rush to embrace new communication technologies has not been matched by a concomitant reconsideration of diplomacy. Cohen worries, in particular, that "twenty-first century statecraft" is confused with public diplomacy as a new means of informing foreign publics, where "technology is just about more effectively and innovatively communicating and advocating our policy. I think technology is a valuable tool for that, but to me that's public diplomacy 2.0."[123] Cohen comes off as skeptical of public diplomacy that is something other than communication about the United States in order to cultivate influence.

Cohen's argument betrays what is arguably a prevalent conceptual confusion over the term public diplomacy in the United States, and in particular, on how it figures within an evolving institutional ideal of diplomacy.[124] For Cohen, the greatest implications of communication technology for diplomacy is in the capacity for diplomacy to accomplish a larger range of objectives and resolve persistent global problems:

> When I think about 21st century statecraft, I think about technology being used as a tool to empower citizens, to promote greater accountability and transparency, to do capacity building. At its core, what technology does is it connects people to information, which is new media; it connects people to each other, which is social media; and then there's a far more exciting path that we're going down now, which is that technology is a tool to connect people to actual resources—like mobile banking or mobile money transfers or telemedicine.[125]

Yet public diplomacy 2.0, as initially advocated by Glassman, outlines that the provision of transparency and connectivity is persuasive in its own right. Indeed, an enduring, historical justification for U.S. international broadcasting efforts is that it does not simply burnish the image of the United States, but demonstrates by example the benefits of a free and objective press.[126]

If the 2010 QDDR and the consequences of Clinton's rhetoric have a lasting institutional impact on U.S. public diplomacy, one important aspect of the United States turn toward communication technologies in public diplomacy may be the gradual *diminishment* of public diplomacy as a distinctive concept in future arguments for the technological practice of statecraft. The State Department is already pushing to integrate how it accomplishes its core mission through ICTs, such as modernizing *internal* communications through message boards and other intra-organizational ICT-based planning tools.[127]

The breakdown of definitional boundaries between public and traditional diplomacy in the United States can be understood as an issue of institutional identity, and would represent a significant break from the inertia of diplomatic tradition. If fully embraced, it could signal a move toward what Ali Fisher describes as "open source" diplomacy—one that acknowledges a radical reorientation toward the stakeholders and constituents of (public) diplomacy: "[Open source] public diplomacy engages in collective effort among peers (both foreign and domestic), whether they are governments, NGO, commercial enterprises, or members of a blogroll or Facebook group."[128] Yet, as is evident, arguments for more communication technologies remain irrevocably linked to the need to justify the particular interests of U.S. policy abroad—a balance of reasons that might ultimately be untenable. Left unresolved, the embrace of technology becomes a symbolic adornment on the more traditional edifice of diplomacy.

The failed Iranian "twitter revolution" already makes the rhetoric of technology for U.S. public diplomacy more problematic. For example, commentator Evgeny Morozov waxes pessimistic about the rush to embrace technology: "You don't win a war of ideas by growing the number of new media staff who sit by their computers and, much like robots, respond to every online thread that mentions U.S. foreign policy with an official position of the State Department."[129] The key point of contention remains the way in which technology is imagined, however unrealistically by its advocates, to circumvent the powers of authoritarian regimes.

The revolutions of the Arab Spring, in contrast, highlight the organizing potential of social media forms as a political tool, yet perhaps not as much as a promotion tool for the United States. Following the logic articulated by Glassman, this doesn't mean that such technologies have no place in public diplomacy. Rather, the Arab Spring indicates that U.S. foreign policy outcomes can be encouraged, if not instigated, by U.S. support of social media and networking technologies.

The *telos* of an ICT-centric strategy of public diplomacy might also dissolve the ultimate authority of diplomacy as a state-centric concept. The expression of Ali Fisher's model of influence in "open source diplomacy" via ICTs is difficult to reconcile with the imperatives of the sovereign nation-state and its parochial goals. As Micah Sifry and Andrew Rasiej of the *Personal Democracy Forum* describe,

> The tricky part of 21st-century statecraft, like 21st-century political campaigning, is this: If you want to engage more people in the process, you have to give up some control[,] and trust that they will help spread your message.[130]

The ICT-charged context of public diplomacy has thus compelled a kind of revisionism for the term within the United States, where the affordances of technology have provided new challenges in the form of media message competition, as well as opportunities to "reach" audiences in the networks that sustain communication credibility among its members.

More importantly, the technological context of public diplomacy imposes very real sociological limitations on the possibilities of influence. If technologically enabled networks sustain particular bonds of legitimacy of credibility, then how can a *government* entity enter into these relational spaces as some form of persuasive interlocutor? The significance of communication context seemingly demands both a tactical shift in the practices of influence (how nation-states would attempt to engage audiences) as well as a strategic shift in the possibilities of statecraft. Yet it is also clear that the prevalence of ICTs, the networks they engender, and the kinds of political agency they can cultivate have shifted the strategic priorities of public diplomacy (and indeed diplomacy more generally) toward the facilitation of democratic and civil society objectives.

The reliance on technology does not mean that the impact of relationships or interpersonal contacts are therefore neglected by U.S. public diplomacy institutions. Nor does this suggest that more traditional means of international broadcasting are now abandoned. Skeptics such as Evgeny Morosov and John Brown rightly point out that a public diplomacy cannot rely too heavily on the potential of technological platforms. Yet the volume of the discourse on technology appears to overshadow continued debates over public diplomacy reform.

The rhetoric that celebrates the affordances of technology for public diplomacy seem to resonate across contexts and seep into the larger discursive construction of U.S. diplomacy. What defines the possibilities of social networking technologies for connection and relationship building also define arguments for a transformational diplomacy that revisions the role of the diplomat and the scene of diplomacy as what Melissen has termed "the management of complexity." Put another way, there is a latent intertextuality between talk of technology and talk of diplomacy, where the ethics and practices of one field find purchase in the other.

The discourse and subsequent implementation of programs reliant on communication technologies also reflect a definitive set of assumptions about soft power that are predominantly American in character. And considering the scope of U.S. public diplomacy activities, many of the assumptions about the strategic requirements of soft power that supposedly justify public diplomacy are often at odds with each other.

The ascendance of "twenty-first-century statecraft" and public diplomacy 2.0–styled initiatives conveys a profoundly subject-oriented depiction of the *scope* of soft power. These developments manifest in American sense of soft power in two ways. First, this means that the intended reach of soft power is an overwhelmingly inclusive depiction of the global audience—nearly all who are "connected" have some sort of stake in U.S. diplomatic efforts. The disconnected, by extension, are also subject to American soft power appeals.

Second, the *agency* bestowed to subjects is significant. While the legacies of transmission-oriented communication and message-management continue to crop up in official statements and arguments for improving U.S. public diplomacy, the implications of public diplomacy 2.0 are based on the presumption that messaging in the service of image promotion is insufficient at best, and at worst can actively damage U.S. credibility.[131]

Subjects to American soft power are rendered as increasingly capable of assessing and evaluating the value of soft power resources and communication messages more generally. This is a significant difference from the prevailing assumptions about persuasion that animated public diplomacy during the Cold War, which relied upon the logic that exposure to information-starved audiences was sufficient. Interestingly, during the Cold War and after, the sociological significance of media communication remained an implicit requirement in the U.S. capacity to cultivate influence. Meaning, the concern was not with the message so much as the context and the preponderance of that message.

Yet, the ascendance of technology in U.S. soft power rhetoric reflects a differing set of expectations for how persuasion and influence can conceivably cultivate influence across disparate cultural contexts and in audiences skeptical of U.S. motives. Put simply, the *mechanisms* of U.S. soft power are anticipated to work differently after the effective public diplomacy strategies of the Bush administration. Previous attempts to amplify U.S. political values as somehow compelling in their own right were roundly criticized by successive U.S. GAO audits. Attempts to set the agenda may have succeeded in terms of global attention to U.S. strategic goals, at the expense of a precipitous loss of identification—or attraction—with the United States as a credible international actor.

In the place of ill-advised efforts of engagement, such as Karen Hughes's 2005 listening tour, public diplomacy 2.0 initiatives seek to convert soft power resources by example and demonstration and not by elaboration. Attempts to facilitate communication through the provision of communication capacity in programs such as Tech@State, or in direct forms of outreach via social media platforms, attempt to scale back promotional intention in order to listen to the needs and demands of the audience. In other words, U.S. soft power appears to be moving toward a long-term strategy of identification through attraction, by providing institutions and technological capacities for disparate global stakeholders to address pressing local issues, such as economic development, international criminal activity, and education.

The *outcomes* associated with American soft power appear evenly divided between immediate parochial interests and the long-term normative management of the international system. Glassman's arguments, in particular, offer that the more appropriate concern for public diplomacy is its potential to contribute to foreign policy objectives that may have nothing to do with explaining U.S. intentions or influencing foreign publics in ways that have a direct impact on the image of the United States. Rather, Glassman suggests that the nature of the global communication environment necessitate that the United States abandon the goal of direct message management. Instead, the United States can effectively "win the war of ideas" by enabling others to share in the benefits of a pluralistic and diverse global media sphere.

Of course, the collaborative language of facilitation remains tempered by the persistence of militaristic metaphors in U.S. foreign policy discourse. U.S. Representative Mac Thornberrry, a staunch advocate of U.S. public diplomacy efforts, grounds the strategic significance of public diplomacy as a matter of security:

> Unlike traditional kinds of diplomacy, such as education and cultural exchanges, the goal of the war of ideas is not to persuade people to like America and its policies. Instead, the aim is to make sure negative attitudes toward America and its allies do not take the form of violent extremism. These efforts are often called "strategic communication."[132]

U.S. Representative Dana Rohrbacher likewise offers that the principal justification for public diplomacy is not facilitation, but the amplification of American interests through communication. "First and foremost, American strategic communications and public diplomacy should seek to promote the national interest of the United States through informing and influencing foreign audiences."[133] In a similar conception of public diplomacy that does not appeal to a loftier "architecture of cooperation," U.S. Representative Ros-Lehtinen argued that the purpose of U.S. public diplomacy aimed at Cuba was purely about American interest. "It is not a 'Let's have all this diversity of thought,' The mission is clear: It's to advance our U.S.-Cuba policy."[134]

This seems at odds with Nye's caution that soft power (as a form of influence) is increasingly difficult to purposively cultivate in a manner that telegraphs self-serving interests of the soft power agent.[135] Nye, for his part, remains optimistic that U.S. efforts to facilitate communication and community remains a significant resource convertible to soft power. For Nye, the diffusion of power renders narrow and exclusive efforts to cultivate power ineffective and potentially counterproductive:

> I think the more we have contacts with other peoples, the more you get face-to-face contacts, the more essentially we're able to get an understanding of American values. It's not by broadcast, it's by these contacts. You have 750,000 foreign students at this country every year. That's a great source of soft power for us.[136]

While an American "working definition" of soft power may, 10 years after the 9/11 attacks, continue to wrestle with the limits of persuasion by monological communication methods and overt, coordinated government promotion—a more enduring characteristic of American soft power is its relative stability as an asset.

This is not to argue that U.S. soft power has not declined relative to other countries like China in the wake of a decade of unpopular foreign interventions. However, there still remains the perceived potential that the United States has soft power resources that can be converted into something influential. And very often, this *faith* translates into inaction.

As former CIA analyst Paul Pillar has argued, the notion of soft power does not receive significant attention in U.S. public discourse because soft power does not appear as a set of assets that are contingent. "It is not a form of power that seems to require the United States to *do* anything. The United States just *is*."[137] As Pillar states, much of this has to do with the prevalent belief in the inherent political appeal of U.S. institutions and founding documents—as a standard for universal values: "[T]he point is that it is also a basis for Americans finding it difficult to understand how foreigners could perceive as less than noble America's motives in exercising its power, and specifically hard power."[138]

Pillar's arguments presents a distinct problem for reconceptualizing U.S. public diplomacy, because to seriously reform the practice of public diplomacy would involve problematizing the very assets that U.S. discourse on public diplomacy often portrays as inviolate. Pillar blames much of the "hand-wringing" in Washington over attempts to reform public diplomacy as fundamentally misrecognizing the core reason for anti-Americanism and the inability of the United States to counter persistent negative views circulating in global media.

> Soft power is seen as an asset—but exactly that: as an asset, more than as a policy instrument. It is seen as flowing out of America's essential goodness rather than out of any concerted effort, apart from messaging, to shape whatever it is that gives rise to the soft power in the first place and can be used as a tool of influence. It is, in short, taken for granted more than it is seen as something in need of nurturing and shaping.[139]

The significant attention to facilitative technologies for public diplomacy and "twenty-first-century statecraft" does suggest a shift away from simplistic, monological models for strategic influence and persuasive communication. However, what remains largely unconsidered or contested is the very nature of U.S. soft power resources, and the capacity of such resources to bring about soft power outcomes. Soft power, in the American context, is overshadowed by a focus on technological solutions that will translate *in themselves* to a kind of influence, by providing a different "route" of elaboration for an uncritical set of soft power resources: American culture, values, and legiti-macy. The United States represents a cautionary reflection on what nation-states can expect from adopting ICT-based solutions for public diplomacy, and how the tension between facilitation of communicative agency and the imperatives of international influence may be difficult to reconcile in a coher-ent strategy of influential communication.

NOTES

* While there are several report "summaries" available, the Defense Science Board Report on Strategic Communication (2004) provides a thoughtful attempt to synthe-size policy recommendations with broader theoretical implications.

1. Geraldo Zahran, "From Hegemony to Soft Power: Implications of a Concep-tual Change," in *Soft Power and U.S. Foreign Policy: Theoretical, Historical and Contemporary Perspectives*, eds. Leonardo Ramos, Inderjeet Parmar, and Michael Cox (New York: Taylor & Francis, 2010), 12–31.

2. Paul Pillar, "The American Perspective on Hard and Soft Power," *The National Interest Blog*, January 4, 2011, http://nationalinterest.org/blog/paul-pillar/the-american-perspective-hard-soft-power-4669.

3. Brian Hocking, "Rethinking the 'New' Public Diplomacy," in *The New Public Diplomacy: Soft Power in International Relations*, eds. Jan Melissen and Paul Sharp (Palgrave Macmillan, 2005), 28.

4. Joseph S. Nye Jr., "Public Diplomacy and Soft Power," *The ANNALS of the American Academy of Political and Social Science* 616, no. 1 (March 2008):94–109.

5. Nancy Snow, "Rethinking Public Diplomacy," in *Routledge Handbook of Pub-lic Diplomacy*, eds. Nancy Snow and Phillip Taylor (New York: Routledge, n.d.), 3–11.

6. Kathy R. Fitzpatrick, *The Future of U.S. Public Diplomacy: An Uncertain Fate* (Brill, 2010), 101.

7. Kennon Nakamura and Matthew C. Weed, *U.S. Public Diplomacy: Back-ground and Current Issues* (Washington D.C.: Congressional Research Service, December 18, 2009).

8. Craig Hayden, "Promoting America: U.S. Public Diplomacy and the Limits of Exceptionalism," in *The Rhetoric of American Exceptionalism: Critical Essays*, eds. Jason A. Edwards and David Weiss (McFarland, 2011), 189–210.

9. John Robert Kelley, "The New Diplomacy: Evolution of a Revolution," *Diplomacy & Statecraft* 21, no. 2 (2010):286.

10. James K. Glassman, "Public Diplomacy 2.0: A New Approach to Global Engagement" (Speech presented at the New America Foundation, Washington, DC, December 1, 2008).

11. James W. Carey, "A Cultural Approach to Communication," in *Communica-tion as Culture: Essays on Media and Society* (Taylor & Francis, 2008), 15.

12. Fitzpatrick, *The Future of U.S. Public Diplomacy*; R. S. Zaharna, *Battles to Bridges: U.S. Strategic Communication and Public Diplomacy after 9/11* (Palgrave

Macmillan, 2009); Geoffrey Cowan and Amelia Arsenault, "Moving from Monologue to Dialogue to Collaboration: The Three Layers of Public Diplomacy," *The ANNALS of the American Academy of Political and Social Science* 616, no. 1 (March 1, 2008):10–30; Kelley, "The New Diplomacy"; Nicholas J. Cull, *The Cold War and the United States Information Agency: American Propaganda and Public Diplomacy, 1945–1989* (Cambridge University Press, 2009); Philip M. Seib, *toward a New Public Diplomacy: Redirecting U.S. Foreign Policy* (Macmillan, 2009); Hans N. Tuch, *Communicating with the World: U.S. Public Diplomacy Overseas* (Palgrave Macmillan, 1990); Gifford D. Malone and Dacor Bacon House Foundation, *American Diplomacy in the Information Age* (University Press of America, 1991).

13. Fitzpatrick, *The Future of U.S. Public Diplomacy*, 16.

14. Cull, *The Cold War and the United States Information Agency*; Fitzpatrick, *The Future of U.S. Public Diplomacy*, 17.

15. Fitzpatrick, *The Future of U.S. Public Diplomacy*.

16. Wilson P. Dizard, *Inventing Public Diplomacy: The Story of the U.S. Information Agency* (Lynne Rienner Publishers, 2004).

17. Nakamura and Weed, *U.S. Public Diplomacy: Background and Current Issues*, 4.

18. Ibid., 4–5.

19. Ibid., 4.

20. Ibid., 6.

21. Matthew Armstrong, "Rethinking Smith-Mundt," *Small Wars Journal* (2008).

22. Matthew Armstrong, "Recalling History: Making the Case for U.S. Government Broadcasting," www.MountainRunner.us, August 31, 2010, http://mountainrunner.us/2010/08/selfportrait.html#more.

23. David Ronfeldt and John Arquilla, "The Promise of Noopolitik," *First Monday* 12, no. 8 (August 6, 2007), http://firstmonday.org/htbin/cgiwrap/bin/ojs/index.php/fm/article/viewArticle/1971/1846%C2%A0%C2%A0.

24. Cull, *The Cold War and the United States Information Agency*.

25. R. S. Zaharna, "The Network Paradigm of Strategic Public Diplomacy," *Foreign Policy in Focus* 10 (April 2005), www.fpif.org.

26. Matthew Armstrong, "Recalling History: Secretary of State Testifies before House Appropriations," www.MountainRunner.us, 010 2010, http://mountainrunner.us/2010/01/marshall_1948_approps.html.

27. Shawn J. Parry-Giles, *The Rhetorical Presidency, Propaganda, and the Cold War, 1945–1955* (Greenwood Publishing Group, 2002).

28. Armstrong, "Recalling History: Secretary of State Testifies before House Appropriations."

29. Hayden, "Promoting America: U.S. Public Diplomacy and the Limits of Exceptionalism."

30. Shawn Parry-Giles, "Rhetorical Experimentation and the Cold War, 1947–1953: The Development of an Internationalist Approach to Propaganda," *The Quarterly Journal of Speech* 80, no. 4 (1994):448–468.

31. Ibid., 450.

32. Leo Bogart, *Cool Words, Cold War: A New Look at the USIA's Premises for Propaganda* (Washington D.C.: American University Press, 1995), Xxvii.

33. Parry-Giles, "Rhetorical Experimentation and the Cold War, 1947–1953: The Development of an Internationalist Approach to Propaganda," 451.

34. E. Barrett, *Truth Is Our Weapon* (New York: Funk & Wagnalls, 1953), lx.

35. Giles Scott-Smith, "The Heineken Factor? Using Exchanges to Extend the Reach of U.S. Soft Power," *American Diplomacy*, June 13, 2011, www.unc.edu/depts/diplomat/item/2011/0104/comm/scottsmith_heineken.html#_ednref3.

36. Nakamura and Weed, *U.S. Public Diplomacy: Background and Current Issues.*

37. Craig Hayden, "Arguing Public Diplomacy: The Role of Argument Formations in U.S. Foreign Policy Rhetoric," *The Hague Journal of Diplomacy* 2 (October 2007):229–254.

38. Nakamura and Weed, *U.S. Public Diplomacy: Background and Current Issues.*

39. Hayden, "Arguing Public Diplomacy."

40. Kristin M. Lord, "Voices of America: U.S. Public Diplomacy for the 21st Century—Brookings Institution," *Brookings Institution*, November 2008, www.brookings.edu/reports/2008/11_public_diplomacy_lord.aspx.

41. Hayden, "Arguing Public Diplomacy."

42. Ibid.

43. Anne-Marie Slaughter, "America's Edge: Power in the Networked Century," *Foreign Affairs* 88 (2009):7.

44. Kennon Nakamura and Susan Epstein, *Diplomacy for the 21st Century: Transformational Diplomacy* (Washington D.C.: Congressional Research Service, August 23, 2007).

45. Ibid.

46. R. S. Zaharna, "The Soft Power Differential: Network Communication and Mass Communication in Public Diplomacy," *Hague Journal of Diplomacy* 2, no. 3 (2007):213–228; Zaharna, *Battles to Bridges.*

47. Christopher Paul, *Whither Strategic Communication?: A Survey of Current Proposals and Recommendations* (Rand Corporation, 2009).

48. Dizard, *Inventing Public Diplomacy.*

49. Slaughter, "America's Edge: Power in the Networked Century."

50. Robin Brown, "Diplomacy, Public Diplomacy and Social Networks" (presented at the International Studies Association, New Orleans, LA, 2010).

51. Kristin Lord and Marc Lynch, "America's Extended Hand: Assessing the Obama Administration's Global Engagement Strategy" (Center for New American Security, 2010).

52. *U.S. Public Diplomacy: Key Issues for Congressional Oversight*, United States Government Accountability Office Report to Congressional Committees (United States Government Accountability Office, May 27, 2009), www.gao.gov/new.items/d09679sp.pdf.

53. Nye Jr., "Public Diplomacy and Soft Power," 99.

54. Manuel Castells, "Communication, Power, and Counter-Power in the Network Society," *International Journal of Communication* 1 (2007):239.

55. Ronald Deibert, *Parchment, Printing, and Hypermedia: Communication in World Order Transformation* (New York: Columbia University Press, 1997); Eytan

Gilboa, "Searching for a Theory of Public Diplomacy," *The ANNALS of the American Academy of Political and Social Science* 616, no. 1 (March 1, 2008):55–77; Elizabeth Hanson, *The Information Revolution and World Politics* (Lanham: Rowman & Littlefield, 2008); Evan H. Potter, "Web 2.0 and the New Public Diplomacy: Impact and Opportunities," in *Engagement: Public Diplomacy in a Globalized World*, eds. Jolyon Welsh and Daniel Fearn (London: UK Foreign Commonwealth Office, 2008), 120–134, www.fco.gov.uk/resources/en/pdf/pd-engagement-jul-08.

56. Donna Marie Oglesby, "Statecraft at the Crossroads: A New Diplomacy," *SAIS Review* 29, no. 2 (2009):8.

57. Ibid., 7.

58. Monroe E. Price, "Changing International Broadcasting in the Obama Era? I USC Center on Public Diplomacy I Newswire—CPD Blog," *Center For public Diplomacy*, November 6, 2008, http://uscpublicdiplomacy.org/index.php/newswire/cpdblog_detail/changing_international_broadcasting_in_the_obama_era/.

59. Glassman, "Public Diplomacy 2.0: A New Approach to Global Engagement."

60. Ibid.

61. Peter Buxbaum, "White House 2.0: Spreading Its Message / ISN," *International Relations and Security Network/ISN ETH Zurich*, July 1, 2009, www.isn.ethz.ch/isn/Current-Affairs/Security-Watch/Detail/?ots591=4888CAA0-B3DB-1461–98B9-E20E7B9C13D4&lng=en&id=102624.

62. Judith A. McHale, "Opening Remarks at the Council on Foreign Relations: A Review of U.S. Public Diplomacy" (New York, June 21, 2011).

63. Ibid.

64. Ibid.

65. Ibid.

66. Richard G. Lugar, "Twitter vs. Terror," *Foreign Policy*, January 6, 2010, www.foreignpolicy.com/articles/2010/01/06/twitter_vs_terror.

67. Ibid.

68. Ibid.

69. Michael Doran, "Remarks of Michael Doran to the 2009 Symposium on Smith-Mundt Act: A Discourse on America's Discourse" (Washington, DC, January 13, 2009).

70. Sandra Ball-Rokeach, "A Theory of Media Power and a Theory of Media Use: Different Stories, Questions, and Ways of Thinking," *Mass Communication and Society* 1, no. 1/2 (1998):5–40.

71. Lugar, "Twitter vs. Terror."

72. Christina Larson, "State Department Innovator Jared Cohen Goes to Google," Foreign Policy.com, September 7, 2010, www.foreignpolicy.com/articles/2010/09/07/jared_cohen?page=0,3.

73. Ibid.

74. Jared Cohen, "State Department Guru Talks Twitter Diplomacy: NPR," *NPR*, October 17, 2009, www.npr.org/templates/story/story.php?storyId=113876776.

75. Ibid.

76. Ibid.

77. Eric Schmidt and Jared Cohen, "Eric Schmidt and Jared Cohen on the Digital Disruption," *Foreign Affairs*, November 4, 2010, www.foreignaffairs.com/discussions/news-and-events/eric-schmidt-and-jared-cohen-on-the-digital-disruption.

78. Walter Isaacson, "From Samizdat to Twitter," *Foreign Policy*, February 28, 2011, www.foreignpolicy.com/articles/2011/02/07/from_samizdat_to_twitter?print=yes&hidecomments=yes&page=full.

79. Oliver Barrett, "Tweets from Secretary Clinton," *Foreign Policy Association*, April 19, 2011, http://foreignpolicyblogs.com/2011/04/19/tweets-from -secretary-clinton/.

80. "Remarks at the Global Technology Symposium," n.d., www.state.gov/r/remarks/2011/159141.htm.

81. Judith A. McHale, "Remarks at the Global Technology Symposium," March 24, 2011, www.state.gov/r/remarks/2011/159141.htm.

82. Ibid.

83. Ali Fisher, "Music for the Jilted Generation: Open-Source Public Diplomacy," *The Hague Journal of Diplomacy* 3, no. 2 (September 2008):129–152.

84. "Staying ahead of the Digital Curve: U.S. Global Engagement in the New Media Era," Press Release, *Broadcasting Board of Governors*, February 16, 2011.

85. Middle East Broadcasting Networks, Inc., "MBN Launches a New Mobile Site," June 29, 2011.

86. Alicia M. Cohn, "State Department Shifts Digital Resources to Social Media," *The Hill's Hillicon Valley*, April 24, 2011, http://thehill.com/blogs/hillicon-valley/technology/157501-state-dept-shifts-digital-resources-to-social-media.

87. N. Kralev, "Arabic Speakers Monitor Net Chats; U.S. Seeks to Fix Misconceptions," *Washington Times*, March 9, 2007.

88. Neil Macfarquhar, "At State Dept., Blog Team Joins Muslim Debate," *The New York Times*, September 22, 2007, sec. Washington, www.nytimes.com/2007/09/22/washington/22bloggers.html?_r=1.

89. Walter Pincus, "State Dept. Tries Blog Diplomacy," November 19, 2007, www.washingtonpost.com/wp-dyn/content/article/2007/11/18/AR2007111801114.html.

90. Jessica Jerrell. "Muddled Public Diplomacy: Examining Conflicting Approaches to U.S. Public Diplomacy through the State Department's Digital Outreach Team." Significant Research Paper, School of International Service, American University, Washington, DC. 2009.

91. Ibid.

92. "Democracy Video Challenge Winners Announced." Dipnote: U.S. Department of State Official Blog. June 17 2009. blogs.state.gov/index.php/archive/entry/democracy_video_challenge_votes.

93. "U.S. Department of State and the Adobe Foundation to launch Online Video Contest to Amplify U.S. Public Diplomacy." CSR Press Release Nov. 25, 2008. www.csrwire.com/press_releases/13746-U-S-Department-of-State-and-the-Adobe-Foundation-to-Launch-Online-Video-Contest-to-Amplify-U-S-Public-Diplomacy.

94. "Secretary Clinton Presents 2010 Democracy Video Challenge Award to Ethiopian Filmmaker Yared Shumete," September 10, 2010, http://ethiopia.usembassy.gov/

secretary_clinton_presents_2010_democracy_video_challenge_award_to_ethiopian_filmmaker_yared_shumete09/10/10.html.

95. "U.S. GAO—Engaging Foreign Audiences: Assessment of Public Diplomacy Platforms Could Help Improve State Department Plans to Expand Engagement," July 21, 2010, www.gao.gov/products/GAO-10–767.

96. Ali Fisher. *Mapping the Great Beyond: Identifying Meaningful Networks in Public Diplomacy.* (Los Angeles: Figueroa Press, April 2010).

97. Ibid., 12.

98. Ibid.

99. "U.S. GAO—Engaging Foreign Audiences: Assessment of Public Diplomacy Platforms Could Help Improve State Department Plans to Expand Engagement."

100. Judith A. McHale, "Remarks at Reception for the @america Center," December 1, 2010, www.state.gov/r/remarks/2010/152313.htm.

101. Hillary Clinton, "Remarks at the Forum for the Future," November 3, 2009, www.state.gov/secretary/rm/2009a/11/131236.htm.

102. "Tech@State," n.d., www.state.gov/statecraft/tech/index.htm.

103. Hillary Clinton, "Remarks on Internet Freedom," January 21, 2010, www.state.gov/secretary/rm/2010/01/135519.htm.

104. Anne Applebaum, "Internet Freedom: The State Department Can Combat Internet Censorship, but It's Not. What Gives?" *Slate Magazine*, April 4, 2011, www.slate.com/id/2290334/.

105. Hillary Clinton, "Remarks by Secretary of State Clinton on Internet Freedom" (Washington, DC, February 15, 2011), www.america.gov/st/texttrans-english/2011/February/20110215155718su0.3556896.html.

106. Ibid.

107. Arnold Wolfers, *Discord and Collaboration: Essays on International Politics* (Baltimore, MD: Johns Hopkins University Press, 1962).

108. United States National Security Council, *National Framework for Strategic Communication* (Washington, D.C., 2009).

109. Ibid.

110. Ibid.

111. Christopher Paul. "'Strategic Communication' Is Vague: Say What You Mean." *Joint Forces Quarterly* 56 (2010): 10–13.

112. Brown, "Diplomacy, Public Diplomacy and Social Networks"; Kelley, "The New Diplomacy."

113. Hillary Clinton, "Citizen Engagement, Foreign Policy Objectives, Discussed at Western Hemisphere Diplomacy Briefing," December 11, 2009, www.alliance-exchange.org/policy-monitor/12/14/2009/citizen-engagement-foreign-policy-objectives-discussed-western-hemisphere-.

114. Alec Ross, "U.S. Diplomacy in the Age of Facebook and Twitter: An Address on 21st Century Statecraft" (Brookings Institute, Washington, DC, December 17, 2009).

115. Ibid.

116. Ibid.

117. Hillary Clinton, "Leading through Civilian Power," *Foreign Affairs*, December 2010, www.foreignaffairs.com/articles/66799/hillary-rodham-clinton/leading-through-civilian-power.

118. Ibid.

119. Walter Isaacson, "Walter Isaacson: America's Voice Must Be Credible and Must Be Heard," *Radio Free Europe/Radio Liberty*, September 29, 2010, sec. Communications / Press Releases, www.rferl.org/content/press_release_isaacson_newseum/2170998.html.

120. Ibid.

121. R.S. Zaharna, "The Network Paradigm of Strategic Public Diplomacy." *Foreign Policy in Focus* 10 (April 2005): 1–4.

122. Isaacson, "From Samizdat to Twitter."

123. Larson, "State Department Innovator Jared Cohen Goes to Google."

124. Brown, "Diplomacy, Public Diplomacy and Social Networks"; Bruce Gregory, "Public Diplomacy: Sunrise of an Academic Field," *The ANNALS of the American Academy of Political and Social Science* 616, no. 1 (March 1, 2008):274–290.

125. Larson, "State Department Innovator Jared Cohen Goes to Google."

126. Cull, *The Cold War and the United States Information Agency*; Dizard, *Inventing Public Diplomacy*.

127. Joe B. Johnson, "Gaps in New Media for Diplomacy?" Blog, *JJohnson47's Weblog*, December 28, 2009, http://jjohnson47.wordpress.com/2009/12/28/gaps-in-new-media-for-diplomacy/.

128. Fisher, "Music for the Jilted Generation: Open-Source Public Diplomacy," 12.

129. Evgeny Morozov, "The Future of 'Public Diplomacy 2.0,'" *Net Effect*, June 9, 2009, http://neteffect.foreignpolicy.com/posts/2009/06/09/the_future_of_public_diplomacy_20.

130. Micah L. Sifry and Andrew Rasiej, "P2P2G: The Rise of e-Diplomacy," POLITICO.com, June 4, 2009, www.politico.com/news/stories/0609/23310.html.

131. Rami Khouri, "Karen Hughes' Two-Year Halloween," *Daily Star*, November 3, 2007, www.dailystar.com.lb/Opinion/Commentary/Nov/03/Karen-Hughes-two-year-Halloween.ashx#axzz1SEgeKEJ5.

132. Mac Thornberry, "Establishing the Strategic Communication and Public Diplomacy Caucus," — www.MountainRunner.us, March 7, 2010, http://mountainrunner.us/2010/03/thornberry.html.

133. Richard Solash, "U.S. Congressional Committee Questions Role of U.S.-Funded Broadcasters," *Radio Free Europe / Radio Liberty*, April 11, 2011, www.rferl.org/content/us_congressional_committee_questions_role_us_funded_broadcasters/3549829.html.

134. Ibid.

135. Joseph S. Nye Jr., *The Future of Power*, 1st ed. (PublicAffairs, 2011).

136. Charlie Rose, "Charlie Rose — Joseph Nye," February 28, 2011, www.charlierose.com/view/interview/11509#frame_top.

137. Pillar, "The American Perspective on Hard and Soft Power."

138. Ibid.

139. Ibid.

REFERENCES

Applebaum, Anne. "Internet Freedom: The State Department Can Combat Internet Censorship, but It's Not. What Gives?" *Slate Magazine*, April 4, 2011. www.slate.com/id/2290334/.

Armstrong, Matthew. "Recalling History: Making the Case for U.S. Government Broadcasting." www.MountainRunner.us, August 31, 2010. http://mountainrunner.us/2010/08/selfportrait.html#more.

———. "Recalling History: Secretary of State Testifies before House Appropriations." www.MountainRunner.us, 010 2010. http://mountainrunner.us/2010/01/marshall_1948_approps.html.

———. "Rethinking Smith-Mundt." *Small Wars Journal* (2008).

Ball-Rokeach, Sandra. "A Theory of Media Power and a Theory of Media Use: Different Stories, Questions, and Ways of Thinking." *Mass Communication and Society* 1, no. 1/2 (1998):5–40.

Barrett, E. *Truth Is Our Weapon*. New York: Funk & Wagnalls, 1953.

Barrett, Oliver. "Tweets from Secretary Clinton." *Foreign Policy Association*, April 19, 2011. http://foreignpolicyblogs.com/2011/04/19/tweets-from-secretary-clinton/.

Bogart, Leo. *Cool Words, Cold War: A New Look at the USIA's Premises for Propaganda*. Washington D.C.: American University Press, 1995.

Brown, Robin. "Diplomacy, Public Diplomacy and Social Networks." New Orleans, LA, 2010.

Buxbaum, Peter. "White House 2.0: Spreading Its Message / ISN." *International Relations and Security Network/ISN ETH Zurich*, July 1, 2009. www.isn.ethz.ch/isn/Current-Affairs/Security-Watch/Detail/?ots591=4888CAA0-B3DB-1461–98B9-E20E7B9C13D4&lng=en&id=102624.

Carey, James W. "A Cultural Approach to Communication." In *Communication as Culture: Essays on Media and Society*, 11–28. Taylor & Francis, 2008.

Castells, Manuel. "Communication, Power, and Counter-Power in the Network Society." *International Journal of Communication* 1 (2007):238–266.

Clinton, Hillary. "Citizen Engagement, Foreign Policy Objectives, Discussed at Western Hemisphere Diplomacy Briefing," December 11, 2009. www.alliance-exchange.org/policy-monitor/12/14/2009/citizen-engagement-foreign-policy-objectives-discussed-western-hemisphere-.

———. "Leading through Civilian Power." *Foreign Affairs*, December 2010. www.foreignaffairs.com/articles/66799/hillary-rodham-clinton/leading-through-civilian-power.

———. "Remarks at the Forum for the Future," November 3, 2009. www.state.gov/secretary/rm/2009a/11/131236.htm.

———. "Remarks by Secretary of State Clinton on Internet Freedom," Washington, DC, February 15, 2011. www.america.gov/st/texttrans-english/2011/February/20110215155718su0.3556896.html.

———. "Remarks on Internet Freedom," January 21, 2010. www.state.gov/secretary/rm/2010/01/135519.htm.

Cohen, Jared. "State Department Guru Talks Twitter Diplomacy: NPR." *NPR*, October 17, 2009. www.npr.org/templates/story/story.php?storyId=113876776.

Cohn, Alicia M. "State Department Shifts Digital Resources to Social Media." *The Hill's Hillicon Valley*, April 24, 2011. http://thehill.com/blogs/hillicon-valley/technology/157501-state-dept-shifts-digital-resources-to-social-media.

Cowan, Geoffrey, and Amelia Arsenault. "Moving from Monologue to Dialogue to Collaboration: The Three Layers of Public Diplomacy." *The ANNALS of the American Academy of Political and Social Science* 616, no. 1 (March 1, 2008):10–30.

Cull, Nicholas J. *The Cold War and the United States Information Agency: American Propaganda and Public Diplomacy, 1945–1989*. Cambridge University Press, 2009.

Deibert, Ronald. *Parchment, Printing, and Hypermedia: Communication in World Order Transformation*. New York: Columbia University Press, 1997.

Dizard, Wilson P. *Inventing Public Diplomacy: The Story of the U.S. Information Agency*. Lynne Rienner Publishers, 2004.

Doran, Michael. "Remarks of Michael Doran to the 2009 Symposium on Smith-Mundt Act: A Discourse on America's Discourse," Washington, DC, January 13, 2009.

Fisher, Ali. "Music for the Jilted Generation: Open-Source Public Diplomacy." *The Hague Journal of Diplomacy* 3, no. 2 (September 2008):129–152.

Fitzpatrick, Kathy R. *The Future of U.S. Public Diplomacy: An Uncertain Fate*. Brill, 2010.

Gilboa, Eytan. "Searching for a Theory of Public Diplomacy." *The ANNALS of the American Academy of Political and Social Science* 616, no. 1 (March 1, 2008):55–77.

Glassman, James K. "Public Diplomacy 2.0: A New Approach to Global Engagement." Speech presented at the New America Foundation, Washington, DC, December 1, 2008.

Gregory, Bruce. "Public Diplomacy: Sunrise of an Academic Field." *The ANNALS of the American Academy of Political and Social Science* 616, no. 1 (March 1, 2008):274–290.

Hanson, Elizabeth. *The Information Revolution and World Politics*. Lanham: Rowman & Littlefield, 2008.

Hayden, Craig. "Arguing Public Diplomacy: The Role of Argument Formations in U.S. Foreign Policy Rhetoric." *The Hague Journal of Diplomacy* 2 (October 2007):229–254.

———. "Promoting America: U.S. Public Diplomacy and the Limits of Exceptionalism." In *The Rhetoric of American Exceptionalism: Critical Essays*, eds. Jason A. Edwards and David Weiss, 189–210. McFarland, 2011.

Hocking, Brian. "Rethinking the 'New' Public Diplomacy." In *The New Public Diplomacy: Soft Power in International Relations*, eds. Jan Melissen and Paul Sharp. Palgrave Macmillan, 2005.

Isaacson, Walter. "From Samizdat to Twitter." *Foreign Policy*, February 28, 2011. www.foreignpolicy.com/articles/2011/02/07/from_samizdat_to_twitter?print=yes&hidecomments=yes&page=full.

——. "Walter Isaacson: America's Voice Must Be Credible and Must Be Heard." *Radio Free Europe/Radio Liberty*, September 29, 2010, sec. Communications / Press Releases. www.rferl.org/content/press_release_isaacson_newseum/2170998 .html.

Johnson, Joe B. "Gaps in New Media for Diplomacy?" Blog. *JJohnson47's Weblog*, December 28, 2009. http://jjohnson47.wordpress.com/2009/12/28/gaps-in-new-media -for-diplomacy/.

Kelley, John Robert. "The New Diplomacy: Evolution of a Revolution." *Diplomacy & Statecraft* 21, no. 2 (2010):286.

Khouri, Rami. "Karen Hughes' Two-Year Halloween." *Daily Star*, November 3, 2007. www.dailystar.com.lb/Opinion/Commentary/Nov/03/Karen-Hughes-two-year-Halloween.ashx#axzz1SEgeKEJ5.

Kralev, N. "Arabic Speakers Monitor Net Chats; U.S. Seeks to Fix Misconceptions." *Washington Times*, March 9, 2007.

Larson, Christina. "State Department Innovator Jared Cohen Goes to Google." Foreign Policy.com, September 7, 2010. www.foreignpolicy.com/articles/2010/09/07/ jared_cohen?page=0,3.

Lord, Kristin M. "Voices of America: U.S. Public Diplomacy for the 21st Century." *Brookings Institution*, November 2008. www.brookings.edu/reports/2008/11_public _diplomacy_lord.aspx.

Lord, Kristin, and Marc Lynch. "America's Extended Hand: Assessing the Obama Administration's Global Engagement Strategy." Center for New American Security, 2010.

Lugar, Richard G. "Twitter vs. Terror." *Foreign Policy*, January 6, 2010. www.foreign policy.com/articles/2010/01/06/twitter_vs_terror.

Macfarquhar, Neil. "At State Dept., Blog Team Joins Muslim Debate." *New York Times*, September 22, 2007, sec. Washington. www.nytimes.com/2007/09/22/ washington/22bloggers.html?_r=1.

Malone, Gifford D., and Dacor Bacon House Foundation. *American Diplomacy in the Information Age*. University Press of America, 1991.

McHale, Judith A. "Opening Remarks at the Council on Foreign Relations: A Review of U.S. Public Diplomacy," New York, June 21, 2011.

——. "Remarks at Reception for the @america Center," December 1, 2010. www .state.gov/r/remarks/2010/152313.htm.

——. "Remarks at the Global Technology Symposium," March 24, 2011. www .state.gov/r/remarks/2011/159141.htm.

Middle East Broadcasting Networks, Inc. "MBN Launches a New Mobile Site," June 29, 2011.

Morozov, Evgeny. "The Future of 'Public Diplomacy 2.0.'" *Net Effect*, June 9, 2009. http://neteffect.foreignpolicy.com/posts/2009/06/09/the_future_of_public _diplomacy_20.

Nakamura, Kennon, and Susan Epstein. *Diplomacy for the 21st Century: Transformational Diplomacy*. Washington D.C.: Congressional Research Service, August 23, 2007.

Nakamura, Kennon, and Matthew C. Weed. *U.S. Public Diplomacy: Background and Current Issues*. Washington D.C.: Congressional Research Service, December 18, 2009.

Nye, Joseph S. Jr. "Public Diplomacy and Soft Power." *The ANNALS of the American Academy of Political and Social Science* 616, no. 1 (March 2008):94–109.

———. *The Future of Power*. 1st ed. PublicAffairs, 2011.

Oglesby, Donna Marie. "Statecraft at the Crossroads: A New Diplomacy." *SAIS Review* 29, no. 2 (2009):93–106.

Parry-Giles, Shawn J. *The Rhetorical Presidency, Propaganda, and the Cold War, 1945–1955*. Greenwood Publishing Group, 2002.

Parry-Giles, Shawn. "Rhetorical Experimentation and the Cold War, 1947–1953: The Development of an Internationalist Approach to Propaganda." *The Quarterly Journal of Speech* 80, no. 4 (1994):448–468.

Paul, Christopher. *Whither Strategic Communication? A Survey of Current Proposals and Recommendations*. Rand Corporation, 2009.

Pillar, Paul. "The American Perspective on Hard and Soft Power." *The National Interest Blog*, January 4, 2011. http://nationalinterest.org/blog/paul-pillar/the-american-perspective-hard-soft-power-4669.

Pincus, Walter. "State Dept. Tries Blog Diplomacy," November 19, 2007. www.washingtonpost.com/wp-dyn/content/article/2007/11/18/AR2007111801114.html.

Potter, Evan H. "Web 2.0 and the New Public Diplomacy: Impact and Opportunities." In *Engagement: Public Diplomacy in a Globalized World*, eds. Jolyon Welsh and Daniel Fearn, 120–134. London: UK Foreign Commonwealth Office, 2008. www.fco.gov.uk/resources/en/pdf/pd-engagement-jul-08.

Price, Monroe E. "Changing International Broadcasting in the Obama Era?" *USC Center on Public Diplomacy*, November 6, 2008. http://uscpublicdiplomacy.org/index.php/newswire/cpdblog_detail/changing_international_broadcasting_in_the_obama_era.

"Remarks at the Global Technology Symposium," n.d. www.state.gov/r/remarks/2011/159141.htm.

Ronfeldt, David, and John Arquilla. "The Promise of Noopolitik." *First Monday* 12, no. 8 (August 6, 2007). http://firstmonday.org/htbin/cgiwrap/bin/ojs/index.php/fm/article/viewArticle/1971/1846%C2%A0%C2%A0.

Rose, Charlie. "Charlie Rose—Joseph Nye," February 28, 2011. www.charlierose.com/view/interview/11509#frame_top.

Ross, Alec. "U.S. Diplomacy in the Age of Facebook and Twitter: An Address on 21st Century Statecraft," Brookings Institute, Washington, DC, December 17, 2009.

Schmidt, Eric, and Jared Cohen. "Eric Schmidt and Jared Cohen on the Digital Disruption." *Foreign Affairs*, November 4, 2010. www.foreignaffairs.com/discussions/news-and-events/eric-schmidt-and-jared-cohen-on-the-digital-disruption.

Scott-Smith, Giles. "The Heineken Factor? Using Exchanges to Extend the Reach of U.S. Soft Power." *American Diplomacy*, June 13, 2011. www.unc.edu/depts/diplomat/item/2011/0104/comm/scottsmith_heineken.html#_ednref3.

"Secretary Clinton Presents 2010 Democracy Video Challenge Award to Ethiopian Filmmaker Yared Shumete," September 10, 2010. http://ethiopia.usembassy.gov/secretary_clinton_presents_2010_democracy_video_challenge_award_to_ethiopian_filmmaker_yared_shumete09/10/10.html.

Seib, Philip M. *Toward a New Public Diplomacy: Redirecting U.S. Foreign Policy.* Macmillan, 2009.

Sifry, Micah L., and Andrew Rasiej. "P2P2G: The Rise of e-Diplomacy." POLITICO.com, June 4, 2009. www.politico.com/news/stories/0609/23310.html.

Slaughter, Anne-Marie. "America's Edge: Power in the Networked Century." *Foreign Affairs* 88 (2009):94–113.

Snow, Nancy. "Rethinking Public Diplomacy." In *Routledge Handbook of Public Diplomacy*, eds. Nancy Snow and Phillip Taylor, 3–11. New York: Routledge, n.d.

Solash, Richard. "U.S. Congressional Committee Questions Role of U.S.-Funded Broadcasters." *Radio Free Europe / Radio Liberty*, April 11, 2011. www.rferl.org/content/us_congressional_committee_questions_role_us_funded_broadcasters/3549829.html.

"Staying ahead of the Digital Curve: U.S. Global Engagement in the New Media Era." Press Release. *Broadcasting Board of Governors*, February 16, 2011.

"Tech@State," n.d. www.state.gov/statecraft/tech/index.htm.

Thornberry, Mac. "Establishing the Strategic Communication and Public Diplomacy Caucus."—www.MountainRunner.us, March 7, 2010. http://mountainrunner.us/2010/03/thornberry.html.

Tuch, Hans N. *Communicating with the World: U.S. Public Diplomacy Overseas.* Palgrave Macmillan, 1990.

"U.S. GAO—Engaging Foreign Audiences: Assessment of Public Diplomacy Platforms Could Help Improve State Department Plans to Expand Engagement," July 21, 2010. www.gao.gov/products/GAO-10-767.

U.S. Public Diplomacy: Key Issues for Congressional Oversight. United States Government Accountability Office Report to Congressional Committees. United States Government Accountability Office, May 27, 2009. www.gao.gov/new.items/d09679sp.pdf.

United States National Security Council. *National Framework for Strategic Communication.* Washington, D.C., 2009.

Wolfers, Arnold. *DIscord and Collaboration: Essays on International Politics.* Baltimore, MD: Johns Hopkins University Press, 1962.

Zaharna, R. S. *Battles to Bridges: U.S. Strategic Communication and Public Diplomacy after 9/11.* Palgrave Macmillan, 2009.

———. "The Network Paradigm of Strategic Public Diplomacy." *Foreign Policy in Focus* 10 (April 2005). www.fpif.org.

Zaharna, R. S. "The Soft Power Differential: Network Communication and Mass Communication in Public Diplomacy." *Hague Journal of Diplomacy* 2, no. 3 (2007):213–228.

Zahran, Geraldo. "From Hegemony to Soft Power: Implications of a Conceptual Change." In *Soft Power and U.S. Foreign Policy: Theoretical, Historical and Contemporary Perspectives*, eds. Leonardo Ramos, Inderjeet Parmar, and Michael Cox, 12–31. New York: Taylor & Francis, 2010.

Chapter 7

Conclusion

"To say we live in a changing world is either the greatest understatement of our time, or the most frequently made statement by public officials today. Both may be true. But in the context of public diplomacy, it cannot be stated enough."

—Judith McHale, U.S. Undersecretary of State
for Public Diplomacy and Public Affairs[1]

How do public diplomacy and strategic communication programs reflect the way in which the concept of soft power has been adapted and adopted outside the confines of its academic origins? This is the central question posed in this book. It is an attempt to chart how aspects of soft power have been picked up as strategically viable, and reflected in the ways that nation-states consider their ability to translate soft power assets into expected gains through a broadly defined range of public diplomacy and strategic communication initiatives. This process of translation, or what Nye calls "conversion," is also freighted with a host of assumptions about communication and politics that convey idealized views of media effects, the persuasive nature of symbols, messages, and culture, and finally the possibilities that soft power can offer to the stewards of national strategy. At a more practical level, the policies and practices of public diplomacy reflect the "contextual intelligence" of each state discussed in this book.[2]

Yet soft power is also a frustratingly vague concept.[3] Nye has attempted to account for this vagueness with further clarification to distinguish between *resources* and *behaviors*, but the concept remains short on precision. This book attempts to introduce a flexible framework through which to understand what is at stake in the deployment of soft power discourse and programs

277

designed to augment soft power. This framework is intended to be a guide to understanding the ways in which resources and behaviors are intended to "work" in a practical way. The primary evidence used for the analysis is available public discourse and policy argumentation, coupled with descriptions of existing programs of strategic influence that draw upon the tenets of soft power—either explicitly or implicitly.

But does soft power *matter* as a conceptual category? Clearly, the growing awareness of public diplomacy as a tool of statecraft, coupled with the unavoidable proliferation of information and communication technologies, suggest that the international environment imposes some kind of attention to influence to be gained from communication-based action. But does this global context suggest that soft power most effectively describes what nation-states confront both as a tool of leverage and as subjects to another agent's power?

Soft power is the focus of analysis here, because it comes closest to distinguishing a nonmaterial form of influence from the material, the coercive, and the otherwise nonmanipulative forms of appeal. As discussed earlier, soft power may not be the most clearly articulated and tidy concept, but it is clearly sufficient to suggest that something other than force and economics is at stake in the management of international relations.

SCOPE

The idea of scope was introduced in order to capture a diversity of ways in which those subject to soft power are portrayed *as* subjects. Scope is intended to include two distinct aspects of soft power discourse. First, scope represents the idealized audiences to soft power efforts—who matters as important to an agent's attempts to cultivate some kind of influence, whether through agenda-setting, persuasion, or some form of attraction.

In the case of the United States and China, the intended audience is a complex of foreign audiences pertinent to a variety of foreign policy objectives. China obviously has interests in sustaining influence in particular regions that are pertinent to its economic development and regional interests. On this level, the scope of China's soft power discourse comprises subjects in developing regions such as Africa, the Middle East, Latin America, and Southeast Asia.[4] For the United States, the immediately crucial audiences are those populations that have some sort of influence on its extended military presence around the world and its position on the Israel–Palestine conflict.

In the case of Japan, the scope of its soft power activities is predominately limited to its strategic security partners, and to its regional political and economic relations. However, it is also possible to argue that the scope of Japanese soft power comprises the global networks of its fan culture, the otaku and other pop culture enthusiasts that admire Japan's creative output. While Japan is arguably concerned with a global level of soft power, its global presence as a soft power is considered a resource in itself as much as an intended object of policy intention. Japan's soft power rhetoric has translated into a concern with global consumers for its content industries and concern for the national brand, eclipsing developments in pop culture diplomacy that have defined recent soft power initiatives in Japan.[5]

Likewise, Venezuela's Bolivaran Republic has global ambitions in the promotion of its antagonism toward the United States, yet its regional interests more accurately define the scope of its soft power ambitions. While sympathetic nation-states are courted around the world, Venezuela also has very explicit soft power objectives in creating regional identification with its soft power institutions such as ALBA.

Scope *also* refers to the manner in which audiences are rendered as subjects. So, for example, are the audiences to public diplomacy portrayed in strategic discourse as "targets" susceptible to persuasive manipulation, or effectively cast as rational and discerning "publics" or "citizens" who are skeptical of intentional efforts to cultivate soft power through promotional communication? As Philip Napoli argues, how audiences are *rationalized* as an institution within strategic influence activities may be highly suggestive of their capacity to be influenced, how they consume mediated messages, and the kind of political agency they possess.[6] More importantly, how audiences are rationalized through soft power discourse anticipates the kind of programs designed to influence them.

In the case of the United States and Japan, there is an increasing trend toward recognition of the audience's power. This manifests in a number of assumptions. Japan presents the likely strongest case for conceiving the audiences for soft power as *agentic* and capable of reasoned consideration of symbolic inducement and other forms of appeal. As Saichi Kondo argues, this is a definitive aspect of Japanese public diplomacy and soft power, which is presentation-oriented rather than promotional.[7] Kondo distinguishes this position from the United States and points to the failed efforts at U.S. public diplomacy during the Bush administration as evidence.

Yet the rise of facilitative public diplomacy efforts in the United States—such as increased use of social media platforms and, significantly, the provision of communicative capacity to non-governmental stakeholders through programs like Tech@State—is suggestive of changing attitudes toward expected media communication effects. The governing model for U.S. public diplomacy and strategic communication is no longer the "magic bullet"—to which audiences simply need be exposed—but addressing audiences in the media spaces that matter to them. Yet the United States retains a significant amount of faith in its own soft power resources as inherently influential—that the United States reflects universal values as much as promotes them.[8] For its part, appeals to its soft power subjects are mostly defined by attention to the communication environment itself. Rather than craft a better message, U.S. public diplomacy programs and related discourse convey the belief that influence is a relational consequence of network structure.

In the case of China, the conception of the audience is much more suggestive of its perceived vulnerabilities. While there are certainly exceptions, the preponderant view of communication to foreign publics is conditioned by an extensive history of domestic political communication and information control. While the overriding concern with China's image in its soft power discourse conveys some sense of audience "power"—the solution to this concern is very often to manage the global information flows in much the same way. The incredible investment in Chinese international broadcasting is suggestive of this belief—that China needs a "voice," regardless of whether its perspective serves as useful to its global audience.[9] More generally, the model of communication effects is also straightforward. Chinese attention to news and cultural flows implies a direct effect from selective exposure to Chinese content. Even the Confucius Institute interventions anticipate gains in much the same way.

For Venezuela, its soft power efforts at "communicational hegemony" is illustrative of subjects conceived as susceptible to ideological manipulation and information intervention. Venezuelan efforts to appeal to regional audiences is predicated on the assumption that they are already subject to propaganda from Western, capitalist media outlets. This attitude within the Bolivaran government is likely bound up in its own political history of political turmoil carried out through factional media.[10]

Yet the very same vulnerability implied in Venezuelan claims about its influence is not a straightforward indictment of audiences as media dupes *per se*. Rather, soft power in the Venezuelan sense can be cultivated through media outlets because media is perceived as crucial to the means by which communities of shared identification are sustained. Media is, rather, a significant *social* sphere within which influence and power must be sustained.

MECHANISM

The term mechanism is used in this study to collapse some of the confusing terminology deployed in various depictions of soft power. Soft power mechanisms reflect the way in which strategic discourse links what Nye calls soft power *resources* with soft power *behaviors*. The reason for this linkage is relatively straightforward. Soft power resources, in Nye's depiction, include aspects of an agent's culture, political ideas or values, and foreign policy legitimacy. Soft power behaviors include agenda-setting, framing, persuasion, and attraction.[11]

These categories, when described as individual aspects of resources and behaviors, are difficult to depict as wholly separate or distinct, because they are so contingent on circumstance and equally difficult to pin down post hoc as a causal mechanism. It is argued here that the notion of soft power resources and behaviors becomes much more useful when presented as paired concepts, in order to capture the combination that an agent deploys to achieve an outcome. Nye's own description of resources and behaviors is fraught with caveats and conditions, which suggests that thinking about resources and behaviors as meaningful when they are linked in practice is perhaps more useful. Nye makes the case for this implicitly by arguing that the crucial factor is an agent's contextual intelligence—its ability to comprehend its strategic situation and convert resources into outcomes effectively.[12]

Outside of specific case studies that carefully piece together historical factors in an episode of soft power, contextual intelligence is most observable in the ways that agents discuss and reason about soft power, as well as in programs designed to deal with an anticipated strategic scenario or accomplish a set of foreign policy objectives. A specific program or policy conveys much about the strategic logic that justifies such interventions.

The case of the United States conveys a number of competing strategic assumptions about appropriate mechanisms to cultivate soft power. And as a result, it is difficult to typify the "behaviors" that make up U.S. soft power ambitions. Part of this may be the inertia of historical ideas about international persuasion that has carried over from the Cold War. When U.S. policy interlocuters argue for the necessity of message management to promote influence or persuasion, they reveal assumptions of programs that "worked" under previous conditions and circumstances. R. S. Zaharna argues that the implicit logics of influence in public diplomacy programs are also cultural in nature.[13] So when the United States expects some form of soft power attraction to accrue from the provision or facilitation of communication platforms, the anticipated effect is drawn from the expected value of liberalized attitudes toward information flows. At a more fundamental level, the way in which the United States seeks to empower individual citizens through its public diplomacy program and its broader "freedom to connect" agenda contains cultural attitudes toward the primacy of the individual over the community, that ultimately mark U.S. soft power mechanisms as culturally inflected.

Yet despite the diversity of public diplomacy and strategic communication programs managed by the U.S. federal government, much of what the United

States seeks to "leverage" from its soft power resources is based in political values and ideals. While the United States engages in cultural diplomacy, the larger scope of U.S. public diplomacy programs appear geared toward explaining, demonstrating, or modeling aspects of U.S. political values and institutions. And this is strongly reflected in increasingly value-laden justifications for reliance on technological platforms to carry out U.S. public diplomacy initiatives.

Venezuela's soft power programs reveal a similar preference. The official discourse describing Venezuela's international broadcasting strategy, as well as justifications for its regional institution-building, are geared to promote the benefits and credibility of the Bolivaran Republic's political and social values. Indeed, the premise that underscores much of the Venezuelan communication policy is predicated on the possibility of offering a political identity in contrast to Western, capitalist democracy.

Venezuelan's "conversion" strategy thus reveals a significant amount of expected appeal from the Bolivaran narrative, and that those potentially subject to its soft power are actively seeking alternatives to the hardships imposed by the United States and U.S.-sympathetic, capitalist-oriented media outlets. The conversion strategy also relies heavily on the significance of broadcast media as a means of interaction. Though President Hugo Chavez has recently embraced social media as a platform of Venezuelan appeals, Venezuelan attempts to cultivate soft power through communication seem strongly defined by explanation, rather than dialogue. The preponderance of the Venezuelan message of Bolivaran solidarity also fundamentally frames its other symbolic strategies of diplomatic engagement and regional institution building. Simply put, Venezuela's communication, economic, and political-based foreign policies appear designed as soft power initiatives as much as other forms of power.

Both China's and Japan's mechanisms for soft power are slated strongly toward the conversion of cultural resources into expected influence. For China, concern for soft power manifests as part of a strategic fixation on enhancing "comprehensive national power." Chinese arguments for soft power suggest an intrinsic value to its cultural heritage and history, in a way that anticipates a waiting global audience for an alternative to Western political and social ideals. For Japan, the expected returns to culture are much more modest. Japanese soft power policy does not seek to shape the boundaries of legitimate norms for international relations or to seriously challenge the "hegemony" of Western cultural expression. Rather, Japan's reliance on culture as a resource for soft power reflects the existing popularity of its popular culture, as a "bridge" to its historical cultural heritage.[14]

For China, its cultural resources can be leveraged through an aggressive "go global" strategy that develops its domestic cultural industries in order to grow a larger footprint in global cultural flows.[15] This effort is complemented by the growth of its Confucius Institutes—partnerships with education institutions around the world that aim to cultivate interest in Chinese culture and language instruction. Culture figures prominently in Chinese discourse about soft power—so much so that some advocates have called for a "cultural soft power."

But culture is not the only resource perceived as available to China's soft power ambitions. The large-scale investment in China's international communication outlets suggests a considerable emphasis on the expected value of agenda-setting and framing. Indeed, much of the discourse on soft power in China reflects an abiding concern with the way in which China's international image is constrained by Western media outlets. This concern shares some conceptual similarity to the U.S. fixation on the "war of ideas," in that it concludes that China must have a voice to compete in the space of global news and information flows. To cultivate soft power is to be able to communicate to audiences that have yet to hear China's unadulterated perspective.

This is not to suggest that Chinese soft power does not derive from its substantial economic development and investment around the world. There is likely to be considerable symbolic benefits from the kind of aid that China continues to provide in the form of nonrestrictive bilateral trade agreements and in infrastructure investment projects.[16] China's international communication initiatives, however, appear most prominently justified as soft power interventions—enabling China to seek agenda-setting capabilities with its increasingly global news services and to help shape long-term perceptions of its motivations and legitimacy as a rising power.

OUTCOMES

The idea of soft power outcomes appears initially to be quite similar to the notion of soft power behaviors. The ability of a soft power agent to effectively set the international agenda or to cultivate the appeal of its institutions and policies can certainly be seen as soft power objectives in their own right. Yet such behaviors are very often also means to larger ends.

Soft power outcomes range from the immediate or tangible objective to the more abstract, institutional, or system-focused. This range is accounted for in Barnett and Duvall's distinction of direct versus diffuse power, and in Wolfer's possession versus milieu goals.[17] Put simply, nation-states and other international actors anticipate that certain outcomes are *possible* given the available soft power mechanisms and subjects to soft power.

It would be futile to categorize an exhaustive list of soft power outcomes, because such outcomes are inevitably driven by the context of an agent's strategic ambitions. Soft power outcomes are not predetermined as a list of strategic possibilities, but a reflection of how culture, values, and credibility are imagined as crucial to strategic ends. What is systemic for one nation-state may be an immediate, parochial interest for another. Additionally, it would not be useful to artificially restrict the range of the possible combinations that agents could seek out as a consequence of their "conversion" strategies—since such a restriction would offer little more than speculation about the potency of soft power. As is evident in the cases explored in this study, nation-states imagine quite a different range of possibilities for the deployment of soft power.

China's expected outcomes for its soft power have been well documented.[18] As both Wuthnow and Li observe, China seeks to present itself as a legitimate global power and regional leader, to promote its culture, and to highlight its assistance to developing countries. These result in longer-term, systemic changes that allow China to more effectively promote its own economic development and secure the necessary resources it requires. This kind of flexibility that China seeks within international politics manifests as a concern for "sovereignty," or the ability of China to achieve its development objectives without normative or material sanction from other international actors. Ultimately, China's wide spectrum of soft power activities (some of which may be short-term in appearance) contribute to a longer-term goal of shaping the international milieu to its advantage.

For Japan, this ambition is far less apparent. Japan's turn to soft power rests primarily on a desire to preserve its economic and political power through alternative means. This has manifest as a concern over the *brand* of Japan, and the expected gains from the promotion of its "contents industry."[19] Japan is not actively seeking a normative realignment away from Western conceptions of international relations. Soft power is increasingly appealing as an option after over a decade of economic malaise—with the prospects of an ODA-based "checkbook" diplomacy less likely in the wake of a rising Chinese economic power.

Venezuela's soft power outcomes are readily apparent in the narratives that its soft power initiatives promote. Venezuela seeks regional power, through the cultivation of shared identification with the principles of Bolivaran social democracy. This serves the functional effect of establishing regional political and economic institutions that are separate from those established or sustained by partnership with the United States. It also signifies establishing an alternative *communication* infrastructure, to compete with corporate-dominated news and information flows that have long been portrayed as the enemy to Bolivaran ideals. Venezuela soft power "works" in effect by opposing the presence of an omnipresent enemy—an insidious capitalism that is coterminous with the machinations of the United States, its principal antagonist. Venezuela's soft power objectives are both immediate—the creation of alternative regional institutions—and milieu-based in the foundation of an alternative communication order to guarantee the symbolic resources of an imagined Bolivaran community.

For the United States, its soft powers ambitions are equally divided between shaping the immediate contexts of its presence abroad and sustaining its credibility and legitimacy as a global power. Much like public diplomacy—soft power can be cultivated in the short and long term through government action. Yet much of what the United States does in terms of public diplomacy appears unmoored from a coherent set of objectives, which has likely contributed to repeated calls for a public diplomacy strategy that clearly reflects U.S. goals.

But the steady fusion of public diplomacy and diplomacy in the United States reveals a more obvious trajectory toward a soft power outcome. While lawmakers continue to quibble in the United States over the exact mission of its international broadcasters, the facilitative turn in U.S. diplomacy signals a deeper conceptual shift in the role of diplomatic institutions that act in partnership with publics and non-state actors to manage complex global problems. Advocates for so-called twenty-first-century statecraft may balk at the notion that the concept reflects a decidedly soft power set of assumptions—namely, that U.S. foreign policy concerns are increasingly contingent on how global stakeholders perceive the legitimacy of such concerns. Twenty-first century statecraft reflects a set of programs that directly engage a variety of non-state actors in order to deal with transnational issues. In contrast, public diplomacy 2.0 reflects innovative technological approaches to communication about twenty-first century statecraft.

Both practices rely increasingly on social and new media technologies, and both stake out the claim that the United States can accrue credibility and legitimacy by demonstrating its values. In the case of public diplomacy 2.0 programs, soft power is expected from the manner in which audiences are addressed: not as targets in a promotional campaign, but as peers in an increasingly pluralistic and diverse marketplace of ideas embedded in ubiquitous network relations.[20] Twenty-first-century statecraft relies on technologies of cooperation and collaboration to facilitate outcomes that benefit both the United States and local stakeholders.[21] For James Glassman, both these terms constitute the ultimate purpose of public diplomacy and, by extension, the possibilities afforded by American soft power.

It is important, however, to reiterate that the characterizations of each nation-state examined in this volume are painted in broad strokes—there are certainly exceptions to the ideal typifications of soft power presented. The vibrant debate

within Chinese discourse about soft power makes it difficult to claim defini-
tively that Chinese soft power is ultimately about a specific resource translated
into influence via a specific instrument of influence. Likewise, the state of the
debate within the United States reflects very different conceptions of how audiences should be addressed as well as the primary purpose of its public diplomacy initiatives. Even in Venezuela, the contextual intelligence behind its soft
power evolves in reaction to perceived changes in the field of communication-
based influence. In 2010, Chavez reversed his public aversion to social media
platforms as somehow infiltrated by Western powers, and embraced Twitter as
another point of contact to the outside world.

Obviously, there are some important limitations to a study of contempora-
neous public diplomacy and strategic communication programs. In particular,
the "cases" presented are not deeply reflective of historical trajectories that
likely inform the translation of soft power into public diplomacy initiatives.
This study is a horizontal slice of time—a snapshot of a moment for four
international actors that grapple with the perceived necessity of contending
with the impact of global public opinion, the power of media framing, and
the opportunities that soft power offers through noncoercive and nonmaterial
forms of influence.

Which is to say, this book is inherently a single step in a larger project of
understanding the ways in which soft power–inspired assumptions about the
requirements of international politics have transformed the relative salience
of public opinion, global communication flows, and fundamental relations
between states, citizens, and foreign publics. There is no definitive interpretation of soft power, but a series of adaptations roughly drawing on the insight
of Joseph Nye's concept that reflect the indigenization of the concept. The
story of soft power as part of a nation-state's *strategic culture* is likely to be
far richer and more extensive than the short summary presented here. But just
as the environment that increasingly necessitates some form of soft power
changes (e.g., the rapid diffusion of social media technologies) so, too, does
the discourse used to justify how to deal with that environment.

SOFT POWER AND PUBLIC DIPLOMACY

This book is about the connection between soft power and public diplomacy.
Specifically, it is about how inherent assumptions that draw upon the analytical concept of soft power have been translated into public diplomacy,
strategic communication, and other forms of communication-based appeal
to foreign publics. Soft power and public diplomacy, however, are not the
same thing.[22]

Nation-states can certainly cultivate soft power through action that cannot be classified as public diplomacy—such as through development aid, through the public rhetoric of its leaders, and through the symbolic effects of its foreign policy. As Nye offers, soft power can also be passive. Nation-states can effectively benefit from soft power without actively seeking to cultivate it. Similarly, soft power can be cultivated through decidedly "non-soft" efforts. As Christopher Layne argues, the luxury of soft power is typically a consequence of other kinds of material or hard power.[23]

But the active efforts to cultivate soft power are very often represented by public diplomacy and strategic communication, and this is the focus of the present study. How nation-states view messages and actions as persuasive or influential is made apparent in its discourse and its actions. In this sense, soft power is inevitably a construction of a particular context.

This observation is not a call for simple relativism, where soft power is too contingent a strategic concept to merit categorical explanation. What the various cases in this book reveal, rather, is how the analytical abstractions of soft power are inevitably translations, inflected by domestic experiences, internal political tensions over foreign policy, and cultural attitudes toward the practice of communication. As a constructivist concept, soft power is also an intersubjective notion, a developing norm of what states should be engaged in as responsible nation-states. China's attention to soft power, for example, did not arise solely out of internal pressures, but was very much influenced by its observations of U.S. strategic thinking after the Cold War, and again during the rise of anti-Americanism leading up to the invasion of Iraq in 2003.[24]

The study of public diplomacy, therefore, is also an implicit study of how the soft power concept has chained out as a set of rhetorical justifications on the necessity of influencing, informing, or managing foreign publics. There is clearly *something* compelling to scholars and practitioners about the notion of soft power, despite its conceptual ambiguity. The same can be said for public diplomacy. Despite persistent debate among policymakers and scholars, there is no consistent definition of public diplomacy. In the United States, this debate tracks with a historical ambivalence to the notion of strategic communication and public diplomacy as a core aspect of foreign policy. This ambivalence, coupled with the unease expressed by international broadcasting practitioners saddled with the mandate for cultivating influence, suggests that public diplomacy is a blanket term signifying the necessity of influential international communication—from interpersonal to mass media—but without a consistent strategic reason or justification.

In the United States, public diplomacy is alternatively about the facilitation of expression as much as it is about the communication of a message intended to influence. In China, public diplomacy is about the maintenance of a global image and the management of information flows. In Japan, public diplomacy is about establishing connections that lay the foundation for greater appreciation of Japan, its policies, and its creative industries. In Venezuela, what is effectively public diplomacy is the provision of a compelling story, through which Venezuela can lead a path toward regional integration.

If there is a consistent aspect to the rhetoric of soft power discussed in this book, it is the centrality of *influence*. Indeed, it could be argued that soft power is but another term for a species of influence. Lurking behind even the most modest ambitions of Japanese public diplomacy is the possibility that particular assets can be leveraged for instrumental gain. This is not surprising, given that soft power is still a form of *power*. Soft power is useful analytically, however, because it draws together a conception of power as both a resource and outcomes—soft power encapsulates the entirety of the influence exchange. This quality is not unique to *soft* power, but as Nye has been forced to successively articulate about what is going in a soft power transaction, he has filled out a set of assumptions about influence that are readily applicable to policy planners.

Yet the rhetoric of soft power is also suggestive of something more than the intentional designs of contemporary public diplomacy. As academic treatments of structural and social power suggest, the tools of soft power reflect more than "the available tools of persuasion," but the capacity to use these tools on the larger structure of international relations.[25] Soft power, in this sense, is a kind of generative power. By intervening on the "rules of the game," soft power transforms what Bourdieu might call the *habitus* of power, the dispositions that lead nation-states and other global actors to consider certain actions as legitimate and others as beyond the pale.[26] For Van Ham, this notion reflects his concept of social power—but a more flexible interpretation of soft power could easily accommodate this perspective.

Soft power as expressed in public diplomacy is a barometer of the strategic field of international politics—what is required of strategic action, which actors are considered relevant, and what kinds of resources are available as assets to be leveraged. Yet soft power is also a reflection of the perceived requirements of influence and importantly, persuasion; the concept of soft power, intentionally or not, reflects the inherently communicative and symbolic dimension of international relations. In making the observation that publics can matter—and that soft power is a means to conduct international politics by other means—Nye clarified the argument for American policymakers that the post–Cold War world was there to be remade with the cultural and political resources available to the United States. While Nye might question this characterization, it could be argued that soft power was at least initially an exercise in applied constructivism.

While better terms and analytical concepts may emerge to capture the significance of image, communication, and culture to international relations, soft power remains a considerable rhetorical resource—a complex of strategic assumptions and arguments that has inspired a host of disparate practices. Public diplomacy, strategic communication, cultural soft power, cultural diplomacy, place branding, nation branding, and a host of related terms owe much of their strategic significance—their justificatory "power"—to the enduring terministic impact of soft power on the policy imagination of foreign policy leaders around the world.

NOTES

1. Judith A. McHale, "Opening Remarks at the Council on Foreign Relations: A Review of U.S. Public Diplomacy" (New York, June 21, 2011).

2. Joseph S. Nye, Jr., *The Future of Power*, 1st ed. (PublicAffairs, 2011), 24.

3. Edward Lock, "Soft Power and Strategy: Developing a 'Strategic' Concept of Power," in *Soft Power and U.S. Foreign Policy: Theoretical, Historical and Contemporary Perspectives*, eds. Inderjeet Parmar and Michael Cox (New York: Taylor & Francis, 2010), 32–50; Steven Lukes, "Power and the Battle for Hearts and Minds," *Millennium—Journal of International Studies* 33, no. 3 (June 1, 2005):477–493; Janice Bially Mattern, "Why 'Soft Power' Isn't so Soft: Representational Force and the Sociolinguistic Construction of Attraction in World Politics," *Millennium—Journal of International Studies* 33, no. 3 (June 2005):583–612.

4. Carola McGiffert, ed., *Chinese Soft Power and Its Implications for the United States: Competition and Cooperation in the Developing World: A Report of the CSIS Smart Power Initiative* (Washington D.C.: CSIS, 2009); Douglas Farah and Andy Mosher, *Winds from the East: How the People's Republic of China Seeks to Influence the Media in Africa, Latin America, and Southeast Asia* (Washington, D.C.: Center for International Media Assistance, September 8, 2010).

5. Kenjiro Monji, "Pop Culture Diplomacy," *Public Diplomacy Magazine*, 2010.

6. Philip M. Napoli, *Audience Evolution: New Technologies and the Transformation of Media Audiences* (Columbia University Press, 2010).

7. Seichi Kondo, "Wielding Soft Power: The Key States of Transmission and Receptions," in *Soft Power Superpowers: Cultural Assets of Japan and the United States*, eds. Yasushi Watanabe and David McConnell (Armonk, NY: M.E. Sharpe, 2008), 191–206.

8. Kathy R. Fitzpatrick, *The Future of U.S. Public Diplomacy: An Uncertain Fate* (Brill, 2010).

9. Kim Andrew Elliott, "Perhaps Too Much Sleep Is Lost over the 'Seduction, Prestige, and Omnipresence' of China's International Media Campaign," *Kim Andrew Elliott reporting on International Broadcasting*, April 14, 2011, http://kimelli.nfshost.com/index.php?id=11080.

10. James Painter, *Counter-Hegemonic News: A Case Study of Al-Jazeera English and Telesur*, RISJ Challenges (Oxford, 2006).

11. Nye Jr., *The Future of Power*, 81–109.

12. Ibid., 24.

13. R. S. Zaharna, *Battles to Bridges: U.S. Strategic Communication and Public Diplomacy after 9/11* (Palgrave Macmillan, 2009).

14. Monji, "Pop Culture Diplomacy."

15. Shanthi Kalathil, *China's Soft Power in the Information Age: Think Again*, ISD Working Papers in Diplomacy (Washington, D.C.: Georgetown University, May 2011), http://isd.georgetown.edu/files/Kalathil_Chinas_Soft_Power.pdf.

16. Deborah Brautigam, *The Dragon's Gift: The Real Story of China in Africa* (Oxford University Press U.S., 2009).

17. Michael Barnett and Raymond Duvall, "Power in International Politics," *International Organization* 59, no. 1 (2005):39–75; Arnold Wolfers, *Discord and Collaboration: Essays on International Politics* (Baltimore: Johns Hopkins University Press, 1962).

18. Mingjiang Li, "China Debates Soft Power," *The Chinese Journal of International Politics* 2, no. 2 (December 21, 2008):287–308.

19. Nissim K. Otmazgin, "Contesting Soft Power: Japanese Popular Culture in East and Southeast Asia," *International Relations of the Asia-Pacific* 8, no. 1 (May 2007):73–101.

20. James K. Glassman, "Public Diplomacy 2.0: A New Approach to Global Engagement" (speech presented at the New America Foundation, Washington, DC, December 1, 2008).

21. Donna Marie Oglesby, "Statecraft at the Crossroads: A New Diplomacy," *SAIS Review* 29, no. 2 (2009):93–106.

22. Nancy Snow, "Rethinking Public Diplomacy," in *Routledge Handbook of Public Diplomacy*, eds. Nancy Snow and Phillip Taylor (New York: Routledge, n.d.), 3–11.

23. Christopher Layne, "The Unbearable Lightness of Soft Power," in *Soft Power and U.S. Foreign Policy: Theoretical, Historical and Contemporary Perspectives*, eds. Inderjeet Parmar and Michael Cox (New York: Taylor & Francis, 2010), 51–82.

24. Yiwei Wang, "Public Diplomacy and the Rise of Chinese Soft Power," *The ANNALS of the American Academy of Political and Social Science* 616, no. 1 (March 1, 2008):257–273.

25. Lock, "Soft Power and Strategy: Developing a 'Strategic' Concept of Power"; Peter Van Ham, *Social Power in International Politics* (Taylor & Francis, 2010).

26. Loic Wacquant, "Towards a Reflexive Sociology: A Workshop with Pierre Bourdieu," *Sociological Theory* 7, no. 1 (spring 1989):26–63.

REFERENCES

Barnett, Michael, and Raymond Duvall. "Power in International Politics." *International Organization* 59, no. 1 (2005):39–75.

Bially Mattern, Janice. "Why 'Soft Power' Isn't so Soft: Representational Force and the Sociolinguistic Construction of Attraction in World Politics." *Millennium— Journal of International Studies* 33, no. 3 (June 2005):583–612.

Brautigam, Deborah. *The Dragon's Gift: The Real Story of China in Africa.* Oxford University Press U.S., 2009.

Elliott, Kim Andrew. "Perhaps Too Much Sleep Is Lost over the 'Seduction, Prestige, and Omnipresence' of China's International Media Campaign." *Kim Andrew Elliott reporting on International Broadcasting*, April 14, 2011. http://kimelli. nfshost.com/index.php?id=11080.

Farah, Douglas, and Andy Mosher. *Winds from the East: How the People's Republic of China Seeks to Influence the Media in Africa, Latin America, and Southeast Asia.* Washington, D.C.: Center for International Media Assistance, September 8, 2010.

Fitzpatrick, Kathy R. *The Future of U.S. Public Diplomacy: An Uncertain Fate.* Brill, 2010.

Glassman, James K. "Public Diplomacy 2.0: A New Approach to Global Engagement". Speech presented at the New America Foundation, Washington, DC, December 1, 2008.

Van Ham, Peter. *Social Power in International Politics.* Taylor & Francis, 2010.

Kalathil, Shanthi. *China's Soft Power in the Information Age: Think Again.* ISD Working Papers in Diplomacy. Washington, D.C.: Georgetown University, May 2011. http://isd.georgetown.edu/files/Kalathil_Chinas_Soft_Power.pdf.

Kondo, Seichi. "Wielding Soft Power: The Key States of Transmission and Receptions." In *Soft Power Superpowers: Cultural Assets of Japan and the United States*, eds. Yasushi Watanabe and David McConnell, 191–206. Armonk, NY: M.E. Sharpe, 2008.

Layne, Christopher. "The Unbearable Lightness of Soft Power." In *Soft Power and U.S. Foreign Policy: Theoretical, Historical and Contemporary Perspectives*, eds. Inderjeet Parmar and Michael Cox, 51–82. New York: Taylor & Francis, 2010.

Li, Mingjiang. "China Debates Soft Power." *The Chinese Journal of International Politics* 2, no. 2 (December 21, 2008):287–308.

Lock, Edward. "Soft Power and Strategy: Developing a 'Strategic' Concept of Power." In *Soft Power and U.S. Foreign Policy: Theoretical, Historical and Contemporary Perspectives*, eds. Inderjeet Parmar and Michael Cox, 32–50. New York: Taylor & Francis, 2010.

Lukes, Steven. "Power and the Battle for Hearts and Minds." *Millennium—Journal of International Studies* 33, no. 3 (June 1, 2005):477–493.

McGiffert, Carola, ed. *Chinese Soft Power and Its Implications for the United States: Competition and Cooperation in the Developing World: A Report of the CSIS Smart Power Initiative.* Washington D.C.: CSIS, 2009.

McHale, Judith A. "Opening Remarks at the Council on Foreign Relations: A Review of U.S. Public Diplomacy" (New York, June 21, 2011).

Monji, Kenjiro. "Pop Culture Diplomacy." *Public Diplomacy Magazine*, 2010.

Napoli, Philip M. *Audience Evolution: New Technologies and the Transformation of Media Audiences.* Columbia University Press, 2010.

Nye, Joseph S. Jr. *The Future of Power*. 1st ed. PublicAffairs, 2011.

Oglesby, Donna Marie. "Statecraft at the Crossroads: A New Diplomacy." *SAIS Review* 29, no. 2 (2009):93–106.

Otmazgin, Nissim K. "Contesting Soft Power: Japanese Popular Culture in East and Southeast Asia." *International Relations of the Asia-Pacific* 8, no. 1 (May 2007):73–101.

Painter, James. *Counter-Hegemonic News: A Case Study of Al-Jazeera English and Telesur*. RISJ Challenges. Oxford, 2006.

Snow, Nancy. "Rethinking Public Diplomacy." In *Routledge Handbook of Public Diplomacy*, eds. Nancy Snow and Phillip Taylor, 3–11. New York: Routledge, n.d.

Wacquant, Loic. "Towards a Reflexive Sociology: A Workshop with Pierre Bourdieu." *Sociological Theory* 7, no. 1 (spring 1989):26–63.

Wang, Yiwei. "Public Diplomacy and the Rise of Chinese Soft Power." *The ANNALS of the American Academy of Political and Social Science* 616, no. 1 (March 1, 2008):257–273.

Wolfers, Arnold. *Discord and Collaboration: Essays on International Politics*. Baltimore: Johns Hopkins University Press, 1962.

Zaharna, R. S. *Battles to Bridges: U.S. Strategic Communication and Public Diplomacy after 9/11*. Palgrave Macmillan, 2009.

Index

CPSIA information can be obtained at www.ICGtesting.com
Printed in the USA
BVOW070820161211

278496BV00002B/5/P

9 780739 142592